A Spy Among Friends

ALSO BY BEN MACINTYRE

Forgotten Fatherland
The Napoleon of Crime
A Foreign Field
Josiah the Great
Agent Zigzag
For Your Eyes Only
The Last Word
Operation Mincemeat
Double Cross

A Spy Among Friends

Kim Philby and the Great Betrayal

Ben Macintyre

SIGNAL

McCLELLAND
& STEWART

Library and Archives of Canada Cataloguing in
Publication is available upon request

ISBN: 978-0-7710-5550-8
ebook ISBN: 978-0-7710-5551-5

Printed and bound in the United States of America

Book design: Donna Sinisgalli
Jacket design: based on an original by David Mann
Jacket photographs: (Kim Philby) © Popperfoto / Getty
Images; (men in coats) © Mark Owen / Arcangel Images;
(London) © cristapper, (Red Square) © Braindrops,
both iStockphoto.com

McClelland & Stewart,
a division of Random House of Canada Limited,
a Penguin Random House Company
www.randomhouse.ca

1 2 3 4 5   18 17 16 15 14

In memory of Rick Beeston

Friends: noun, general slang for members of an intelligence service; specifically British slang for members of the Secret Intelligence Service [or MI6].

—INTERNATIONAL SPY MUSEUM

If I had to choose between betraying my country and betraying my friends, I hope I should have the guts to betray my country. Such a choice may scandalize the modern reader, and he may stretch out his patriotic hand to the telephone at once and ring up the police. It would not have shocked Dante, though. Dante places Brutus and Cassius in the lowest circle of Hell because they had chosen to betray their friend Julius Caesar rather than their country Rome.

—E. M. FORSTER, 1938

Contents

Preface

There is a voluminous literature on Kim Philby, including the invaluable pioneering work of writers such as Patrick Seale, Phillip Knightley, Tom Bower, Anthony Cave Brown, and Genrikh Borovik. But to many readers Philby remains opaque, like the cold war itself, often alluded to but little understood. Moreover, in recent years the release of much previously classified material, along with authorized histories of MI5 and MI6, has shed new light on both that conflict and Philby's place within it.

This is not another biography of Kim Philby. Rather, it is an attempt to describe a particular sort of friendship that played an important role in history, told in the form of a narrative. It is less about politics, ideology, and accountability than personality, character, and a very British relationship that has never been explored before. Since the MI6, CIA, and KGB files remain closed, much source material is secondary: the evidence of third parties, often expressed in retrospect. Spies are particularly skilled at misremembering the past, and the protagonists in this story are all guilty, to some extent, of distorting their own histories. Many of the "facts" about the Philby case are still hotly disputed, and theories, conspiratorial and otherwise, abound. Some of the more contentious issues are discussed in the endnotes. Much that has been written about Philby derives from memory or speculation without documentary support; some is colored by propaganda, and some is pure fantasy. Until and unless the official files are released in their entirety, a degree of mystery will always be attached to these events. For the narrative historian this creates particular challenges. Presented with conflicting accounts, different view-points, and divergent recollections, I have had to make judgments about the credibility of different sources and choose which of the many strands of evidence seem to run closest to reality. Others will doubtless disagree with my choices. This is not an exact science, but what follows is as close to a true story as I can make it.

This book does not purport to be the last word on Kim Philby. Instead, it seeks to tell his story in a different way, through the prism of personal friendship, and perhaps arrive at a new understanding of the most remarkable spy of modern times.

A Spy Among Friends

Introduction

Beirut, January 1963

TWO MIDDLE-AGED SPIES ARE SITTING IN AN APARTMENT IN THE Christian Quarter, sipping tea and lying courteously to each other, as evening approaches. They are English—so English that the habit of politeness that binds them together and keeps them apart never falters for a moment. The sounds of the street waft up through the open window, car horns and horses' hooves mingling with the clink of china and the murmured voices. A microphone, cunningly concealed beneath the sofa, picks up the conversation and passes it along a wire, through a small hole in the wainscoting, and into the next room, where a third man sits hunched over a turning tape recorder, straining to make out the words through Bakelite headphones.

The two men are old friends. They have known each other for nearly thirty years. But they are bitter foes now, combatants on opposing sides of a brutal conflict.

Kim Philby and Nicholas Elliott learned the spy trade together during the Second World War. When that war was over, they rose together through the ranks of British intelligence, sharing every secret. They belonged to the same clubs, drank in the same bars, wore the same well-tailored clothes, and married women of their own tribe. But all that time, Philby had one secret he never shared: he was covertly working for Moscow, taking everything he was told by Elliott and passing it on to his Soviet spymasters.

Elliott has come to Beirut to extract a confession. He has wired up the apartment and set watchers on the doors and street.

He wants to know how many have died through Philby's betrayal of their friendship. He wants to know when he became a fool. He needs to know the truth, or at least some of the truth. And once he knows, Philby can flee to Moscow or return to Britain or start anew as a triple agent or drink himself to death in a Beirut bar. It is, Elliott tells himself, all the same to him.

Philby knows the game, for he has played it, brilliantly, for three decades. But he does not know how much Elliott knows. Perhaps the friendship will save him, as it has saved him before.

Both men tell some truth, laced with deception, and lie with the force of honest conviction. Layer upon layer, back and forth.

As night falls, the strange and lethal duel continues, between two men bonded by class, club, and education but divided by ideology; two men of almost identical tastes and upbringing but conflicting loyalties; the most intimate of enemies. To an eavesdropper their conversation appears exquisitely genteel, an ancient English ritual played out in a foreign land; in reality it is an unsparing, bare-knuckle fight, the death throes of a bloodied friendship.

Chapter One

Apprentice Spy

ONE MOMENT NICHOLAS ELLIOTT WAS AT ASCOT RACECOURSE, watching the favorite, Quashed, come romping home at 7–2, and the next, rather to his own surprise, he was a spy. The date was June 15, 1939, three months before the outbreak of the deadliest conflict in history. He was twenty-two.

It happened over a glass of champagne. John Nicholas Rede Elliott's father, Sir Claude Aurelius Elliott, OBE, was headmaster of Eton (England's grandest public school), a noted mountaineer, and a central pillar of the British establishment. Sir Claude knew everybody who was anybody and nobody who wasn't somebody, and among the many important men he knew was Sir Robert Vansittart, chief diplomatic adviser to His Majesty's government, who had close links to the Secret Intelligence Service (SIS), better known as MI6, the agency responsible for intelligence gathering abroad. Nicholas Elliott arranged to meet "Van" at Ascot and, over drinks, mentioned that he thought he might like to join the intelligence service.

Sir Robert Vansittart smiled and replied: "I am relieved you have asked me for something so easy."

"So that was that," Elliott wrote many years later.

The old boys' recruitment network had worked perfectly.

Nicholas Elliott was not obviously cut out to be a spy. His academic record was undistinguished. He knew little about the complexities of international politics, let alone the dextrous and dangerous game being played by MI6 in the run-up to war. Indeed, he knew nothing whatsoever about espionage, but he thought spying sounded exciting and important and exclusive. Elliott was self-confident as only a well-bred, well-heeled young Etonian, newly graduated from Cambridge University, with all the right social connections, can be. He was born to rule (though he would never have expressed that belief so indelicately), and membership in the most selective club in Britain seemed like a good place to start doing so.

The Elliotts were part of the backbone of the empire; for generations, they had furnished military officers, senior clerics, lawyers, and colonial administrators who ensured that Britain continued to rule the waves—and much of the globe in between. One of Nicholas Elliott's grandfathers had been the lieutenant governor of Bengal; the other, a senior judge. Like many powerful English families, the Elliotts were also notable for their eccentricity. Nicholas's great-uncle Edgar famously took a bet with another Indian Army officer that he could smoke his height in cheroots every day for three months, then smoked himself to death in two. Great-aunt Blanche was said to have been "crossed in love" at the age of twenty-six and thereafter took to her bed, where she remained for the next fifty years. Aunt Nancy firmly believed that Catholics were not fit to own pets since they did not believe animals had souls. The family also displayed a profound but frequently fatal fascination with mountain climbing. Nicholas's uncle, the Reverend Julius Elliott, fell off the Matterhorn in 1869, shortly after meeting Gustave Flaubert, who declared him "the epitome of the English gentleman." Eccentricity is one of those English traits that look like frailty but mask a concealed strength; individuality disguised as oddity.

Towering over Nicholas's childhood was his father, Claude, a man of immovable Victorian principles and ferocious prejudices. Claude loathed music, which gave him indigestion, despised all forms of heating as "effete," and believed that "when dealing with foreigners the best plan was to shout at them in English." Before becoming headmaster of Eton, Claude Elliott had taught history at Cambridge University, despite an ingrained distrust of academics and an aversion to intellectual conversation. The long university vacations gave him plenty of time for mountain climbing. He might have become the most celebrated climber of his generation, but for a kneecap broken by a fall in the Lake District, which prevented him from joining Mallory's Everest expedition. A dominating figure physically and psychologically, Claude was nicknamed "the Emperor" by the boys at Eton. Nicholas regarded his father with awed reverence; in return, Claude alternately ignored or teased his only child, believing, like many fathers of his time and class, that displaying affection would make his son "soft" and quite possibly homosexual. Nicholas grew up convinced that "Claude was highly embarrassed by my very existence." His mother avoided all intimate topics of conversation, according to her only son, including "God, Disease and Below the Waist."

The young Elliott was therefore brought up by a succession of nannies and then shunted off to Durnford School in Dorset, a place with a tradition of brutality extreme even by the standards of British prep schools: every morning the boys were made to plunge naked into an unheated pool for the pleasure of the headmaster, whose wife liked to read improving literature out loud in the evenings with her legs stretched out over two small boys while a third tickled the soles of her feet. There was no fresh fruit, no toilets with doors, no restraint on bullying, and no possibility of escape. Today such an institution would be illegal; in 1925 it was considered "character-forming." Elliott left his prep school with the conviction that "nothing as unpleasant could ever recur," an ingrained contempt for authority, and a hardy sense of humor.

Eton seemed like a paradise after the "sheer hell" of Durnford, and having his father as headmaster posed no particular problem for Nicholas, since Claude continued to pretend he wasn't there. Highly intelligent, cheerful, and lazy, the young Elliott did just enough work to get by: "The increased legibility of his handwriting only serves to reveal the inadequacy of his ability to spell," noted one report. He was elected to his first club, Pop, the Eton institution reserved for the most popular boys in the school. It was at Eton that Elliott discovered a talent for making friends. In later life he would look back on this as his most important skill, the foundation of his career.

Basil Fisher was Elliott's first and closest friend. A glamorous figure with an impeccable academic and sporting record, Fisher was captain of the First XI, the chairman of Pop, and son of a bona fide war hero, Basil senior having been killed by a Turkish sniper at Gaza in 1917. The two friends shared every meal, spent their holidays together, and occasionally slipped into the headmaster's house, when Claude was at dinner, to play billiards. Photographs from the time show them arm in arm, beaming happily. Perhaps there was a sexual element to their relationship, but probably not. Hitherto, Elliott had loved only his nanny, "Ducky Bit" (her real name is lost to history). He worshipped Basil Fisher.

In the autumn of 1935 the two friends went up to Cambridge. Naturally, Elliott went to Trinity, his father's old college. On his first day at the university, he visited the writer and poet Robert Gittings, an acquaintance of his father, to ask a question that had been troubling him: "How hard should I work, and at what?" Gittings was a shrewd judge of character. As Elliott remembered: "He strongly advised me to use my three years at Cambridge to enjoy myself in the interval before the next war"—advice that Elliott followed to the letter. He played cricket, punted, drove around Cambridge in a Hillman Minx, and attended and gave some very good parties. He read a lot of spy novels. On weekends he went shooting or to the races at Newmarket. Cambridge in the 1930s boiled with ideological conflict; Hitler had taken power in 1933; the Spanish civil war would erupt in the summer of 1936; extreme Right and extreme Left fought it out in university rooms and on the streets. But the fervid political atmosphere simply passed Elliott by. He was far too busy having fun. He seldom opened a book and emerged after three years with many friends and a third-class degree, a result he considered "a triumph over the examiners."

Nicholas Elliott left Cambridge with every social and educational advantage and absolutely no idea what he wanted to do. But beneath a complacent and conventional exterior and the "languid, upper-class manner" lay a more complex personality, an adventurer with a streak of subversion. Claude Elliott's Victorian rigidity had instilled in his son a deep aversion to rules. "I could never be a good soldier because I am insufficiently amenable to discipline," he reflected. When told to do something, he tended to "obey not the order which he had actually been given by a superior, but rather the order which that superior would have given if he had known what he was talking about." He was tough—the brutality of Durnford had seen to that—but also sensitive, bruised by a lonely childhood. Like many Englishmen, he concealed his shyness behind a defensive barrage of jokes. Another paternal legacy was the conviction that he was physically unattractive; Claude had once told him he was "plug ugly," and he grew up believing it. Certainly Elliott was not classically handsome, with his gangly frame, thin face, and thick-rimmed glasses, but he had poise, a barely concealed air of mischief, and a resolute cheerfulness that women were instantly drawn to. It took him many years to conclude that he "was no more or less odd to look at than a reasonable proportion of my fellow creatures." Alongside a natural conservatism he had inherited the family propensity for eccentricity. He was no snob. He could strike up a conversation with anyone from any walk of life. He did not believe in God or Marx or capitalism; he had faith in King, country, class, and club (White's Club, in his case, the gentleman's club in St James's). But above all he believed in friendship.

In the summer of 1938 Basil Fisher took a job in the City, while Elliott wondered idly what to do with himself. The old boys soon solved that. Elliott was playing in a cricket match at Eton that summer when, during the tea interval, he was approached by Sir Nevile Bland, a senior diplomat and family friend, who tactfully observed that Elliott's father was concerned by his son's "inability to get down to a solid job of work." (Sir Claude preferred to speak to his son through emissaries.) Sir Nevile explained that he had recently been appointed Britain's minister at The Hague, in the Netherlands. Would Nicholas like to accompany him as honorary attaché? Elliott said he would like that very much, despite having no idea what an honorary attaché might actually do. "There was no serious vetting procedure," Elliott later wrote. "Nevile simply told the Foreign Office that I was all right because he knew me and had been at Eton with my father."

Before leaving, Elliott underwent a code training course at the Foreign Office. His instructor was one Captain John King, a veteran cipher clerk who was also, as it happened, a Soviet spy. King had been passing Foreign Office telegrams to Moscow since 1934. Elliott's first tutor in secrecy was a double agent.

Elliott arrived at The Hague in his Hillman Minx in the middle of November 1938 and reported to the legation. After dinner, Sir Nevile offered him a warning—"in the diplomatic service it is a sackable offense to sleep with the wife of a colleague"—and some advice—"I suggest you should do as I do and not light your cigar until you have started your third glass of port." Elliott's duties were hardly onerous—a little light bag carrying for the minister, some coding and decoding in the wireless room, and attendance at formal dinners.

Elliott had been in the Netherlands only four months when he got his first taste of clandestine work and an "opportunity to see the German war machine at first hand." One evening, over dinner, he fell into conversation with a young naval officer named Glyn Hearson, the assistant naval attaché at the embassy in Berlin. Commander Hearson confided that he was on a special mission to spy on the port of Hamburg, where the Germans were believed to be developing midget submarines. After a few more glasses, Hearson asked Elliott if he would care to join him. Elliott thought this a splendid idea. Sir Nevile gave his approval.

Two days later, at three in the morning, Elliott and Hearson broke into Hamburg's port by climbing over the wall. "We discreetly poked our noses all over the place for about an hour" taking photographs, Elliott recalled, before "returning to safety and a stiff drink." Elliott had no diplomatic cover and no training, and Hearson had no authority to recruit him for the mission. Had they been caught, they might have been shot as spies; at the very least, the news that the son of the Eton headmaster had been caught snooping around a German naval dockyard in the middle of the night would have set off a diplomatic firestorm. It was, Elliott happily admitted, "a singularly foolhardy exploit." But it had been most enjoyable and highly successful. They drove on to Berlin in high spirits.

April 20, 1939, was Hitler's fiftieth birthday, a national holiday in Nazi Germany and the occasion for the largest military parade in the history of the Third Reich. Organized by propaganda minister Joseph Goebbels, the festivities marked a high point of the Hitler cult, a lavish display of synchronized sycophancy. A torchlight parade and cavalcade of fifty white limousines, led by the Führer, was followed by a fantastic five-hour exhibition of military muscle involving fifty thousand German troops, hundreds of tanks, and 162 warplanes. The ambassadors of Britain, France, and the United States did not attend, having been withdrawn after Hitler's march on Czechoslovakia, but some twenty-three other countries sent representatives to wish Hitler a happy birthday. "The Fuhrer is feted like no other mortal has ever been," gushed Goebbels in his diary.

Elliott watched the celebrations, with a mixture of awe and horror, from a sixth-floor apartment in the Charlottenburger Chaussee belonging to General Nöel Mason-MacFarlane, the British military attaché in Berlin. "Mason-Mac" was a whiskery old warhorse, a decorated veteran of the trenches and Mesopotamia. He could not hide his disgust. From the balcony of the apartment there was a clear view of Hitler on his saluting podium. The general remarked under his breath to Elliott that Hitler was well within rifle range: "I am tempted to take advantage of this," he muttered, adding that he could "pick the bastard off from here as easy as winking." Elliott "strongly urged him to take a pot shot." Mason-MacFarlane thought better of the idea, though he later made a formal request to be allowed to assassinate Hitler from his balcony. Sadly for the world, the offer was turned down.

Elliott returned to The Hague with two newly minted convictions: that Hitler must be stopped at all costs and that the best way of contributing to this end would be to become a spy. "My mind was easily made up." A day at Ascot, a glass of fizz with Sir Robert Vansittart, and a meeting with an important person in Whitehall did the rest. Elliott returned to The Hague still officially an honorary attaché but in reality, with Sir Nevile Bland's blessing, a new recruit to the Secret Intelligence Service, or MI6. Outwardly his diplomatic life continued as before; secretly he began his novitiate in the strange religion of British intelligence.

Sir Robert Vansittart, the Foreign Office mandarin who smoothed Elliott's way into MI6, ran what was, in effect, a private intelligence agency outside the official orbit of government but with close links to both MI6 and MI5, the Security Service. Vansittart was a fierce opponent of appeasement, convinced that Germany would start another war "just as soon as it feels strong enough." His network of spies gathered copious intelligence on Nazi intentions, with which he tried (and failed) to persuade Prime Minister Neville Chamberlain of the looming confrontation. One of his earliest and most colorful informants was Jona von Ustinov, a German journalist and fierce secret opponent of Nazism. Ustinov was universally known as "Klop," Russian slang for bedbug, a nickname that derived from his rotund appearance, of which he was, oddly, intensely proud. Ustinov's father was a Russian-born army officer; his mother was half Ethiopian and half Jewish; his son, born in 1921, was Peter Ustinov, the great comic actor and writer. Klop Ustinov had served in the German army during the First World War, winning an Iron Cross, before taking up a post with the German Press Agency in London. He lost his job in 1935 when the German authorities, suspicious of his exotically mixed heritage, demanded proof of his Aryanism. That same year he was recruited as a British agent, code-named "U35." Ustinov was fat and monocled, with a deceptively bumbling demeanor. He was "the best and most ingenious operator I had the honor to work with," declared Dick White, his case officer, who would go on to head both MI5 and MI6.

Elliott's first job for MI6 was to help Ustinov run one of the most important and least known prewar spies. Wolfgang Gans Edler Herr zu Putlitz was the press attaché at the German embassy in London, a luxury-loving aristocrat, and a flamboyant homosexual. Ustinov recruited Gans zu Putlitz and began to extract what was described as "priceless intelligence, possibly the most important human-source intelligence Britain received in the prewar period" on German foreign policy and military plans. Gans zu Putlitz and Ustinov shared Vansittart's conviction that the policy of appeasement had to be reversed: "I was really helping to damage the Nazi cause," Gans zu Putlitz believed. When Gans zu Putlitz was posted to the German embassy at The Hague in 1938, Klop Ustinov discreetly followed him, posing as the European correspondent of an Indian newspaper. With Ustinov as go-between, Gans zu Putlitz continued to supply reams of intelligence, though he was frustrated by Britain's apparent unwillingness to confront Hitler. "The English are hopeless," he complained. "It is no use trying to help them to withstand the Nazi methods which they so obviously fail to understand." Gans zu Putlitz began to feel he was "sacrificing himself for no purpose."

In The Hague, Klop Ustinov and Nicholas Elliott established an instant rapport and would remain friends for life. "Klop was a man of wide talents," wrote Elliott, "bon viveur, wit, raconteur, mimic, linguist—endowed with a vast range of knowledge, both serious and ribald." Ustinov put Elliott to work boosting the spirits of the increasingly gloomy and anxious Wolfgang Gans zu Putlitz.

Gans zu Putlitz was a "complicated man," Elliott wrote, torn between his patriotism and his moral instincts. "His motivation was solely idealistic and he went through acute mental torture at the knowledge that the information he gave away could cost German lives." One evening in August, Elliott took Gans zu Putlitz to dinner at the Royale Hotel. Over dessert he remarked that he was thinking of taking a holiday in Germany: "Is Hitler going to start the war before we get back at the end of the first week of September?" he asked, half in jest. Gans zu Putlitz did not smile. "On present plans the attack on Poland starts on 26 August but it may be postponed for a week, so if I were you, I'd cancel the trip." Elliott swiftly reported this "startling statement" to Klop, who passed it on to London. Elliott called off his holiday. On

September 1, just as Gans zu Putlitz had predicted, German tanks rolled into Poland from the north, south, and west. Two days later Britain was at war with Germany.

Not long afterward, the German ambassador to The Hague showed Wolfgang Gans zu Putlitz a list of German agents in the Netherlands; the list was identical to one that Gans zu Putlitz had recently handed over to Klop Ustinov and Nicholas Elliott. Clearly, there must be a German spy within the MI6 station, but no one for a moment suspected Folkert van Koutrik, an affable Dutchman working as assistant to the station chief, Major Richard Stevens. Van Koutrik had "always displayed perfectly genuine faithfulness," according to his colleagues. Secretly he was working for the Abwehr, German military intelligence, and "by the autumn of 1939, the Germans had a pretty clear picture of the whole SIS operation in Holland." Van Koutrik had obtained the list of German spies Putlitz had passed to MI6 and passed it back to German intelligence.

Gans zu Putlitz knew "it could only be a matter of time before he was discovered and dealt with." He immediately requested asylum in Britain but insisted he would not leave without his valet, Willy Schneider, who was also his lover. Gans zu Putlitz was whisked to London on September 15 and lodged in a safe house.

The loss of such a valuable agent was bad enough, but worse was to follow.

On November 9 the head of station, Major Stevens, Elliott's new boss, set off for Venlo, a town on the Dutch border with Germany, in the expectation that he would shortly bring the war to a speedy and glorious conclusion. He was accompanied by a colleague, Sigismund Payne Best, a veteran military intelligence officer. Elliott liked Stevens, considering him a "brilliant linguist and excellent raconteur." Best, on the other hand, he regarded as "an ostentatious ass, blown up with self-importance."

Some months earlier, Stevens and Best had secretly made contact with a group of disaffected German officers plotting to oust Hitler in a military coup. At a meeting arranged by Dr. Franz Fischer, a German political refugee, the leader of the group, one

Hauptmann Schämmel, explained that elements within the German High Command, appalled by the losses suffered during the invasion of Poland, intended to "overthrow the present regime and establish a military dictatorship." The prime minister was informed of the anti-Hitler conspiracy, and Stevens was encouraged to pursue negotiations with the coup plotters. "I have a hunch that the war will be over by the spring," wrote Chamberlain. Stevens and Best, accompanied by a Dutch intelligence officer, headed to Venlo in high spirits, convinced they were about to link up with "the big man himself," the German general who would lead the coup. In fact, "Schämmel" was Walter Schellenberg of the Sicherheitsdienst (SD), the Nazi Party intelligence agency, a canny and ruthless master spy who would eventually take over German intelligence; Dr. Fischer was in Gestapo pay. The meeting was a trap, personally ordered by SS Reichsführer Heinrich Himmler.

Shortly before 11:00 a.m. they arrived at the rendezvous point, Café Backus, on the Dutch side of the frontier, a few yards from the border post. "No one was in sight except a German customs officer," wrote Stevens, "and a little girl who was playing ball with a big dog in the middle of the road." Schellenberg, standing on the café veranda, beckoned them over by waving his hat. That was the signal. As they climbed out of their car, the British officers were immediately surrounded by SS commandos in plain clothes, firing machine guns in the air. The Dutch officer drew his revolver and was shot down.

"Our number's up," muttered Stevens.

"The next moment," recalled Best, "there were two fellows in front of each of us, one holding a pistol to our heads and the other putting handcuffs on. Then the Germans shouted at us 'March!,' and prodding us in the back with their pistols and calling 'Hup! Hup! Hup!,' they rushed us along toward the German frontier." The Germans bundled the captives into waiting cars, dragging the dying Dutch officer with them.

"At one stroke," wrote Elliott, "all British intelligence operations in Holland were compromised." Worse still, Stevens had been carrying in his pocket, idiotically, a list of intelligence sources in

Western Europe. MI6 scrambled to extract its network of agents before the Germans pounced.

The Venlo incident was an unmitigated catastrophe. Since the Dutch were clearly involved and had lost an officer, Hitler could claim that Holland had violated its own neutrality, providing an excuse for the invasion of Holland that would follow just a few months later. The episode left the British with an ingrained suspicion of German army officers claiming to be anti-Nazi, even when, in the final stages of the war, similar such approaches were genuine. Stevens and Best were imprisoned for the rest of the war. By December, through information derived from the British captives and the double agent Van Koutrik, the Germans were "able to construct detailed and largely accurate charts of [MI6's] agent networks," as well as the structure of MI6 itself. It was the first and most successful German Double Cross operation of the war. Oddly, it was also one of the last.

Looking back on the Venlo incident, Elliott blamed the "intense ambition" of Stevens, who had scented the "possibility of winning the war off his own bat, and this completely clouded his operational judgment." Instead of maintaining the fiction of a resistance cell inside Nazi High Command, Schellenberg sent a crowing message: "Corresponding with conceited and foolish people becomes boring in the long run. You will understand our breaking off relations. Best wishes from your good friends the German Opposition." It was signed "German Secret Police."

In his first six months as a spy, Elliott had learned a salutary lesson in the forgery and fraud that is the currency of espionage. His boss was now in a German prison, having fallen for an elaborate deception; a valuable spy had fled to London, betrayed by a double agent; the entire intelligence network in Holland had been fatally compromised. Even the innocuous Captain John King, the cipher clerk who had taught Elliott coding, was now in prison, serving a ten-year sentence for spying, after a Soviet defector revealed that he had been "selling everything to Moscow" for cash.

Far from being repelled by the duplicity around him, Elliott felt ever more drawn to the game of skulduggery and double cross.

The Venlo debacle had been "as disastrous as it was shameful," but he also found it fascinating, an object lesson in how highly intelligent people could be duped if persuaded to believe what they most wanted to believe. He was learning quickly. He even made up a ditty in celebration:

Oh what a tangled web we weave
When first we practise to deceive.
But when you've practised quite a bit
You really get quite good at it.

At 3:00 a.m. on May 9, 1940, Elliott was awoken by the arrival of an emergency telegram from London. He extracted the code books from the ambassador's safe, sat down at the embassy dining table, and began to decode the message: "Information has been received that the Germans intend to attack along the entire Western Front. . . ." The phony war was over, and the real one had started. The next day Germany attacked France and Holland. "It soon became apparent," wrote Elliott, "that the Dutch, bravely though they fought, would not last out for long."

The British prepared to flee. Elliott and his MI6 colleagues made a swift bonfire of compromising files in the embassy courtyard. Another officer seized most of Amsterdam's industrial diamond stocks and smuggled them to Britain. The Dutch queen sailed to safety on a Royal Navy destroyer, along with her cabinet, her secret service, and her gold. Elliott's principal task, he found, was to evacuate the terrified dancers of the Vic-Wells Ballet Company, which he did by loading them onto a dredger commandeered at IJmuiden. On May 13 a British destroyer, HMS *Mohawk*, anchored off the Hook of Holland, waiting to carry the last British stragglers to safety. As he raced in a convoy toward the coast, Elliott watched as flames from burning Rotterdam lit up the horizon. He was one of the last to climb aboard. The following day the Dutch surrendered. As the young MI6 officer alighted in Britain, he was greeted by the words "We're in the final now."

Elliott had expected to find a nation in crisis, but he was struck by the "normality and calmness" of London. From that moment, he wrote, it "never occurred to me for one moment that we might lose the war." Within days he was commissioned into the Intelligence Corps, and then, to his astonishment, he found himself behind bars.

Wormwood Scrubs, the Victorian prison in West London, had been adopted as the wartime headquarters of the security service, MI5, and was now expanding rapidly to cope with the threat of German espionage. The falls of France and the Netherlands were attributed in part to Nazi fifth columnists, enemy spies working from within to aid the German advance. The threat of a German invasion set off an intense hunt for spies in Britain, and MI5 was swamped by reports of suspicious activity. "England was gripped by spy fever," wrote Elliott, who was seconded to MI5 to "give evidence of what I had seen at first hand of Fifth Column activity in Holland." The fifth-column threat never materialized, for the simple reason that it did not exist—Hitler had not intended to go to war with Britain, and little effort had been made to prepare the ground for a German invasion. The Abwehr soon set about making up the deficit. Over the next few months, so-called invasion spies poured into Britain by boat, parachute, and submarine; ill trained and underequipped, they were duly and swiftly rounded up. Some were imprisoned, and a handful executed, but a number were recruited as double agents to feed false information back to their German handlers. This was the embryo of the great Double Cross system, the network of double agents whose importance would steadily expand as the war progressed. Under interrogation, many of these spies provided information of vital interest to MI6, the Secret Intelligence Service. Elliott was appointed liaison officer between the sister services and based in Wormwood Scrubs. It was a bizarre place to work: malodorous and dingy, the prison still contained a few inmates, including an Old Etonian contemporary of Elliott's, Victor Hervey, the future 6th Marquess of Bristol, a notorious playboy who had been jailed in 1939 for robbing a Mayfair jeweler. Elliott worked from a soundproofed jail cell with no door handle on the inside; if his last visitor of the day accidentally turned the outside handle on leaving, he was locked in until morning.

Elliott loved his new life, in prison by day and at liberty at night, in a city under siege and threatened with invasion but pulsating with energy. He moved into a flat in Cambridge Square, Bayswater, belonging to the grandmother of another friend from Eton, Richard Brooman-White, who was also in MI6. Basil Fisher was now a fighter pilot with 111 Squadron, flying Hurricanes out of Croydon. Whenever Fisher was on leave, the three friends would gather, usually at White's Club. The Blitz hammered down, and Elliott was elated by the "feeling of camaraderie" as he sat with his friends in the smoky, mahogany-paneled luxury of London's oldest and most exclusive gentlemen's club. "My only moment of real danger was when drinking a pink gin in the bar of the club. A bomb fell on the building next door, upsetting my gin and knocking me flat. I got another pink gin with the compliments of the barman." Elliott was enjoying his war. Then, three months after returning to London, he discovered what war is about.

On August 15, 111 Squadron was scrambled to intercept a formation of Luftwaffe Messerschmitts that had crossed the Channel at Dungeness. In the ferocious, sky-sprawling dogfight that followed, one of the fiercest engagements in the Battle of Britain, seven of the German fighter-bombers were shot down. Basil Fisher's plane was seen peeling away with smoke and flames streaming from the fuselage. He managed to bail out over the village of Sidlesham in West Sussex, with his parachute on fire. The cables burned through, and Elliott's friend tumbled to earth. The pilotless Hurricane crashed into a barn. The body of Flying Officer Basil Fisher was found in Sidlesham pond. He was buried in the churchyard of the Berkshire village where he had been born.

Elliott was quietly but utterly distraught. Like many upperclass Englishmen, he seldom spoke about his feelings, but in its taut, agonized understatement, his private epitaph for Basil Fisher said more than any number of emotive words. The mask of flippancy slipped. "Basil Fisher was killed in action. I felt this very deeply. He had been virtually a brother to me. This was the first time I had been hit by tragedy."

Elliott was still dazed by grief when, just a few weeks later, he met another new recruit to the secret world, a product of Westminster School, a fellow graduate of Trinity College, Cambridge, and a man who would define the rest of his life: Harold Adrian Russell Philby, better known as Kim.

Chapter Two

Section V

THE WORD MOST CONSISTENTLY USED TO DESCRIBE KIM PHILBY was "charm," that intoxicating, beguiling, and occasionally lethal English quality. Philby could inspire and convey affection with such ease that few ever noticed they were being charmed. Male and female, old and young, rich and poor, Kim enveloped them all. He looked out at the world with alert, gentle blue eyes from under an unruly forelock. His manners were exceptional: he was always the first to offer you a drink, to ask after your sick mother and remember your children's names. He loved to laugh, and he loved to drink—and to listen, with deep sincerity and rapt curiosity. "He was the sort of man who won worshippers," said one contemporary. "You didn't just like him, admire him, agree with him; you worshipped him." A stutter, which came and went, added to his appeal, betraying an attractive glimmer of fragility. People waited on his words, for what his friend, the novelist Graham Greene, called his "halting stammered witticisms."

Kim Philby cut a dashing figure in wartime London. As the *Times* correspondent in the Spanish civil war, reporting from the rebel Nationalist side, he had narrowly cheated death in 1937 when a Republican shell landed near the car he was sitting in (eating chocolates and drinking brandy), killing all three of the other passengers. Philby escaped with a minor head wound and a reputation for "great pluck." General Franco himself had pinned a medal, the Red Cross of Military Merit, on the young war reporter. Philby had been one of only fifteen newspaper correspondents selected to join the British Expeditionary Force sent to France on the outbreak of the Second World War. From the continent he wrote wry, distinctive dispatches for the *Times* as he waited with the troops for the fighting to start: "Many express disappointment at the slow tempo of the overture to Armageddon. They expected danger, and they have found damp." Philby continued reporting as the Germans advanced and quit Amiens with the panzers already rumbling into the city. He took ship for England with such haste that he was forced to leave behind his luggage. His expenses claim for lost items became a Fleet Street legend: "Camel-hair overcoat (two years' wear), fifteen guineas; Dunhill pipe (two years old, and all the better for it), one pound ten shillings." It is a measure of his reputation that the *Times* compensated its star correspondent for the loss of an old pipe. Philby was a fine journalist, but his ambitions lay elsewhere. He wanted to join MI6, but like every would-be spy he faced a conundrum: how do you join an organization to which you cannot apply, because it does not formally exist?

In the end, Philby's entry into the secret services turned out to be as straightforward as that of Elliott, and by much the same informal route: he simply "dropped a few hints here and there" among influential acquaintances and waited for an invitation to join the club. The first sign that his signals had been picked up came on the train back to London after the retreat from France, when he found himself in a first-class compartment with a journalist named Hester Harriet Marsden-Smedley, of the *Sunday Express*. Marsden-Smedley was thirty-eight years old, a veteran of foreign wars, and as tough as teak. She had come under enemy fire on the Luxembourg border and witnessed the German surge across the Siegfried Line. She knew people in the secret services and was said to do a little spying on the side. She found Philby charming. She did not beat about the bush.

"A person like you has to be a fool to join the army," she said. "You're capable of doing a lot more to defeat Hitler."

Philby knew exactly what she was alluding to and stammered that he "didn't have any contacts in that world."

"We'll figure something out," said Hester Marsden-Smedley.

Back in London, Philby was summoned to the office of the foreign editor of the *Times*, to be told that a Captain Leslie Sheridan of the "War Department" had called, asking if Philby was available for "war work" of an unspecified nature. Sheridan, the former night editor of the *Daily Mirror*, ran a section of MI6 known as D/Q, responsible for black propaganda and disseminating rumors.

Two days later, Philby sat down to tea at St Ermin's Hotel off St James's Park, just a few hundred yards from MI6 headquarters at 54 Broadway, with another formidable woman: Sarah Algeria Marjorie Maxse, chief of staff for MI6's Section D, which specialized in covert paramilitary operations. The *D* stood for "destruction." Miss Marjorie Maxse was chief organization officer for the Conservative Party, a role that apparently equipped her to identify people who would be good at spreading propaganda and blowing things up. Philby found her "intensely likeable." She clearly liked him too, for two days later they met again, this time with Guy Burgess, an old friend and Cambridge contemporary of Philby's who was already in MI6. "I began to show off, name-dropping shamelessly," wrote Philby. "It turned out I was wasting my time, since a decision had already been taken." MI5 had conducted a routine background check and found "nothing recorded against" him: young Philby was clean. Valentine Vivian, the deputy head of MI6, who had known Philby's father when they were both colonial officials in India, was prepared to vouch personally for the new recruit, giving what may be the quintessential definition of Britain's old boys' network: "I was asked about him, and said I knew his people."

Philby resigned from the *Times* and duly reported to a building near MI6 headquarters, where he was installed in an office with a blank sheaf of paper, a pencil, and a telephone. He did nothing for two weeks except read the newspaper and enjoy long, liquid lunches with Burgess. Philby was beginning to wonder if he had really joined MI6 or some strange, inactive offshoot, when he was assigned to Brickendonbury Hall, a secret school for spies deep in Hertfordshire where an oddball collection of émigré

Czechs, Belgians, Norwegians, Dutchmen, and Spaniards were being trained for covert operations. This unit would eventually be absorbed into the Special Operations Executive (SOE), the organization created, in Winston Churchill's words, to "set Europe ablaze" by operating behind enemy lines. In its early days, the only thing the agents seemed likely to ignite was Brickendonbury Hall and the surrounding countryside. The resident explosives expert mounted a demonstration for visiting Czech intelligence officers but set fire to a wood and nearly immolated the entire delegation. Philby was soon transferred to SOE itself, and then to another training school at Beaulieu in Hampshire, specializing in demolition, wireless communication, and subversion. Philby gave lectures on propaganda, for which, having been a journalist, he was considered suitably trained. He was champing at the bit, eager to join the real wartime intelligence battle. "I escaped to London whenever I could," he wrote. It was during one of these getaways that he encountered Nicholas Elliott.

Elliott could never recall exactly where their first meeting took place. Was it at the bar in the heart of the MI6 building on Broadway, the most secret drinking hole in the world? Or perhaps it was at White's, Elliott's club. Or the Athenaeum, which was Philby's. Perhaps Philby's future wife Aileen, a distant cousin of Elliott's, brought them together. It was inevitable that they would meet eventually, for they were creatures of the same world, thrown together in important clandestine work, and remarkably alike in both background and temperament. Claude Elliott and Philby's father, St John, a noted Arab scholar, explorer, and writer, had been contemporaries and friends at Trinity College, and both sons had obediently followed in their academic footsteps—Philby, four years older, left Cambridge the year Elliott arrived. Both lived under the shadow of imposing but distant fathers whose approval they longed for and never quite won. Both were children of the empire: Kim Philby was born in the Punjab when his father was a colonial administrator; his mother was the daughter of a British official in the Rawalpindi Public Works Department. Elliott's father had been born in Simla. Both had been brought up largely by nannies, and both were unmistakably molded by their schooling: Elliott wore his Old Etonian tie with pride; Philby cherished his Westminster School scarf. And both concealed a certain shyness, Philby behind his impenetrable charm and fluctuating stammer, and Elliott with a barrage of jokes.

They struck up a friendship at once. "In those days," wrote Elliott, "friendships were formed more quickly than in peacetime, particularly amongst those involved in confidential work." While Elliott helped to intercept enemy spies sent to Britain, Philby was preparing Allied saboteurs for insertion into occupied Europe. They found they had much to talk about, within the snug confines of absolute secrecy.

The void in Elliott's life left by the death of Basil Fisher was filled by Philby. "He had an ability to inspire loyalty and affection," wrote Elliott. "He was one of those people who were instinctively liked but more rarely understood. For his friends he sought out the unconventional and the unusual. He did not bore and he did not pontificate." Before the war, Philby had joined the Anglo-German Fellowship, an organization with pro-Nazi leanings, but now, like Elliott, he was committed to battling "the inherent evil of Nazism." The two friends "very rarely discussed politics" and spent more time debating "the English batting averages and watching the cricket from the Mound Stand at Lord's"—home to the Marylebone Cricket Club, the central citadel of cricket, of which Elliott was a member. Philby seemed to share Elliott's firm but simple British loyalties, uncomplicated by ideology. "Indeed," wrote Elliott, "he did not strike me as a political animal." Philby was only twenty-eight when they met, but to Elliott he seemed older, matured by his experience of war, confident, competent, and agreeably louche.

MI6 enjoyed a reputation as the world's most redoubtable intelligence agency, but in 1940 it was in a state of flux, rapidly reorganizing under the pressure of war. Philby seemed to bring a new air of professionalism to the job. He was plainly ambitious but hid his drive, as English manners required, behind a "pose of amiable, disengaged worldliness."

Hugh Trevor-Roper was another new recruit to wartime intelligence. One of the cleverest and rudest men in England, Trevor-Roper (later the historian Lord Dacre) had hardly a good word for any of his colleagues ("by and large pretty stupid, some of them very stupid"). But Philby was different: "An exceptional person: exceptional by his virtues, for he seemed intelligent, sophisticated, even real." He appeared to know exactly where he was going. When Philby spoke about intelligence matters, Elliott thought he displayed impressive "clarity of mind," but he was neither drily academic nor rule-bound: "He was much more a man of practice than of theory." Philby even dressed distinctively, eschewing both the Whitehall stiff collar with pinstripe and the military uniform to which, as a former war correspondent, he was entitled. Instead, he wore a tweed jacket with patches at the elbows, suede shoes, and a cravat, and sometimes a coat of green fabric lined with bright red fox fur, a gift from his father, who had received it from an Arab prince. This eye-catching outfit was topped off with a homburg and a smart, ebony-handled umbrella. Malcolm Muggeridge, another writer recruited to wartime intelligence, noted Philby's unique sartorial swagger: "The old Secret Service professionals were given to spats and monocles long after they passed out of fashion," but the new intake of officers could be seen "slouching about in sweaters and gray flannel trousers, drinking in bars and cafés and low dives . . . boasting of their underworld acquaintances and liaisons. Philby may be taken as a prototype and was indeed, in the eyes of many of them, a model to be copied." Elliott began to dress like Philby. He even bought the same expensive umbrella from James Smith & Sons of Oxford Street, an umbrella that befitted an establishment man of the world, but one with panache.

Through Philby, Elliott was introduced to a fraternity of ambitious, clever, hard-drinking intelligence officers, the "Young Turks" of MI5 and MI6. This informal group often gathered, in off-duty hours, at the home of Tomás Harris, a wealthy, half-Spanish art dealer who worked in MI5, where he would play a central role in the great Double Cross deception as the case officer for double agent "Garbo," Juan García Pujol. Harris and his wife, Hilda, were generous hosts, and their Chelsea home, with its large wine cellar, became an open-house salon for spies. "You'd drop in to see who was around," Philby remembered. Here, in an "atmosphere of *haute cuisine* and *grand vin*," might be found Philby's friend Guy Burgess, extravagant in his homosexuality, frequently drunk, faintly malodorous, and always supremely entertaining. Here too came their friend Anthony Blunt, a Cambridge art scholar now ensconced at the heart of MI5. Other regulars included Victor, Lord Rothschild, the aristocratic chief of countersabotage at MI5, and Guy Liddell, MI5's head of counterintelligence, whose diaries from the period offer an extraordinary glimpse into this private dining and drinking club within the secret world. From MI6 came Tim Milne, who had been at Westminster with Philby (and was the nephew of Winnie-the-Pooh creator A. A. Milne), Richard Brooman-White, now head of MI6's Iberian operations, and, of course, Nicholas Elliott. Hilda Harris served up sumptuous Spanish meals. Liddell, who had once contemplated a professional career as a musician, would sometimes pick up his cello. Burgess, usually accompanied by his latest rent boy, added scandalous unpredictability. And among them moved Philby, with his aura of smiling charm, holding forth on intelligence matters, provoking arguments ("out of fun rather than malice," Elliott insisted), and dispensing Harris's fine wine in torrential quantities.

Even by the heavy-drinking standards of wartime, the spies were spectacular boozers. Alcohol helped to blunt the stress of clandestine war, serving as both a lubricant and a bond, and the gentlemen's clubs were able to obtain supplies for their members far beyond the reach of ordinary rationed folk. Dennis Wheatley, a novelist who worked in the deception section of British intelligence, described a typical lunch with fellow officers: "To start with we always had two or three Pimm's at a table in the bar, then a so-called 'short-one' well-laced with absinthe. . . . There would be smoked salmon or potted shrimps, then a Dover sole, jugged hare, salmon or game, and a Welsh rarebit to wind up with. Good red or white wine washed this down, and we ended with port or

Kümmel." After this blowout, Wheatley tended to sneak off to bed "for an hour to sleep it off" before returning to work.

No one served (or consumed) alcohol with quite the same joie de vivre and determination as Kim Philby. "He was a formidable drinker," Elliott wrote, and held to the arcane theory that "serious drinkers should never take exercise or make sudden or violent movements" since this would provoke a "violent headache." Philby sucked down the drink, and poured it into others, as if on a mission.

Elliott was flattered to find himself in such company and relaxed. Englishmen are naturally reticent. Englishmen of Elliott's class and character even more so, and an upper-class English spy, in wartime, may be the most discreet human being imaginable, his stiff upper lip buttoned down inflexibly. Members of the secret services were forbidden to tell their friends, wives, parents, or children what they did, yet many were drawn to this closed clique, bound by shared secrets others must never know. In the civilian world Elliott never breathed a word about his job. But inside the secular monastery that is MI6, and particularly at Harris's raucous soirees, he was among people he could trust utterly and speak to openly in a way that was impossible outside. "It was an organisation in which a large proportion of one's colleagues, male and female, were personal friends," wrote Elliott. "A sort of convivial camaraderie prevailed, rather like a club, in which we all called each other by our first names, and saw a lot of one another outside the office."

The friendship between Philby and Elliott was not just one of shared interests and professional identity, but something deeper. Nick Elliott was friendly to all but emotionally committed to few. The bond with Philby was unlike any other in his life. "They spoke the same language," Elliott's son Mark recalls. "Kim was as close a friend as my father ever had." Elliott never openly expressed, or demonstrated, this affection. Like so much of importance in the masculine culture of the time, it was left unsaid. Elliott hero-worshipped Philby, but he also loved him, with a powerful male adoration that was unrequited, unsexual, and unstated.

Their relationship grew still closer when both were plucked from the outer reaches of British intelligence and placed at the very center, in Section V of MI6, the division devoted to counterintelligence. MI5 was responsible for maintaining security, including the combating of enemy espionage, within the UK and the British Empire. MI6 was responsible for gathering intelligence and running agents abroad. Within MI6, Section V played a specific and vital role: collecting information on enemy intelligence in foreign parts, by means of spies and defectors, and furnishing MI5 with advance warning of espionage threats to Britain. A vital link between Britain's secret services, Section V's task was to "negate, confuse, deceive, subvert, monitor or control the clandestine intelligence collection operations and agents of foreign governments or agencies." Before the war, the section had devoted most of its energies to monitoring the spread of international communism and battling Soviet espionage, but as the war progressed, it came to focus almost exclusively on the intelligence operations of the Axis powers. The Iberian peninsula was a particular concern. Neutral Spain and Portugal stood on the front line of the espionage war. Many of the German intelligence operations directed at Britain were launched from these two countries, and in 1941 MI6 began beefing up the Iberian operation. One evening Tommy Harris told Philby that the bosses were looking for someone "with a knowledge of Spain to take charge of the expanded sub-section." Philby immediately expressed an interest; Harris spoke to Richard Brooman-White, Elliott's old friend, the chief of MI6's Iberian operations; Brooman-White spoke to the head of MI6. "The old boy network began to operate," as Philby put it, and within days he was summoned to see the head of Section V.

Major Felix Cowgill was the model of the old-style intelligence officer: a former officer in the Indian police, he was rigid, combative, paranoid, and quite dim. Trevor-Roper dismissed him as a "purblind, disastrous megalomaniac," and Philby, privately, was equally scathing. "As an intelligence officer, he was inhibited by lack of imagination, inattention to detail and sheer ignorance of the world." Cowgill was "suspicious and bristling" toward anyone

outside his section, blindly loyal to those within it, and no match
for the Philby charm.

Philby never formally applied for the job, and Cowgill never
formally offered it, but after one long, bibulous evening, Philby
emerged as the new head of Section V's Iberian department, a
job that, as Philby happily noted, entailed wider responsibilities
as well as "personal contacts with the rest of SIS and MI5." Before Philby took up the post, however, Valentine Vivian, known as
"Vee-Vee," the deputy head of MI6, decided to have another chat
with Philby's father. Hillary St John Bridger Philby was a figure of
considerable notoriety. As adviser to Ibn Saud, the first monarch
of Saudi Arabia, he had played (and would continue to play) a key
role in the oleaginous politics of that region. He had converted to
Islam, taking the name Sheikh Abdullah, spoke Arabic fluently,
and would eventually marry, as his second wife, a slave girl from
Baluchistan presented to him by the Saudi king. He remained,
however, quintessentially English in his tastes and wildly unpredictable in his opinions. The elder Philby's opposition to the war
had seen him arrested and briefly imprisoned, an episode that
did no harm to his own social standing or his son's career prospects. Over lunch at the club, Colonel Vivian asked St John Philby
about his son's politics.

"He was a bit of a communist at Cambridge, wasn't he?"

"Oh that was all schoolboy nonsense," Jack Philby airily replied. "He's a reformed character now."

Nicholas Elliott, meanwhile, was making a parallel career
move. In the summer of 1941 he was also transferred to Section V,
with responsibility for the Netherlands. Henceforth Philby would
be fighting German espionage in the Iberian peninsula, and Elliott would be doing the same in Nazi-occupied Holland, from the
next-door office. Each would be paid a salary, in cash, of six hundred pounds a year and neither, in accordance with long-standing
secret-services rules, would pay any tax. Philby and Elliott were
now fighting shoulder to shoulder in the "active pursuit and liquidation of the enemy intelligence services."

Section V was not housed in London with the rest of MI6 but headquartered in Glenalmond, a large Victorian house in St Albans, some twenty miles north of the capital, code-named "War Station XB." Kim Philby and Aileen rented a cottage on the outskirts of the town.

Philby had been introduced to his future wife, on the day war was declared, by Flora Solomon, a friend from Cambridge. The daughter of a Jewish-Russian gold tycoon, Solomon was another exotic bloom in the colorful hothouse of Philby's circle: as a young woman she had had an affair with Aleksandr Kerensky, the Russian prime minister deposed by Lenin in the October Revolution, before going on to marry a British First World War general. In 1939, she was hired to improve working conditions at Marks & Spencer, and here she met and befriended Aileen Furse, a store detective in the shop's Marble Arch branch. "Aileen belonged to that class, now out of fashion, called 'county,'" wrote Solomon. "She was typically English, slim and attractive, fiercely patriotic." Working undercover, in her twinset and raincoat, she was virtually invisible when discreetly policing the aisles of Marks & Spencer. Aileen tended to disappear in a crowd, hanging back, watchful and careful. Her upbringing in the Home Counties had been strictly conventional, boring, and quite lonely. Secretly, she was "subject to depressions." Aileen Furse and Kim Philby met over drinks at Solomon's Mayfair home. Philby began talking about his experiences as a newspaper correspondent during the Spanish civil war. "He found an avid listener in Aileen," wrote Solomon, and "the next I knew they were sharing a flat."

Their union, it seemed to Elliott, was an ideal one, founded on a shared love of good company. Elliott liked Aileen almost as much as he liked Philby, an affection that deepened after Elliot developed diabetes and she gently nursed him back to health. "She was highly intelligent," wrote Elliott, "very human, full of courage and had a pleasant sense of humor." Indeed, Aileen was just the sort of wife he hoped for himself: loyal, discreet, patriotic, and willing to laugh at his jokes. The Philbys' first child, a daughter, was born in 1941; a son followed the next year, and another the year after that. Philby was a doting father, Elliott noted approvingly, bursting with "parental pride."

The Philby home became a gathering place for the young intelligence officers of Section V, an out-of-town version of the Harris salon in London, where the doors, and various bottles, were always open. Graham Greene, then one of Philby's deputies, recalled the "long Sunday lunches in St Albans when the whole subsection relaxed under his leadership for a few hours of heavy drinking." Philby was adored by his colleagues, who recalled his "small loyalties," his generosity of spirit, and his distaste for petty office politics. "He had something about him—an aura of lovable authority like some romantic platoon commander—which made people want to appear at their best in front of him. Even his senior officers recognized his abilities and deferred to him."

Section V was a tight-knit little community, just a dozen officers and their deputies and a similar number of support staff. Officers and secretaries were on Christian-name terms, and some were on more intimate terms than that. Philby's "merry band" included his old school friend Tim Milne, a jovial eccentric named Trevor Wilson who had formerly been "a purchaser of skunk excrement in Abyssinia for the French perfume company Molyneux," and Jack Ivens, a fruit exporter who spoke fluent Spanish. The local townsfolk were led to believe that the educated young men and women in the big house were a team of archaeologists from the British Museum, excavating the ruins of Verulamium, the Roman name for St Albans. Mrs. Rennit, the cook, served solid English fare and fish-and-chips on Fridays. On the weekends they played cricket on the pitch behind Glenalmond before repairing to the King Harry pub next door. Colonel Cowgill was the boss, but Philby was the animating spirit of the group: "The sense of dedication and purpose to whatever he was doing gleamed through and inspired men to follow him." Elliott was not alone in his adulation. "No one could have been a better chief than Kim Philby," wrote Graham Greene. "He worked harder than anyone else and never gave the impression of labor. He was always relaxed, completely unflappable." In even the most casual bureaucracies there is room for jockeying, but Philby was the epitome of loyalty. "If one made an error of judgment he was sure to minimise it and cover it up, without criticism." Desmond Bristow, a new Spanish-speaking recruit, arrived at Glenalmond in September 1941 and was welcomed by Philby, "a gentle-looking man with smiling eyes and an air of confidence. My first impression was of a man of quiet intellectual charm. . . . He had a spiritual tranquillity about him." The "cosiness" of Section V distinguished it from other, more reserved parts of MI6. The team members kept few secrets from one another, official or otherwise. "It was not difficult to find out what colleagues were doing," wrote Philby. "What was known to one would be known to all."

The admiration of his subordinates was echoed by the approbation of Philby's superiors. Felix Cowgill called him "a good cricket umpire." There could be no higher praise. Here was a man who played by the most honorable rules. But some saw a flicker of something else in Philby, something harder and deeper, a "calculating ambition," a ruthless "single-mindedness." Like Elliott, he used humor to deflect inquiry. "There was something mysterious about him," wrote Trevor-Roper. "He never engaged you in serious conversation—it was always irony."

As head of the Iberian section, Philby faced a formidable challenge. Although Spain and Portugal were officially neutral non-combatants in the war, in reality both countries tolerated, and even actively encouraged, German espionage on a grand scale. Wilhelm Leissner, the Abwehr chief in Spain, presided over a well-funded, sprawling intelligence network made up of more than two hundred officers (more than half the German diplomatic presence), with some fifteen hundred agents deployed around the country. Leissner's principal target was Britain: recruiting and dispatching spies to the UK, bugging the British embassy, bribing Spanish officials, and sabotaging British shipping. Portugal was another hotbed of espionage, although Abwehr operations were less efficient under the command of a dissolute German aristocrat named Ludovico von Karsthoff. The Abwehr poured spies and cash into Spain and Portugal, but in his duel with Leissner and Karsthoff, Philby had one overwhelming advantage: Bletchley Park, the top secret decoding station where intercepted German wireless messages were decrypted, furnishing a priceless insight into Nazi intelligence. "It was not long before we had a very full picture of the Abwehr in the Peninsula," wrote Philby. That information would soon be put "to good use in disrupting, or at least seriously embarrassing, the enemy on his own chosen ground."

Nicholas Elliott's task of attacking German intelligence in the Netherlands, his former stomping ground, was a different proposition, and even harder. The Abwehr in Nazi-occupied Holland was highly effective, recruiting, training, and dispatching a stream of spies to Britain. By contrast, infiltrating agents into Holland was exceptionally difficult. The few networks that had survived the Venlo incident were riddled with Nazi informers.

In a plot that smacks of James Bond (and has all the hallmarks of an Elliott ruse), a Dutch agent named Peter Tazelaar was put ashore near the seafront casino at Scheveningen, wearing full evening dress and covered with a rubber suit to keep him dry. Once ashore, Tazelaar peeled off his outer suit and began to "mingle with the crowd on the front" in his dinner jacket, which had been sprinkled with brandy to reinforce the "party-goer's image." Formally dressed and alcoholically perfumed, Tazelaar successfully made it past the German guards and picked up a radio previously dropped by parachute. The echo of 007 may not be coincidental: among the young blades of British intelligence at this time was a young officer in naval intelligence named Ian Fleming, the future author of the James Bond books. Ian Fleming and Nicholas Elliott had both experienced the trauma of being educated at Durnford School; they became close friends.

Peter Tazelaar was one of the few to make it back to Britain. Of the fifteen agents sent into Holland between June 1940 and December 1941, only four survived, thanks to the brutal efficiency of Major Hermann Giskes, the head of Abwehr counterintelligence in Holland, Elliott's opposite number. In August 1941 Giskes intercepted a team of Dutch SOE agents shipped into Holland by fast torpedo boat and forced them, under threat of execution, to send encrypted wireless messages back to Britain, luring more spies across the water. Some fifty-five Dutch agents were subsequently captured and dozens executed, in a Double Cross operation code-named *Englandspiel* ("The England Game"), before two managed to escape and alert the British to the fact that they were being hoaxed. Winding up the operation, Giskes sent a final, mocking wireless message: "This is the last time you are trying to make business in Netherlands without our assistance Stop we think this rather unfair in view our long and successful co-operation as your sole agents Stop but never mind whenever you will come to pay a visit to the Continent you may be assured that you will be received with the same care and result as all those who you sent us before Stop so long." The episode was "an operational disaster," in Philby's words, but almost equally alarming was the discovery that German intelligence in Holland had managed to slip at least one spy into Britain undetected.

In the spring of 1941 the body of a Dutchman was found in an air-raid shelter in Cambridge. His name, unimprovably, was Engelbertus Fukken. In his pockets and suitcase were found a Dutch passport, a forged identity card, and one shilling and sixpence. He had parachuted into Buckinghamshire five months earlier, passed himself off as a refugee, and shot himself in the head when he ran out of money. No Nazi spy had managed to remain at large for so long, and there was no trace of him in the Bletchley Park intercepts, which raised, for Elliott, the worrying possibility that there might be others at large.

Under Cowgill's relaxed regime, the officers of Section V could visit London "virtually at will." Philby and Elliott seized every opportunity to do so, in order to cultivate "contacts with other SIS sections, with MI5 and with other government departments" while also visiting their clubs and, in the summer, watching cricket together at Lord's. Both volunteered for "fire-watching nights" once or twice a month at MI6 headquarters, monitoring the telegrams that came in overnight from around the world, which offered a fascinating insight into British intelligence operations. Among the secret brethren, Elliott and Philby were the closest of siblings, reveling in the shared risks, hard work, and ribaldry.

One morning in 1941, Kim Philby caught the train to London, taking with him, as usual, a "bulging briefcase and a long visiting list." He also carried a detailed description of the workings of Section V and its personnel, aims, operations, failures, and successes, written out in "longhand, in neat, tiny writing." After completing his round of meetings at MI5 and MI6, Philby did not head to the bar beneath MI6, nor to his club, nor to the Harris home for an evening of drinking and secret sharing. Instead he descended into the St James's Park Underground station. He let the first train leave without boarding. Then he waited until every other passenger had boarded the next train before slipping on just as the doors closed. Two stops later, he alighted and caught a train in the opposite direction. Then he hopped on a moving bus. Finally certain that he was not being followed ("dry-cleaned," in spy jargon), Philby made his way to a park, where a stocky, fair-haired man was waiting for him on a bench. They shook hands; Philby handed over the contents of his briefcase and then headed to King's Cross to catch the train home to St Albans.

Had Nick Elliott examined the report about Section V written by his best friend, he would have been amazed and then mortified. One passage read: "MR NICHOLAS ELLIOTT. 24, 5ft 9in. Brown hair, prominent lips, black glasses, ugly and rather pig-like to look at. Good brain, good sense of humor. Likes a drink but was recently very ill and now, as a consequence, drinks little. He is in charge of Holland."

Elliott would have been still more astonished to discover that the man hurrying away into the night with the bundle of papers was an officer of the NKVD, Stalin's intelligence agency (the predecessor organization to the KGB), and that his friend Kim Philby was an experienced Soviet spy of eight years' standing, code-named "Sonny."

Chapter Three

Otto and Sonny

PHILBY'S FATHER NICKNAMED HIS SON KIM AFTER THE EPONY-
mous hero in the popular Rudyard Kipling novel. Brought up by
an Indian nanny, Philby's first language was a sort of nursery Pun-
jabi; like Kipling's Kim, he was a white child who could pass for an
Indian. The name stuck forever, but its aptness would not emerge
for years. The fictional Kim has two distinct personalities; he is a
two-sided man:

> Something I owe to the soil that grew
> More to the life that fed,
> But most to Allah Who gave me two
> Separate sides to my head.

The soil that grew Kim Philby had produced a conventional
upper-class, public school–educated Englishman; the life that fed
him had created something entirely different, and it was a life that
his dear friend Nicholas Elliott knew nothing about.

He did not know that Philby had become a Soviet agent in the
very year that Elliott had gone up to Cambridge; he did not know
that Philby's idyllic marriage was a fraud or that his friend was
really married to an Austrian communist spy; he did not know
that Philby had joined MI6 not as an eager patriot like himself
but rather, in Philby's own words, as a "penetration agent working in the Soviet interest." And he did not know that during the
convivial Sunday lunches in St Albans, the boozy evenings at the
Harris home, and the drinks in the basement of MI6 and the bar

at White's, Philby was hard at work, absorbing his friends' secrets as fast as the gin and then passing them all to Moscow.

The seeds of Philby's double life lay in his childhood, his father, his upbringing, and the intense ideological conversion that shaped him in early adulthood. Philby maintained that his dual existence emerged from an unwavering belief in a set of political principles that he discovered at the age of eighteen and never abandoned: what Philby's enemies described as betrayal he saw as loyalty. But there was more to Philby than mere ideology. Like many late-empire products of the establishment, he had an inborn faith in his ability, and right, to change and rule the world. This he shared with Elliott, though their views of how the world should be run could not have been more opposed. Both were imperialists, but for rival empires. Beneath Philby's golden charm lay a thick substratum of conceit; the charmer invites you into his world, though never too far and only on his terms. The English love their secrets, the knowledge that they know a little more than the man standing next to them; when that man is also a secret keeper, it redoubles what Trevor-Roper called "the exquisite relish of ruthless, treacherous, private power." Philby tasted the drug of deception as a youth and remained addicted to infidelity for the rest of his life.

Kim was his father's pet and project. Like Claude Elliott, St John Philby was ambitious for his son but showed him little affection. He molded him for Westminster and Cambridge and was proud when his son achieved those goals, but mostly he was absent, charging around the Arab world courting controversy and searching for celebrity. "My ambition is fame, whatever that may mean," he said. St John Philby was a notable scholar, linguist, and ornithologist, and he did achieve fame of a sort, but he might have found more lasting appreciation had he not been so profoundly irritating, willful, and arrogant. He was a man who regarded his opinions, however briefly adopted, as revealed truth: he never backed down, or listened, or compromised. He was equally swift to give and take offense and ferociously critical of everyone except himself. He alternately neglected and hectored his wife, Dora. He was snobbish and in many ways conventional, but also instinctively contrarian, forever bucking the system and then complaining furiously when the system failed to reward him. Kim idolized him—and loathed him.

At school the young Philby was "constantly aware of his father's long shadow." Alongside his fine academic record and general popularity, the boy showed a small streak of mendacity, prompting some parental disquiet: "He should always be careful to be truthful whatever the consequences," observed his father. Kim arrived at Cambridge at the age of seventeen on a history scholarship, having inherited both his father's intellectual self-confidence and his determination to swim against the tide.

The violent ideological currents sweeping Cambridge in the 1930s had created a vortex that quickly swept up Philby and many other clever, angry, alienated young men. He made friends on the political left and some on the extreme left. Fascism was on the march in Europe, and only communism, it seemed to many, could oppose it. Late at night, over copious drinks, in paneled rooms, young students argued, debated, tried on one ideological outfit or another, and, in a small handful of cases, embraced violent revolution. The most significant, and certainly the most colorful, of Philby's radical new friends was Guy Francis de Moncy Burgess—amoral, witty, supremely dangerous, and loud in his advocacy of communism. Another was Donald Maclean, a clever young linguist destined for the Foreign Office. Philby joined the Cambridge University Socialist Society. He canvassed on behalf of the Labor Party. But there was no "sudden conversion," no revolutionary epiphany wherein the religion of communism seized his soul. Instead, the student Philby moved slowly leftward, and then faster after visiting Berlin in 1933 and witnessing at first hand, like Elliott, the brutality of Nazism during an anti-Jewish rally. Unlike many of his friends, Philby never joined the Communist Party. His beliefs were radical but simple: the rich had exploited the poor for too long; the only bulwark against fascism was Soviet communism, "the inner fortress of the world movement"; capitalism was doomed and crumbling; the British establishment was poisoned by Nazi leanings. "I left the university," he wrote, "with the conviction that my life must be devoted to communism." Yet he wore his convictions so lightly they were all but invisible. With the fourteen pounds he was awarded for his degree, he bought the collected works of Karl Marx. But there is no evidence he ever studied them in depth, or even read them. Though politics would dictate his life, he was not greatly interested in political theory. As Elliott later observed: "I can hardly see him as a lecturer in dialectical materialism."

Before leaving Cambridge Philby sought out his supervisor, the Marxist economist Maurice Dobb, and asked him how best he might "devote his life to the communist cause." It was a measure of how deeply Marxism had penetrated the university that Philby felt no danger in asking such a loaded question, and Dobb had no qualms in answering it. Dobb directed him to Louis Gibarti, a Paris agent of the Comintern, the international communist organization, who in turn furnished an introduction to the Austrian communist underground. It was that easy: the radical Left had its own old boys' network.

In the autumn of 1933 Philby traveled to Vienna, ostensibly to improve his German before applying to join the Foreign Office, in reality to witness, and if possible take part in, the battle between Left and Right then under way in the Austrian capital. Engelbert Dollfuss, Austria's extreme right-wing dictator, had already suspended the constitution and outlawed strikes and demonstrations in his efforts to suppress the socialist movement. A full-scale conflict was imminent, and the situation, as Philby put it, was "at a crisis point." Philby made his way to the address provided by Gibarti and introduced himself to its occupants, Israel and Gisella Kohlman and their daughter Alice—with whom he promptly fell in love. Alice, known as Litzi, was twenty-three, dark-haired, Jewish, vivacious, direct to the point of bluntness, and newly divorced, having married at eighteen. When Philby met Litzi, he was still a virgin and a political naïf; she swiftly attended to both deficiencies. Litzi was a fully committed revolutionary and, according to one contemporary, a "tremendous little sexpot."

Litzi was active in the Viennese underground, and in contact with Soviet intelligence. She had spent two weeks in prison for subversive activities. Philby was instantly besotted. They made love in the snow. ("Actually quite warm, once you get used to it," he recalled.) Philby had been in Austria for only a few weeks when Dollfuss moved to crush the leftists, arresting socialist leaders, banning trade unions, and catapulting Austria into a brief but vicious civil war. Philby and Litzi plunged into the fray on behalf of the Revolutionary Socialists, the short-lived alliance of socialists and communists, passing messages, drafting leaflets, and helping to smuggle wanted men and women out of the country. The Left was crushed in four days; 1,500 people were arrested, and the Socialist leaders were executed. Litzi was on the wanted list, and the police were closing in, but Philby's British passport would offer her protection: on February 24, 1934, he married Litzi in Vienna Town Hall. This was more than just a marriage made in Marxism. Litzi may be the only woman to whom Philby remained both ideologically and sexually faithful. "Even though the basis of our relationship was political to some extent, I truly loved her and she loved me."

A few weeks later, the newlyweds arrived in London, where they lodged with Philby's mother. Conventional Dora Philby, desperate to keep up appearances despite a perennial shortage of money, was not best pleased to find her son married to a foreign communist. She regarded his politics as another passing adolescent phase, like acne. "I do hope Kim gets a job to get him off this bloody communism," Mrs. Philby wrote to her husband in Saudi Arabia. "He's not quite extreme yet, but may become so." St John was unconcerned by his son's radicalism: "Excess can always be toned down afterwards," he declared.

Just a few weeks after his return from Vienna, Philby sat on a bench in Regent's Park, waiting to meet a "man of decisive importance" who, Litzi had promised, would change his life. When Philby had asked her who he was and what made him so important, she had clammed up.

Out of the June sunshine appeared a short, stout man in his

early thirties with curly, fair hair and intelligent eyes. He spoke English with a strong Eastern European accent and introduced himself as Otto. Philby never forgot their first conversation. Otto spoke about art and music, his love of Paris, and his dislike of London. This, Philby reflected, was a "man of considerable cultural background." Philby was entranced: "He was a marvellous man. Simply marvellous. I felt that immediately. The first thing you noticed about him were his eyes. He looked at you as if nothing more important in life than you and talking to you existed at that moment." That was a quality many found in Philby too. Gradually their conversation drifted toward politics, and then the works of Marx and Lenin, which Otto seemed to know by heart. Philby, in turn, described his political experiences in Cambridge, his activities in Vienna, and his wish to join the Communist Party. They spoke in euphemisms, with Otto hinting that he could put "important and interesting work" in Philby's direction. As with most espionage relationships, this one began not with politics but with friendship. "I trusted him from the start," wrote Philby. "It was an amazing conversation." They agreed to meet again.

Otto's real name, which Philby would not learn for decades, was Arnold Deutsch. He was the chief recruiter for Soviet intelligence in Britain, the principal architect of what would later become known as the Cambridge spy ring. Born of Czech Jewish parents, Deutsch had moved with his family to Austria when he was a child. Prodigiously clever, he emerged from Vienna University after just five years with a doctorate in chemistry, a fervent commitment to communism, and a passionate interest in sex. His first career was as publisher and publicist for the German sexologist Wilhelm Reich, the "prophet of the better orgasm," who sought to bring sexual enlightenment to the prudish Viennese as part of the "Sex-Pol" (sexual politics) movement, which equated sexual repression with fascist authoritarianism. Reich developed the radical, though slightly implausible, theory that "a poor man's sexual performance led him to fascism." While promoting Reich's idea that better sex makes better revolutionaries, Deutsch was also secretly working for Soviet intelligence, having undergone a training course in Moscow. The Gestapo arrested Deutsch briefly in 1933; the antipornography section of the Vienna police was also on his trail, on account of his Sex-Pol activities. A year later he arrived in Britain to begin a postgraduate degree in phonetics and psychology at University College London while working as a spy recruiter. Deutsch had relatives in the UK, notably his wealthy cousin Oscar, the founder of the Odeon cinema chain, which was said to stand for "Oscar Deutsch Entertains Our Nation." One Deutsch was doing well out of British capitalism; the other was hellbent on destroying it.

Deutsch was an "illegal," espionage parlance for a spy operating without diplomatic status. His mission was to recruit radical students at the best universities (using his academic work as cover) who might later rise to positions of power and influence. Deutsch was on the hunt for long-term, deep-cover, ideological spies who could blend invisibly into the British establishment, for Soviet intelligence was playing a long game, laying down seed corn that could be harvested many years hence or left dormant forever. It was a simple, brilliant, durable strategy of the sort that only a state committed to permanent world revolution could have initiated. It would prove staggeringly successful.

Philby's introduction to Deutsch appears to have been arranged by Edith Tudor-Hart, an Austrian communist friend of Litzi's. Born Edith Suschitzky and the daughter of a wealthy Viennese publisher, Edith married an English doctor and fellow communist named Alexander Tudor-Hart, and moved to England in 1930, where she worked as a photographer and part-time talent scout for the NKVD, under the remarkably unimaginative codename "Edith." She had been under MI5 surveillance since 1931, but not, fatefully, on the day she led Philby to meet Deutsch in Regent's Park.

Philby was just the sort of recruit Deutsch was looking for. He was ambitious, well connected, and devoted to the cause, but unobtrusively: unlike others, Philby had never made his radical views obvious. He sought a career in diplomacy, journalism, or the civil service, all excellent perches for a spy. Deutsch was also under the impression that St John Philby was an agent of British intelligence, with access to important secret material.

At their second meeting, Deutsch asked Philby if he was willing to act as an undercover agent for the communist cause. Philby did not hesitate: "One does not look twice at an offer of enrolment in an elite force," he wrote. That was a most telling remark: the attraction of this new role lay in its exclusivity. In some ways, Philby's story is that of a man in pursuit of ever more exclusive clubs. In a brilliant lecture written in 1944, C. S. Lewis described the fatal British obsession with the "inner ring," the belief that somewhere, just beyond reach, is an exclusive group holding real power and influence, which a certain sort of Englishman constantly aspires to find and join. Westminster School and Cambridge University are elite clubs; MI6 is an even more exclusive fellowship; working secretly for the NKVD within MI6 placed Philby in a club of one, the most elite member of a secret inner ring. "Of all the passions," wrote Lewis, "the passion for the Inner Ring is most skillful in making a man who is not yet a very bad man do very bad things."

"My future looked romantic," Philby wrote. Deutsch laid out a vision of that future: Philby and Litzi must break off all communist contacts; rather than join the party, he should establish a new political image as a right-winger, even a Nazi sympathizer. He must become, to all outward appearances, a conventional member of the very class he was committed to opposing. "By background, education, appearance and manners you are an intellectual, a bourgeois. You have a marvelous career ahead of you. A bourgeois career," Deutsch told him. "The anti-fascist movement needs people who can enter into the bourgeoisie." Hidden inside the establishment, Philby could aid the revolution in a "real and palpable way." Deutsch began to instruct Philby on the rudiments of tradecraft: how to arrange a meeting; where to leave messages; how to detect if his telephone was bugged; how to spot a tail and how to lose one. He presented Philby with a new subminiature Minox camera and taught him how to copy documents. Philby memorized Deutsch's lessons "like poetry." His double life had begun.

Deutsch gave Philby the affectionate code name "Sonny" ("Söhnchen" in German) and reported his catch to the London *rezident*, the regional control officer of the NKVD, who passed on the news to Moscow Center, the Soviet intelligence headquarters: "We have recruited the son of an Anglo agent, advisor to Ibn-Saud, Philby." Moscow was impressed: "What are his prospects for a diplomatic career? Are they realistic? Will he choose his own path or will his father 'suggest' he meet someone and discuss it? That would be good." Deutsch instructed his new protégé to draw up a list of acquaintances and contemporaries, from Oxford as well as Cambridge, who might also be recruited to the cause. He told him to discreetly explore whatever documents St John Philby kept in his office at home and to photograph "the most interesting."

Asking Philby to spy on his own father was surely a test of his commitment, and Philby passed it easily. He did what was asked of him without hesitation. Deutsch reported that his new recruit "refers to his parents, who are well-to-do bourgeois, and his entire social milieu with unfeigned contempt and hatred." Philby was doubtless putting on a display of class-warrior zeal for Deutsch, for he was spellbound by his spymaster, "his marvelous education, his humanity, his fidelity to building a new society." They met often, always in "the remoter open spaces in London" and once in Paris. Deutsch flattered and inspired his young ward. When Philby's relationship with Litzi began to falter, the older man dispensed marital advice. ("His wife was his first lover in his life," Deutsch reported to Moscow, keen, as ever, to establish a link between sex and socialist zeal. "When difficulties arose in their relationship, they would confide in me and both followed my advice.") Philby was bonded, ideologically and emotionally, to his charismatic Soviet controller. "I sometimes felt we had been friends since childhood," he wrote. "I was certain that my life and myself interested him not so much professionally as on a human level." The fatal conceit of most spies is to believe they are loved, in a relationship between equals, and not merely manipulated. Deutsch made a careful study of Philby's psychology, the flashes of insecurity beneath the debonair exterior, the unpredictable stammer, his veiled resentment of a domineering father. Deutsch reported to Moscow Center that Philby had potential but needed "constant encouragement": "Söhnchen comes from a peculiar family. His father is considered at present to be the most distinguished expert on the Arab world. . . . He is an ambitious tyrant and wanted to make a great man out of his son." Deutsch noted his acolyte's intellectual curiosity, his fluctuating moods, his old-world manners, and his resolve: "It's amazing that such a young man is so widely and deeply knowledgeable. . . . He is so serious he forgets that he is only 25."

Deutsch urged Philby to get a job in journalism—"Once you're inside, you'll look around and then decide which way to go"—and he reassured Moscow that Philby's family contacts would ensure swift promotion. "He has many friends from the best homes." Philby soon obtained a job as a subeditor at the *World Review of Reviews*, a literary and political monthly, before moving on to the *Anglo-German Trade Gazette*, a magazine devoted to improving economic relations between Britain and Germany that was partly financed by the Nazi government. Completing this lurch from extreme Left (secretly) to extreme Right (publicly), he joined the Anglo-German Fellowship, a society formed in 1935 to foster closer understanding with Germany. A sump for the forces of appeasement and Nazi admiration, the fellowship included politicians, aristocrats, and business leaders, some naive or gullible, others rampantly fascist. With views diametrically opposed to his own, such people offered Philby ideal political camouflage, as well as information, eagerly received in Moscow, about links between the Nazis and their British sympathizers. Philby traveled regularly to Berlin on behalf of the fellowship and even met the German foreign minister, Ribbentrop. He later claimed to have found playing the part of a keen young fascist "profoundly repulsive" because "in the eyes of my friends, even conservative ones, but honest conservatives, I looked pro-Nazi." Former friends from the Left were aghast at his apparent conversion, and some shunned him. Deutsch commiserated, telling Philby he knew "how difficult it is to leave old friends." Litzi and Philby's commitment to communism proved more durable than their commitment to each other; they separated, without rancor, and she moved to Paris.

To Moscow's surprise, Philby found nothing of intelligence value among his father's papers. The NKVD was convinced that someone as well connected as St John Philby who traveled widely and freely must be a spy. "It seems unlikely that his father . . . would not be a close and intimate collaborator with the Intelligence Service." Not for the last time, Moscow elevated its erroneous expectations into fact. Meanwhile Philby dutifully handed over a list of potential recruits among his left-wing Cambridge friends, including Donald Maclean and Guy Burgess.

Maclean, still a committed communist, was by now in the Foreign Office. Philby invited him to dinner and hinted that there was important clandestine work to be done on behalf of the party. "The people I could introduce you to are very serious." Philby instructed Maclean to carry a book with a bright yellow cover into a particular café on a given day. "Otto" was waiting for him and duly signed up this "very serious and aloof" young man with "good connections." Code-named "Orphan," Maclean too began to shed his radical past. "Sonny has high praise for Orphan," Deutsch reported to Moscow. Burgess seemed a more dubious prospect: "Very smart . . . but a bit superficial and could let slip in some circumstances." Characteristically, Burgess sensed he was being denied admission to a most enjoyable and risky party and brazenly barged his way in. One night he confronted Maclean: "Do you think that I believe for even one jot that you have stopped being a communist? You're simply up to something." A little reluctantly, Deutsch added Burgess to his roster. Burgess duly announced, with maximum fanfare, that he had swapped Marx for Mussolini and was now a devotee of Italian fascism. It was Burgess who subsequently introduced Deutsch to yet another recruit, Anthony Blunt, already an art historian of note. Slowly, discreetly, with paternal diligence and Philby's help, Deutsch added one link after another to the Cambridge spy chain.

While Deutsch handled recruitment, much of the day-to-day management of the spies was carried out by another "illegal,"

Theodore Stephanovich Maly, a Hungarian former monk who, as an army chaplain during the First World War, had been taken prisoner in the Carpathians and witnessed such appalling horrors that he emerged a revolutionary: "I lost my faith in God and when the revolution broke out I joined the Bolsheviks. I became a communist and have always remained one." After training as an agent-runner, he arrived in London in 1932 under the alias "Paul Hardt." For a spy, Maly was conspicuous, standing six feet four inches tall with a "shiny grey complexion" and gold fillings in his front teeth. But he was a most subtle controller who shared Deutsch's admiration for Philby, describing him as "an inspirational figure, a true comrade and idealist." The feeling was reciprocated; in Philby's mind the bewitching personalities of his handlers were indistinguishable from their political allure: "Both of them were intelligent and experienced professionals, as well as genuinely very good people."

Philby's work for the *Anglo-German Trade Gazette* came to an abrupt end in 1936 when the Nazis withdrew financial support. But by then, Moscow Center had other plans for him. Civil war had erupted in Spain between the Soviet-backed Republican forces and the fascist-backed Nationalists under General Franco. Philby was instructed to spy on the Nationalists, using freelance journalism as a cover, and to report back on troop movements, communications, morale, and the military support being supplied to Franco's forces by Germany and Italy. Moscow would pay for his passage. Philby "handles our money very carefully," Deutsch told his bosses. In Spain, Philby quickly ingratiated himself with Franco's press officers and began sending well-informed articles to British newspapers, notably the *Times*. On a return trip to Britain he persuaded its most influential paper to appoint him special correspondent in Spain: "We have great difficulty getting any information at all from the Franco side," Ralph Deakin, the *Times*'s foreign editor, told Philby.

Meanwhile Philby assiduously gathered intelligence for his Soviet spymasters on "unit strengths and locations, gun calibres, tank performance," and other military information. This he sent in code to "Mademoiselle Dupont" in Paris (to an address that he later learned was the Soviet embassy itself). He began an affair with Frances Doble, Lady Lindsay-Hogg, an aristocratic former actress ten years his senior, a supporter of Franco, and "a royalist of the most right-wing kind," who gave him access to Franco's inner circle. "I would be lying if I said I started the affair only for the sake of my work," he later observed. Philby was untroubled about making love to someone whose opinions he despised.

Philby's controller in Paris, a Latvian named Ozolin-Haskins, was full of praise: "He works with great willingness [and] always knows what might be of interest to us. He never asks for money. He lives modestly." Nor did Philby neglect his role as a recruiter for the cause. During a return trip to London, he lunched with Flora Solomon, the Marks & Spencer executive who would later introduce him to Aileen. Despite her inherited wealth and marriage to a general-turned-stockbroker, Flora Solomon was firmly on the left. According to one MI5 officer, she had "obviously been in the thick of things in mid 1930s, part inspiration, part fellow accomplice, and part courier." During the conversation, Philby remarked, in an intense undertone, that he was "doing a very dangerous job for peace and that he needed help. Would she help him in his task? It would be a great thing if she would join the cause." He did not specify what his "important work for peace" entailed but insisted, "You should be doing it too, Flora." Solomon, surprised at what was unmistakably an invitation to join him in working secretly for communism, turned down the offer but told Philby "he could always come to her if he was desperate." She would not forget that strange exchange.

In Moscow a still more radical plan was being hatched for Agent Sonny. Philby had already been asked to report on General Franco's security arrangements. Now Moscow Center wondered whether he might be able to get close enough to the *Caudillo* to kill him, delivering a devastating blow to the Nazi-backed Nationalists. The officer with the unenviable task of passing on this idea was Theodore Maly, who knew that it was virtually impossible to achieve and, even if possible, suicidal. Maly discussed the proposal

with Philby but then sent a message to the Center quashing the
idea, fully aware that in doing so he was inviting Moscow's mortal
displeasure. "Even if he had been able to get close to Franco . . .
then he, despite his willingness, would not be able to do what is
expected of him. For all his loyalty and willingness to sacrifice
himself, he does not have the physical courage and other qualities
necessary." The plan was quietly dropped, but it was another mark
of Philby's growing status in Soviet eyes: in just four years he had
gone from a raw recruit to a potential assassin.

The *Times* was also impressed with his performance: "They
are very pleased with Kim, they have the highest opinion of him,"
the diarist Harold Nicolson told Guy Burgess. "He has made a
name for himself very quickly." That reputation expanded hugely
when, the day before his twenty-sixth birthday, New Year's Eve
1937, Philby narrowly avoided being killed by a Republican shell
(of Russian manufacture) while covering the battle of Teruel. The
award of a medal from Franco himself convinced the Nationalists
that Philby was, as one Spanish officer put it, "a decent chap."

In the summer of 1939, with Franco victorious in Spain, Philby
returned to London to a warm reception from his colleagues at
the *Times*. There was no equivalent welcome from his Soviet spy
friends, for the simple reason that they were all dead or had disappeared, swept away by Stalin's Terror. In the wild, murderous
paranoia of the Purges, anyone with foreign links was suspected
of disloyalty, and the outposts of Soviet intelligence came under
particular suspicion. Theodore Maly was among the first to be
recalled to Moscow, an obvious suspect on account of his religious
background: "I know that as a former priest I haven't got a chance.
But I've decided to go there so that nobody can say 'That priest
might have been a real spy after all.'" Maly was tortured in the
cells of the Lubyanka, headquarters of the secret police, until he
eventually confessed to being a German spy and was then shot
in the head. The fate of Arnold Deutsch has never been fully explained. Philby would later claim he had died when a ship taking
him to America, the *Donbass*, was torpedoed by a U-boat, thus

making him a victim of Hitler's aggression rather than Stalin's. The KGB history reports he died en route to South America, but another KGB report claims he was heading to New York. It seems just as probable that bright-eyed "Otto," founder-recruiter of the Cambridge spy ring, shared Maly's fate. As a foreign-born, Jewish intellectual who had spent years abroad, he was a likely candidate for purging. The task of running the Cambridge spies was taken over by one Grigori Grafpen, until he too was arrested and sent to the Gulag. Philby's controller in Paris, Ozolin-Haskins, was shot in Moscow in 1937. His successor, Boris Shapak, lasted two more years before he too was ordered home to be killed. A few defected before they could be seized, further fueling Stalin's paranoia, but most submitted to the inevitable. As Maly put it: "If they don't kill me there, they will kill me here. Better to die there." One by one, Philby's handlers were declared enemies of the people. Philby knew they were nothing of the sort. He had revered them for their "infinite patience" and "intelligent understanding," their "painstaking advice, admonition and encouragement." But in later life he expressed little sadness over the murder of these "marvellous men" and offered no criticism of the tyranny that killed them. Only the politics mattered.

By 1939, however, politics was becoming extremely complicated. In August the foreign ministers of the Soviet Union and Germany signed a nonaggression pact. Philby had become a Soviet agent in order to fight fascism; under the Molotov-Ribbentrop pact, communism and fascism were now effectively in alliance. For the first and only time in his life, Philby seems to have experienced an ideological wobble: "What's going to happen to the single-front struggle against fascism now?" he asked his new Soviet controller. The relationship cooled markedly. Philby complained that he was not receiving sufficient political instruction. The replacement case officer did not know him and may not have trusted him. For a time contact was broken off for reasons that still remain obscure.

That same year, the head of MI5 blandly declared that Soviet "activity in England is nonexistent, in terms of both intelligence and political subversion." He could not have been more wrong, for the Soviet network in Britain was not only far more substantial than anything Germany could muster but was also developing new tactics and encouraging its spies to seek positions within British intelligence itself, where they would have access to secrets of the greatest importance. Anthony Blunt would soon join MI5. Burgess had talked his way into MI6, known as "the Hotel" in Soviet spy code, and helped to haul in Philby after him. "I had been told in pressing terms by my Soviet friends that my first priority must be the British secret service," Philby wrote. Obediently, he began putting out feelers.

The coolness between Philby and his Soviet handlers was short-lived. In the spring of 1940, the *Times* sent its star correspondent to France to join the British Expeditionary Force as the paper's accredited correspondent. Philby had already memorized elaborate instructions for contacting Soviet intelligence in Paris. He should stand near the Thomas Cook office in Place de la Madeleine with a copy of the *Daily Mail*; the Soviet contact would be carrying a copy of the same newspaper. Philby would ask him: "Where is the Café Henri round here?" The man would reply: "It's near the Place de la République." Having performed this mini-drama, Philby passed on information he had gathered in the course of his reporting about British military strength and weaponry, as well as French forces behind the Maginot Line—information of great interest to Moscow and of even greater interest to Berlin. But whatever qualms he may have felt about the Nazi-Soviet pact seem to have evaporated. Returning to London after the retreat, he hastened to contact Maclean, saying he had brought back "extraordinarily valuable materials" that he wanted to pass to "the appropriate hands." Philby's loyalties were unchanged, his determination undimmed, and his hints about wanting to join the secret services already bearing fruit, in the shape of Hester Marsden-Smedley.

This, then, was the man who met and befriended Nicholas Elliott in 1940, a two-sided man who used one side to disguise the other. Elliott loved and admired Philby, the upper-crust,

Cambridge-educated *bon viveur,* the charming, happily married, conservative clubman, the battle-scarred war correspondent now playing a vital part in the thrilling world of espionage. Elliott had no inkling of the other Philby, the veteran communist spy, and it would be many more years before he finally met him.

Chapter Four

Boo, Boo, Baby, I'm a Spy

SIR STEWART MENZIES, THE HEAD OF MI6, WAS VERY NEARLY A caricature of what a spy chief ought to be: aristocratic, wily, and enigmatic. Some said he was the illegitimate son of Edward VII, a rumor almost certainly untrue that he did nothing to gainsay. Like all chiefs of MI6, he was known as "C," a tradition begun by the last initial of the earliest chief, Mansfield Cumming. Menzies was a member of White's Club, rode to hounds, mixed with royalty, never missed a day at Ascot, drank a great deal, and kept his secrets buttoned up behind a small, fierce mustache. He preferred women to men and horses to both. He was impenetrably polite and entirely ruthless: enemy spies, foxes, and office rivals could expect no quarter. Nicholas Elliott revered "the Chief" for what he called his "true sense of values"—which was his way of saying that Menzies, an Old Etonian and a friend of his father, shared his own view of the world. Outwardly, Kim Philby was equally admiring of Menzies; privately he considered him a prime specimen of the doomed ruling-class elite. "His intellectual equipment was unimpressive," Philby later wrote, "his knowledge of the world, and views about it, were just what one would expect from a fairly cloistered son of the upper levels of the British establishment." C was ripe for manipulation.

Like many small, sealed, self-replicating communities, MI6 was riven with internecine feuding. Its senior officers loathed one another and intrigued ferociously. Claude Dansey, the assistant chief, was described by Hugh Trevor-Roper as "an utter shit, corrupt, incompetent, but with a certain low cunning." Valentine Vivian, "Vee-Vee," who had eased Philby's entry into the secret world, was an old-style veteran of colonial policing, a stickler for form and protocol who, as the son of a mere portrait painter, lived in a state of permanent social anxiety. He reacted to the smallest slight, real or perceived, with fury. "Vivian was long past his best if, indeed, he had ever had one," observed Philby. "He had a reedy figure, carefully dressed crinkles in his hair, and wet eyes." Dansey hated Vivian, and Vivian hated Dansey; Philby's boss, Felix Cowgill, feuded with both and was detested in turn. Philby cultivated, flattered, and despised them all while nurturing his relationships with other branches of intelligence, most notably MI5. The security service was the main customer for his counterintelligence gatherings, but more than that it was responsible for counterespionage within Britain: if Philby ever came under suspicion, then MI5 would come hunting. It was, therefore, an important place to make friends. Philby's closest contact within MI5 was Guy Liddell, the refined, cello-playing head of counterintelligence and a regular at the Harris spy salon. A rumpled, genial figure, Liddell looked more like a country banker than a spymaster. "He would murmur his thoughts as if groping his way towards the facts of a case, his face creased in a comfortable, innocent smile," wrote Philby. "But behind the façade of laziness, his subtle and reflective mind played over a storehouse of photographic memories." Philby admired Liddell's professionalism and feared it.

Secrets are the currency of intelligence work, and among professional spies a little calculated indiscretion raises the exchange rate. Philby took to passing on tidbits to selected colleagues, off the record, and they would respond in kind. As Philby put it: "The rewards of such unorthodoxy were often generous." A secret shared was a friend made, and friendship, or its simulacrum, was the best way to extract more secrets. Philby became a familiar and popular figure in the corridors of both MI5 and MI6, always happy to exchange pleasantries, gossip, or confidences, always ready for a drink after work, and then another. Philby's Soviet handler reported smugly that Agent Sonny was probably "the only man in The Hotel without any enemies."

Menzies saw Philby and Elliott as his protégés, his "golden lads" representing a new generation of intelligence officers, far removed from the whiskery ex-policemen and military leftovers who had dominated the prewar MI6. They were keen, ambitious, and well educated (but not intellectuals—C had little time for those). They belonged to the right clubs and spoke with the right accents. It soon became apparent that both young men were being groomed for promotion by Menzies, who fought off every attempt to lure them away. When the Foreign Office inquired whether Philby might be seconded to the diplomatic service, C rejected the request with a tart note: "You know as well as I do the valuable work which Philby is doing for me. . . . The essential nature of Philby's contribution to the war effort compels his present employers regretfully to refuse to let him go." Similarly, the King's private secretary, Tommy Lascelles, sent a note to Guy Liddell telling him that Elliott was being considered for employment as a secretary to the monarch and asking for his opinion. Liddell replied that he had gotten to know Elliott "in the hurly-burly of the Scrubs" and found him "a pleasant personality highly recommended by Nevile Bland." He might make a fine courtier. Menzies, whose mother was a lady-in-waiting to Queen Mary, quashed that idea too. He wanted his lads in the inner circle, and Philby and Elliott, for rather different reasons, were only too happy to remain there.

The work of Section V, battling German espionage around the world, was fascinating, complicated, and frequently frustrating. "For every lead that produced results . . . a dozen lured us tortuously into dead ends." Elliott found the "monstrous" volume of paperwork—an essential part of intelligence—particularly tedious and tried to emulate Philby's brisk memo-writing style, "a model of economy and lucidity." The officers of Section V might complain about the hours, but they formed a tight-knit group with their own bonding rituals and routine: Sunday lunch at the Philbys', cricket on weekends, drinks at the King Harry, a club dinner in London from time to time, and occasional weekends at Eton. "I had the advantage of being able to invite these friends to spend a night from time to time with my parents, who were fortunate enough to have some old retainers to help cope with a very large house," wrote Elliott.

Philby seemed to be working twice as hard as anyone else, which was unsurprising, since he was working for two masters or, more precisely, appearing to serve one for the benefit of the other. As Philby's influence on British intelligence grew, so did his importance to the NKVD. Moscow Center sent a message to its London *rezident,* describing Sonny as "an interesting and promising agent" and ordering that he be put to greater use. Philby responded with devoted diligence. On night duty in Broadway, he combed incoming telegrams for anything of interest to the Soviets; messages between London and the military mission in Moscow were "especially valuable." He described everyone in Section V with waspish precision. Elliott was not the only colleague who would have been shocked to discover Philby's secret opinion: his boss Felix Cowgill had "few social graces"; his school friend Tim Milne was "inclined towards inertia"; Trevor Wilson, the former skunk-dung collector, had a "weakness [for] women"; and young Desmond Bristow was "the weak link . . . owing to immaturity and inferior brain."

Every evening, Philby took home a "fat briefcase" and sat in his study laboriously copying out files while Aileen cooked dinner and looked after the children. He even reported on Aileen, like some commissar assessing the ideological weakness of his nearest kin: "Her political views are Socialistic, but like the majority of the wealthy middle class, she has an almost ineradicable tendency towards a definite form of philistinism (petite bourgeoisie) namely: she believes in upbringing, the British navy, personal freedom, democracy, the constitutional system, honor etc. . . . I am certain that I can cure her of these confusions, although of course I haven't yet attempted to do so; I hope that the revolutionary situation will give her the necessary shake-up and cause a correct revolutionary response." Marriage, family, friendships: all were subservient to the demands of revolutionary orthodoxy.

Philby did whatever his Soviet controllers asked, although he found it "difficult, exhausting and often very ordinary, even boring work that required enormous patience, will-power and control." It was also nerve-racking. Philby suffered "twinges of panic," his controller reported, which was hardly surprising, since he was playing an astonishingly dangerous game. If just one Soviet intelligence officer switched sides and identified him to the British secret services, he was doomed. One had very nearly done so.

In 1937 a Soviet intelligence officer named Walter Krivitsky had defected to the West, bringing with him a dowry of top-level intelligence, including the identities of no fewer than seventy Soviet intelligence personnel working abroad. Krivitsky's defection had led to the arrest and trial of John King, Elliott's former coding instructor. But much of his information was contradictory and fragmentary. In 1940 he was debriefed by MI5 officer Jane Archer, in St Ermin's Hotel, where Philby had been recruited to MI6. The interview did not start well when Krivitsky (alias "Mr. Thomas") was offered a saccharin tablet for his tea (sugar was rationed). He immediately assumed this was a poison pill and that he was being murdered by the British secret services, albeit rather obviously and very politely. Once that moment of social embarrassment had passed, Krivitsky opened up and revealed an important new nugget of information: during the Spanish civil war, Soviet intelligence had sent an agent to kill General Franco. Krivitsky could not provide a name or any other specifics, but described the would-be assassin as "a young Englishman, a journalist of good family, an idealist and fanatical anti-Nazi." MI5 launched an investigation, but there had been several well-born journalists in Spain in the 1930s, and the inquiry fizzled out. No one thought to connect the tip with Philby. The clue would rattle around British intelligence for years before assuming vast significance many years later.

Philby was slaving for the Soviet cause, risking his life and prepared to report on whatever interested Moscow, including his father, his wife, and his best friend. Yet Moscow was not happy. The Cambridge spies—Guy Burgess in MI6, Donald Maclean in the Foreign Office, Anthony Blunt in MI5, John Cairncross in Bletchley Park, and Kim Philby in Section V—were producing top-level intelligence. But their very productivity posed a conundrum. In the insanely distrustful world of Soviet espionage, the quality, quantity, and consistency of this information rendered it suspect. A misgiving began to take root in Moscow that British intelligence must be mounting an elaborate, multilayered deception through Philby and his friends; they must all be double agents. Moreover, Philby's story failed to meet firmly held Soviet preconceptions: MI6 was supposed to be impregnable, yet Philby had practically sauntered into the organization; he had been a left-winger at university, yet supposedly rigorous background checks had failed to pick this up; he had been asked to find evidence that his own father was a spy and had failed to do so.

Was Philby a plant? Was he shielding his father? Was he too an enemy of the people, masquerading as a friend? To find out, a test was set. The information provided by Philby was all very well, but what interested Moscow most was the identity of British spies within the Soviet Union; who had MI6 recruited in the USSR, what were their names, and what Soviet secrets had they revealed? If Philby exposed these spies, then he was reliable and loyal; but if not, then Moscow would draw its own conclusions. Philby politely pointed out that his role in MI6 was catching enemy spies, not agent running, which was the responsibility of a different section in a completely different place. But Moscow was adamant: "We told him he must use whatever plausible and reasonable pretexts in order to get these files." As his former controller Theodore Maly had discovered to his cost, in the warped logic of Stalinism, refusing to do something just because it was impossible was a sign of disloyalty. Philby obediently set to work.

The Central Registry was the memory and reference library of MI6, housed at Prae Wood in St Albans, next door to Section V headquarters. The registry source books collated the personal files of all current British secret agents and every agent who had spied for Britain since the creation of MI6 in 1909, including names, code names, aliases, character, performance, and pay—a running tally of MI6 spies across the world. Presiding over this fabulously valuable (and exceedingly dangerous) trove of secrets was Captain William Woodfield, the chief registrar, a puce-faced former policeman whose drinking habits were extreme even by MI6 standards. In a description for his Soviet controller, Philby described Woodfield with typical concision: "About 58, 5 feet 6 inches, slight build, dark hair, bald on top, wears glasses, long narrow face formerly attached for some years to Special Branch." Woodfield liked dirty jokes and pink gin: Philby made a point of seeking him out at the King Harry pub and supplying him with copious quantities of both. Soon they were the best of drinking buddies, and when Philby asked to see the source books for Spain and Portugal, Woodfield signed them out without question. The Iberian peninsula was Philby's sphere of work, and he had every reason to be interested in the MI6 agents in the region. Next Philby requested the source books for the Soviet Union. Again Woodfield obliged, never pausing to wonder why his amiable new pub chum was digging into an area so far removed from his allotted patch.

Philby duly sent a report to Moscow. It described Britain's spies in the Soviet Union with typical bluntness: "There aren't any." The station chief of MI6 in Moscow had not recruited a single major spy in the Soviet Union, Philby reported, and had only a few minor informants, mostly Poles. The USSR, moreover, was "tenth on the list of countries to which agents are to be sent." The files showed there was no British spy network in Soviet Russia, no MI6 espionage campaign, and "no Soviet citizens whatsoever who worked as secret agents either in Moscow or anywhere else on Soviet territory." The report was received with incredulity; Moscow's paranoia and sense of self-importance combined to provoke a reaction of furious disbelief. The Soviet Union was a world power and MI6 was the most feared intelligence organization in the world; it therefore stood to reason that Britain *must* be spying on the USSR. If Philby said otherwise, then he *must* be lying. That Britain could conceivably relegate the mighty Soviet state to number ten on its espionage target list was an "obvious absurdity" (and frankly quite wounding). An outraged Soviet intelligence officer took a red pen and scrawled two large and angry question marks over the report. Philby's assertion was "highly suspicious"; his failure to corroborate expectations was "dubious"; henceforth he must be "tested and retested." In truth, British intelligence was overwhelmingly focused on the Nazi threat, and since Moscow had become an ally the Foreign Office had imposed strict restrictions on covert activities inside the Soviet Union. But when Anthony Blunt confirmed that MI6 had no secret agents in the USSR, he too fell under suspicion; Philby and Blunt must be in league. And so began a bizarre situation in which Philby told Moscow the truth and was disbelieved because the truth contradicted Moscow's expectations.

Philby's successful and unauthorized foray into the Soviet files was a remarkable feat of espionage and a complete waste of time: it not only deepened Moscow's suspicions but very nearly ended Philby's career. One morning, Bill Woodfield of the beetroot complexion sent a polite note asking him to return the Soviet source books; Philby responded that he had already done so. Woodfield, a sloppy drunk but a meticulous librarian, said that there was only one Soviet source book on the shelves, and the registry had no record of the second volume being returned. Philby was convinced the books had been sent back to the repository but nonetheless turned his office "upside down" in a fruitless search for the missing volume. He met Woodfield at the King Harry "to discuss the mystery over a few pink gins" and discovered, to his horror, that under registry rules C would have to be informed of the missing records. This was Friday. Woodfield said he would send a memo on Monday. Nothing to worry about, said Bill: just paperwork. Philby was now in deep peril. Menzies might understand, even applaud, his interest in MI6 agents in Spain and Portugal, but he would surely wonder what on earth his protégé was doing with material on the Soviet Union, an area "far outside the normal scope of [his] duties." At best Philby would have some tricky explaining to do; at worst he was sunk. After a weekend of simmering panic, Monday came, and with it a last-minute reprieve. Woodfield's secretary, who had been ill with the flu for a few days, returned to work and explained that she had amalgamated the two source books into one volume to save shelf space. Philby had indeed returned the files. Woodfield offered profuse apologies for the embarrassing mix-up over "another flood of pink gin." Had Woodfield's secretary been ill slightly longer, or had Woodfield been a little less pickled, then Philby's story would have ended then and there. But his luck held: he had escaped a Republican shell in Spain, dodged the clue furnished by the defector Krivitsky, and narrowly avoided exposure for trawling the Soviet files. "Luck played an enormous role in my life," he later wrote. "But you have to know how to use luck."

Nicholas Elliott was becoming restless. Life in St Albans was pleasant enough but "cloistered." Running counterintelligence operations in occupied Holland involved a great deal of memo writing for meager results and nothing in the way of action. The world of intelligence, he concluded, was divided into "those who sit at desks at home analysing and evaluating the information as it comes in, and those who go out into the highways and byways of the world in order to get hold of it." Philby was of the former sort, a gifted analyst and collator of facts, but Elliott belonged to the latter type, and he was "anxious to get away to another theatre of war." He longed to travel, partly in reaction to his father's acute distrust of "abroad." ("All foreigners are bloody unless they climb mountains," Claude insisted, "and Germans are bloody even if they do.") Elliott hungered for risk. With Philby's support, he began lobbying for a more active role in the field, preferably somewhere dangerous. In the spring of 1942 Elliott was summoned to Cowgill's office and told he would soon be heading to Cairo, and from there to Istanbul as Section V's representative in Turkey. At the age of twenty-six, Nicholas Elliott would be running counterespionage operations in an espionage hothouse, for Turkey was neutral and, like Spain and Portugal, the scene of a fierce, secret war. "I was delighted," he wrote. Philby threw a farewell party for him. The next day, May 11, 1942, Acting Lieutenant Elliott climbed, somewhat unsteadily, up the gangplank of a five-thousand-ton passenger-cargo vessel in Liverpool docks, part of a forty-ship convoy bound for Africa.

Elliott spent the three-week passage to Lagos playing bridge with an SOE officer "who was being sent out to Angola to blow things up," taking his turn to man the ancient Japanese gun mounted on the stern, and tucking into a "well-stocked bar." Although never a drinker in Philby's league, Elliott was a keen tippler—despite his diabetes, which he treated merely by avoiding sugar. Most of his colleagues were entirely unaware that he was diabetic; with typical recklessness, Elliott was not about to let his health stand in the way of a good time. When the ship put in at Freetown, he was greeted on the quayside by Graham Greene, who was now the somewhat disgruntled MI6 representative in Sierra Leone—a good place to gather material for fiction but an intelligence backwater. Greene took one look at Elliott and proclaimed him "the tattiest army officer I had ever seen." Over a drink, Greene explained that his principal concern was "the shortage of contraceptives in Sierra Leone," a problem Elliott "managed to alleviate through the generosity of some of our passengers." Elliott assumed these were for Greene's personal use: in fact, the future novelist had set up a "roving brothel" to entice secrets out of "two lonely Germans suspected of spying on British shipping," and his brothel workers were demanding protection from venereal disease.

In Lagos Elliott transferred to a Dakota transport plane, and five days later he reached Cairo, after hopscotching across Africa via Kano, Fort-Lamy, El Fasher, and Khartoum. On reporting to intelligence headquarters, Elliott was informed that his first job was to take a truckload of confidential files to Jerusalem for safekeeping before traveling on to Beirut. He would then catch the fabled Taurus Express to Turkey.

The elderly train puffed slowly up the Taurus Mountains and then ambled gently across the Anatolian plateau to Ankara and on to Istanbul, never exceeding thirty miles an hour and stopping frequently for no discernible reason. The food in the restaurant car was excellent, and Elliott found the journey a "delight" made more pleasant still by the company of his new secretary, a young Englishwoman named Elizabeth Holberton.

Elliott was rather struck by Miss Holberton. She had spent the early part of the war in the Motorised Transport Corps, driving Jeeps in the desert, before becoming a secretary at General Headquarters (GHQ) in Cairo. She was quick-witted, resourceful, beautiful in a demure sort of way, a devoted Catholic, and quite posh. Her father was a former managing director of the Bombay Burmah Trading Company and her mother descended from a long line of Irish judges. They got on famously. When the train ran out of supplies of water, the conductor brought Elizabeth a bottle of Turkish Cointreau with which to brush her teeth. She declared the experience refreshing. Elliott liked that.

Ankara was the diplomatic capital of Turkey, but the major powers kept embassies in Istanbul, on the cusp between Europe and Asia; this was where the serious spying was done. Britain's ambassador to Turkey was Sir Hughe Montgomery Knatchbull-Hugessen, a diplomat of the old school who spent much of his time on the ambassadorial yacht and was, perhaps inevitably, an Old Etonian friend of Elliott's father. Hugessen adopted an attitude of "pained tolerance" toward the activities of British intelligence in Turkey. Formally a junior diplomat, Elliott joined a swiftly expanding, multilayered British intelligence force under the overall command of Lieutenant Colonel Harold Gibson, a veteran MI6 professional of "great ability and energy." "Gibbie" oversaw a vast system of intelligence gathering and agent running extending from Turkey into Romania, Bulgaria, Greece, Yugoslavia, and Hungary. As the representative of Section V, Elliott's task was to undermine enemy intelligence operations, principally those of the Abwehr. Gibson gave Elliott a fairly free rein to explore and attack espionage targets in Turkey, and there were plenty to choose from.

Istanbul was "one of the great espionage entrepôts of the war," in the words of MI6's official historian. The city was just forty miles from Nazi-occupied Bulgaria; it was Germany's gateway to the Middle East and an access point for the Allies into occupied Europe. The Turks feared the Germans, distrusted the Soviets, and felt little love for either the British or the Americans. But the authorities were prepared to tolerate espionage by foreign powers, so long as this did not impinge on Turkish sovereignty and the spies did not get caught. By 1942 some seventeen different intelligence organizations had converged on Istanbul to mix and mingle, bribe, seduce, and betray, and with them came a vast and motley host of agents and double agents, smugglers, blackmailers, arms dealers, drug runners, refugees, deserters, black-marketeers, pimps, forgers, hookers, and con artists. Rumors and secrets, some of them true, whirled around the bars and back alleys. Everyone spied on everyone else; the Turkish secret police, the Emniyet, spied on all. Some Turkish officials were prepared to cooperate on intelligence sharing if the price was right, but every so often, if the spying became too brazen or insufficiently remunerative, the Emniyet would stage an arrest. The spy battle was intense and oddly intimate. The head of the Abwehr was on nodding terms with his opposite numbers in MI6 and Soviet intelligence. "Everyone was well informed as to the identity of everyone else," wrote Elliott. When one or another of the intelligence chiefs entered the ballroom of the Park Hotel, the band would strike up the song "Boo, Boo, Baby, I'm a Spy":

> I'm involved in a dangerous game,
> Every other day I change my name,
> The face is different but the body's the same,
> Boo, boo, baby, I'm a spy!
> You have heard of Mata Hari,
> We did business cash and carry,
> Poppa caught us and we had to marry,
> Boo, boo, baby, I'm a spy!
> Now, as a lad, I'm not so bad,
> In fact, I'm a darn good lover,
> But look my sweet, let's be discreet,
> And do this under cover.
> I'm so cocky I could swagger,

The things I know would make you stagger,
I'm ten percent cloak and ninety percent dagger,
Boo, boo, baby, I'm a spy!

But the dagger beneath the cloak was razor sharp. Just two months before Elliott's arrival, a Macedonian student had attempted to assassinate the German ambassador, Franz von Papen, but the bomb exploded prematurely, blowing up the assassin and only injuring the German diplomat. Moscow blamed the Gestapo; the Germans blamed the Allies; Papen suspected the British. The plot was almost certainly the work of the Soviet NKVD. A year earlier, a German suitcase bomb planted in the lobby at the Pera Palace hotel had killed a member of the British consular staff and badly injured the vice-consul, Chantry Hamilton Page. Espionage in Istanbul, as the MI6 station chief Harold Gibson observed, was "not a kid glove affair."

Elliott was immediately seduced by Istanbul's sleazy glamour. He moved into an office in the embassy "crammed from top to bottom with intelligence operatives engaged in various aspects of skulduggery," and with a garden surprisingly full of copulating tortoises, and plunged into the espionage fray. On his first evening he was swept up by Major Bernard O'Leary, an enormous multilingual former cavalry officer, "extremely erudite, but irredeemably idle," who was responsible for liaison with Turkish intelligence. O'Leary announced they were going to Taksim's, the spy center of Istanbul, a cross between a restaurant, a nightclub, a cabaret, and a casino. "Its clientele," wrote Elliott, "combined the representatives—mainly engaged in espionage—of all the Axis and Allied powers." Taksim's was run by a charming White Russian who accepted bribes from everyone without favoritism and endeavored to place rival spies at adjacent tables to facilitate eavesdropping. The waitresses were said to be former czarist duchesses. Nothing at Taksim's was quite as it seemed. One night Elliott was admiring the club's resident belly dancer, a stunning creature with "white coloured skin and jet black hair," when she fell off the stage, twisted an ankle, and swore loudly in a thick northern English accent. She was from Bradford. When not at Taksim's, Elliott might be found at Ellie's Bar, a favorite watering hole of British military personnel that served "a ferocious dry martini with the kick of a horse." Ellie was buxom, blond, and thought to be Romanian. She "spoke excellent English, and purported to fear and hate the Germans." In fact, Elliott discovered, she was in German pay, employed by the Abwehr to get British officers as drunk as possible in the hope that they would eventually divulge valuable information.

Elliott set about making friends with the sort of people who would have made his father shudder. In later years he wrote that "the capacity for friendship is a particularly important characteristic" in an intelligence officer. "A large amount of intelligence work in the field is all about the establishment of personal relationships; of gaining other people's confidence and on some occasions persuading people to do something against their better judgment." He befriended the Russian maître d' at Taksim's and the waiters at Ellie's Bar; he went drinking with a former czarist guards officer called Roman Sudakov, who was plugged into Russian intelligence and agreed to work for MI6; he got to know the porters at the embassies, the consular officials, and the clerks at the telegraph office. He made contacts among the press corps and the Lars fisherman who plied the Bosphorus and did a little smuggling and information gathering to supplement the catch. He made a particular point of befriending the conductors on the wagon-lits of the Taurus Express, who were much in demand as couriers for the intelligence organizations, since the railway was the only reliable way of getting from Turkey to the Middle East. The conductors would supply information about who was traveling where, report gossip, smuggle documents, and even, for an additional consideration, steal travel papers. They were for sale to the highest bidder but to none exclusively: "One particularly remarkable man at one stage was working for both the Abwehr and the SD [German security intelligence] (each unknown to the other); for the Italians, and for the Japanese; as well as for the British."

At the other end of Istanbul society, Elliott mixed with high-ranking officials, military officers, diplomats, and religious leaders. The papal legate, Monsignor Angelo Giuseppe Roncalli, who would later become Pope John XXIII, proved to be a fund of good intelligence and a vigorous antifascist. Like so many in wartime Istanbul, Roncalli was playing a double game, dining with Papen and taking his wife's confession while using his office to smuggle Jewish refugees out of occupied Europe. A few months after they became friends, Elliott discovered that Roncalli's assistant, one Monsignor Rici, "a most unattractive little man," was a spy "operating a clandestine wireless set on behalf of the Italian military intelligence." Elliott tipped off the Turkish secret police and had Rici arrested. When he informed Roncalli, with some embarrassment, that his assistant was likely to be spending a considerable period breaking rocks in an Anatolian penal colony, the future pope merely shrugged, leaving Elliott with the strong impression that he "was not altogether displeased."

After just a few months in Istanbul, Elliott concluded there were "more people involved in various forms of skulduggery per head of population than any other city in the world." And he had identified a good proportion of them: German intelligence officers, Italian agents, Polish, Czech, and Yugoslavian informers, Free French and Jewish Agency spies, and officers of the NKVD and the GRU (Soviet military intelligence). "All were kept under close observation by the Turks, who ran their own informers."

Elliott's energetic counterintelligence activities met with approval in London. Sir Stewart Menzies had always had what Philby called a "schoolboyish" attitude to counterespionage: "bars, beards and blondes." Elliott was experiencing plenty of all three, and his stock rose still higher when one of his informants on the Taurus Express handed over a bomb, saying he had been given the device by the Japanese military attaché, Colonel Tateishi, with instructions to detonate it on the line between Aleppo and Tripoli. Elliott gingerly handed the package over to the countersabotage section in Istanbul and paid his informant a large bonus; the informant told Colonel Tateishi the bomb had failed to detonate and demanded another bonus. Everyone was happy.

Elliott relished his new posting. Even a nasty bout of foot-and-mouth disease picked up on his travels could not blunt his happiness. And he was falling in love. Elizabeth Holberton was proving to be more than just an excellent secretary. Her Catholicism and his cordial aversion to all religion did nothing to hinder a blossoming relationship. They went everywhere together and drank quantities of Egyptian Bordeaux, which Elliott declared "the worst claret I have ever drunk." Shy beneath his bonhomie, it took Elliott months to summon up the courage to say what was on his mind. A cocktail made for spies finally did the trick. "After three of Ellie's volcanic martinis we decided to get married." Marriages between officers and their secretaries were something of a tradition in MI6, where secrecy bred a special sort of intimacy. Even C was conducting a long-running affair with his secretary.

Elliott dashed off a letter to Sir Edgar Holberton saying that he planned to marry his daughter and "hoping he didn't mind." Even if Sir Edgar had minded, it would have made no difference, for Elliott had no intention of waiting for a reply. Roman Sudakov, his best man, threw a stag party for him at the Park Hotel—an event made even more auspicious by the presence at the next table of Papen, the German ambassador, and his military attaché. After the ceremony, on April 10, 1945, performed by Monsignor Roncalli in the papal legate's private chapel, the newlyweds moved into a flat with a view of the Golden Horn—accompanied by a tiny Russian cook named Yaroslav Stenko Popovski, who made vodka in the bath and began teaching Elliott to speak Russian.

Philby was delighted by Elliott's success, his growing reputation, and the news of his marriage. Nicholas Elliott was a rising star in the service and a valued friend, and no one understood the value of friendship better than Kim Philby.

Chapter Five

Three Young Spies

PHILBY'S LIFE IN THE ENGLISH SUBURBS SEEMED DRAB IN COMPARISON to Elliott's colorful experiences on the front line of the espionage battle. St Albans was a long way from Istanbul. In Philby's opinion, it was too far from anywhere, including London, where the important intelligence decisions were being made and the most valuable secrets might be found. Early in 1943 Felix Cowgill announced that Section V would be moving to new premises on Ryder Street, in the heart of St James's. Philby was elated, since the new office would be just "two minutes from MI5 and 15 from Broadway," the MI6 headquarters. He would now be closer to his club, closer to the gossipy parties hosted by Tommy Harris, and closer to his Soviet handlers. Ryder Street was also the ideal vantage point from which to assess, befriend, and manipulate an important new force in the wartime intelligence battle.

The attack on Pearl Harbor catapulted America into the war and brought into being the Office of Strategic Services, a new and well-funded intelligence service presided over by the extroverted, hard-driving lawyer William "Wild Bill" Donovan. The OSS would eventually evolve into the CIA, the most powerful intelligence service in the world, but in 1942 America was still new to the game of wartime intelligence, long on resources and energy but short on expertise. The first OSS officers began arriving in London, keen to learn, late in 1942, and occupied offices in Ryder Street. Malcolm Muggeridge compared them to innocent young maidens about to be deflowered in "the frowsty old intelligence brothel" that was MI6. Philby was unimpressed with the first American

arrivals, "a notably bewildered group." Even their leader, Norman Holmes Pearson, a Yale academic, was scathing about his
own team, describing them as "a bunch of amateur bums." Nov-
ices they may have been, but they were also frightfully keen in a
way the hardened veterans of MI6 found rather quaint. "They lost
no opportunity of telling us that they had come to school," wrote
Philby, who, as a respected three-year veteran of the service, was
about to become one of their most influential instructors, briefing
the Americans on the work of MI6's counterespionage section, the
structure of the British secret services, and decoding operations
at Bletchley Park. Philby dismissed these eager Americans as a
"pain in the neck," but there was one who stood out from the rest:
a tall, intense, cadaverously thin young man who wrote poetry,
cultivated tropical plants, and studied the minutiae of espionage
with the dedication of a true obsessive. His name was James Jesus
Angleton and he would rise, in time, to become one of the most
powerful and controversial spies in history.

Angleton was the product of a romantic and unlikely marriage between Hugh Angleton, a soldier–turned–cash register
salesman, and Carmen Mercedes Moreno, an uneducated, fiery,
and exceptionally beautiful woman from Nogales, Arizona, with
a mixture of Mexican and Apache blood. The two had met in
1916, when Hugh Angleton was serving as a cavalry officer under
General Pershing during the campaign against the Mexican rebel
Pancho Villa. James Angleton was born in 1917 in Boise, Idaho,
and given the middle name "Jesus" by his Catholic mother—he
hated it, but with his ascetic looks and oddly spiritual air, the
name fit him. The boy was fourteen when his father moved to
Italy to run, and then own, the Milan branch of the National Cash
Register Company. The young Angleton was sent to England for
his education, first at a prep school in Buckinghamshire and then
at Malvern College, a British public school firmly in the Victorian
tradition. He became a Boy Scout and a prefect and joined the
Officer Training Corps. These were, in Angleton's words, his "formative years": he left Malvern with courteous manners, a sense
of fair play, an air of cultivated eccentricity, and a faint English

accent that never left him. The boy from Idaho was already "more English than the English," a disguise he would wear, along with his Savile Row suits, for the rest of his life. He enrolled at Yale in 1937 to study English literature but spent most of his time listening to jazz, chasing girls, and running a literary magazine, *Furioso*, which published the work of such notable poets as Ezra Pound and e. e. cummings, both of whom became his friends. An insomniac night owl, Angleton developed a reputation as a fierce anticommunist and an aesthete: he wrote romantic verse, most of it execrable, and was nicknamed the Poet. His classmates found him enigmatic, "a mysterious person, with dark mysterious looks." Soon after Pearl Harbor, he enlisted in the U.S. Army, and through his former English professor, Norman Pearson, was offered work in London in the newly formed OSS. Before heading to England, he married a twenty-one-year-old heiress to a Minnesota lumber fortune. It was a slightly odd thing to do, but then much of what Jim Angleton did was unexpected. "What a miracle of momentous complexity is The Poet," wrote e. e. cummings.

Angleton was attached to X-2, the OSS counterintelligence section and the direct counterpart of MI6's Section V. X-2 would eventually expand to take up an entire floor of the Ryder Street building, while Section V occupied the floor above. Philby was drafted in to lecture the newcomers on the "arts and crafts" of counterespionage, penetration of enemy intelligence organizations, and the running of double agents. As one American officer observed, "I do remember being very impressed. He really knew what he was doing."

Philby took a shine to the twenty-four-year-old American and later wrote that Angleton "earned my respect by openly rejecting the Anglomania" of so many of the new American arrivals. Angleton did not need to be an Anglophile since he was, in many ways, so very English already. The extent of the friendship between Philby and Angleton at this point is hard to gauge since Angleton's allies later tried to downplay it, just as his enemies tended to exaggerate it. According to Angleton's biographer, "Philby may have felt he had a mentoring relationship with Angleton; Angleton may have shared that feeling." The two men became patron and protégé, the expert and the prodigy. "Philby was one of Angleton's instructors, his prime tutor in counter-intelligence; Angleton came to look up to him as an elder-brother figure." Philby enjoyed having acolytes, and Angleton may have filled a gap left by Nicholas Elliott's absence. The new arrivals and the old hands got to know one another over drinks, lots of them. "Our European friends were formidable consumers of alcoholic beverages, with apparently little effect," recalled one OSS officer. Angleton could drink with a Philby-like determination, but then he did everything with an intensity that others found impressive and slightly odd. He moved a cot-bed into his Ryder Street office and seemed to spend most of the night studying the esoteric secrets of counterespionage with devout fervor, "as if they contained the secret of the Trinity." He mixed with writers and poets, including William Empson and T. S. Eliot, and occasionally inserted a poem into his reports. Empson noted his "restless appetite for organising things." Colleagues in the OSS found him "extremely brilliant, but a little strange . . . full of impossible, colossal ideas." Angleton was a little like one of the rare orchids he would later cultivate with such dedication: an exotic hybrid, a Mexican-Apache-Midwestern English-sounding poet-spy, rare and remarkable, alluring to some but faintly sinister to those who preferred simpler flora. The bosses recognized that Angleton, for all his peculiarities, had found a vocation, and after six months he was promoted to the rank of second lieutenant and made chief of the Italian desk of X-2, controlling counterintelligence operations in the country where he had spent much of his youth. His rapid ascent was due in part to Philby's tutelage and patronage, and Angleton would later cite him as an inspiration. "Once I met Philby, the world of intelligence that had once interested me consumed me," he said. "He had taken on the Nazis and Fascists head-on and penetrated their operations in Spain and Germany. His sophistication and experience appealed to us. . . . Kim taught me a great deal."

With his mixture of charm and competence, Philby's stature within Allied intelligence continued to grow, along with his responsibilities. Late in 1942 Cowgill asked him to take over counterintelligence operations in North Africa, an area of key importance given the impending Allied invasion of French Morocco and Algeria. The region had previously been the responsibility of Captain Felix Russi, a former soldier from Gibraltar whom Philby described to his Soviet handlers as "an almost total moron." Philby was happy to colonize his region. "We had achieved a fair stranglehold on the Abwehr in Spain and Portugal," he wrote, and "there was no reason why I should not shoulder additional responsibilities." A few months later his brief expanded yet again, to include counterespionage in Italy (the region James Angleton would soon cover, in parallel, for OSS). Soon after the move to London, Cowgill asked Philby to act as his deputy "in all intelligence matters" while he paid a three-week visit to the United States on MI6 business. Philby reflected, with wry false modesty, that he was "beginning to make a career in the secret service." Promotion, however, was only a means to an end. "I regarded my SIS appointments purely in the light of cover jobs, to be carried out sufficiently well to ensure my attaining positions in which my service to the Soviet Union would be most effective."

Even the most ideologically driven people usually need to test their convictions, to have others understand them, support them, or challenge them. Philby never shared his beliefs; he never discussed politics, even with his fellow Soviet spies; after his early ideological discussions with Arnold Deutsch, the subject of communism was seldom raised with his Soviet handlers. He had persuaded himself of the rectitude of his course back in 1934, and after that the subject was closed. He retained and sustained his certainties in perfect isolation.

One of the richer ironies of Philby's position is that while he could do no wrong in British eyes, in Moscow he continued to be viewed with mistrust. The main source of Soviet suspicion was a plump, blond, highly intelligent, politically doctrinaire, and fabulously paranoid NKVD analyst named Elena Modrzhinskaya, the head of the British department at Moscow Center. As was true of many who lived through Stalin's Purges, fear, propaganda, and obedience had left a deep residue of mistrust in the soul of Modrzhinskaya, one of the very few women in a senior position within Soviet intelligence. She suspected a gigantic plot: she simply could not credit the "incomprehensible" risks the Cambridge spies claimed they were taking on behalf of the Soviets; it was surely impossible that men with communist pasts could enter the British secret service so easily and rise so fast; the British were known to be foisting an elaborate deception on the Nazis, and it stood to reason that they must be attempting to do the same thing to Moscow. In short, she simply could not, and would not, believe that Philby was what he proclaimed himself to be: "a straight penetration agent working in the Soviet interest." Philby was a plant, an impostor, a double-crosser: "He is lying to us in a most insolent manner." Anatoliy Gorsky, the new *rezident* in London, was instructed to find out exactly what disinformation was being spread by Philby and the other British double agents. In time Moscow Center would even dispatch undercover agents to trail them and collect incriminating evidence. The surveillance team spoke no English and got repeatedly lost, a problem they ascribed to brilliant spy craft on the part of Philby and the others, rather than to their own inability to read a map. The Soviets set out to find evidence that did not exist and, when they failed to find it, assumed this must be proof of how well that evidence had been hidden. In the end, Philby's very Englishness rendered him suspect. As Yuri Modin, the Soviet officer who would take over the Cambridge spy network, observed: "He was so completely, psychologically and physically, the British intelligence officer that I could never quite accept that he was one of us, a Marxist in the clandestine service of the Soviet Union." The very attributes that made his spying invisible to Elliott and MI6 made Moscow mistrustful.

Modrzhinskaya's suspicions of disloyalty did not outwardly alter the way Philby was handled by his Soviet controllers. Gorsky was ordered to maintain contact with the British spies "in such a manner as to reinforce their conviction that we trust them completely." Here, then, was a truly bizarre situation: Philby was telling Moscow the truth and was disbelieved but allowed to go on thinking he was believed; he was deceiving the British in order to aid the Soviets, who suspected a deception and were in turn deceiving him. Moscow's faith in Philby seemed to ebb and flow; sometimes he was considered suspect, sometimes genuine, and sometimes both simultaneously.

Britain and the USSR had been allies ever since Hitler's attack on the Soviet Union in the summer of 1941. Philby could argue that, by passing on information to Moscow, he was simply helping an ally and supporting the "single-front struggle against fascism." His colleagues in MI6 and OSS would not have seen matters that way. Some high-grade intelligence was already passing between London and Moscow, but in restricted form, for both sides continued to view each other with deep suspicion. Philby was passing on secrets that his bosses in MI6 would never have dreamed of sharing with Stalin: deception operations, the identities of agents and officers, and a detailed (and damning) picture of the very structure of the secret services themselves. There was also the danger—never confirmed or disproved—that German spies had penetrated Soviet intelligence and information supplied by the Cambridge network was passing back to Berlin. If that possibility crossed Philby's mind, it does not seem to have worried him. His loyalty was to Moscow; what Moscow did with the information he provided was not his concern. He knew he was committing treason by spying for a foreign power and the implications of doing so. If caught, he would almost certainly be prosecuted under the Treachery Act of 1940, which carried the death penalty.

Death was part of the game. Philby had accepted the liquidation of his much-loved Soviet handlers with the acquiescence of a true believer. More than a dozen spies intercepted through the Bletchley Park decrypts had ended their lives on the gallows or in front of a firing squad. British intelligence was not above "bumping off" enemy spies, to use the cheery euphemism favored by MI6. Philby would later claim that he had done his "modest bit towards helping to win the war" by killing large numbers of Germans. He saw himself as a combatant, albeit one who fought from behind a desk, with all the risks that war involves. But as the war headed to its climax, Philby's espionage career was about to enter a new and much more lethal phase, in which he would help to destroy not Nazi spies but ordinary men and women whose only crime was to oppose the political creed he had espoused. Philby would soon kill for the communist cause, and Nicholas Elliott, unwittingly, would help him.

ELLIOTT'S PRINCIPAL ADVERSARY in the Istanbul spy battle was a tall, bald, bespectacled, urbane, and probably homosexual lawyer named Paul Leverkühn. Plucked from his comfortable legal practice in Lübeck to be the Abwehr chief in Turkey, Leverkühn was an unlikely spymaster. He had studied law at Edinburgh University and worked in New York and Washington. "Moody and nervous," he disliked Turkey and, like many Abwehr officers, had little time for the brutality and vulgarity of Nazism. He looked more like an academic than a spy. But he was a first-class espionage operative and, as Elliott was discovering, a worthy enemy with a formidable spy network employing German expatriates and Turkish informants, as well as Russian thugs, Persian hit men, Arab informants, and even an Egyptian prince. "The city is riddled with their agents," warned an OSS report. Germany had broken Turkey's diplomatic codes early in the war. Leverkühn's spies, tipsters, and honey traps could be found wherever secrets might be gleaned. Hildegard Reilly, the attractive German widow of an American officer, haunted Taksim's, where she "specialised in making Britons and Americans more talkative." Wilhelmina Vargasy, a blond, blue-eyed Hungarian, prowled Ellie's bar and was said to have seduced no less than six Allied soldiers. Leverkühn ran agents into the Middle East, gathering information on Allied military forces in Palestine, Jordan, Egypt, and Iraq, and infiltrated spies into the Soviet Union to foment revolution against Moscow—just as the CIA and MI6 would seek to do after the war.

Elliott's work frequently took him to Ankara, where he stayed in the ambassador's residence as a guest of the Knatchbull-Hugessens. On these occasions, the obliging British ambassador even lent Elliott his personal valet, an Albanian named Elyesa Bazna, to help him dress for dinner. "I remembered him vividly," wrote Elliott, a "small roundish man with a high forehead, thick black hair and a large drooping mustache." Before joining the domestic staff of the British embassy, Bazna had been a low-level criminal, a servant in the Yugoslav embassy, and valet to a German diplomatic official, who had caught him reading his letters and fired him. Bazna was also a spy for the Germans.

Sir Hughe Knatchbull-Hugessen had developed the extremely unsafe habit of bringing official papers home to the ambassador's residence in his dispatch box and reading them in bed before turning in for the night. Elliott liked the ambassador but later conceded that he should have been "instantly dismissed" for this flagrant breach of security. Bazna identified the nature of his boss's bedtime reading and spotted a moneymaking opportunity. In October 1943 (at about the time that Elliott first encountered Bazna laying out his dinner jacket) the Albanian valet made contact with German intelligence and offered to hand over photographs of the documents in exchange for cash, lots of it. Over the next two months Bazna made some ten deliveries of documents and was paid a fortune in cash, which he carefully stashed away, unaware that the Germans had taken the precaution of paying him in forged notes. Since he spoke almost no English, Bazna was ignorant of precisely what secrets he was spilling, but he knew what the word "secret" meant: reports on British diplomatic efforts to bring Turkey into the war against the Germans, infiltration of Allied personnel into Turkey, and U.S. military aid to the USSR. The Albanian spy—code-named "Cicero" by the Germans—even furnished accounts of decisions taken by Churchill, Roosevelt, and Stalin at the Tehran Conference and the code name of the impending D-day invasion: "Overlord." The impact of these revelations was limited by German skepticism: having been badly misled by the deception plans covering the Sicily invasion (most famously "Operation Mincemeat," in which a dead body carrying false papers was put ashore in Spain), there were some in the German High Command who suspected that Cicero might be another fiendish British ruse to mislead them at a crucial juncture in the war. The Bletchley Park intercepts and a spy in the German Foreign Office eventually alerted the British to the leakage at the British embassy in Ankara. Suspicion swiftly focused on Bazna, who, sensing the danger, shut down his espionage operations. He survived the war and later tried to sue the West German government when he discovered that he had been paid in worthless notes. He gave singing lessons, sold used cars, and ended his life working as a doorman at one of Istanbul's seedier hotels. The Cicero affair was an embarrassing debacle and further evidence of Germany's proficient spy network in Turkey. British propaganda later tried to claim that Bazna had been a double agent, but Elliott was under no illusions: "The information obtained by Cicero was completely genuine," he wrote, and "the plain truth is that the Cicero case was probably the most serious diplomatic security leak in British history."

British intelligence fought back, reinforced in 1943 by the arrival of the OSS. The head of Turkish operations for American intelligence was Lanning "Packy" Macfarland, an extroverted Chicago banker with a taste for trouble and a spy's wardrobe, including a trench coat and slouch hat: "If he had not been a spy, dressed like that he would have had to become one," remarked a fellow officer. Aided by British intelligence, Macfarland began setting up his own agent network, starting with a Czech businessman named Alfred Schwartz, code-named "Dogwood," who claimed to have access to anti-Nazi resistance groups inside Germany, Austria, and Hungary. Elliott liked Macfarland, despite his "penchant for involving himself in unfortunate escapades," and established an effective working relationship with the Americans. Together they successfully introduced a Turkish informant into one of Leverkühn's sabotage cells. "The names of the Azerbaijanis, Persians and Caucasians who work for German intelligence are now known," reported OSS officer Cedric Seager, "where they congregate of an evening, where they work and what they look like."

Iraq was a particular focus of Abwehr interest. In 1941 British forces had invaded the country, fearing that a pro-Axis government in Baghdad might cut off oil supplies. Elliott discovered that Leverkühn was attempting to foment anti-British rebellion among Iraq's Kurdish tribes while encouraging and financing the revolutionary underground. Three German agents were parachuted into Iraq and intercepted soon after they landed. Next Elliott planted a double agent within the revolutionary cell, codenamed "Zulu." On September 3, 1943, Leverkühn picked up Zulu in his Mercedes at a prearranged rendezvous in Istanbul. As they drove around the city, Leverkühn delivered a propaganda lecture, insisting that "the Arab cause depended on German victory," before instructing the agent on how to identify British military units in Iraq and handing over a radio code along with two thousand dollars in cash. The British authorities in Baghdad duly rounded up the entire revolutionary ring.

The duel between Nicholas Elliott and Paul Leverkühn was ferocious and unrelenting, but it was also oddly gentlemanly. If Elliott spotted his rival dining in Taksim's, he would always send over a bottle with his compliments. Each side wanted the other to know who was on top and sometimes made the point in ways that were deeply silly. When Leverkühn discovered that Britain's secret wireless code for Germany was "1200," he immediately informed his colleagues: henceforth, whenever Elliott or another British intelligence officer walked into an Istanbul bar where German officers were drinking, they faced a humiliating chorus of "Twelve-land, Twelve-land, *über alles.*" The tit-for-tat battle raged without a clear winner. But as 1943 drew to a close, Elliott pulled off a feat of espionage so remarkable that it rocked the Third Reich, tipped Hitler into a towering rage, crippled the Abwehr, and sent Elliott's stock soaring at MI6. The first hint that such a spectacular coup might be in the offing came from Kim Philby.

Chapter Six

The German Defector

IN THE SPRING OF 1943 KIM PHILBY LEARNED THAT A YOUNG GER-
man named Erich Vermehren had turned up in Lisbon, where
his mother was working as a journalist, and made a tentative approach to British intelligence. The Vermehrens were a prominent
family of Lübeck lawyers with known anti-Nazi leanings, and
Erich Vermehren hinted that he was thinking of defecting to the
British. This first contact went no further. Vermehren had little of
intelligence value to offer, his wife was still in Berlin, and he soon
returned there. But the approach was intriguing, and Philby filed
it away for future use.

Erich Vermehren was one of those rare people whose conscience expands and strengthens under stress. In body he was
fragile, the result of a gunshot injury suffered as a youth; but his
soul was made of some tensile, almost impossibly resilient material that never broke or even bent in its certainty. Patriotic and
pious, Vermehren was convinced of his own moral rectitude. In
1938, at the age of nineteen, he won a Rhodes Scholarship to
Oxford but was prevented from taking it because his repeated
refusal to join the Hitler Youth had rendered him, in Nazi eyes,
"unfit to represent German youth." Hitler himself is said to have
ordered that Vermehren's name be struck off the list of scholars.
Unfit to serve in the army on account of his injury, he worked
in a prisoner-of-war camp. In 1939 he converted to Catholicism
and married the aristocratic Countess Elisabeth von Plettenburg,
a devout Catholic thirteen years his senior whose loathing for Nazism was as staunch as his own. Elisabeth had come to Gestapo

attention before the war for distributing religious tracts critical of the pagan Nazis. The Plettenburgs were deeply implicated in the anti-Nazi resistance, as were the Vermehrens. Adam von Trott zu Solz, a German foreign office official who would become a key player in the plot to oust Hitler, was Vermehren's cousin. The marriage of Erich and Elisabeth thus brought together two wings of the secret anti-Nazi resistance—which was, in part, a family affair. In this small band of German resisters, religious and moral outrage fused with politics. These were not liberals: they were deeply conservative, often wealthy, fiercely anticommunist, old-fashioned German families, fearful that Hitler was leading Germany into a calamity that would usher in rule by the godless Bolsheviks. The plotters dreamed of ousting Hitler, making peace with Britain and the United States, and then defeating the red menace from the East to create a new German state that was democratic, anticommunist, and Christian. Erich and Elisabeth Vermehren decided, along with a handful of like-minded conspirators, that Hitler must be destroyed before he destroyed Germany.

In late 1943, with the help of Trott, Erich Vermehren was assigned to the Abwehr, given two weeks' training in the use of wireless codes and secret inks, and then deployed to Istanbul as personal assistant to Paul Leverkühn, a friend and legal colleague of his father's from Lübeck. Officially, wives were not allowed to accompany their husbands on diplomatic postings, to discourage any possibility of defection. Elisabeth, already a marked woman, remained in Berlin, in effect held hostage. Vermehren arrived in Istanbul in early December and began work at the Abwehr office under Leverkühn. Two weeks later he again made contact with British intelligence; Harold Gibson of MI6 passed his name on to Section V; Kim Philby's Iberian section had flagged his earlier approach in Lisbon; the Vermehren file was forwarded to Elliott in Istanbul, and the wheels began to turn.

On December 27, 1943, at seven o'clock in the evening, Erich Vermehren made his way to an address on Istiklal Caddesi, the main street of Pera. A servant with a strong Russian accent answered the door to the apartment, showed the young German into the sitting room, and handed him, unbidden, a large Scotch. A few moments later, a lanky, bespectacled man emerged from behind a sliding door and stuck out his hand with a friendly grin. "Erich Vermehren?" he said. "Why, I believe you were coming up to Oxford." Nicholas Elliott had done his homework.

Vermehren vividly recalled that moment and Elliott's unmistakable, reassuring Englishness. "I had a sense of tremendous relief. I felt almost as if my feet rested already on English soil."

The two men talked while Elizabeth Elliott served dinner, and they continued talking through the night. Vermehren explained that he was anxious to strike a blow against Hitler but agonized at the thought that he might be betraying his country. He insisted he could not leave without his wife, who would certainly be arrested and probably killed if he defected. Elliott detected "signs of instability" in the young man. He coaxed and cajoled him; he summoned Elizabeth to stress the moral responsibility incumbent on Vermehren through his Catholic faith; he explained that it would take some time to arrange the false paperwork, but when the moment was right he would spirit the Vermehrens out of Turkey and bring them safely to Britain. Vermehren's defection, Elliott promised, would strike a devastating blow to Nazism. When the German still hesitated, Elliott's voice took on a harder edge. Vermehren was in too deep to back out now. As dawn broke over Istanbul, Vermehren rose to his feet and shook Elliott's hand. He would do what Elliott, and God, required of him.

In his report to MI6, Elliott described Vermehren as "a highly strung, cultivated, self-confident, extremely clever, logical-minded, slightly precious young German of good family" who was "intensely anti-Nazi on religious grounds." Elliott was "fully convinced" of Vermehren's sincerity.

Vermehren flew back to Berlin and told his wife to prepare for the moment they had long discussed. Trott had arranged a job for her at the German embassy in Istanbul, where her cousin, Franz von Papen, was the German ambassador. This might provide some protection if the Gestapo demanded to know how husband and wife had traveled abroad together in violation of the rules. Elisabeth divided her bank accounts among her siblings, and the Vermehrens set off by rail for Istanbul. But as the train trundled through Bulgaria they learned, to their horror, that the man occupying the wagon-lit compartment next door was a Gestapo officer. They were already under surveillance. Sure enough, at the Bulgarian border, Elisabeth was arrested and taken to the German embassy in Sofia. Erich had no choice but to continue on to Istanbul alone. After a wait of two weeks, again with the help of Adam von Trott zu Solz, Elisabeth wangled her way onto a courier plane to Istanbul and was finally reunited with her husband. Leverkühn knew Frau Vermehren was on the Gestapo blacklist, and he was distinctly alarmed to find her turning up unannounced in his city; he instructed Vermehren to write a memo to Berlin explaining exactly how and why his wife had come to Istanbul.

The Vermehrens had to move fast, and so did Elliott. Under the pretense of familiarizing himself with the office paperwork, Vermehren began extracting what seemed to be the most important Abwehr files, including an organogram of "the complete Abwehr setup in Istanbul" and a "quantity of detailed information" about Abwehr operations in the Near and Middle East. These were photographed by Elliott and then returned to the Abwehr office by Vermehren. Leverkühn gave his new assistant full access to the files, and Vermehren was soon passing on huge quantities of information every night. But time was running out. On January 25, one of Elliott's informants in the Turkish police tipped him off that they knew Vermehren was in contact with the British; Leverkühn had his own police spies, and "it would not be long, therefore, before the Germans got wind" of what was afoot.

Two days later Erich and Elisabeth Vermehren attended a cocktail party at the Spanish embassy. As the couple left the building, they were seized by two men and bundled into a waiting car. The scene was stage-managed by Elliott to make it appear that they had been kidnapped, in order to buy time and perhaps limit reprisals against their families. The Vermehrens were driven southeast to the coast near Smyrna and transferred to a fast motor launch, which then accelerated into the Mediterranean darkness. Twenty-four hours later they were in Cairo, still wearing their party clothes.

Paul Leverkühn reacted to the Vermehrens' disappearance with bafflement, followed by anger, and then sheer, paralyzing panic. The Abwehr chief, MI6 reported happily, was in "a hell of a flap." Papen cut short a skiing holiday in the Bursa Mountains to take personal command of the crisis and demanded that the Turkish police track down the fugitives. The Turks politely agreed to help, and did nothing at all. Leverkühn was ordered back to Berlin. As the Germans scoured Istanbul, Ernst Kaltenbrunner, Hitler's brutal security chief, gave orders that the Istanbul Abwehr be thoroughly investigated and purged, since more enemy spies must be lurking there. He was right. Several of Leverkühn's colleagues now also decided to bolt. Karl Alois Kleczkowski, a forty-three-year-old journalist who had worked as a German propagandist and a rumor collector for the Abwehr, went into hiding in a safe house on the city's outskirts. Wilhelm Hamburger, the heir to an Austrian paper fortune, was one of Leverkühn's most trusted deputies. Posing as a flax buyer, he had spent much of the war gathering intelligence on the Middle East while seldom leaving his table at the Park Hotel. He was also in touch with the Allied intelligence services. On February 7 he was woken by two German officers and told he was under arrest. Hamburger asked if he could call his most important Turkish agent "lest his disappearance provoke controversy." Bizarrely, he was allowed to do so: Hamburger dialed a prearranged number, got through to his OSS contact, and uttered the following words: "I am going to Berlin for a week and will be back. *Tell it to the Marines.*" (Slang for nonsense.) Half an hour later, with Hamburger still packing and stalling, a car pulled up outside his house. Hamburger raced out the front door before his captors could stop him, jumped in the backseat, and was driven at high speed to the British consulate, where "he was given breakfast and a new identity." The two defectors followed the Vermehrens' secret escape route to Egypt. Packy Macfarland of the OSS sent a jubilant message to Washington, reporting that

Cairo was in danger of being "swamped by an invasion of evaders and turncoats." Kaltenbrunner conveyed the bad news to Hitler: Vermehren's defection had "gravely prejudiced the activities not only of the Abwehr-Istanbul but of our other military agencies in Turkey. The entire work of the Abwehr station has been exposed and its continuation seems impracticable."

Having spirited no fewer than four defectors out of Istanbul, Elliott followed them to Britain. He traveled by train to Lebanon and then on by air via Cairo, Algiers, and Casablanca before finally arriving at Newquay, Cornwall, after an "exceedingly tedious and uncomfortable" journey lasting more than a week.

Kim Philby, ever helpful, had offered the use of his mother's Kensington flat as a place to house the Vermehrens on their arrival in London. The defection was so secret that not even MI5 knew they were in the country. Elliott went straight to Dora Philby's flat in Drayton Gardens, South Kensington, where he was greeted by a beaming Philby and reunited with the Vermehrens. Over the next fortnight, Philby and Elliott put the couple through a friendly, detailed, and rigorous debriefing. Vermehren had worked for the Abwehr for only a few months, yet the information he had to impart was supremely valuable: the structure of German intelligence, its operations in the Middle East, the identities of its officers and agents; Elisabeth Vermehren furnished chapter and verse on the Catholic underground resistance in Germany. The Vermehrens' piety made them quite irritating. Whereas most spies are compelled by a variety of motives, including adventure, idealism, and avarice, and can thus be manipulated, the Vermehrens served only God, which made them unpredictable and occasionally uncooperative. "They are so God-awful conscientious you never know what they're going to do next," Elliott complained to Philby in exasperation after sitting through another of Vermehren's religious homilies. Vermehren was code-named "Precious," because that is what he was, in more ways than one.

During a break in the debriefing process, Elliott at last had an opportunity to meet his parents-in-law, which might have been a confusing experience for someone less familiar with the eccentricities of the British upper class. Sir Edgar Holberton turned out to be convivial, pompous, and distinctly odd. Years in the tropics had left him with a peculiar verbal habit: every so often, and quite without warning, he would say something entirely inappropriate. Elliott met Sir Edgar for lunch at his club. The older man launched into an exceptionally boring disquisition on the Chilean economy and then suddenly observed, without breaking stride: "I don't mind telling you, my boy, that I too kept a Burmese girl in Rangoon. Didn't cost me a penny more than £20 a month." Conversation with Sir Edgar, Elliott reflected, was an "obstacle race with frequent jumps."

Some of the material extracted from the Vermehrens was deemed of sufficient value to be passed on to Britain's allies. Moscow was informed that Vermehren had revealed that certain Turkish officials were passing information to the Abwehr. The Soviets protested loudly over this violation of Turkish neutrality, and Turkey immediately ceased all "German-Turkish intelligence exchanges regarding the USSR." But many of the defectors' revelations, notably those relating to the anticommunist resistance organization in Germany, were considered far too sensitive to be shared with the Soviet Union. More than a year later, Moscow was still complaining that it had not seen a full account of Vermehren's debriefing.

The news of Vermehren's defection was carefully leaked. The Associated Press reported: "The 24-year-old attaché and his wife declared that they had deserted the Germans because they were disgusted with Nazi brutality. He is said to possess detailed information of the greatest value." MI5 was annoyed to discover that the defection was being exclusively handled by MI6. "If an enemy alien is to be brought here solely for the purposes of his being pumped for information he should, I think, be under our control," wrote Guy Liddell. This was pure professional jealousy. In securing Vermehren's defection, MI6 trumpeted that Elliott had struck an "outstanding blow" against the enemy: the information he brought was useful enough in terms of intelligence, but the symbolic impact of his defection on Germany was quite shattering.

Hitler is said to have "exploded" when told of Vermehren's defection. For some time he had suspected (rightly) that Admiral Wilhelm Canaris and many of his fellow Abwehr officers were less than fully loyal to the Nazi project and secretly conspiring with the enemy. Here was proof. Hitler also believed (wrongly) that Vermehren had taken the Abwehr's secret codebooks with him. Anyone who had aided, or even merely known, the Vermehrens was now under suspicion. Vermehren's father, mother, sisters, and brother were all rounded up and imprisoned in concentration camps. Hitler summoned Canaris for a ferocious dressing-down and told him the Abwehr was falling apart. With more bravery than tact, Canaris replied that this was "hardly surprising given that Germany was losing the war." Two weeks later Hitler abolished the Abwehr and created a new, overarching intelligence service under Himmler's SD. Canaris was shuffled into a meaningless job, placed under effective house arrest, and finally, following the failure of the July Plot in 1944, executed. The Abwehr might have been corrupt, inefficient, and partly disloyal, but it was, at least, a functioning worldwide intelligence service. The defections set off a chain reaction that destroyed it utterly, just three months before D-day. In the words of the historian Michael Howard, German intelligence was "thrown into a state of confusion just at the moment when its efficient functioning was vital to the survival of the Third Reich."

Nicholas Elliott was now the darling of MI6. An internal assessment concluded that he had handled the case with "consummate skill and sympathy, but with just the necessary touch of firmness." Some of the glory rubbed off on Philby, who had helped orchestrate the defections from afar and then debriefed the Vermehrens in his mother's flat. The operation, it seemed, had ended in complete triumph. Elliott would "dine out" on this success for a very long time, but the wining and dining began immediately, in celebration of Elliott's "dazzling coup."

It was through Philby that Elliott met the gaunt but convivial young American James Jesus Angleton. The three intelligence officers became firm friends and spent a good deal of time in one another's company, from which Elliott emerged "formidably impressed both by Jim's intellect and his personality, as well as by his enjoyment and capacity for food and drink." Angleton had taken to wearing a homburg, like Philby, and he peered out from underneath it through heavy-lidded eyes. "Beneath the rather sinister mystique was a very likable man," Elliott recorded, "with a formidable personality and breadth of vision." Angleton and Elliott had much in common: fierce ambition, daunting fathers, and, of course, a shared admiration for Kim Philby.

Before heading back to Istanbul, Elliott was summoned to MI6 headquarters by the head of security, a former soldier newly appointed to oversee vetting and secrecy procedures within the diplomatic service and MI6. This was an issue that had never been raised before with Elliott, who was almost pathologically discreet. "At that time, secrets were secrets," he wrote. But he now wondered if he had let his guard down in some way or spilled some information to the wrong person. He need not have worried. The ensuing conversation, which he wrote down afterward, said a great deal about the organization of which Elliott was now a most valued part.

SECURITY OFFICER: "Sit down, I'd like to have a frank talk with you."

NICHOLAS ELLIOTT: "As you wish colonel."

OFFICER: "Does your wife know what you do?"

ELLIOTT: "Yes."

OFFICER: "How did that come about?"

ELLIOTT: "She was my secretary for two years and I think the penny must have dropped."

OFFICER: "Quite so. What about your mother?"

ELLIOTT: "She thinks I'm in something called SIS, which she believes stands for the Secret Intelligence Service."

OFFICER: "Good God! How did she come to know that?"

ELLIOTT: "A member of the War Cabinet told her at a cocktail party."

OFFICER: "Then what about your father?"

ELLIOTT: "He thinks I'm a spy."

OFFICER: "Why should he think you're a spy?"

ELLIOTT: "Because the Chief told him in the bar at White's."

And that, once again, was that.

Elliott and Philby existed within the inner circle of Britain's ruling class, where mutual trust was so absolute and unquestioned that there was no need for elaborate security precautions. They were all part of the same family. "For centuries the Office had operated on trust," said George Carey Foster, the Foreign Office security officer. "In that family atmosphere they couldn't conceive that there was a wrong 'un among them." Elliott trusted his wife to keep a secret; Elliott's employer trusted his father to keep a secret; and Elliott trusted his friend Philby to keep his secrets, never suspecting that those secrets were now being put to murderous use.

The information passed on by the Vermehrens included a detailed description "of all their contacts in the Catholic underground in Germany, and the role they could play in a post-war democratic and Christian Germany." This was intelligence of the greatest value, since it listed the names, addresses, and occupations of all those who, like the Vermehrens, opposed Hitler but wished to prevent a communist takeover of their country—the "leading Catholic activists who could be instrumental in the post-war period in helping the Allies establish an anti-communist government in Germany." For obvious reasons, with the Red Army poised to march into Germany from the East, MI6 did not pass this list on to Moscow.

But Philby did.

After the war, Allied officers went in search of the anticommunist activists identified by the Vermehrens, people who "could have formed the backbone of a Conservative Christian post-war German political leadership." They found none of them: "All had been deported or liquidated." The final months of the war were bloody and chaotic: Nazi loyalists killed some five thousand people in the wake of the July Plot, including many in the Catholic resistance. It was not until years later that MI5 worked out what had really happened: Philby had passed the list to his Soviet controller, who had passed it to Moscow Center, which had sent in the killers with a ready-made shopping list of influential ideological opponents to be eliminated as Stalin's armies advanced. "Because Moscow had decided to eliminate all non-communist opposition in Germany, these Catholics had been shot."

No one knows how many died as a consequence of Philby's actions, because MI5 and MI6 have never released Vermehren's list. In his diary Liddell of MI5 noted reports that Soviet forces were liquidating opposition in East Germany in the "drive against the Catholic Church, which the Russians recognize as the most powerful international force in opposition to communism." Years later Philby observed: "I was responsible for the deaths of a considerable number of Germans." It was assumed he was referring to Nazis, but among his victims were also an unknown number of German anti-Nazis, who perished because they did not share Philby's politics. Any lingering doubts Moscow may have had about Philby seem to have evaporated at this moment.

The Vermehrens believed they were alerting the Allies to the men and women who might save Germany from communism; unwittingly, they were handing them over to Moscow. Through Philby's betrayal, Elliott's greatest triumph was a secret, sordid tragedy.

Chapter Seven

The Soviet Defector

D-DAY WAS APPROACHING, THE ALLIES WERE ADVANCING, AND KIM Philby, Nick Elliott, and their OSS colleague James Jesus Angleton, like so many others who had come of age in war, began to wonder what they would do with their lives when it was over. Each was determined to remain in the intelligence game and make a career of it; each had found success in the arcane art of espionage, and all three were destined for rapid promotion, two through merit and one by an office putsch.

As the Nazi threat receded, the fear of Soviet espionage revived. Before the war MI5 and MI6 had expended considerable energy, resources, and anxiety on combating the communist menace, both inside and outside Britain. But the overwhelming challenge of the war with Germany and the alliance with Stalin had diverted attention from Moscow's covert activities. By 1944 the Soviet espionage threat was coming back into sharp focus. "We've been penetrated by the communists," Sir Stewart Menzies told Angleton, "and they're on the inside, but we don't know exactly how." Waking up to the threat of communism from within, the chiefs of British intelligence were increasingly aware that new weapons and a restructured service would be needed to take on "the next enemy," the Soviet Union. The battle lines of the cold war were being drawn.

In March 1944 Philby suggested to C that the time had come to resume the fight against communist spies, by establishing a new section, Section IX, for the "professional handling of any cases coming to our notice involving Communists or people concerned in Soviet espionage." C was enthusiastic, and so was the Foreign Office, "provided you do not do anything in the USSR itself (despite Soviet espionage in this country)." An MI5 officer, Jack Curry, was initially placed in charge, but the obvious person to run the new division in the long term was the experienced head of Section V, Felix Cowgill. Philby later claimed that Moscow ordered him to elbow aside Cowgill, a task he did not relish: "I must do everything, but *everything*, to ensure that I become head of Section IX," Philby wrote. "Cowgill must go." It seems more likely that Philby suggested the setting up of Section IX with the firm intention of taking it over, and Cowgill was in the way.

The removal of Cowgill was carried out with surgical detachment and no remorse. Philby carefully stoked the antagonism between Cowgill and his senior colleagues, brittle Valentine Vivian and venomous Claude Dansey; he whispered darkly to those in authority of the sour relations between Cowgill and MI5; and he maneuvered himself into a position as prime candidate to take over Section IX in Cowgill's stead. Finally, in September 1944, Philby was summoned to C's office, received with "great warmth," and told that he would be running the new Soviet section. Philby accepted with pleasure, but not before planting a small and suitably deferential suggestion in C's mind. Since Cowgill's dealings with MI5 had been so bad, might it be sensible to ensure the sister service had no objection to his own appointment? Philby was not remotely fearful that MI5, where he had many friends, would actually challenge his promotion. He merely wanted to be sure that MI5's fingerprints were all over this decision; that way, if the security service should ever investigate how he had come to be in such a powerful position, he could point out that they had helped to put him there. Menzies swiftly became convinced that "the idea was his own." When Cowgill discovered he had been passed over for the top job, he resigned in fury, as Philby had known he would.

Section IX was originally envisaged as a counterintelligence unit to attack Moscow's espionage efforts abroad, but it would soon expand to include running intelligence operations *against* the Soviet bloc, as well as monitoring and secretly attacking communist movements in Europe. Philby, the veteran Soviet spy, was now in charge of Britain's anti-Soviet intelligence operations, in a position to inform Moscow not only of what Britain was doing to counter Soviet espionage but also of Britain's own espionage efforts against Moscow. The fox was not merely guarding the henhouse but building it, running it, assessing its strengths and frailties, and planning its future construction. As a contemporary later observed, "At one stroke he got rid of a staunch anti-communist and ensured that the whole post-war effort to counter communist espionage would become known in the Kremlin. The history of espionage offers few, if any, comparable masterstrokes."

The reaction in Moscow was, naturally, ecstatic. "The new appointment is hard to over-estimate," the British section of the NKVD reported, noting that Philby was "moving up in his institution, he is respected and valued." Soviet suspicion of Philby had already waned and now dispersed altogether, in part because Elena Modrzhinskaya, the doyenne of conspiracy theory, had retired with the rank of colonel to give lectures at the Soviet Institute of Philosophy on the evils of cosmopolitanism. Notwithstanding her suspicions, Philby and the other Cambridge spies had been loyal throughout the war—and astonishingly productive. Philby had reported on the "Manhattan" atomic-bomb program, the plans for D-day, Britain's Polish policy, OSS operations in Italy (thanks to Angleton), MI6 activities in Istanbul (thanks to Elliott), and much more, all perfectly truthfully. In the course of the war an estimated ten thousand documents, political, economic, and military, were sent to Moscow from the London office of the NKVD. Modrzhinskaya stands as a symbol of Stalinism at its oddest: she was consistently ideologically correct while being utterly, hilariously wrong.

Philby's latest Soviet case officer was Boris Krötenschield, a young workaholic code-named "Max," a "jovial, kindly man" who spoke an antique, courtly English that made him sound like a tweedy country squire. Krötenschield was closer in mentality and character to the men who had recruited Philby back in 1934, "a splendid professional and a wonderful person" to whom he could "unburden" his thoughts and feelings. Some of his former hero worship was returning. The Center showered him with praise and presents. "I must thank you once again for the marvelous gift," Philby wrote in December 1944. "The prospects that have opened before me in connection with my recent change at work inspire me to optimistic thoughts." Philby's new job in MI6 was coincidentally reflected in a change of spy name: agent "Sonny" was now agent "Stanley."

In Istanbul Elliott remained oblivious to the way Philby had ousted their old boss. He knew only that his friend had landed an important new job as head of MI6's powerful Soviet counterespionage section, and Elliott was rising through the ranks in tandem. After a few months back in Turkey, Elliott was summoned to London and told by C that he had been appointed MI6 station chief in neutral Switzerland, a crucial intelligence battleground during the war that would acquire even greater importance as the cold war grew hotter.

After a long and difficult journey across newly liberated, war-ravaged France, Elliott crossed the Swiss frontier in early April 1945 and checked into Geneva's Hôtel Beau-Rivage as night was falling. "After the gloom of London and France it was an extraordinary contrast to be shown up to a clean bedroom with a view across the lake and to relax in a hot bath with a whisky and soda." After Turkey, Switzerland seemed disconcertingly civilized, tidy, and regulated, an almost artificial world. Here were no dodgy nightclubs where spies swapped secrets with belly dancers, no bomb-throwing assassins or corrupt officials ready to sell truth and lies for the same inflated price. Elliott was nettled to hear the Swiss complain of their wartime privations, when the war seemed to have swept around and over Switzerland. But beneath a placid, neutral surface, the place was riddled with spies. Swiss efforts to discourage espionage during the war failed utterly: Allied, Axis, and freelance agents had converged on the country as a base from which to launch intelligence operations into enemy territory. The Soviets had run at least two linked spy networks based in Switzerland, the Rote Kapelle (Red Orchestra) and the Lucy Ring, extracting top secret information from Nazi Germany and funneling it to Moscow. In 1943 an anti-Nazi German diplomat named Fritz Kolbe had turned up in Bern and offered his services to the Allies: first to the British embassy, which turned him away, and then to the OSS station chief Allen Dulles (who would go on to become director of the CIA). Kolbe became, in Dulles's words, "not only our best source on Germany but undoubtedly one of the best secret agents any intelligence service has ever had." He smuggled more than 2,600 secret Nazi documents into Switzerland, including German plans before D-day and designs for Hitler's secret weapons, the V1 and V2 rockets. As Hitler's regime crumbled, Switzerland became a magnet for defectors, resisters, and rats leaving the sinking Nazi ship, all clutching their secrets. During the war, the Soviets ran their own networks, and the British and Americans ran theirs, in wary cooperation. But with the coming of peace, Soviet and Western intelligence forces would turn on each other.

In Bern Elliott rented a flat on the Dufourstrasse, not far from the British embassy, in which he installed his family, which now included a baby daughter, Claudia. (Elliott had insisted that the baby be born on English soil; had she arrived on her due date, VE Day, May 8, 1945, she would have been christened Victoria Montgomeriana in patriotic tribute to the British general. Luckily for her, she arrived late.) The baby was the responsibility of "Nanny Sizer," the widow of a sergeant major, who had enormous feet, drank gin from a bottle labeled "Holy Water," and doubled as Elliott's informal bodyguard. Officially, Elliott was second secretary at the British embassy and passport control officer; in reality, at the age of thirty, he was Britain's chief spy in another espionage breeding ground. In the summer of 1945, after only a few months in post, he was invited to meet Ernest Bevin, the new foreign secretary. One of Britain's earliest cold warriors, Bevin remarked over lunch: "Communists and communism are vile. It is the duty of all members of the service to stamp upon them at every possible opportunity." Elliott never forgot those words, for they mirrored the philosophy he would take into his new role.

While Elliott settled in to Switzerland, James Angleton took up residence in neighboring Italy. In November 1944 the young OSS officer was appointed head of "Unit Z" in Rome, a joint U.S.-UK counterintelligence force reporting to Kim Philby in London. A few months later, at the age of twenty-seven, he was made chief of X-2 (counterespionage) for the whole of Italy, with responsibility for mopping up remaining fascist networks and combating the growing threat of Soviet espionage. With an energy bordering on mania, Angleton set about building a counterespionage operation of extraordinary breadth and depth. It was said that during the final months of the war he captured "over one thousand enemy intelligence agents" in Italy. Philby kept Angleton supplied with the all-important Bletchley Park decrypts. The American was "heavily dependent on Philby for the continuation of his professional success."

Angleton's fevered approach to his work may have reflected a poetic, if misplaced, conviction that, like Keats, he was destined to die of consumption in Rome and had little time to waste. He chatted up priests and prostitutes, ran agents and double agents, and tracked looted Nazi treasures. An "enigmatic wraith" in sharp English tailoring, he "haunted the streets of Rome, infiltrating political parties, hiring agents, and drinking with officers of the Italian Secret Service." At night he was to be found among his files, noting, recording, tracking, plotting, and wreathed in cigarette smoke. "You would sit on a sofa across from the desk and he would peer at you through this valley of papers." He smiled often, but seldom with his eyes. He never seemed to sleep.

Over the coming years, as Soviet intelligence penetrated deeper into Western Europe, James Angleton and Nicholas Elliott worked ever more closely with Philby, the coordinator of Britain's anti-Soviet operations. Yet the separate sides of Philby's head created a peculiar paradox: if all his anti-Soviet operations failed, he would soon be out of a job; but if they succeeded too well, he risked inflicting real damage on his adopted cause. He needed to recruit good people to Section IX, but not too good, for these might actually penetrate Soviet intelligence and discover that the most effective Soviet spy in Britain was their own boss. Jane Archer, the officer who had interrogated Krivitsky back in 1940, joined the section soon after Philby himself. He considered her "perhaps the ablest professional intelligence officer ever employed by MI5" and a serious threat. "Jane would have made a very bad enemy," he reflected.

As the war ended, a handful of Soviet officials with access to secret information began to contemplate defection, tempted by the attractions of life in the West. Philby was disdainful of such deserters. "Was it freedom they sought, or the fleshpots?" In a way, he too was a defector, but he was remaining in place (though enjoying the fleshpots himself). "Not one of them volunteered to stay in position and risk his neck for 'freedom,'" he later wrote. "One and all, they cut and ran for safety." But Philby was haunted by the fear that a Soviet turncoat would eventually emerge with the knowledge to expose him. Here was another conundrum: the better he spied, the greater his repute within Soviet intelligence and the higher the likelihood of eventual betrayal by a defector.

In September 1945 Igor Gouzenko, a twenty-six-year-old cipher clerk at the Soviet embassy in Ottawa, turned up at a Canadian newspaper office with more than one hundred secret documents stuffed inside his shirt. Gouzenko's defection would be seen, in hindsight, as the opening shot of the cold war. This trove was the very news Philby had been dreading, for it seemed entirely possible that Gouzenko knew his identity. He immediately contacted Boris Krötenschield. "Stanley was a bit agitated," Krötenschield reported to Moscow with dry understatement. "I tried to calm him down. Stanley said that in connection with this he may have information of extreme urgency to pass to us." For the first time, as he waited anxiously for the results of Gouzenko's debriefing, Philby may have contemplated defection to the Soviet Union. The defector exposed a major spy network in Canada and revealed that the Soviets had obtained information about the atomic-bomb project from a spy working at the Anglo-Canadian nuclear research laboratory in Montreal. But Gouzenko worked for the GRU, Soviet military intelligence, not the NKVD; he knew little about Soviet espionage in Britain and almost nothing of the Cambridge spies. Philby began to relax. This defector, it seemed, did not know his name. But the next one did.

In late August 1944 Chantry Hamilton Page, the vice-consul in Istanbul, received a calling card for Konstantin Dmitrievich Volkov, a Soviet consular official, accompanied by an unsigned letter requesting, in very poor English, an urgent appointment. Page discussed this odd communication with the consul and concluded that it must be a "prank": someone was taking Volkov's name in vain. Page was still suffering from injuries he had sustained in the bomb attack on the Pera Palace hotel, and he was prone to memory lapses. He failed to answer the letter, then lost it, and finally forgot about it. A few days later, on September 4, Volkov appeared at the consulate in person, accompanied by his wife, Zoya, and demanded an audience with Page. The Russian couple were ushered into the vice-consul's office. Mrs. Volkov was in a "deplorably nervous state," and Volkov himself was "less than rock steady." Belatedly realizing that this visit might presage something important, Page summoned John Leigh Reed, first secretary at the embassy and a fluent Russian speaker, to translate. Over the next hour Volkov laid out a proposal that promised, at a stroke, to alter the balance of power in international espionage.

Volkov explained that his official position at the consulate was cover for his real job as deputy chief of Soviet intelligence in Turkey. Before coming to Istanbul, he explained, he had worked for some years on the British desk at Moscow Center. He and Zoya now wished to defect to the West. His motivation was partly personal, a desire to get even after a blazing row with the Russian ambassador. The information he offered was priceless: a complete list of Soviet agent networks in Britain and Turkey; the location of the NKVD headquarters in Moscow and details of its burglar alarm system, guard schedules, training, and finance; wax impressions of keys to the files; and information on Soviet interception of British communications. Nine days later Volkov was back, now with a letter laying out a deal.

The Russian had "obviously been preparing his defection for a long time," for his terms were precise: he would furnish the names of 314 Soviet agents in Turkey and a further 250 in Britain; copies of certain documents handed over by Soviet spies in Britain were now in a suitcase in an empty apartment in Moscow. Once a deal was agreed, and Volkov and his wife were safely in the West, he would reveal the address and MI6 could collect the papers. In exchange for this haul, Volkov demanded £50,000 (equivalent to about £1.6 million today) and political asylum in Britain under a new identity. "I consider this sum as a minimum considering the importance of the material given to you, as a result of which all my relatives living in the territory of the USSR are doomed." The Russian provided just enough detail to prove that his information was genuine: among the Soviet spies in important positions in Britain, he revealed, were seven in the British intelligence services or the Foreign Office. "I know, for instance, that one of these agents is fulfilling the functions of head of a section of the British counter-espionage service in London."

Volkov insisted on several more conditions. On no account should the British allude to him in wireless messages, since the Soviets had broken the British codes and were reading everything sent through official channels; the Russians also had a spy inside the British embassy, so any paperwork relating to his offer should be closely guarded and handwritten. All further communications would be through Chantry Page, who could contact him on routine consular business without raising suspicions among his Soviet colleagues. If he did not hear from Page within twenty-one days, he would assume the deal was off and take his information elsewhere. Volkov's nervousness was entirely understandable. As a veteran NKVD officer, he knew exactly what Moscow Center would do, and how quickly, if it got wind of his disloyalty.

The new British ambassador to Turkey, Sir Maurice Peterson, was allergic to spies. His predecessor, Knatchbull-Hugessen, had come horribly unstuck through the work of the spy Cicero. Peterson wanted nothing to do with such people, and his reaction to Volkov's approach was to shovel the whole thing, as fast as possible, onto MI6: "No one's going to turn my embassy into a nest of spies. . . . Do it through London." Even the MI6 station chief in Istanbul, Cyril Machray, was kept in the dark. John Reed wrote up a report by hand and put it in the diplomatic bag. It landed on the desk of Sir Stewart Menzies ten days later. C immediately summoned his head of Soviet counterespionage, Kim Philby, and handed him the report. Here was another potential intelligence coup, a trove of information that might, like the Vermehren defection two years earlier, change the game completely.

Philby read the memo with mounting, if hidden, horror. Volkov's allusion to the Soviet spy running a counterintelligence section in London could only refer to him. Even if Volkov did not know his identity, he had promised to hand over "copies of the material provided" to Moscow, which would soon be traced back to him. The spies Volkov threatened to uncover in the Foreign Office must be Guy Burgess, now working in the news department, and Donald Maclean, first secretary at the British embassy in Washington. This lone defector had enough information to break up the entire Cambridge spy ring, expose the inner workings of Soviet intelligence, and destroy Philby himself. Struggling to compose his features, Philby stalled, telling C the Volkov approach was "something of the greatest importance." He would ponder the memo overnight, he said, and report back in the morning.

"That evening I worked late," Philby wrote many years later. "The situation seemed to call for urgent action of an extracurricular nature." The insouciant tone is misleading: Philby was close to panic. He arranged a hasty meeting with Krötenschield and told him what had happened. Max tried to calm him, in language that sounds like one Englishman discussing a cricket match with another: "Don't worry, old man. We've seen a lot worse. The score will be settled in our favor." Philby should prevaricate, said Krötenschield, and try to control the situation. That evening British radio interceptors picked up (but failed to attach any significance to) a sudden surge in coded radio messages passing from London to Moscow, followed by another increase in traffic between Moscow and Istanbul.

The next morning Philby was back in C's office, full of enthusiasm, since any hint of reluctance would look deeply suspicious if matters came to the crunch. "Someone fully briefed should be sent out to take charge of the case on the spot," he said, with the task of "meeting Volkov, bedding him down with his wife in one of our safe houses in Istanbul, and spiriting him away, with or without the connivance of the Turks, to British-occupied Egypt." C agreed. In fact, he had met just the man for the job at White's Club the night before: Brigadier Sir Douglas Roberts, head of Security Intelligence (Middle East) (SIME) based in Cairo, who happened to be in London on leave. Roberts was an experienced intelligence officer and a veteran anti-Bolshevik. Born in Odessa to an English father and Russian mother, he spoke Volkov's language fluently. Indeed, he was the only Russian-speaking intelligence officer in either the Middle East or London, which says much about MI6's state of preparation for the cold war. Roberts would be able to smuggle Volkov out of Istanbul with ease, and Philby knew it. All he could do was hope that his "work the night before would bear fruit before Roberts got his teeth into the case."

Once again, Philby's uncanny good fortune intervened. Brigadier Roberts was a brave man, a veteran of the First World War, but he had one fear: flying. Indeed, so extreme was his aviophobia that his job description explicitly excused him from having to fly anywhere. When asked to head to Istanbul at once and take over the Volkov case, he barked: "Don't you read my contract? I don't fly."

The obvious replacement for Roberts was Nicholas Elliott. From Bern he could reach Istanbul, his old stomping ground, in a matter of hours. He had done a fine job of extracting Vermehren two years earlier and had excellent contacts in Turkey. He even appears to have met Volkov at some point during his stint in Istanbul. But Elliott, precisely because of his suitability, was the last person Philby wanted to handle the case. For once, instead of delicately planting an idea on the boss and waiting for him to believe he had coined it, Philby directly intervened and suggested that C send him to Turkey to extract Volkov in person. Menzies agreed, "with obvious relief" at this bureaucratic problem solved. Philby now gave the impression of busily making preparations, while dragging his feet as slowly as possible. He first underwent a crash course in wireless coding, to ensure he could bypass the penetrated embassy systems, and then dawdled for three more days. When his plane finally took off for Cairo, it was diverted to Tunis, causing further delay. He was still en route when the Turkish consulate in Moscow issued visas for two Soviet "diplomatic couriers" traveling to Istanbul.

Philby finally arrived in Turkey on September 26, twenty-two days after Volkov's initial contact. The city was looking particularly beautiful in the late-summer sun, but Philby grimly reflected that if he failed to prevent Volkov's defection, "this might be the last memorable summer I was destined to enjoy." When Reed asked him why MI6 had not sent someone sooner, Philby lied blandly: "Sorry, old man, it would have interfered with leave arrangements." Reed later found himself pondering the "inexplicable delays and evasions of Philby's visit," but at the time the Foreign Office man held his tongue. "I thought he was just irresponsible and incompetent."

The following Monday, with Philby standing over him, Chantry Page picked up the telephone, dialed the number of the Soviet consulate, and asked the operator for Konstantin Volkov. Instead, he was put through to the consul general. Page phoned again. This time, after a lengthy pause, the telephone was answered by someone who claimed to be Volkov but who spoke good English, which Volkov did not. "It wasn't Volkov," said Page. "I know Volkov's voice perfectly well. I've spoken to him dozens of times." The third call got no further than the telephone operator.

"She said he was out," complained Page. "A minute ago, she put me on to him." Page's face was "a study in puzzlement." Silently, Philby rejoiced. The next day Page called the Soviet consulate again. "I asked for Volkov, and the girl said 'Volkov's in

Moscow.' Then there was a sort of scuffle and slam, and the line went dead." Finally, Page marched over to the Soviet consulate in person and returned enraged. "It's no bloody good. I can't get any sense out of that madhouse. Nobody's ever heard of Volkov." Philby was silently triumphant. "The case was dead." And so, by this point, was Volkov.

The two "diplomatic couriers," hit men dispatched by Moscow Center, had worked with crisp efficiency. A few hours earlier two figures, bandaged from head to foot, were seen being loaded onto a Soviet transport aircraft "on stretchers and heavily sedated." In Moscow Volkov was taken to the torture cells of the Lubyanka, where, under "brutal interrogation," he confessed that he had intended to reveal the identities of hundreds of Soviet agents. Volkov and his terrified wife, Zoya, were then executed.

Philby later reflected that the episode had been "a very narrow squeak," the closest he had yet come to disaster. As for Volkov, Philby dismissed the Russian as a "nasty piece of work" who "deserved what he got."

Konstantin Volkov left no traces: no photograph, no file in the Russian archives, no evidence about whether his motives were mercenary, personal, or ideological. Neither his family nor that of his wife, Zoya, have ever emerged from the darkness of Stalin's state. He had been right to assume that his relatives were doomed. Volkov was not merely liquidated; he was expunged.

Philby sent a coded message to Menzies, explaining that Volkov had vanished and requesting permission to wind up the case. In a subsequent report he proffered several plausible explanations for Volkov's disappearance: perhaps he had changed his mind about defecting or had gotten drunk and talked too much. If the Soviets bugged the consulate telephones, they might have discovered the truth that way. At no point did he even hint at the possibility of a tip-off from the British side. Menzies, comfortable with Philby's explanations, concluded it was "extremely unlikely" that "indiscretion in the British embassy in Istanbul was the cause. The more probable explanation is that Volkov betrayed himself. . . . It is quite possible that his quarrels [with the Soviet ambassador] led to him being watched, and that either he or his wife, or both, made some mistake."

On his way home Philby stopped off in Rome to visit James Angleton. The strain of the Volkov scare had rattled him, and he proceeded to get extremely drunk. American intelligence knew of the failed defection, and Philby's desire to see Angleton may have been partly to "test the waters" and find out how the story was playing in Washington. Angleton listened attentively to Philby's account and "expressed sympathy that so promising a case had been lost." But the American seemed more preoccupied with his own concerns: he was worried about "the effect his work was having on his marriage," since he had not seen his wife, Cicely, for over a year and "felt guilty about it." Philby was sympathetic. "He helped me to think it through," Angleton said. After three days of bibulous secret sharing and mutual support, Angleton poured Philby onto a plane, "worse for wear of the considerable amount of alcohol he had consumed."

Settling into his new job, Philby's life developed a pattern of duality, in which he consistently undermined his own work but never aroused suspicion. He made elaborate plans to combat Soviet intelligence and then immediately betrayed them to Soviet intelligence; he urged ever greater efforts to combat the communist threat and personified that threat; his own section worked smoothly, yet nothing quite succeeded. Information from the defector Igor Gouzenko had enabled MI5 to identify Alan Nunn May, another secret communist recruited at Cambridge, as a Soviet mole working on nuclear research in Canada. May's method of contacting his Soviet controller was to stand outside the British Museum carrying a copy of the *Times*. A trap was set, but neither May nor his handler turned up. Philby had tipped off Moscow, just as he almost certainly "warned the Center about other agents identified by Gouzenko who were under British and American surveillance."

Philby worked alongside the other panjandrums of the secret

elite on the powerful Joint Intelligence Committee; in formal meetings and private parties he mixed with the cream of the secret services, people intensely secretive outside this charmed circle and so indiscreet inside it. Philby's Section IX gathered information to discredit Soviet dignitaries, it labored to stimulate defections, it gleaned secrets from former Soviet prisoners of war, and it eavesdropped on diplomats and spies. Philby approved every move in the game and then told Krötenschield, who told the Center. From his contacts in MI5 and MI6, from Elliott and Angleton, Menzies and Liddell, from every corner of the intelligence machine, Philby extracted secrets to bolster the revolution and stymie the West and passed on everything, "without reserve," to Moscow.

During the war, the Bletchley Park decoders had enabled Britain to discover what German intelligence was doing. Philby's espionage went one better: he could tell his Soviet handlers what Britain's spymasters were intending to do before they did it; he could tell Moscow what London was *thinking*. "Stanley informed me of a plan to bug simultaneously all the telephone conversations of all staff in Soviet institution [the embassy] in England," reported Krötenschield. Thanks to Philby, the Russians were not one step ahead but two. And they were grateful: "Stanley is an exceptionally valuable source. . . . His eleven years of flawless work with us is irrefutable proof of his sincerity. . . . Our goal is to protect him from discovery."

Spies love to receive medals they can never wear in public, secret rewards for secret acts. In 1945 Elliott was awarded the U.S. Legion of Merit, although with typical modesty he joked that he had probably been given the medal for rescuing Packy Macfarland, his OSS counterpart in Turkey, drunk, from an Istanbul bar. Early the following year a grateful Britain appointed Kim Philby to the Order of the British Empire for his wartime work. A few months previously in Moscow, Philby had been secretly recommended for the Soviet Order of the Red Banner in recognition of his "conscientious work for over ten years." He already had his Red Cross from General Franco. By the end of 1946 Philby had achieved something no other spy could boast: the award of three separate medals from nationalist Spain, the communist Soviet Union, and Britain.

Kim Philby, OBE, was increasingly seen by his colleagues in British intelligence as a man marked out for great things: the consummate intelligence professional, the captivating star of the service who had worsted the Germans at the intelligence game and was now leading the fight against Soviet espionage. Stewart Menzies had served throughout the war as Britain's spy chief, but eventually C would have to pass the torch. "I looked around," wrote waspish Hugh Trevor-Roper, "at the part-time stockbrokers and retired Indian policemen, the agreeable epicureans from the bars of White's and Boodle's, the jolly, conventional ex–Navy officers and the robust adventurers from the bucket shop; and then I looked at Philby. . . . He alone was real. I was convinced that he was destined to head the service."

Chapter Eight

Rising Stars

WITH THE COMING OF PEACE, THE DENIZENS OF THE SECRET WORLD emerged onto a new political landscape fraught with uncertainty and ripe with opportunity. James Angleton, anticommunist to the core, was elated at the prospect of doing battle with the Soviet spy machine: "I believed we were in the dawn of a new millennium," he later recalled. Nicholas Elliott moved easily from loathing Nazism to hating communism; both threatened the British way of life he cherished, and both were therefore evil. In Elliott's mind, the threat from Russia represented a stark choice: "the continuation of a civilization mainly fit to live in, or Armageddon." For Kim Philby too the political frontiers shifted, though his convictions altered not at all. For most of the war he had spied on behalf of Britain's ally; now he was spying for Britain's sworn enemy, and from within the very heart of the British intelligence machine.

Elliott plunged into his role as Britain's spy chief in spy-saturated Switzerland with the enthusiasm of a schoolboy—which, in many ways, he remained. He was now a husband, a father (a son, Mark, would arrive in 1947), and a career intelligence officer, an MI6 professional with weighty responsibilities, yet there was still something boyish about him, an engaging combination of worldliness and naïveté, as he waded cheerily through the moral and ethical quicksand of espionage. He found the challenge of intelligence gathering not merely enjoyable but frequently absurd. "I'm in it for the belly-laughs," he said. He knew his tendency to see the funny side in the worst situations was "a form of defence mechanism," a way of holding back reality with jokes, the dirtier the better. Elliott's character was a distinctly English combination of the staid and the unconventional, conservatism and oddity: he was popular with colleagues, for he was unfailingly courteous and never raised his voice. "Verbal abuse is not the right course of action," he once reflected. "Except perhaps in dealing with Germans." Elliott could not abide bureaucracy, administration, or rules. His knack for intelligence gathering relied on personal contact, risk, hunch, and what he called "the British tradition of somehow muddling through despite the odds." Jocular, old-fashioned, amateurish, and eccentric, Elliott struck some as a posh bumbler. It was a useful disguise.

As he had in Istanbul, Elliott gathered around him a collection of more or less motley characters, agents, informers, and tipsters; he cultivated new friends and imported old ones. "One of the joys of living in Switzerland in the immediate post-war period was to be able to have friends out to stay from deprived England and feed them up." The spare bedroom in Dufourstrasse became temporary home to a succession of British and American spies crisscrossing Europe. Richard Brooman-White, Elliott's chum who had eased Philby into Section V, came to stay in 1946 and was very nearly immolated when a waitress in Elliott's favorite restaurant attempted to flambé an omelet at the table by pouring brandy onto a heated pan, causing a violent explosion that set fire to the hair of a Swedish diner. Elliott extinguished her with three glasses of white wine. Philby made a point of stopping off in Switzerland during his regular tours of Europe for working holidays with Elliott involving copious drink, Swiss cuisine, and spy gossip. Another frequent visitor was Peter Lunn, one of Elliott's "oldest and closest friends" from Eton. Slight, blue-eyed, and with a pronounced lisp, Lunn had joined MI6 at the same time as Elliott in 1939, but on the whole he preferred skiing to spying. The Lunns were "British skiing aristocracy": Peter's grandfather was a former missionary who spent a lifetime preaching the joys of skiing and founded the ski travel company that still bears his name; his father successfully campaigned to have downhill skiing recognized as an Olympic sport, and Peter himself captained the British ski team at the 1936 Winter Olympics. Under Lunn's instruction, Elliott took to the sport with a typical combination of enthusiasm and recklessness. Where his father had climbed mountains slowly, Elliott discovered the thrill of sliding down them as fast as possible. Most weekends he could be found on the slopes of Wengen or St Moritz.

Elliott's life in Bern was rendered still more pleasurable by the arrival of Klop Ustinov, his old friend and mentor from The Hague. After successfully extracting the spy Wolfgang Gans zu Putlitz from the clutches of the Gestapo, the part-Jewish, part-Ethiopian Russian with the upper-class English accent had spent a fascinating war working for British intelligence, most recently in Germany where, in the uniform of a British colonel, he had proved to be "the ideal person to be entrusted with the interrogation of Nazi suspects." In 1946, Ustinov was sent to Bern to work with Elliott on "attempting to piece together a picture of the post-war Soviet intelligence networks in Europe." Elliott was delighted to be reunited with this spherical, jovial man, whose eye permanently twinkled with merriment behind his monocle. Klop believed that life was a "superficial existence," an attitude that fused perfectly with Elliott's frivolity and taste for danger. The Elliott-Ustinov partnership proved extraordinarily effective but rather fattening: a fine chef, Klop tended to turn up unexpectedly, carrying *rognons de veau à la liégeoise* inside a leather top-hat case.

Elliott and Ustinov focused first on the remnants of the wartime Soviet spy system in Switzerland, notably the network code-named the Rote Kapelle, which at its height had run some 117 agents, including 48 inside Germany, producing high-grade intelligence. One of the most important members of the network was British, a young communist named Alexander Foote. Born in Derbyshire, Foote had served in the RAF before deserting to join the International Brigade during the Spanish civil war. Shortly before the Second World War he was recruited by Soviet military intelligence and sent to Switzerland as a radio operator for the fledgling Rote Kapelle. In January 1945 Foote moved to Moscow, convinced his interrogators of his continued loyalty, and was redeployed to the Soviet sector of postwar Berlin under the pseudonym "Major Grantov." There, in July 1947, he defected to the British. Foote produced a detailed picture of Soviet intelligence methods, offering a "unique opportunity to study the methodology of a Soviet network" from which Elliott and Ustinov were able to draw up a "blueprint for communist activities during the Cold War." Foote's debriefing contained some deeply worrying elements, most notably the revelation that Moscow had many long-term, deeply embedded spies in Britain, some of whom had been recruited long before the war. Elliott and Ustinov concluded that most of these spies were "lifelong communist activists," but not necessarily with any overt connection to the party.

James Angleton had come to see the task of combating Soviet espionage as "not so much an ideology, as a way of life." In the last years of war and the first years of peace, Angleton's agents pervaded every corner of Italy: the civil service, armed forces, intelligence services, and political parties, including the Soviet-backed Italian Communist Party. Like Elliott, Angleton cultivated a brand of high eccentricity: he gave his agents botanical code names such as "Fig," "Rose," or "Tomato" and sported a fur cape with a high collar, which made him look "like a British actor emulating a Thirties spy." Behind his back, colleagues called him "the cadaver" and wondered at his strangeness. "The guy was just in another world," said one. But he was good. By 1946 he had successfully penetrated no fewer than seven foreign intelligence services and had a roster of more than fifty active informants—most of them quite dodgy and some of them entirely so. Among the most glamorous, and least trustworthy, was Princess Maria Pignatelli, the widow of an Italian marquess with links to Mussolini who had offered her services to the OSS as an informant on what remained of Italian fascism. Angleton discovered, however, that she had previously been in contact with the German intelligence service; he was never sure how far he could trust the spy he knew, with only limited affection, as "Princess Pig."

Even more dubious was Virgilio Scattolini, a corpulent Italian journalist who wrote best-selling, semipornographic novels, including one entitled, rather unenticingly, *Amazons in the Bidet.* This sideline did not prevent him from obtaining a job on the Vatican newspaper. In 1944 he offered to supply the OSS in Rome with Vatican diplomatic documents and cable traffic, including copies of reports from the papal nuncio in Tokyo, who was in direct contact with senior Japanese officials. Angleton paid Scattolini a princely retainer of five hundred dollars a month. His reports were sent straight to Roosevelt and were considered so secret that only the president or the secretary of state could authorize access to them. Angleton, however, began to have doubts when it emerged that Scattolini was hawking similar material to other intelligence organizations, including MI6. The crunch came when Scattolini reported a conversation between the Japanese envoy to the Holy See and his American counterpart that the State Department discovered had never taken place. Scattolini was making it up, and he continued to do so even after he was sacked by Angleton. In 1948 he was imprisoned for fabricating two entire volumes purporting to be the "Secret Documents of Vatican Diplomacy."

The Scattolini episode was deeply embarrassing, the first blemish on Angleton's career. It also ingrained his natural propensity for extreme suspicion. His time in Britain observing the successful Double Cross operation against the Germans had taught Angleton "how vulnerable even the most supposedly secure counter-intelligence service is to clandestine penetration." On reflection, he wondered whether Scattolini might have been a Soviet double agent, deployed to plant damaging disinformation. The duplicity of spies like Princess Pig and Virgilio Scattolini seemed to reinforce Angleton's distrust of all but a few intimates; he became increasingly obsessed with double agents and "the Byzantine possibilities open to the counter-intelligence practitioner." On Angleton's visits to Bern, Elliott noted his American friend's deepening mistrust, his compulsive compilation of secret files, his adherence to secrecy as a sort of religion. Every day, Angleton scoured his Rome office for bugs, "crawling around on his hands and knees," convinced the Soviets were attempting to listen in on his conversations, just as he was eavesdropping on theirs. "His real love was unravelling the web of deception, penetration and general intrigue woven by the KGB," wrote Elliott. "Above all, he loved secrecy, perhaps even secrecy for its own sake."

Angleton's only real intimacy was with other spies, and he later remarked on the way friendship, secrecy, and professional comradeship seemed to merge during his years in Rome. "We were . . . damned good friends," he later said. "I feel that's the only way you can keep a service going." There was rivalry between the American and British services in many parts of the world, but Angleton and Elliott kept few secrets from each other and fewer still from Kim Philby.

During one of Philby's visits to Rome, Angleton described one of his proudest achievements: a bugging device planted in the offices of Palmiro Togliatti, the veteran leader of the Italian Communist Party. Togliatti had spent the war in the Soviet Union, making radio broadcasts urging Italian communists to resist the Nazis, before returning to Italy after the fall of Mussolini to serve in a democratic government of national unity. Togliatti's links with Moscow rendered him deeply suspect in American eyes, and Angleton boasted that he was recording every word spoken in the communist leader's office. A few weeks later, Boris Krötenschield sent a message to Moscow Center: "Stanley reported that the counter-intelligence section of the OSS in Italy has set up a microphone in the building where Togliatti works, thanks to which they can monitor all conversations in that building."

In the autumn of 1946, Philby announced that he was marrying Aileen Furse—news that came as a shock to both Elliott and Angleton, who had always assumed that the mother of Philby's children was already his wife. Philby had hitherto refused to marry Aileen, despite her entreaties, for the simple reason that he was already married, to a foreign communist. But as he rose within MI6, Philby concluded that this particular skeleton, in a cupboard packed with such things, would have to be revealed. He approached Valentine Vivian, the man who had so casually waved him into the service in the first place, and explained that, as an impetuous youth, he had married a left-wing Austrian, whom he now planned to divorce in order to make an honest woman of Aileen. The revelation does not seem to have given Vee-Vee a moment's concern.

Philby contacted Litzi, now living in Paris, arranged an uncontested and amicable divorce, and married Aileen a week later, on September 25, in a civil ceremony at the Chelsea registry office. Elliott, occupied with his duties in Switzerland, was unable to attend but sent an enormous bouquet of flowers and a crate of champagne. The witnesses were Tommy Harris, the MI5 double-agent runner, and Flora Solomon, Philby's friend and Aileen's former employer, who had brought them together in 1939. The wedding party then repaired to the Philby family home in Carlyle Square for a bibulous party that lasted long into the night. Many friends and colleagues from MI6 turned up and drank to a delayed marriage that fit Philby's faintly bohemian image. One senior MI6 colleague, Jack Easton, who would go on to become deputy director, observed Kim's obvious pride in his growing family and reflected: "What a very nice chap Kim must be!" Flora Solomon felt an almost proprietary pride in the "happy ending" for the young couple: "Kim, a happy and devoted father, was making a successful career in the Foreign Office, and Aileen seemed stable and content." As for Philby's early communism, Solomon reflected, that "seemed to belong to the misty, juvenile past."

Philby told Aileen nothing about his MI6 work, let alone his activities on behalf of Soviet intelligence. She knew only that he worked for the Foreign Office. But she too was concealing something. For years, unknown to Philby, she had suffered from a psychiatric disorder later known as Munchausen syndrome that manifested itself in episodes of self-harm and bouts of pyromania in order to attract sympathy and attention. As a teenager, she had opened an appendectomy wound and infected it with her own urine, considerably prolonging her recovery. "Awkward of her gestures and unsure of herself in company," Aileen's mental health was deteriorating and the "accidents" and illnesses multiplying. Perhaps Aileen's distress reflected the first stirrings of doubt; she may already have begun to wonder whether her husband was really the charming, uxorious, popular, straight-batting bureaucrat that he seemed. He tended to vanish without warning or explanation, sometimes disappearing for twenty-four hours at a time, returning hungover and tight-lipped. Aileen came from a conventional background of Girl Guides, colonial servants, marital vows, and simple patriotism. Flora Solomon considered her "incapable of disloyalty, either personal or political," but Aileen would not have been human had she not begun to suspect that her husband might be seeing someone else. If she did have her doubts, she told nobody. Mrs. Philby, the former undercover detective at Marks & Spencer, was also good at keeping secrets.

Philby's decision to regularize his domestic arrangements was a sound career move, if he was to become head of MI6. Elliott harbored similar ambitions. But while Elliott had already spent time in the field, in Istanbul and Bern, Philby had so far spent most of his intelligence career behind a desk. Late in 1946 Menzies informed Philby that in order to gain "all round experience" he would be following in Elliott's footsteps, to Turkey, as MI6 station chief. Section IX was taken over by Douglas Roberts, the veteran officer whose fear of flying had enabled Philby to seize control of the Volkov case. Guy Liddell of MI5 was "profoundly sorry" to learn that Philby was leaving London and doubted his successor would be as good. But Philby was happy to be moving on. Istanbul was the "main southern base for intelligence work against the Soviet Union and socialist countries of the Balkans and central Europe," and his new assignment was a further sign that he was heading for the top. "Kim gave a large farewell party," Liddell of MI5 recorded in his diary, "which consisted mostly of representatives of our office [MI5], SIS [MI6] and the Americans. He is off to Turkey."

On his way Philby stopped off in Switzerland to see Elliott, who provided him with a detailed briefing on what to expect in Istanbul and handed over the contents of his contact book. Istanbul's significance as a spy center was even greater in 1947 than it had been during the war. Tension was mounting between Turkey and the USSR amid fears of a full-scale confrontation between

East and West; from Turkey, Western intelligence sought to infiltrate spies and insurgents into the Soviet Union, and vice versa.
Before leaving London, Philby had been told that if the opportunity arose, he could set himself up as a "coat trailer," spy parlance
for an agent who seeks to be recruited by the enemy in order to
turn double agent. Philby was "given permission to play the full
double game with the Russians." Here was an additional layer of
protection: if Philby was discovered to be in contact with the Soviets, he had a cast-iron explanation.

Philby landed at the very airport from which, two years earlier,
the luckless and insensible Konstantin Volkov had been flown to
his death. He rented a villa in Beylerbeyi, on the shores of the
Bosphorus, installed his growing family, and then, armed with
Elliott's introductions, slipped easily into the spy society of Istanbul. He even inherited the services of Elliott's best man, Roman
Sudakov, "a white Russian of boundless charm and appalling energy," in Philby's estimation. The Turkish authorities, when ade-
quately bribed, still allowed foreign intelligence agencies "a fairly
free hand to spy, so long as they didn't spy on Turkey." Over the
next two years, Philby and his five deputies liaised with the Turkish security services, cultivated exiles, trailed for defectors, coor-
dinated British agents, and conducted a topographical survey of
the Turkish frontier with the Soviet Union—a possible target of
invasion in the event of war. But his first priority was to try to infiltrate agents into the USSR along a broad front, into the Caucasus,
Ukraine, the Crimea, Georgia, Armenia, and Azerbaijan. MI6
believed that Soviet Armenia and Soviet Georgia, in particular,
were ripe for subversion. Hundreds of Georgian and Armenian
émigrés had fled communism to settle in Beirut, Paris, and other
Western cities; if the right candidates could be found, trained,
and then slipped across the borders, these insurrectionists might
form the kernel of a counterrevolutionary cell that could "start
weaving a spy network," foment rebellion against the communist
government, recruit local allies, and eventually roll back the Red
tide. That, at least, was the theory. Such infiltrations would loom
ever larger in the thinking of MI6 and the CIA in coming years,

Harold Adrian Russell "Kim" Philby at the age of eighteen: the secret Cambridge communist.

Philby as a boy of
about eight years old.

The young Philby: "He was the sort
of man who won worshippers."

St John Philby, noted Arab scholar,
explorer, writer, troublemaker, and
demanding father.

Basil Fisher (left) and Nicholas Elliott: their close friendship came to a tragic end when Fisher was shot down in the Battle of Britain.

Elliott, the Eton schoolboy, born to rule, who hid his shyness behind a barrage of jokes.

Claude Elliott, the father of Nicholas, celebrated mountaineer and provost of Eton, accompanies a young Queen Elizabeth II on a tour of the school.

Donald Maclean (right): a talented linguist destined for the Foreign Office.

Anthony Blunt (below, left) with Cambridge friends: a brilliant art historian and a Soviet spy.

Guy Burgess (above): witty, flamboyant, highly intelligent, and pure trouble.

Great Court, Trinity College, Cambridge: the unlikely crucible of communist revolution.

Alice "Litzi" Kohlman, Philby's first love and first wife, an activist in the Viennese communist underground.

Edith Tudor-Hart, an Austrian photographer married to an Englishman, arranged Philby's rendezvous with the Soviet intelligence service.

Street violence erupts in Vienna in 1933, as the extreme right-wing government goes to war with the left.

Nicholas Elliott, as a new recruit to MI6. "A convivial camaraderie prevailed, rather like a club."

James Jesus Angleton, an apprentice intelligence officer in wartime London. An American from Idaho, he was "more English than the English" and an honorary member of the club.

Philby (second from left), *The Times* war correspondent, at a lunch with Lord Gort (to Philby's left), commander of the British Expeditionary Force in France, 1939.

Arnold Deutsch, alias "Otto," Philby's charismatic recruiter and spymaster.

Theodore Maly, Philby's NKVD controller, later murdered in Stalin's Purges.

Yuri Modin, the subtle and ingenious handler of the Cambridge spy network.

Klop Ustinov, Russian-born German journalist, secret agent for Britain and father of the actor Peter Ustinov.

Alexander Foote, British-born radio operator for the Soviet spy network Rote Kapelle.

Igor Gouzenko, masked, awaiting interviews with the press after his defection in 1945.

Dick White, a former schoolmaster, was the chief of MI5 counterintelligence in 1951.

Felix Cowgill, chief of Section V, the MI6 counterintelligence unit based in St Albans.

Victor Rothschild, MI5 head of counterintelligence and friend of Kim Philby.

C: Sir Stewart Menzies, the wartime head of MI6.

Guy Liddell: MI5 head of counterintelligence and diarist.

Valentine Vivian, known as Vee-Vee, the deputy chief of MI6 who vouched for Philby: "I knew his people."

Hester Harriet Marsden-Smedley, the *Sunday Express* war correspondent who steered Philby into MI6.

Sarah Algeria Marjorie Maxse, organization officer for the Conservative Party and recruiter for MI6. Philby found her "intensely likeable."

Elizabeth Holberton, Nicholas Elliott's
MI6 secretary, confidante, and finally wife.

The Elliotts on their
wedding day, outside
the Park Hotel, Istanbul,
April 10, 1943.

Erich and Elisabeth
Vermehren. The Vermehrens'
defection, organized by
Elliott, plunged the German
intelligence service into crisis.

Kim Philby (left) was appointed the MI6 station chief in Washington in September 1949. The RMS *Caronia* (above), the luxury Cunard liner nicknamed the "Green Goddess" on which he sailed to New York. "Philby was a great charmer. He came to us with an enormous reputation," said one CIA colleague.

Guy Burgess, Philby's problematic lodger: frequently drunk, faintly malodorous, and always entertaining.

James Angleton, poet, orchid-enthusiast, CIA chief of counterintelligence and America's most powerful mole hunter.

Bill Harvey of CIA counterintelligence, the former FBI agent and Philby's most dangerous opponent in the United States.

Harvey's Oyster Salon, the smart Washington restaurant where Philby and Angleton lunched together: "Philby picked him clean."

Enver Hoxha, Albania's hardline communist ruler.

David de Crespigny Smiley, an aristocratic British Army officer with a legendary taste for derring-do, seen here with Yemeni resistance fighters.

The *Stormie Seas*, a forty-three-ton schooner disguised as a pleasure boat, carrying enough munitions to start a small war.

En route to the Albanian coast for the start of "Operation Valuable," one of the most catastrophic secret operations of the Cold War.

The "pixies" prepare for action: three of the four men in this photograph were killed within hours of landing on the Karaburun Peninsula.

The "wanted" poster issued for Donald Maclean and Guy Burgess, after the two men fled from Britain in May 1951.

WANTED

Donald D. Maclean

Date of birth: 25 May 1913

Home: Beacon Shaw Tatsfield, Kent. England

PP Nr. Br. C 36575, Issued in Rome, 20 July 1949

Discription:

6'3", normal built, short hair, brushed back, part on left side, slight stoop, thin tight lips, long thin legs, sloppy dressed, chain smoker, heavy drinker.

WANTED

Guy Francis De Money Burgess

Date of birth: 6 April 1911

Home: Unknown

PP.Nr. 1674591, Issued in London, 20 July 1950

Discription:

5'9", slender built, dark complexions, dark curly hair, tinged with gray, chubby face, clean shaven, slightly Pidgeon toed.

Call in case apprehended:
Vohenstrauss 112
Munich Civ. 481688
Munich Military 7401
Herford 2297
Herford 2172

"Maybe using forged pass-ports"

Two typically irreverent cartoons drawn by Guy Burgess in Moscow: Lenin with a chip on his shoulder and a ferocious Stalin declaring: "I'm very human!"

as the policy of "roll-back" became intelligence orthodoxy. Philby was an "energetic enthusiast" for this policy of war by proxy within the Soviet Union. He found his new assignment fascinating. So did Moscow.

Philby did not make direct contact with Soviet intelligence in Istanbul. Instead, he sent whatever information he gleaned to Guy Burgess, now working at the Foreign Office, who passed it on to the Soviets. With one hand Philby set up infiltration operations, and with the other he unpicked them. Moscow knew exactly what to do with Philby's information: "We knew in advance about every operation that took place, by air, land or sea, even in the mountainous and inaccessible regions."

Angleton was also moving on, and up. The Central Intelligence Agency was formally established in September 1947. Three months later, after three years in Rome, Angleton returned to Washington to take up a new role in the Office of Special Operations (OSO) with responsibility for espionage and counter-espionage. Reunited with his long-suffering wife, Cicely, and their young son, Angleton set up home in the Virginia suburbs, and on New Year's Eve he formally applied to join the CIA, the intelligence organization he would serve, shape, and dominate for almost three decades.

The OSO was the intelligence-gathering division within the fledgling CIA, and from here Angleton began to carve out his own empire, working day and night, driving himself, his colleagues, and his secretaries with manic determination. He started in a small office with a single secretary; within a year he had been promoted, rated "excellent," and awarded a pay raise and a much larger office; two years later he was deploying six secretaries and assistants and amassing a vast registry of files on the British model, which would become "the very mechanism through which the CIA organized the secret war against the Soviet Union." As that war expanded, so did Angleton's power. "He was totally consumed by his work. There was no room for anything else," said his secretary. On weekends he fished, usually alone, or tended his orchids. Astonishingly, Cicely not only put up with his peculiarities but loved him for them. "We rediscovered each other," she recalled. For all his eccentricities, there was something deeply romantic about the gaunt-faced, half-Mexican, hard-drinking poet-spy who cultivated his secrets, in private, like the rarest blooms.

If the Angletons' marriage was now on firmer ground, that of the Philbys, outwardly so solid, was beginning to come apart. Aileen Philby had become convinced that her husband was having an affair with his secretary, Edith Whitfield, who was young, pretty, and a friend of Guy Burgess, whom Aileen deeply disliked. As he had in London, Philby would sometimes disappear overnight without warning or explanation. On his trips around the country, Edith always accompanied him. Aileen's suspicions, almost certainly justified, tipped her into deeper depression. She became seriously ill. Secretly, she injected herself with urine, causing her body to erupt with boils. Her health became so precarious that after ten months in Istanbul, she had to be hospitalized. While in the clinic she was badly burned after a fire mysteriously started in her bedroom.

Aileen was back in Beylerbeyi, and seemed to be recovering, when Philby arrived home one evening and announced with a grin: "I've got sitting in my Jeep outside one of the most disreputable members of the British Foreign Office." Guy Burgess had arrived, unannounced, for a holiday. He would stay for almost a month. The two old chums and fellow spies painted the town a deep shade of red, with Edith Whitfield in tow. In a single evening at the Moda Yacht Club, they polished off fifty-two brandies. At the end of the evening Burgess could be heard singing, to the tune of Verdi's "La donna è mobile":

> Little boys are cheap today
> Cheaper than yesterday
> Small boys are half a crown
> Standing up or lying down

Excluded from the revelries, deeply suspicious, and upset by the presence in her home of this drunken reprobate to whom her husband seemed so deeply attached, Aileen was heading for complete breakdown.

Philby did not seem unduly concerned or even aware of the impending crisis. He was the same charming, cheerful figure, roué enough to raise the eyebrows of the more straitlaced members of the diplomatic fraternity but not nearly so wicked as to damage his career prospects in the secret services. In the eyes of MI6: "He was both efficient and safe." And besides, he was doing important work, taking the fight to the Reds, even if the results of his efforts to penetrate the Soviet Union were proving less than successful.

A meeting in Switzerland (probably arranged by Elliott), with a Turk representing a number of exiled groups from Georgia and Armenia, secured a verbal agreement that MI6 would be "willing to back them with training and finance" if the émigrés could furnish suitable counterrevolutionaries. But finding the right people to foment rebellion behind the iron curtain was proving tricky: many had been born abroad or exiled for so long they barely knew their native countries, while others were tainted by association with Nazi efforts to destabilize the USSR during the war. Philby originally envisaged sending half a dozen groups of five or six "insurrectionists" into Soviet Georgia and Soviet Armenia for several weeks at a time. Finally, among the exiled Georgian community in Paris, just two candidates were selected, "energetic lads," aged twenty, who were ready to undertake this mission to a homeland neither had ever seen. One was called Rukhadze; the name of the other has never been discovered.

The two young men were trained in London for six weeks and then dispatched to Istanbul to be met by Philby. The operation, code-named "Climber," was a "tip and run" exercise, an exploratory foray to assess the possibilities of mounting a rebellion in Georgia: the two agents would establish communication lines with potential anticommunist rebels and then slip across the border back into Turkey. The young men struck Philby as "alert and intelligent," convinced they were striking a blow to liberate Georgia from Soviet oppression. One of them, however, perhaps realizing he faced certain death if caught, seemed "notably subdued." The party traveled to Erzurum in eastern Turkey, where Philby bustled around briefing the two agents and issuing them weapons, radio equipment, and a bag of gold coins. "It was essential I should be seen doing everything possible to ensure the success of the operation," he later wrote. He had, of course, ensured exactly the opposite. The spot chosen for the infiltration was Posof, in the far northeast of Turkey on the border with Georgia. In the dead of night, the pair were taken to a remote section of the frontier and slipped into Soviet territory.

Within minutes, a burst of gunfire rang out from the Georgian side. One of the men went down in the first volley. The other, Rukhadze, was spotted in the half-light, "striding through a sparse wood away from the Turkish frontier." He did not get far and was soon in the hands of Soviet intelligence. It is doubtful whether the torturers got much out of him before he died; he had little to reveal. Years later, Philby discussed the fate of the Georgians with the chief of the Georgian KGB: "The boys weren't bad," he said. "Not at all. I knew very well that they would be caught and that a tragic fate awaited them. But on the other hand it was the only way of driving a stake through the plans of future operations." This ill-conceived, badly planned operation might well have failed anyway; but Philby could not have killed them more certainly if he had executed them himself. Their deaths did not trouble him, now or later. If there was a blot on his happy horizon, it was the increasingly erratic behavior of his wife.

One evening in March 1949, Aileen Philby was found lying beside a country road with a gash in her head. When she regained consciousness, she explained that while taking a walk she had been viciously attacked by a Turkish man, who hit her with a rock. Several potential culprits were rounded up and brought to her hospital bedside "in chains," but Aileen could not positively identify her assailant. The Turkish police were baffled; so were the doctors when septicemia set in. Aileen was now extremely unwell. In this moment of crisis, Philby turned to his old friend.

Philby contacted Nicholas Elliott in Bern and told him that Aileen seemed to be "dying of some mysterious ailment." Would Elliott find a Swiss doctor who could discover what was wrong with her? Elliott sprang into action. After an intensive trawl, he told Philby he had found just the man: a distinguished Swiss medical professor who had listened to Aileen's symptoms and believed he could cure her. The Philbys immediately flew to Geneva and traveled on by ambulance to Bern: Aileen was settled into a comfortable clinic, while Philby moved in with the Elliotts. Just days after her arrival, Aileen tried to set her room on fire and then slashed her arm with a razor blade. The Swiss doctor swiftly established that Aileen's original injury had been self-inflicted, then self-infected. The story of the roadside attack was fictitious. Aileen's doctor in London, Lord Horder, confirmed a history of self-harm dating back to her teenage years, and Aileen was committed to a psychiatric clinic under close observation. Elliott was deeply shocked to discover that this "charming woman and loving wife and mother suffered, unknown to others, from a grave mental problem." The Elliotts nursed her with tender solicitude; Nicholas Elliott sat at her bedside, feeding her grapes and jokes. Slowly, Aileen regained her strength and a measure of mental composure.

Philby was livid, a reaction that struck Elliott as distinctly odd. He had expected Philby to be relieved that his wife had been diagnosed at last. Instead, his friend complained bitterly that Aileen had hoodwinked him and vowed he would never forgive her. "It was an intense affront to Philby's pride," Elliott concluded, that he, an intelligence professional schooled in deception, "had been tricked for so many years" by his own wife. "He had to return to Istanbul knowing that all the years he had been living with Aileen, he had himself been deceived." Elliott would never have criticized Philby, particularly with regard to women. He knew about Philby's extramarital affairs and passed no judgment. Indeed, Elliott had his own mistress, a Swedish woman he kept carefully hidden from Elizabeth. A chap's marriage was his own business, and in Nick Elliott's eyes Kim Philby could do no wrong. Still, it seemed strange that his friend should be so angered by a deception that was, in the end, medical rather than moral. From that moment on, Elliott reflected sadly, "the marriage steadily deteriorated."

Aileen had been back in Istanbul less than a month when Philby announced that the family was on the move again: he had been offered, and had accepted, one of the most important jobs in British intelligence: MI6 chief in Washington, DC.

The Berlin blockade had thrown the escalating cold-war tension into sharp relief, and the power balance in the intelligence relationship between Britain and the United States was shifting. The time when MI6 could patronize the American amateurs, new to the game of espionage, was long gone, and in Whitehall Britain's spy chiefs wrestled with the novel and uncomfortable sensation that the Americans were now calling the shots, running a new kind of war against the Soviets, and paying the bills for it. For most of the Second World War the United States had been the junior partner on intelligence issues, grateful to follow the British lead. That relationship was now reversing, but the veterans of MI6 were determined to prove that Britain was still a master of the intelligence game, despite mounting evidence of an empire in steep decline. One way to stop the rot was to send a young star to Washington, a decorated wartime intelligence hero with a dazzling record, as living proof that British intelligence was just as vigorous and effective as it had always been.

In the United States Philby would be responsible for maintaining the Anglo-American intelligence relationship, liaising with the CIA and the FBI, and even handling secret communications between the British prime minister and the president. MI6 could hardly have offered him a more emphatic vote of confidence. Philby's had been one of three names in the running for this coveted post, and it had been left to the Americans to choose their preferred candidate. According to CIA historian Ray Cline, "It was James Jesus Angleton who selected Philby's name."

Aileen was not consulted about the new job. Philby did not even wait for the approval of his Soviet handlers. He accepted this irresistible new posting exactly half an hour after it was offered.

"At one stroke, it would take me right back into the middle of intelligence policy making and it would give me a close-up view of the American intelligence organisations," he wrote. It also offered "unlimited possibilities" for fresh espionage on behalf of his Soviet masters.

News of Philby's appointment was greeted with sadness by his colleagues in Istanbul, who had grown used to his combination of conviviality and efficiency. "Who am I supposed to work with now?" wondered the ambassador, Sir David Kelly. In London the appointment was seen as a natural progression for a man destined for the top. Elliott was delighted, and if he felt a twinge of envy that his friend seemed to be climbing the ladder faster than he was, he was much too British to show it.

Philby flew back to London in early September to be briefed on his new role. He made a point of looking up old contacts in both MI5 and MI6 and inviting each of them to come and stay with him in Washington. "I was lunched at many clubs," he wrote. "Discussions over coffee and port covered many subjects." Those very same subjects were also discussed by Philby in a series of meetings, no less cheerful but even more clandestine, in various London parks. Boris Krötenschield was pleased by his agent's new appointment and deeply impressed by the dedication of this double-sided man: "One side is open to family and friends and everyone around them," Krötenschield reported to Moscow Center. "The other belongs only to himself and his secret work."

Much of Philby's time in London was spent discussing Albania.

Most citizens of Britain, America, and the USSR, if they thought about Albania at all, imagined a wild country on the edge of Europe, a place of almost mythical irrelevance to the rest of the world. But Albania, sandwiched between Yugoslavia, Greece, and the Adriatic, was poised to become a key cold-war battlefield. After the war, Albania's King Zog was deposed as the country came under the iron rule of Enver Hoxha, the ruthless and wily leader of the communist partisans, who set about transforming Albania into a Stalinist state. By 1949 Albania presented a tempting target for the anticommunist hawks in British and American intelligence: separated from the Soviet bloc by Yugoslavia (itself split from the USSR), Albania was poor, feudal, sparsely populated, and politically volatile. Many exiled Albanian royalists and nationalists were itching to return to their homeland and do battle with the communists. Viewed from London and Washington through a veil of wishful thinking, Albania appeared ready to shake off communism: trained guerrillas would be slipped into Albania to link up with local rebel groups, eventually sparking civil war and toppling Hoxha. If Albanian communism was successfully undermined, it was believed, this would set off a "chain reaction that would roll back the tide of Soviet Imperialism." The SOE had played an important role in Albania during the war, and it was therefore agreed that Britain should take the lead in training the Albanian rebels, with the United States as an enthusiastic partner. Philby was fully briefed on the plans. The first wave of insurgents would be sent in by boat from Italy in October 1948; the mission was code-named "Valuable."

The Albanian operation was an example of gung-ho wartime thinking wrongly applied to the more nuanced circumstances of the cold war. But within MI6 it was seen as the opening salvo in a new, covert war. Stalin had backed a communist insurgency in Greece, engineered the communist takeover of Czechoslovakia, and blockaded Berlin. Albania would be the target of a counterattack, in direct contravention of international law but in keeping with the new mood of aggression. Many greeted the prospect with glee. Richard Brooman-White, Elliott's friend in MI6, even imagined a situation whereby the Albanian campaign could spark "formal British and American armed intervention." Philby would be responsible for coordinating Albanian plans with the Americans.

Before leaving for the United States, Philby was indoctrinated, with due reverence, into perhaps the most closely guarded secret of the cold war. Between 1940 and 1948 American cryptanalysts had intercepted some three thousand Soviet intelligence telegrams written in a code that was, theoretically, unbreakable. In 1946, however, due to a single blunder by the Soviets, a team of code breakers led by the brilliant American cryptanalyst Meredith Gardner had begun to unpick the messages that had passed between the United States and Moscow. What they revealed was staggering: more than two hundred Americans had become Soviet agents during the war; Moscow had spies in the treasury, the State Department, the nuclear Manhattan Project, and the OSS. The code-breaking operation, code-named "Venona" (a word that, appropriately, has no meaning) was so secret that President Truman himself was not informed of its existence for more than three years; the CIA did not learn about Venona until 1952. But it is a measure of the trust between the British and American intelligence agencies that news of the breakthrough and its chilling implications were immediately shared with MI6, because the intercepts also revealed that Soviet spies had penetrated the British government. In particular, the Venona team uncovered evidence of a Soviet agent, code-named "Homer," who was leaking secrets from within the British embassy in Washington in 1945. The identity of this mole was still a mystery, but it was assumed that, like "Cicero" in Turkey during the war, Homer was probably an embassy employee—a cleaner, perhaps, or a clerk. Philby knew better: Donald Maclean, his Cambridge friend and fellow spy, had been first secretary at the Washington embassy between 1944 and 1948. Maclean was Homer.

The first flicker of a shadow, as yet no more than a mote in the far distance, fell across Philby's long and sunny run of luck.

Chapter Nine

Stormy Seas

BIDO KUKA CROUCHED IN THE HOLD OF THE *STORMIE SEAS*, HUD-dled alongside the other fighters clutching their German Schmeis-ser submachine guns, as the boat rose and fell queasily in the dark Adriatic swell. Kuka felt patriotic, excited, and scared. Mostly he felt seasick. A pouch filled with gold sovereigns was strapped in-side his belt. Taped to the inside of his wristwatch was a single cyanide pill, for use should he fall into the hands of the Albanian secret police, the Sigurimi. In his knapsack he carried a map, medical supplies, hand grenades, enough rations to survive for a week in the mountains, Albanian currency, propaganda leaflets, and photographs of the émigré anticommunist leaders to show to the people and inspire them to rise up against the hated dictator, Enver Hoxha. Through the porthole the jagged cliffs of Karabu-run rose blackly against the moonless night sky, the edge of a country Kuka had not seen for three years. The Englishmen could be heard on deck, whispering muffled orders as the boat drew in-shore. They were strange, these Englishmen, huge, sun-reddened men who spoke an incomprehensible language and laughed when there was nothing funny to laugh at. They had brought along a dog called Lean-To; one had even brought his wife. They were pre-tending to be on a boating holiday. The man called "Lofty" kept his binoculars trained on the cliffs. The one called "Geoffrey" rehearsed once more the procedure for operating the wireless, a bulky contraption powered by a machine that looked like a bicycle without wheels. Kuka and his eight companions smoked in nervy silence. The *Stormie Seas* edged toward the Albanian shore.

Six months earlier Bido Kuka had been recruited for Operation Valuable in a displaced-persons camp outside Rome. Kuka was a "Ballist," a member of the Balli Kombëtar, the Albanian nationalist group that had fought the Nazis during the war and then the communists after it. With the communist takeover of Albania hundreds of Ballists had been arrested, tortured, and killed, and Kuka had fled with other nationalists to Italy. Since then he had spent three miserable years in Fraschetti Camp, nursing his loathing of communism, rehearsing the Balli Kombëtar motto, "Albania for the Albanians, Death to the Traitors," and plotting his return. When he was approached by a fellow émigré and asked to join a new guerrilla unit for secret anticommunist operations inside Albania, he did not hesitate. As another recruit put it: "There was no question of refusing. When your life is devoted to your country you are prepared to do anything to help it." On July 14, 1949, Kuka and a fellow Ballist named Sami Lepenica boarded a military plane in Rome and flew to the British island of Malta in the Mediterranean. They had no travel documents. A British officer, flapping a red handkerchief by way of a recognition signal, marched them past the customs barrier and into a car. An hour later the bemused Albanians arrived at the gateway to a large castle surrounded by a moat: Fort Bingemma, a Victorian citadel on the island's southwest corner, selected by British intelligence as the ideal place from which to launch an anticommunist counterrevolution.

Over the next three months, Kuka and some thirty other Albanian recruits underwent intensive training under the watchful (if slightly mad) eye of Lieutenant Colonel David de Crespigny Smiley, an aristocratic British army officer with a legendary taste for derring-do. During the war, Smiley had fought the Italians in Abyssinia as part of the Somaliland Camel Corps, foiled a German-backed coup to unseat the King of Iraq, fought alongside Siamese guerrillas, and liberated four thousand prisoners ("all absolutely stark naked except for a ball bag") from the Japanese camp at Ubon. But it was in Albania that he earned his reputation for raw courage: in 1943 he parachuted into northern

Greece and set about blowing up bridges, ambushing German troops, and training guerrillas. He emerged from the war with a deep love of Albania, a loathing for Hoxha and the communists, a Military Cross, and facial scars from a prematurely exploding briefcase. When MI6 needed someone to equip, train, and infiltrate anticommunist fighters into Albania, Smiley was the obvious choice. He was imperialist, fearless, romantic, and unwary, and in all these respects he was a neat reflection of Operation Valuable.

The training program was brief but intensive and conducted amid rigid secrecy. A series of British instructors, including an eccentric Oxford don, provided lessons in map reading, unarmed combat, machine-gun marksmanship, and operating a radio with a pedal generator. Since the instructors spoke no Albanian, and the Albanians spoke not a word of English, training was conducted in sign language. This explains why Kuka's conception of his mission was somewhat vague: get into Albania, head for his hometown near the Greek border, sound out the possibilities for armed insurrection, then get out and report back. None of the recruits were officers, and few had any military training. Life in the camps had left some with malnutrition, and all were quite small. The British, with more than a hint of condescension, called them "the pixies."

In late September Bido Kuka and eight other recruits were taken to Otranto on the Italian coast, fifty-five miles across the Adriatic from Albania. Disguised as local fishermen, they were loaded into a fishing vessel, and at a rendezvous point twenty miles off the Albanian coast they were transferred to the *Stormie Seas*, a forty-three-ton schooner painted to resemble a pleasure boat but containing a mighty ninety-horsepower engine, concealed fuel tanks, and enough munitions to start a small war. The *Stormie Seas* was commanded by Sam Barclay and John Leatham, two intrepid former Royal Navy officers who had spent the previous year running supplies from Athens to Salonika for the forces fighting the Greek communist guerrillas. MI6 had offered them the sum of fifty pounds to transport the insurgents to the Albanian coast,

which Leatham thought was more than generous: "We were looking only for free adventure and a living."

Shortly after 9:00 p.m. on October 3, two hundred yards off
the Karaburun Peninsula, the heavily armed pixies clambered
into two rubber boats and headed toward a cove, rowed by two
stout former marines, "Lofty" Cooling and Derby Allen. The
Karaburun was barely inhabited, a wild place of goat tracks and
thorny scrub. Having dropped off the men and their equipment,
the Englishmen rowed back to the *Stormie Seas*. Looking back
at the retreating coast, they saw a light flash suddenly at the cliff
top and then go out again.

The nine pixies were already heading up the cliff. The going
was slow in the deep darkness. As dawn broke, they split into two
parties. Bido Kuka and four others, including his friend Ramis
Matuka and his cousin Ahmet, headed south toward his home
region while the remaining four, led by Sami Lepenica, headed
north. As they separated, Kuka was struck by a sudden forebod-
ing, the sensation, intense but unfocused, "that the communists
were ready and waiting for them."

After a day spent hiding in a cave, Kuka and his men set off
again at nightfall. In the morning they approached the village of
Gjorm, a wartime center of resistance and home to many Balli
Kombëtar sympathizers. As they drew near, a young girl ran
toward them shouting: "Brothers, you're all going to be killed!"
Breathlessly she explained that the other group had already been
ambushed by government forces: three of the four had been
killed, including Lepenica, and the fourth had vanished. Two
days earlier no less a personage than Beqir Balluku, the Albanian
army chief of staff, had arrived with hundreds of troops, and the
Karaburun ridge was crawling with government forces scouring
every village, track, cave, and gully for the "fascist terrorists."
Local shepherds had been instructed to report anything suspicious, on pain of death. The Albanian guerrillas thanked the girl,
gratefully seized the bread and milk she offered, and ran.

———

AT THE VERY moment Bido Kuka was scrambling for his life through the Albanian mountains, Kim Philby was steaming toward New York aboard the RMS *Caronia*, the most luxurious ocean liner afloat. His many friends in MI5 and MI6 had given him a "memorable send-off." The *Caronia* was barely a year old, a spectacular floating hotel nicknamed the "Green Goddess" on account of her pale green livery. She was fitted with every modern luxury, including sumptuous art deco interiors, an open-air lido, and terraced decks. The only class of travel was first. Described as "a private club afloat," the liner had four hundred catering staff for seven hundred passengers. On arriving in his paneled cabin with private bathroom, Philby had found a crate of champagne awaiting him, a gift from a "disgustingly rich friend," Victor Roth-schild. Philby might have disapproved of Rothschild's riches, but he thoroughly approved of his champagne. The seven-day voyage was made all the more pleasant by the company of the cartoon-ist Osbert Lancaster, an affable clubland acquaintance of Philby's with a walrus mustache and a terrific thirst. Philby and Lancaster settled into the cocktail bar and started drinking their way to America. "I began to feel that I would enjoy my first transatlantic crossing," wrote Philby.

The *Caronia* docked in New York on October 7. The FBI sent out a motor launch to meet Philby; like Bido Kuka, he was whisked through customs without any of the usual formalities. That night he stayed in a high-rise hotel overlooking Central Park before catching the train to Washington, DC. Alongside the track the sumac shrubs were still in flower, but autumn was in the air and the leaves were beginning to turn. Philby's first glimpse of the American landscape took his breath away. The fall, he later wrote, is "one of the few glories of America which Americans have never exaggerated because exaggeration is impossible."

At Union Station he was met by Peter Dwyer of MI6, the outgo-ing station chief, and immediately plunged into a whirlwind of in-troductions and meetings with officials of the CIA, FBI, the State Department, and the Canadian secret service. All were delighted to shake hands with this urbane Englishman whose impressive reputation preceded him—but none more than James Jesus Angleton, his former protégé, now a powerful figure in the CIA. Angleton had prepared the ground, telling his American colleagues about Philby's wartime work and how much he "admired him as a 'professional.'" The Anglo-American intelligence relationship was still close in 1949, and no two spies symbolized that intimacy more than Kim Philby and James Angleton.

Angleton remained in many ways an Englishman. "I was brought up in England in my formative years," he said many years later, "and I must confess that I learned, at least I was disciplined to learn, certain features of life, and what I regarded as duty." Honor, loyalty, handmade suits, strong drinks, deep leather armchairs in smoky clubs: this was the England that Angleton had come to know and admire through Philby and Elliott. There was an element within American intelligence that took a more hard-eyed view of Britain's continuing claims to greatness, a younger generation unmoved by the nostalgic bonds of war, but Angleton was not of that stamp. His time in Ryder Street had left a permanent imprint on him, personally and professionally. Philby had introduced him to the arcane mysteries of the Double Cross system, the strange, endlessly reflecting conundrum of counterintelligence, and the very British idea that only a few, a select few, can be truly trusted. Philby was Angleton's souvenir of war, a time of duty, unshakable alliance, and dependability. Angleton paraded his English friend around Washington like a trophy.

While Philby was clinking glasses in Washington, on the other side of the world David Smiley waited, with mounting unease, for the Albanian guerrillas to make contact. Twice a day, morning and evening, the MI6 radio operator stationed in a large mansion on the coast of Corfu tuned in at the agreed time, but a week had passed with no word from the pixies. Finally a hasty message was picked up, sent from the caves above Gjorm where Kuka and his team were in hiding: "Things have gone wrong . . . three men killed . . . police know everything about us." The Albanians were terrified: the bulky generator gave out a high-pitched whining sound when pedaled at full speed, the noise bouncing off the hills and threatening to reveal them. They were running out of food and dared not descend to the village to beg or steal more. Bido Kuka persuaded the others to make a break for it and try to reach his home village of Nivica just twenty-five miles to the south. The route passed though inhospitable terrain and the government troops were doubtless still out in force, but from Nivica it was only thirty-five miles to the Greek border. A four-day trek, walking at night, skirting patrols, and hiding during daylight, brought them to the home Kuka had last seen three years earlier. He was welcomed, but cautiously. When Kuka explained that they were the vanguard of a British-backed force that would overthrow Hoxha, the villagers were skeptical: Why were they so few in number? Where were the British? Where were the guns? Kuka sensed that even here they faced mortal danger. The group declined offers to spend the night in the village. They retreated instead to the mountains and agreed to push on for the border as fast as possible in two groups: Bido Kuka, Ramis Matuka, and a third man headed south; his cousin Ahmet and the fifth man took a more direct route. Patrols were everywhere; three times Kuka's group narrowly avoided capture. They were still a dozen miles from the border, trudging through a narrow ravine, when a voice boomed out of the darkness demanding that they identify themselves or be shot down. "Who are you?" called Kuka, cocking his machine gun. "Police," came the answer. The three men opened fire. The police, dug in above them, returned fire. Ramis Matuka fell dead. Kuka and his last companion, firing wildly, fled into the woods.

Three days later, exhausted and famished, Kuka and his comrade finally reached the Greek border. They were immediately arrested, jailed by the Greek police, and interrogated. Kuka stuck to his story that he was "Enver Zenelli," the name on his forged Albanian identity card. "We said we were ordinary Albanians fleeing the country." The Greek border guards were disbelieving "and would have shot them for tuppence." After several weeks, a British officer appeared. Kuka uttered the code phrase agreed on back in Malta: "The sun has risen." Finally they were free. The survivors were flown to Athens, lodged in a safe house, and debriefed by two British intelligence officers.

By any objective estimate the first phase of Operation Valuable had been a debacle. Of the nine guerrillas who had landed in October, four were dead, one was almost certainly captured, one had vanished, the others had barely escaped with their lives, and "several Albanian civilians had also been arrested and killed," accused of aiding the guerrillas. A second landing group, arriving soon after the first, had fared little better. The Albanian forces were primed and waiting, clearly aware of the incursion, if not of its precise timing and location.

With understatement verging on fantasy, MI6 described the first phase of the operation merely as "disappointing." The loss of half the initial force was a setback but not a disaster, and the death toll was "judged by wartime standards to be acceptable." Colonel Smiley vowed to press ahead with fresh incursions, better-trained guerrillas, and greater U.S. involvement. Albania would not be won overnight, and "it would be wrong to abandon such an important exercise," particularly now that MI6 had one of its highest fliers installed in Washington, ready and more than willing to liaise with the Americans on the next stage of Operation Valuable.

Just a few days after his arrival in Washington, Philby was appointed joint commander of the Anglo-American Special Policy Committee, responsible for running the Albanian operation with his American opposite number, James McCargar. The Americans would play an increasing role in Operation Valuable (which they code-named, perhaps more realistically, "Fiend"), not least by financing it, but Philby "was the one who made all the operational decisions."

James McCargar was a former journalist from a wealthy California family who had made a name for himself in the postwar period by arranging escape routes out of Hungary for scientists and intellectuals fleeing communism. He smuggled one Romanian woman out in the trunk of his car and then married her. Like many American intelligence officers of the time, McCargar had an exaggerated respect for his British counterparts, and his new colleague came with glowing credentials. "Philby was a great charmer. He came to us with an enormous reputation," recalled McCargar. "One had the feeling one could have confidence in him." Philby seemed to exemplify the sort of qualities that Americans hoped to see in their British allies: cheerful, resolute, witty, and exceedingly generous with the bottle. "He had charm, warmth and an engaging, self-deprecating humor," said McCargar. "He drank a lot, but then so did we all in those days. We floated out of the war on a sea of drink without its having much effect. I considered him a friend."

Philby loved Washington, and Washington loved him. Doors were flung open, the invitations poured in, and few people needed to meet him more than once before they too considered him a friend. Aileen also seemed to find strength in Washington's welcoming atmosphere. The family moved into a large, two-story house at 4100 Nebraska Avenue, which was soon a riot of children's toys, full ashtrays, and empty bottles. In Nicholas Elliott's words, Philby was "undoubtedly devoted to his children," a trait that further endeared him to his new American friends and colleagues: here was a family man, the quintessential English gentleman, a man one could trust. Within weeks, it seems, Philby had made contact with just about everyone of note in American intelligence. To their faces he was politeness personified; behind their backs, vituperative. There was Johnny Boyd, assistant director of the FBI ("by any objective standard, a dreadful man"); Frank Wisner, head of the Office of Policy Coordination ("balding and self-importantly running to fat"); Bill Harvey of CIA counterintelligence ("a former FBI man . . . sacked for drunkenness"); CIA chief Walter Bedell Smith ("a cold, fishy eye"); deputy CIA head and future chief Allen Dulles ("bumbling"); Bob Lamphere of the FBI ("puddingy"); and many more. The house on Nebraska Avenue soon became a gathering place for Washington's intelligence elite. "He entertained a lot of Americans," said another CIA officer. "The wine flowed, and the whisky too." Aileen played the role of salon hostess, tottering around with trays of drinks, and drinking her fair share. One guest recalled only this of Philby's parties: "They were long, and very, very wet."

Philby seemed to invite intimacy. His knowing smile, "suggestive of complicity in some private joke, conveyed an unspoken understanding of the underlying ironies of our work." He made a point of dropping in on the offices of American colleagues and counterparts in the late afternoon, knowing that his hosts would sooner or later (and usually sooner) "suggest drifting out to a friendly bar for a further round of shop talk." Trading internal information is a particular weakness of the intelligence world; spies cannot explain their work to outsiders, so they seize every opportunity to discuss it with their own kind. "Intelligence officers talk trade among themselves all the time," said one CIA officer. "Philby was privy to a hell of a lot beyond what he should have known." The CIA and FBI were rivals, sometimes viciously so, with a peculiar social division between the two arms of American intelligence that was echoed by the competition between MI5 and MI6. Philby characterized CIA operatives as upper-class wine drinkers, while the FBI were earthier beer-drinking types. Philby was happy to drink quantities of both, with either, while trying to "please one party without offending the other." Philby's office was in the British embassy, but he was often to be found at the CIA or FBI headquarters or the Pentagon, where a room was set aside for meetings on the Albanian operation. Few subjects were out of bounds: "The sky was the limit. . . . He would have known as much as he wanted to find out."

James Angleton was now chief of Staff A, in command of foreign intelligence operations, and in Philby's estimation "the driving force" within the intelligence-gathering division of the CIA. A strange mystique clung to Angleton; he used the name "Lothar Metzl" and invented a cover story that he had been a Viennese café pianist before the war. Behind his house in the suburbs of North Arlington he constructed a heated greenhouse, the better to cultivate his orchids and his aura of knowing eccentricity. In the basement he polished semiprecious stones. He carried a gold fob watch; his suits and accent remained distinctly English.

Angleton tended to describe his work in fishing metaphors: "I got a few nibbles last night," he would remark obscurely after an evening trawling the files. In intelligence circles he inspired admiration, gossip, and some fear. "It was the belief within the CIA that Angleton possessed more secrets than anyone else, and grasped their meaning better than anyone else."

Harvey's, on Connecticut Avenue, was the most famous restaurant in the capital, probably the most expensive, and certainly the most exclusive. Harvey's Ladies' and Gentlemen's Oyster Saloon started serving steamed oysters, broiled lobster, and crab imperial in 1820 and had continued to do so, in colossal quantities, ever since. In 1863, notwithstanding the Civil War, Harvey's diners were getting through five hundred wagonloads of oysters a week. Every president since Ulysses S. Grant had dined there, and the restaurant enjoyed an unrivaled reputation as the place to be seen for people of power and influence. The black waiters in pressed white uniforms were discreet, the martinis potent, the napkins stiff as cardboard, and the tables spaced far enough apart to ensure privacy for the most secret conversations. Ladies entered by a separate entrance and were not permitted in the main dining room. Most evenings, FBI director J. Edgar Hoover could be seen at his corner table, eating with Clyde Tolson, his deputy and possibly his lover. Hoover was said to be addicted to Harvey's oysters; he never paid for his meals.

Angleton and Philby began to lunch regularly at Harvey's, at first once a week, then at least every other day. They spoke on the telephone three or four times a week. Their lunches became a sort of ritual, a "habit" in Philby's words, beginning with bourbon on the rocks, proceeding through lobster and wine, and ending in brandy and cigars. Philby was impressed by both Angleton's grasp of intelligence and his appetite for food and drink. "He demonstrated regularly that overwork was not his only vice," wrote Philby. "He was one of the thinnest men I have ever met, and one of the biggest eaters. Lucky Jim!" The two men could be seen hunched in animated conversation, talking, drinking, laughing, and enjoying their shared love of secrecy. Angleton had few close friends and fewer confidants. Philby had many friends and had refined the giving and receiving of confidences to an art form. They fit one another perfectly.

"Our close association was, I am sure, inspired by genuine friendliness," wrote Philby. "But we both had ulterior motives. . . . By cultivating me to the full, he could better keep me under wraps. For my part, I was more than content to string him along. The greater the trust between us overtly, the less he would suspect covert action. Who gained most from this complex game I cannot say. But I had one big advantage. I knew what he was doing for CIA and he knew what I was doing for SIS. But the real nature of my interest was something he did not know." Beneath their friendship was an unspoken competition to see who could outthink—and outdrink—the other. Angleton, according to one associate, "used to pride himself that he could drink Kim under the table and still walk away with useful information. Can you imagine how much information he had to trade in those booze-ups?"

"Our discussions ranged over the whole world," Philby recalled. They spoke of the various covert operations against the Soviet Union, the anticommunist insurgents being slipped into Albania and other countries behind the iron curtain; they discussed the intelligence operations under way in France, Italy, and Germany and resources pouring into anticommunist projects worldwide, including the recruiting of exiles for subversion behind the iron curtain. "Both CIA and SIS were up to their ears in émigré politics," wrote Philby. Angleton explained how the CIA had taken over the anti-Soviet spy network established by Reinhard Gehlen, the former chief of German intelligence on the eastern front who had offered his services to the United States after surrendering in 1945. Gehlen's spies and informants included many former Nazis, but the CIA was not choosy about its allies in the new war against communism. By 1948 the CIA was funneling some $1.5 million (around $14.5 million today) into Gehlen's spy ring. Philby was all ears: "Many of Harvey's lobsters went to provoke Angleton into defending, with chapter and verse, the past record and current activities of the von Gehlen organisation." CIA interventions in

Greece and Turkey to hold back communism; covert operations in Iran, the Baltics, and Guatemala; secret American plans in Chile, Cuba, Angola, and Indonesia; blueprints for Allied cooperation in the event of war with the USSR. All this and more was laid before Philby, between friends, as Angleton gorged and gossiped over the starched tablecloths and full glasses at Harvey's. "During those long, boozy lunches and dinners, Philby must have picked him clean," a fellow officer later wrote.

But Philby and Angleton were also professionals. After every lunch, Angleton returned to his office and dictated a long memo to his secretary, Gloria Loomis, reporting in detail his discussions with the obliging MI6 liaison chief. "Everything was written up," Loomis later insisted. Philby did likewise, dictating his own memo for MI6 to his secretary Edith Whitfield, who had accompanied him to Washington from Istanbul (much to Aileen's annoyance). Later, at home on Connecticut Avenue, Philby would write up his own notes for other eyes.

Philby liked to portray the Russian intelligence service as an organization of unparalleled efficiency. In truth, Moscow Center was frequently beset by bureaucratic bungling, inertia, and incompetence, coupled with periodic bloodletting. Before Philby's arrival, the Soviet spy outpost in Washington had been through a period of "chaotic" turbulence, with the recall of two successive *rezidents*. Initially, Philby had no direct contact with Soviet intelligence in the United States, preferring to send any information via Guy Burgess in London, as he had from Istanbul. Finally, four months after Philby's arrival, Moscow woke up to the realization that it should take better care of its veteran spy.

On March 5 a young man stepped off the ship *Batory*, newly arrived in New York harbor from Gdynia in Poland. His passport proclaimed him to be an American citizen of Polish origin named Ivan Kovalik; his real name was Valeri Mikhailovich Makayev, a thirty-two-year-old Russian intelligence officer with orders to establish himself under cover in New York and arrange a way for Philby to communicate with Moscow Center. Makayev swiftly obtained a job teaching musical composition at New York University and started an affair with a Polish dancer who owned a ballet school in Manhattan. Makayev was a good musician and one of nature's romantics, but he was a hopeless case officer. His bosses had supplied him with $25,000 for his mission, which he proceeded to spend, mostly on himself and his ballerina. Finally, Makayev got word to Philby that he had arrived. They met in New York, and Philby's newly arrived case officer handed over a new camera for photographing documents. Thereafter they would rendezvous at different points between New York and Washington, in Baltimore or Philadelphia. After nine months, Makayev had managed to set up two communication channels to Moscow, using a Finnish seaman as a courier and a postal route via an agent in London. The system was slow and cumbersome; Philby was wary of face-to-face meetings and unimpressed by his new case officer; Makayev was much more interested in ballet than in espionage. Philby was producing more valuable intelligence for Moscow than at any time in his life, yet he had never been run more incompetently.

Frank Wisner, the CIA officer in charge of insurgent operations behind the iron curtain, was baffled: every bid to undermine communism by secretly fomenting resistance within the USSR and among its satellites seemed to be going spectacularly wrong. But Wisner, or "the Whiz," as he liked to be known, refused to be downcast, let alone change tack. Despite a disappointing start, the Albanian operation would continue: "We'll get it right next time," Wisner promised Philby.

But they did not get it right. Instead, it continued to go wrong, and not just in Albania. Funds, equipment, and arms were funneled to the anticommunist resistance in Poland, which turned out to be nothing more than a front operated by Soviet intelligence. Anticommunist Lithuanians, Estonians, and Armenians were recruited and then dropped into their homelands by British and American planes; nationalist White Russians were sent in to continue the fight against the Bolsheviks. Almost all mysteriously disappeared. "We had agents parachuting in, floating in, walking in, boating in," said one former CIA officer. "Virtually all these operations were complete failures. . . . They were all rolled up." The CIA and MI6 kept each other informed of exactly where and when their respective teams were going in, to avoid overlap and confusion. Philby, as the liaison officer in Washington, was responsible for passing on "the timing and geographical coordinates" from one intelligence agency to another, and then another. Ukraine was considered particularly fertile ground for an insurgency, with an established resistance group active in the Carpathian Mountains. In 1949 the first British-trained team of Ukrainian insurgents was sent in with radio equipment. They were never heard from again. Two more teams followed the next year, and then three more six-man units were parachuted to drop points in Ukraine and inside the Polish border. All vanished. "I do not know what happened to the parties concerned," Philby later wrote, with ruthless irony. "But I can make an informed guess."

None of the incursions proved more catastrophic, more spectacularly valueless, than Operation Valuable. Undaunted, the British continued to train the "pixies" in Malta while the CIA established a separate training camp for Albanian insurgents, now including teams of parachutists, in a walled villa outside Heidelberg. "We knew that they would retaliate against our families," said one recruit, "[but] we had high hopes." At the same time, MI6 prepared to drop thousands of propaganda leaflets over Albania from unmanned hot-air balloons: "The boys in London imagined a rain of pamphlets over Albanian towns with thousands of Albanians picking them out of the air, reading them and then preparing themselves for the liberation." The parachutists were flown in by Polish former RAF pilots in late 1950, crossing into Albanian airspace at a height of just two hundred feet to avoid radar.

The communist forces were ready and waiting. Two days earlier, hundreds of security police had poured into the area of the drop zone. A policeman was stationed in every village. They even knew the names of the arriving insurgents. Some of the parachutists were killed on landing, others captured. Only a few escaped. The next drop, the following July, was even more disastrous. One group of four parachutists was mowed down immediately; another was surrounded, with two killed and two captured; the last group of four fled to a house and barricaded themselves in. The police set fire to the building and burned them all to death. British-trained fighters continued to filter into Albania, some by boat and others on foot across the Greek border, only to be intercepted like their predecessors. Meanwhile, across Albania, the Sigurimi began rounding up relatives and friends of the insurgents. A shared surname was enough to invite suspicion. For each guerrilla as many as forty others were shot or thrown into prison. Two captives were "tied to the back of a Jeep and dragged through the streets until their bodies were reduced to a bloody pulp." A handful of the fighters apparently escaped and sent back radio messages urging the British and Americans to send more forces. Only much later did it emerge that the Sigurimi was running a classic double cross: the messages were sent by captives, forced to reveal their codes and transmitting with guns to their heads. Enver Hoxha bragged: "Our famous radio game brought about the ignominious failure of the plans of the foreign enemy. . . . The bands of criminals who were dropped in by parachute or infiltrated across the border at our request came like lambs to the slaughter." Show trials were later staged with captured survivors, propaganda spectacles at which the tortured, semicoherent defendants condemned themselves and cursed their capitalist backers before being sentenced to long prison terms from which few emerged alive.

In London and Washington, as the operation lurched from failure to calamity, morale slumped and suspicions rose. "It was obvious there was a leak somewhere," said one CIA officer. "We had several meetings, trying to figure out where the thing was going wrong. We had to ask ourselves how long we were prepared to go on dropping these young men into the bag." The British privately blamed the Americans, and vice versa. "Our security was very, very tight," insisted Colonel Smiley.

In fact, the secrecy surrounding the operation was anything but secure. Soviet intelligence had penetrated not just the Albanian émigré groups in Europe but every other community of disgruntled exiles. James Angleton learned, through his Italian contacts, that Operation Valuable had been "well and truly blown" from the start: Italian intelligence had been watching the *Stormie Seas* from the moment she set sail for Albania. Journalists had also gotten wind of the story. Once the first teams of guerrillas had been intercepted, the Albanian authorities were naturally braced for more. The operation was flawed from its inception: Hoxha was more firmly entrenched and the opposition to him much weaker than Anglo-American intelligence imagined. The planners had simply believed that "Albania would fall from the Soviet imperial tree like a ripe plum and other fruit would soon follow." And they were simply wrong.

Operation Valuable might well have failed without Philby, but not so utterly nor so bloodily. Looking back, the planners knew whom to blame for the embarrassing and unmitigated failure. "There is little question that Philby not only informed Moscow of overall British and American planning," wrote CIA historian Harry Rositzke, "but provided details on the individual dispatch of agent teams before they arrived in Albania." Yuri Modin, the NKVD controller in London who passed on Philby's messages to Moscow, was also explicit: "He gave us vital information about the number of men involved, the day and the time of the landing, the weapons they were bringing and their precise program of action. . . . The Soviets duly passed on Philby's information to Albanians who set up ambushes."

Philby later gloried in what he had done: "The agents we sent into Albania were armed men intent on murder, sabotage and assassination. They were quite as ready as I was to contemplate bloodshed in the service of a political ideal. They knew the risks they were running. I was serving the interests of the Soviet Union and those interests required that these men were defeated. To the extent that I helped defeat them, even if it caused their deaths, I have no regrets."

The precise death toll will never be known: somewhere between one hundred and two hundred Albanian guerrillas perished; if their families and other reprisal victims are taken into account, the figure rises into the thousands. Years later, those who had deployed the doomed Albanian insurgents came to the conclusion that, over the course of two lunch-filled years, James Angleton "gave Philby over drinks the precise coordinates for every drop zone of the CIA in Albania."

At the heart of the tragedy lay a close friendship—and a great betrayal.

Lunch at Harvey's came with a hefty bill.

Chapter Ten

Homer's Odyssey

THE ANNUAL THANKSGIVING PARTY AT THE ANGLETON HOME IN 1950 was not a sober affair. Jim and Cicely Angleton invited the entire Philby clan to their Arlington house for a turkey dinner with all the trimmings. The other guests included Wilfred Mann, a physicist in the British Embassy's science section. According to some accounts William E. Colby, future head of the CIA, was also present. All four men were deeply involved in the accelerating nuclear arms race and the espionage attendant on it. The Soviet Union had carried out its first nuclear test a year earlier, thanks in part to Moscow's spies penetrating the West's atomic program. The Venona intercepts identified one of the Soviet spies at Los Alamos labs as Klaus Fuchs, a German-born nuclear physicist. Philby had alerted Moscow Center when the trap was closing on Fuchs, but too late to save him: he confessed under questioning and was now serving a fourteen-year prison sentence. A number of other Soviet agents were warned that they too were in danger. Several fled. Two who did not were Julius and Ethel Rosenberg, organizers of a Soviet spy ring in New York. In 1953 they would be executed.

Spies were dying. President Truman was calling for a buildup of weapons to halt the spread of Soviet influence around the globe. There was talk of nuclear war, and the Western intelligence services were locked in increasingly bloody conflict with their Soviet rivals. The opposing sides in that secret war were ranged around Angleton's dinner table, but no hint of discord marred the happy occasion as Philby joined his friends in giving bibulous thanks for America's bounty. "Jim and Kim were very fond of each other," recalled Cicely Angleton. "We all liked him." Philby was only thirty-eight but looked older. There was already something raddled in his handsome features. The eyes remained bright, but the bags beneath them were growing heavier, and the lunches at Harvey's were taking a toll on his waistline. "After a year of keeping up with Angleton," he wrote, "I took the advice of an elderly lady friend and went on a diet, dropping from thirteen stone to eleven in three months."

These were heady times in Washington, the young superpower capital suffused with wealth and self-confidence. Philby moved easily among the leaders of this new world order, a warm and reassuring presence among the cold warriors. Philby was not a greedy man, but he wanted for nothing. "If you have a lot of money," reflected this secret communist at the heart of capitalist power, "you can organise your life in a rather pleasant way." Philby's life could not have been organized more pleasantly. He urged Nicholas Elliott to come and visit him. "The more visitors I had in Washington," he wrote, "the more spies I got my finger into." And Philby wanted a finger in every spy.

On the surface Philby might appear as serene and affable as ever, but inside a small worm of anxiety was burrowing away. The twinge he had felt on learning that a Soviet spy had been located in the wartime embassy grew markedly more uncomfortable in June 1950, when the Venona decrypts revealed a "valuable agent network" operating in Britain in 1945, including a "particularly important" spy code-named "Stanley." The code breakers were gaining ground every day. Philby decided to pay a visit to the U.S. government decoding center at Arlington Hall, Virginia. Meredith Gardner, the chief of the Venona project, welcomed Philby to his secret word laboratory and later recalled the strange intensity with which the Englishman had observed the decryption teams at work, picking away at the vast spy puzzle. "Philby was looking on with no doubt rapt attention but he never said a word, never a word." Philby knew that a single word correctly identifying "Stanley" as him would be enough to sink him.

A joint investigation by the FBI and MI5 had not yet identi-fied the spy code-named "Homer." The investigators seemed convinced that the mole in the British embassy must be a local employee, a janitor or servant, even though the quality of the in-formation Homer had supplied was high. After leaving Washing-ton in 1948, Donald Maclean had moved on to Cairo as counselor and head of chancery at the British embassy. His behavior had become increasingly bizarre under the strain of his double life, yet no one imagined that this urbane, cultured English diplomat might be a spy for Russia. Maclean was the son of a former cabinet minister, a product of public school and Cambridge, a member of the Reform Club. And so he was protected from suspicion, in Philby's words, by the "genuine mental block which stubbornly resisted the belief that respected members of the Establishment could do such things." But that presumption could not shield him forever. As the investigators dug deeper, Philby kept Moscow in-formed of their progress. "Maclean should stay in his post as long as possible," Moscow Center told him, while noting that it might be necessary to extract him "before the net closed in."

Philby laid out his own safety net, knowing that if the Venona decrypts unmasked Maclean, then all his associates would come under suspicion and the trail, eventually, could lead to Philby himself. He discreetly hinted to MI5 that he would like to expand his role in Washington, ostensibly to improve efficiency, in real-ity to ensure even closer monitoring of the Homer investigation. "He clearly feels he is not really getting enough scope," wrote Guy Liddell of MI5. "I thought I discerned a fly thrown over me in the form of a suggestion that it was really unnecessary for us to have a Washington representative and that he could carry the whole business." The counterintelligence chief resisted Philby's veiled offer to represent MI5 as well as MI6, though not out of any suspi-cion of the real motive behind it. Philby also lobbied C in London to notify him in advance of any decoding breakthrough, to "give us more time for studying it"—and, if necessary, more time to get away.

Philby's marriage was under severe strain once more. The

Philby clan was growing, but while Philby told Nicholas Elliott of his "parental pride in being the father of five children," the arrival of another baby increased the burden on Aileen, who was again showing signs of instability. She was now drinking almost as much as her husband. Their relationship took another body blow when a letter arrived from Guy Burgess, announcing cheerily: "I have a shock for you. I have just been posted to Washington." Burgess asked to stay with the Philbys "for a few days" while he looked for somewhere to live. Aileen was appalled. "I know him only too well," she wrote to friends. "He will never leave our house."

Burgess was still in the Foreign Office, although how he had managed to retain employment in that staid and respectable organization remains a mystery. In a career not so much checkered as blotched, he had worked in the news department, as assistant to the minister of state in the Foreign Office, and in the Far Eastern section. Throughout that time he supplied the Russians with every secret document he could lay his hands on, removing them in the evening and returning them in the morning after they had been copied by the Soviets. Burgess was as entertaining as ever and pure, undiluted trouble: he boasted about his espionage contacts, made no attempt to hide his promiscuous homosexuality, and left a trail of chaos in his wake. He was usually drunk and frequently insulting, particularly to important people. He failed to pay his bills, picked fights, identified MI6 officers in public places, and went on a bender in Gibraltar of such scale that the local MI5 officer could not help being impressed: "I do not think that even in Gibraltar have I ever seen anyone put away so much hard liquor in so short a time." On another occasion he got into a fight with a Foreign Office colleague, fell down the marble steps of the Royal Automobile Club, and fractured his skull, after which his behavior grew even more extreme. Burgess was permanently on the point of being sacked. Instead, he was appointed information officer at the British embassy in Washington, a job requiring delicacy and tact for which he was monumentally unsuited. Laughably, Guy Liddell insisted that Burgess "was not the sort of person who would deliberately pass confidential information to

unauthorised persons." It was hoped that Burgess's "eccentricities" (code for his homosexuality) might be less conspicuous in
the United States. But the Foreign Office security chief warned
Sir Robert Mackenzie, the security officer at the Washington embassy, that with Burgess in town he should be prepared for even
worse escapades. Mackenzie was heard to mutter: "What does he
mean *worse*? Goats?"

If the prospect of Burgess arriving in Washington worried
some officials, it positively horrified Aileen. Philby insisted, however, that his old friend must be made welcome and could live in
the basement of their house. Aileen protested, and a furious row
followed, duly reported back, by both parties, to Elliott in Switzerland, who wrote: "Knowing the trouble that would inevitably
ensue—and remembering Burgess's drunken and homosexual
orgies when he had stayed with them in Istanbul—Aileen resisted
this move, but bowed in the end (and as usual) to Philby's wishes."
Burgess hit the U.S. capital and the Philby household like a particularly destructive and volatile meteor. "The inevitable drunken
scenes and disorder ensued," Elliott wrote, "and tested the marriage to its limits."

Philby later depicted his decision to take in Burgess as an act
of loyalty. They had been friends for more than twenty years; they
had discovered communism together and remained locked in
service to Moscow. Burgess was one of the few people to whom
Philby could speak openly. He assured the embassy that he would
"keep an eye" on the renegade—a task that was virtually impossible anyway, but perhaps marginally easier with the man living
under his roof. Philby had his own motive for welcoming Burgess
to Washington. As information officer Burgess would be able to
travel freely without exciting comment; he could therefore act as
a courier, taking information to Philby's Soviet controller, Valeri
Makayev, in New York. Soon after Burgess's arrival, Philby told
him about the hunt for "Homer" and the increasing risk that Maclean might be exposed and confess all, with potentially calami-
tous consequences.

Philby had not seen Maclean since the end of the war, but

their early friendship would not be hard to prove; Burgess knew Maclean much better and was also a close friend of Anthony Blunt; the association between Burgess and Philby was evident; Blunt was also in touch with Maclean. If Maclean cracked, MI5 could swiftly establish the links between the spies, and the chain of suspicion would eventually lead to Philby.

Maclean was heading off the rails at fantastic speed. He had tried to persuade his Soviet handler that he no longer wished to be a Soviet spy, apparently unaware that this was not the sort of club one could resign from. Moscow simply ignored the request. In May 1950 the strain became too much for him: he got drunk, smashed up the Cairo flat of two secretaries at the U.S. embassy, ripped up their underwear, and hurled a large mirror off the wall, breaking a large bath in two. He was sent home, placed under the care of a Harley Street psychiatrist, and then, amazingly, after a short period of treatment, promoted to head the American desk at the Foreign Office. Even drunken, unhinged knicker shredding, it seemed, was no bar to advancement in the British diplomatic service if one was the "right sort." But the short list of suspects was getting shorter, and Maclean's name was on it. He was plainly on the verge of complete nervous collapse. If MI5 pulled him in for questioning, he was almost certain to crack. With Burgess as his go-between, Philby could now be sure of a "secure line of communication to Moscow" if and when the crisis erupted.

Once installed in the Philby home, Burgess began to behave entirely in character: extremely badly. He crashed around Washington dropping names, picking quarrels, downing numberless drinks, and leaving others to pay for them. He wore a filthy old duffel coat, eschewed soap, and loudly declared that Americans were incapable of intellectual thought. Philby introduced Burgess to Angleton as "the most outstanding historian of his time at Cambridge." (Anyone familiar with Cambridge historians can attest that Burgess's personal habits did not entirely negate that claim.) He was certainly outstandingly embarrassing. Some days later, Burgess lurched up to Angleton's table at the Occidental restaurant, sat down without invitation, and demanded a drink of "the cheapest bourbon." He was wearing "a peculiar garb, namely a white British naval jacket which was dirty and stained. He was intoxicated, unshaven, and, by the appearance of his eyes, had not washed since he last slept." Burgess launched into a description of a mad scheme to import jackets like the one he was wearing to sell "for fantastic profits" in New York. Then he demanded to be taken for a ride in Angleton's Oldsmobile and finally asked the CIA officer to lend him some cash. Then he wandered off. There is no evidence Angleton found this behavior objectionable. He liked British eccentrics, and any friend of Kim Philby was a friend of his.

On January 19, 1951, Philby made a fateful decision: with his wife depressed, his dangerous friend careening around Washington, and his own future uncertain, he decided to throw a dinner party. It was, by almost universal agreement, the dinner party from hell.

Philby invited all his senior contacts in American intelligence: the Angletons, of course, and Robert Lamphere, the FBI mole hunter, along with the Manns and several others. Also present were Bill Harvey, a former FBI agent now in charge of CIA counterintelligence, and his high-strung wife, Libby. A hard-driving Ohio native, Bill Harvey was intelligent but also "a bloated alcoholic with the manners of a comically corrupt cop in a Raymond Chandler thriller." The Harveys had already attended a dinner party chez Philby, which had ended with Bill Harvey slumped insensible at the table.

The evening began, as always, with martinis served from a pitcher. There was an acrid mood in the air. Cicely Angleton noticed that Bob Lamphere was the only guest not smoking: "What Freudian impulse causes you not to smoke?" she demanded archly. The drinking continued steadily and, in the case of Libby Harvey, unsteadily. With the meal over (no one could later recall what was said or eaten), the guests moved on to whiskey. At this point Burgess burst in. He was disheveled, loudly inebriated, and itching for an argument. Libby lurched up to the new arrival, cornered him, and demanded that he draw a cartoon of her. Burgess was a talented sketcher, and his caricatures had become objects of admiration on the Washington dinner-party circuit. Burgess demurred. Libby drunkenly insisted. Finally, fed up with her badgering, he picked up a pad and pencil and began to sketch. A few minutes later, with a glinting grin, he handed over the caricature.

Sadly, the finished artwork does not survive, but its broad outlines have been described by witnesses. The woman in the picture was unmistakably Libby Harvey, though her face was "beastily distorted." Her face, however, was not the main focus of the cartoon: her dress was hiked up around her waist, her legs spread, and her naked pudenda bared. Libby stared at it, shrieked, and burst into tears. Bill Harvey threw a punch at Burgess. Uproar ensued. The Harveys stormed out.

Burgess found the incident hilarious. Philby did not. "How could you? How could you?" he demanded before slumping on the sofa. Aileen retired sobbing to the kitchen. Before drifting home, Angleton and Mann lingered outside 4100 Nebraska Avenue like two teenagers after a fight, discussing what Angleton termed "a social disaster."

Philby later sent the Harveys a "handsome" apology for Burgess's insulting behavior.

"Forget it," said Bill Harvey charmlessly. But Harvey didn't forget it.

A few weeks later, at Arlington Hall, came the break the decoders had been hoping for and Philby had been dreading: Meredith Gardner finally decrypted a message dating back to June 1944 indicating that the spy "Homer" had a pregnant wife who was then staying with her mother in New York. Melinda, Maclean's American-born wife, had been expecting a child in 1944; her wealthy, divorced mother lived in Manhattan; therefore Homer must be Donald Maclean.

News of the breakthrough flew to London and then bounced back to Philby in Washington. He was now the closest to exposure since Volkov had threatened to unmask him in 1945. But time was on his side. There was no evidence as yet to connect him directly with Maclean, and the two men had not met for many years.

Moreover, instead of arresting Maclean at once, MI5 opted to wait and watch in the hope of gathering further evidence. The Venona material was simply too secret to be used in court: by tapping his telephone, bugging his office, intercepting his post, and putting him under surveillance, MI5 hoped to catch Maclean in direct contact with his Soviet controller. But the Security Service may also have been suffering from the sort of paralysis that affects organizations when faced with a situation that is deeply embarrassing, potentially ruinous, and entirely unprecedented. Maclean, the most senior spy ever detected inside the British government, would remain at liberty for five more weeks.

Philby immediately relayed the bad news to Makayev and demanded that Maclean be extracted from the UK before he was interrogated and compromised the entire British spy network—and, most important, Philby himself. But with Maclean now under close surveillance, arranging his escape was a delicate task, since any overt contact with the Soviets would trigger his immediate arrest. Maclean must be warned and told to flee by a third party who would not arouse suspicion. The ideal messenger, Philby concluded, was close at hand in the disreputable and disheveled shape of Guy Burgess, whose diplomatic career was about to come to an end in a car crash, almost literally. Whether by accident or by design, he collected no fewer than three speeding tickets in a single day by hurtling around Virginia in a gray Lincoln convertible, claimed diplomatic immunity on all of them, insulted the officers who stopped him, and provoked a furious official protest from both the State Department and the governor of Virginia. It wasn't quite goats, but for the ambassador it was the last straw. Burgess, in disgrace but wholly unrepentant, was instructed to return to London immediately. Philby would later claim that Burgess's recall had been a carefully engineered ploy; it was probably more a lucky accident, but either way it presented an ideal opportunity to warn Maclean that he must flee to Moscow.

The night before Burgess's departure, the two spies dined in a Chinese restaurant in downtown Washington, selected because it had individual booths with piped music to stymie any eavesdroppers. They rehearsed the plan: Burgess would make contact with the Soviets in London, then visit Maclean at his office and, while making innocuous conversation, hand over a sheet of paper setting the time and place for a rendezvous. Burgess had not yet been formally fired, and there would be nothing suspicious in the newly returned information officer from Washington reporting to the head of the American desk. The Soviets would then arrange Maclean's escape. "Don't you go too," said Philby, only half joking, as he dropped Burgess off at Union Station. Burgess, however, was congenitally incapable of doing what he was told.

Burgess arrived back in England on May 7, 1951, and immediately contacted Anthony Blunt, who got a message to Yuri Modin, the Soviet controller of the Cambridge ring: "There's serious trouble," Blunt reported. "Guy Burgess has just arrived back in London. Homer's about to be arrested. . . . It's only a question of days now, maybe hours. . . . Donald's now in such a state that I'm convinced he'll break down the moment they arrest him." Modin informed Moscow and received an immediate response: "We agree to your organizing Maclean's defection. We will receive him here and provide him with whatever he needs."

A graduate of the Leningrad Naval Academy, Yuri Modin had, in his own estimation, "no predisposition to be a spy." But he was very good at it. He had inherited the Cambridge network at a time when it was falling apart, yet he had handled Burgess's drinking and Maclean's volatility with tact and competence. Spiriting Maclean to Moscow, however, was by far the greatest challenge he had yet faced.

MI5's surveillance unit, A4, was known as "the Watchers." In 1951 it numbered about twenty men and three women. Most were former police officers selected for their sharp eyesight, good hearing, and average height ("men who are too short . . . are just as conspicuous as tall men," ruled the chief Watcher). They were expected to dress in trilby hats and raincoats and communicated with one another by hand signals. They stood on street corners, watching and trying to appear inconspicuous. They looked, in short, exactly like surveillance agents. Since the end of the war,

A4 had kept watch on the Soviet intelligence residency in Kensington Palace Gardens, and the Soviets, in turn, had kept a close watch on them. Modin knew that the Watchers did not work in the evenings or over the weekends. He knew too that surveillance of Maclean did not extend beyond London, because MI5 feared that a man hanging around in a trilby might be a giveaway in the countryside. Maclean lived in Tatsfield in rural Kent and commuted to and from London by train. The Watchers trailed after him during the day but, Modin observed, "at Victoria, MI5's men saw the train out of the station, and then headed home like good little functionaries. There was no one at Tatsfield to take up the chase." Modin believed Maclean would be arrested on Monday, May 28. On Friday, May 25, the very day the foreign secretary gave formal approval for Maclean's interrogation, the escape plan swung into action.

That evening, which happened to be Maclean's thirty-eighth birthday, Burgess appeared at the Maclean home in Tatsfield with a rented car, packed bags, and two round-trip tickets, booked in false names, for the *Falaise*, a pleasure boat leaving that night for Saint-Malo in France. He had spent the previous day at his club, talking loudly about a road trip he planned to take to Scotland with a new boyfriend. Burgess had dinner with Donald and Melinda Maclean (who was party to the plan), and the two men set off for Southampton in a state of high excitement and unaccustomed sobriety. They arrived just minutes before the midnight sailing, parked the car askew on the dockside, and scrambled up the gangplank of the *Falaise*. One of the dockworkers shouted that the car door was still open; "Back on Monday!" Burgess shouted back. He may have thought he was telling the truth.

Before Burgess left Washington, Philby had made him promise he would not flee with Maclean to Moscow. "Don't go with him when he goes. If you do, that'll be the end of me. Swear that you won't." Modin, however, had insisted that Burgess accompany Maclean. Burgess had at first objected. He had pointed out that he had no desire to defect and found the prospect of life in Moscow perfectly ghastly. But finally he had agreed, apparently on the understanding that he could steer Maclean to Moscow and then return and resume his life just as before. The Soviets had other plans. As Modin wrote: "The Centre had concluded that we had not one, but two burnt-out agents on our hands. Burgess had lost most of his former value to us. . . . Even if he retained his job, he could never again feed intelligence to the KGB as he had done before. He was finished." Burgess and Maclean were traveling on one-way tickets to Moscow. What the Soviets had failed to take properly into account was the knock-on impact the double defection would have on Kim Philby. Modin later acknowledged that allowing Burgess to leave with Maclean had been an error. In the spy world, nothing is supposed to occur by accident, but in this case Modin's explanation was probably true: "It just happened. . . . Intelligence services do silly things sometimes."

The *Falaise* was popular with wealthy adulterers wanting to take their mistresses on a weekend cross-channel jaunt. There were no passport controls and few questions asked. In theory the ship cruised off the coast of France, but unofficially she always put in at Saint-Malo for a few hours of French food and sightseeing. The ship docked at eleven forty-five the next morning. Burgess and Maclean left their luggage on board, filed down the gangplank with the other passengers, and then slipped away from the crowds. They caught a taxi to the station at Rennes, a train to Paris, and then another train to Bern in Switzerland, where Nicholas Elliott, wholly unaware of the presence of the two fugitives on his patch, was enjoying dinner at the Schweizerhof Hotel.

Elliott considered the hotel restaurant one of the finest in Europe, with particularly good foie gras. "I have never tasted better," Elliott insisted, "even in Strasbourg." The maître d', Théo, was one of Elliott's paid informants and always managed to find him a table. Saturday-night dinner at the Schweizerhof had become something of an Elliott tradition.

On the evening of May 26, while Elliott was tucking into his foie gras, a taxi pulled up outside the Soviet embassy, less than a mile away. Elliott would have recognized both passengers. Burgess had been a frequent guest at the Harris parties, and he, Philby, and Elliott had often dined together at Prunier, a restaurant on Piccadilly. Burgess had once applied for a teaching post at Eton but been turned down when Claude Elliott discovered how unsuitable he was. "It seems a pity the Foreign Office did not take the trouble to make a similar inquiry," Elliott later reflected ruefully. He had also met Maclean on several occasions.

A few hours later, Burgess and Maclean reemerged from the Soviet embassy carrying fake passports in false names. They then took another train to Zurich, where they boarded a plane bound for Stockholm with a stopover in Prague. At the Prague airport, now safely behind the iron curtain, the two men walked out of the arrivals hall and were whisked into a waiting car.

On Monday morning the Watchers watched in vain as the train from Tatsfield pulled into Victoria Station with no Maclean aboard. A little later Melinda Maclean called the Foreign Office to report that her husband had left the house on Friday night with a man named "Roger Styles," and she had not seen him since. The Foreign Office put a call through to MI5. Special Branch reported that a car hired by Guy Burgess had been abandoned at Southampton docks. A flush of dawning horror began to spread across the British government.

The Foreign Office sent out an urgent telegram to embassies and MI6 stations throughout Europe, with instructions that Burgess and Maclean be apprehended "at all costs and by all means." A "wanted" poster gave a description of the fugitives. Maclean: "6' 3", normal built, short hair, brushed back, part on left side, slight stoop, thin tight lips, long thin legs, sloppy dressed, chain smoker, heavy drinker." Burgess: "5' 9", slender built, dark complexion, dark curly hair, tinged with gray, chubby face, clean shaven, slightly Pidgeon-toed." In Bern, Elliott gave orders to his own Watchers to keep a careful eye on the Soviet embassy. One of his colleagues prepared a "decanter of poisoned Scotch," just in case the notoriously thirsty fugitives turned up and needed to be immobilized. By that time Burgess and Maclean were already being toasted in Moscow.

The morning after the discovery of Burgess and Maclean's disappearance, a long, coded telegram arrived at the British embassy in Washington, marked Top Secret. Geoffrey Paterson, the MI5 representative in Washington, called Kim Philby at home to ask if he could borrow his secretary, Edith Whitfield, to help decipher it. Philby was happy to oblige. A few hours later he found Paterson in his embassy office, gray faced.

"Kim," Paterson half-whispered. "The bird has flown."

"What bird?" said Philby, arranging his features to register the appropriate consternation. "Not Maclean?"

"Yes, but there's worse than that. . . . *Guy Burgess* has gone with him."

Philby's alarm was now unfeigned. Burgess had been his houseguest until a few weeks earlier. Philby was one of the few people apprised of the Homer investigation and in a position to warn Maclean. All three had been at Cambridge together. It was only a matter of time—and probably very little time—before MI5 took an interest in his friendship with Burgess and started digging into his past. Philby realized, as his Soviet handlers apparently did not, just how seriously Burgess's flight would threaten his own position. He might be placed under surveillance at any moment, sacked, or even arrested. He had to move fast.

An emergency plan was already in place. If MI5 seemed to be closing in, the Soviets would provide money and false papers, and Philby would escape to Moscow via the Caribbean or Mexico. Makayev in New York had been instructed to leave two thousand dollars and a message at a dead-letter drop for precisely this purpose. He failed to do so. Philby never received the money. Makayev was later disciplined for this failure by his superiors in Moscow, who noted his "lack of discipline" and "crude manners": it seems likely that he simply spent the money on his ballet dancer.

The British embassy was in secret uproar as news spread that not one but two senior Foreign Office officials in Washington had vanished and were probably Soviet spies. Philby and Paterson together broke the embarrassing news to the FBI. Philby carefully observed the reaction of his FBI friends, including Bob Lamphere, his former dinner-party guest, and saw only surprise, tinged with some wry pleasure at the British predicament. So far Philby himself did not seem to be under suspicion. At lunchtime Philby told Paterson he was going home for "a stiff drink," behavior that anyone who knew him would have considered perfectly normal. Back at Nebraska Avenue, Philby headed not for the drinks cabinet but for the potting shed, where he collected a trowel, and then down to the basement that had, until recently, housed Guy Burgess. There he retrieved from a hiding place the Russian camera, tripod, and film given to him by Makayev, sealed the lot in waterproof containers, and placed them in the trunk of his car. Then he climbed in, gunned the engine, and drove north. Aileen was at home with the children; if she thought it strange that her husband should come home from work early, lock himself in the basement, and then drive away without a word, she did not say so.

Philby had traveled the road to Great Falls many times. Angleton had taken him fishing in the Potomac Valley and there was a faux-English pub called the Old Angler's Inn where they had spent several convivial evenings. The road was little used and heavily wooded. On a deserted stretch with woods on one side and the river on the other, Philby parked, extracted the containers and trowel, and headed into the trees. He emerged after a few minutes, casually doing up his fly buttons for the benefit of any passersby, and drove home. Somewhere in a shallow hole in the woods beside the Potomac lies a cache of Soviet photographic equipment that has lain buried for more than sixty years, a secret memorial to Philby's spy craft.

If Philby was going to make his escape and join Burgess and Maclean in exile, then now was the moment. But he did not run. He decided to stay and try to bluff it out. Philby later framed this choice (as he interpreted most of his own behavior) in terms of principle: "My clear duty was to fight it out." But the decision was also calculated: the FBI did not yet suspect him, so presumably the same must be true of MI5. No one had identified "Stanley." If and when they explored his past, the evidence they might find was mostly circumstantial. His early dabblings with left-wing politics were hardly secret, and he had told Valentine Vivian of his marriage to Litzi. His friendship with Burgess looked bad (back in 1940 Burgess had been instrumental in his recruitment by MI6), but then if they were really both Soviet spies, why would Philby have allowed Burgess to live in his home? "There is no doubt that Kim Philby is thoroughly disgusted with Burgess's behavior," wrote Liddell, after Philby contacted him to express horror at his friend's defection.

The very act of staying put would suggest a clear conscience. True, there were some uncomfortable early clues to his real allegiance: the British spy described by the defector Krivitsky who had worked in Spain as a journalist, Volkov's allusion to a counterintelligence officer, and the Russian's subsequent disappearance after Philby took over the case. Going back still further, MI6 might recall the Soviet files he had taken out from the registry at St Albans. But for a legal prosecution MI5 would need harder evidence than this. They might suspect him, interrogate him, urge him to confess, and try to trap him. But they would find it very hard to convict him. And Philby knew it. With a cool head and the luck that seemed to cling to him, he might yet ride out the coming storm. "Despite all appearances, I thought my chances were good."

Philby had one other weapon in his armory, perhaps the most powerful of all, and that was his capacity for friendship. Philby had powerful friends on both sides of the Atlantic, people who had worked with him and trusted him for many years. These people had witnessed his skill as an intelligence officer, shared secrets with him, and drunk his martinis. To accept Philby's guilt would have been, in a way, to implicate themselves. "There must be many people in high positions," Philby reflected, "who would wish very much to see my innocence established. They would be inclined to give me the benefit of the doubt."

Philby knew he could rely on his friends to defend him, two above all: Jim Angleton and Nick Elliott.

Chapter Eleven

Peach

PHILBY'S SUMMONS TO LONDON ARRIVED IN THE FORM OF A PO-
lite, handwritten note from his immediate superior, Jack Easton,
informing him that he would shortly receive a formal telegram
inviting him to come and discuss the disappearance of Burgess
and Maclean. Easton was one of the very few senior officers Philby
respected, a man with a "rapier mind" capable of "deeply subtle
twists." Philby later wondered if the letter was a tip-off intended to
make him flee in order to avoid a scandal. In truth it was probably
just a friendly gesture, a reassurance that there was nothing to
worry about. Before leaving, Philby made the rounds of his CIA
and FBI contacts once more and again detected no overt suspicion. Angleton seemed as friendly as ever. On June 11, 1951, the
evening before Philby's flight, the friends met in a bar.

"How long will you be away?" Angleton inquired.

"About a week," said Philby nonchalantly.

"Can you do me a favor in London?" asked Angleton, explaining that he needed to send an urgent letter to MI6 but had missed
the diplomatic bag that week. Would Philby deliver it by hand?
He pushed over an envelope addressed to the head of counterintelligence in London. Philby later imagined that this too had
been a ruse of some sort, intended to test or trap him. Paranoia
was beginning to gnaw. Angleton had no inkling of suspicion: his
trusted friend would deliver the letter and return in a week, when
they would have lunch together, as usual, at Harvey's. After what
Philby called "a pleasant hour" at the bar, discussing "matters of

mutual concern," Philby boarded the night plane to London. He would never see America or Jim Angleton again.

Dark clouds of doubt were swiftly gathering on both sides of the Atlantic, as Philby knew they would. These would soon blow up into a storm that would knock the "special relationship" off course and set Britain's secret services at each other's throats. The Americans might appear unruffled, but the disappearing diplomats had provoked a "major sensation" in Washington. An investigation was now under way focusing on Guy Burgess and, by association, his friend, protector, and landlord, Kim Philby. CIA chief Walter Bedell Smith ordered any officers with knowledge of the British pair to relate what they knew of Philby and Burgess as a matter of urgency. The first report to arrive on the CIA chief's desk came from Bill Harvey of counterintelligence; the second, arriving a few days later, was written by James Angleton. They were markedly different documents.

Harvey's report—"highly professional, perceptive and accusatory"—was, in effect, a denunciation of Philby. The former FBI agent would later claim to have had his suspicions about Philby long before the Burgess and Maclean defections, and at the FBI he may have had access to the Venona material. Harvey had studied the Englishman's career with meticulous care, and he drew together the strands of evidence with devastating precision over five closely typed pages: he noted Philby's links with Burgess, his part in the Volkov affair, his involvement in the doomed Albanian operations, and his intimate knowledge of the hunt for the spy "Homer," which had placed him in an ideal position to warn Maclean of his impending arrest. None of these alone amounted to proof of guilt, but taken together, Harvey argued, they pointed to only one conclusion: "Philby was a Soviet spy." Philby later described Harvey's condemnation as "a retrospective exercise in spite," personal revenge for the offense given to his wife at Philby's disastrous dinner party just six months earlier.

The second report stood in stark contrast. Angleton described his various meetings with the drunken Guy Burgess, but he noted that Philby had seemed embarrassed by his friend's antics and explained them away by saying that Burgess had "suffered severe concussion in an accident which had continued to affect him periodically." Angleton explicitly rejected any suggestion that Philby might have been in league with the defector and stated his "conviction" that whatever crimes Burgess might have committed, he had acted "without reference to Philby." As one CIA officer put it, "the bottom line was . . . that you couldn't blame Philby for what this nut Burgess had done." In Angleton's estimation, Philby was no traitor but an honest and brilliant man who had been cruelly duped by a friend, who in turn had been rendered mentally unstable by a nasty bump on the head. According to Angleton's biographer, "he remained convinced that his British friend would be cleared of suspicion" and warned Bedell Smith that if the CIA started leveling unsubstantiated charges of treachery against a senior MI6 officer, this would seriously damage Anglo-American relations, since Philby was "held in high esteem" in London.

In some ways the two memos echoed the different approaches to intelligence that were developing on opposite sides of the Atlantic. Bill Harvey's reflected a new, American style of investigation: suspicious, quick to judge, and willing to offend. Angleton's was written in the British MI6 tradition: based on friendship and trust in the word of a gentleman.

Harvey read Angleton's memo, so different in tone and import from his own, and scrawled on the bottom, "What is the rest of this story?"—in effect accusing his fellow CIA officer of turning a blind eye to the truth. The disagreement between Harvey and Angleton over Philby sparked a feud that would last the rest of their lives. A similarly stark divergence of opinion was emerging within British intelligence.

On the afternoon of June 12 Kim Philby arrived at MI5 headquarters in Leconfield House off Curzon Street, feeling exhausted and "apprehensive" but tensed and primed for the coming duel. The adrenaline rush of danger had always stimulated him. Jack Easton insisted on accompanying him to the interview as a supportive presence. The two MI6 men were greeted by Dick

White, the chief of MI5 counterintelligence, who, over the next few hours, would subject Philby to a grilling thinly disguised as a friendly chat. Tea was served. A fug of tobacco smoke filled the room. Civilities were exchanged. Dick White (not to be confused with Richard Brooman-White, Elliott's old friend) was a former schoolmaster, the son of a Kentish ironmonger, a frank, even-tempered, and honorable man who would go on to head MI5 and then MI6. Philby had known White since the war and had always gotten on well with him while privately disparaging what he considered to be his meager intellect and vacillating character. "He did his best to put our talk on a friendly footing." The mood in the room was more embarrassed than confrontational. C had reluctantly agreed to allow one of his officers to be interviewed by MI5 on the understanding that Philby was aiding an inquiry and "might have views on the case." White was at pains to point out that Philby was there simply to help shed light on "this horrible business with Burgess and Maclean."

But beneath the civilized veneer cracks were appearing that would soon split one branch of British intelligence from the other.

MI6 was standing by its man. The files contained nothing to incriminate Philby, only accolades of mounting admiration leading up to his appointment in Washington. "There was no case against him at this time," recalled Easton. At most he could be accused of indiscretion for associating with a degenerate like Guy Burgess. But if that was a crime, many in the Foreign Office and secret services were equally guilty. Philby had not run away, he was happy to help, and he was, importantly, a gentleman, a clubman, and a highflier, which meant he must be innocent. Many of Philby's colleagues in MI6 would cling to that presumption of innocence as an article of faith. To accept otherwise would be to admit that they had all been fooled; it would make the intelligence and diplomatic services look entirely idiotic. MI5, however, had been making inquiries, and already convivial, clubbable Kim Philby was beginning to take on a more sinister shape. The threads of suspicion identified by Bill Harvey in Washington were being pursued with even greater determination in London. In the weeks since the defections, a fat file had been assembled, and it now lay on White's desk, just a few feet away from where Philby sat, sipping tea, smoking his pipe, and trying to appear relaxed.

The conflicting attitudes toward Philby between the sister services of British intelligence would expose a cultural fault line that predated this crisis, long outlasted it, and persists today. MI5 and MI6—the Security Service and the Secret Intelligence Service, broadly equivalent to the FBI and CIA—overlapped in many respects but were fundamentally dissimilar in outlook. MI5 tended to recruit former policemen and soldiers, men who some-times spoke with regional accents and frequently did not know, or care about, the right order to use the cutlery at a formal dinner. They enforced the law and defended the realm, caught spies and prosecuted them. MI6 was more public school and Oxbridge; its accent more refined, its tailoring better. Its agents and officers frequently broke the laws of other countries in pursuit of secrets, and did so with a certain swagger. MI6 was White's Club; MI5 was the Rotary Club; MI6 was upper-middle class (and sometimes aris-tocratic); MI5 was middle class (and sometimes working class). In the minute gradations of social stratification that meant so much in Britain, MI5 was "below the salt," a little common, and MI6 was gentlemanly, elitist, and old school tie. MI5 were hunters; MI6 were gatherers. Philby's patronizing dismissal of Dick White as "nondescript" precisely reflected MI6's attitude to its sister service: White, as his biographer puts it, was "pure trade," whereas Philby was "establishment." MI5 looked up at MI6 with resentment; MI6 looked down with a small but ill-hidden sneer. The looming bat-tle over Philby was yet another skirmish in Britain's never-ending, hard-fought, and entirely ludicrous class war.

White was a decent man, a good administrator, and an adept office politician, but he was no interrogator. The evidence against Philby was still, as he put it, "very sketchy." He was also facing a spy of polished duplicity who had hidden himself in broad daylight for nearly two decades. It would take a cleverer man than White to discover him. Philby assumed the room was bugged. His stammer gave the conversation a strange, halting quality: perhaps evidence of nerves, perhaps to buy time and sympathy. White first asked about Maclean: Philby said he remembered him from Cambridge and knew him by reputation but had not seen him for years and probably would not even recognize him. Then the focus turned to Burgess, and the tension in the room slid up a notch. Philby insisted it was simply unbelievable that any intelligence service, let alone the Russians, would employ someone so wholly unsuited to espionage, "an indiscreet, disorganised, drunken, homosexual reprobate." Philby played his part well, with a careful combination of embarrassment, ingratiation, and self-justification: here was a senior intelligence officer defending himself against the unspoken charge that he had been fooled and the threat that he might lose his job through a disastrous friendship. The question of Philby's own loyalty was never mentioned, never even hinted at, but it hung over the conversation like pipe smoke. The meeting broke up with amicable handshakes. Ever helpful, Philby offered to draw up a summary of the conversation and said he could be contacted at his mother's flat. White hinted that they would probably need to meet again soon.

Both men discussed the conversation with Guy Liddell, who wrote in his diary: "Kim is extremely worried." White, for his part, had not found Philby's answers "wholly convincing." Liddell had been Philby's friend for twenty years. He knew Guy Burgess well. Anthony Blunt was one of his closest chums. Liddell's diary betrays a man struggling with the realization that some, and perhaps all, of his closest friends were spies. "I dined with Anthony Blunt," he wrote. "I feel certain that Blunt was never a conscious collaborator with Burgess in any activities that he may have conducted on behalf of the Comintern." His tone was anything but certain. That Burgess and Maclean might be spies, let alone Philby, was "hard to believe." Because he did not want to believe it.

Two days later Philby was back in White's office, where the atmosphere was now several degrees chillier. In the interim a letter had arrived from CIA chief Walter Bedell Smith, drafted by Bill Harvey and with his indictment attached. Aggressive in tone and addressed to C in person, it stated that under no circumstances would Philby be permitted to return to Washington. The underlying message was blunt: "Fire Philby or we break off the intelligence relationship." The relationship was under strain as never before. Noting that confidence in the Foreign Office had been "severely shaken" by the disappearance of Burgess and Maclean, both of whom were obvious security risks, the United States urged the British government to "clean house regardless of whom may be hurt." Even more insultingly, Washington suggested that such a security breach would never have happened in the United States: "In the State Department repeated drunkenness, recurrent nervous breakdowns, sexual deviations and other human frailties are considered security hazards and persons showing any one or more of them are summarily dismissed."

As Angleton had predicted, MI6 did not take kindly to having one of its officers accused of treachery without hard evidence, let alone the suggestion that the Foreign Office was staffed with drunken, mentally unstable sexual deviants. The bosses of MI6 immediately sent a message to Dick White at MI5 stating "their wholehearted commitment to the protection of their protégé and to the reputation of their service." White was now facing both a looming confrontation with Philby and a showdown with MI6 itself. At the same time, the dossier on Philby was growing. Investigations had revealed his left-wing leanings at Cambridge, his marriage to a communist, his subsequent swing to the far right, and the defector Krivitsky's reference to a Soviet spy working as a journalist in Spain during the civil war. The Volkov case, the wreckage of Operation Valuable, the Homer investigation, and the timing of the Burgess and Maclean defections all seemed to point, circumstantially if not definitively, to Philby's guilt. "While all the points against him are capable of another explanation their cumulative effect is certainly impressive," wrote Liddell. In a mark of the deepening suspicion, Philby was awarded his own code name: "Peach." Code names are supposed to be neutral but very seldom are. It is tempting to see a hidden meaning in the MI5 code name now attached to Philby, for a peach was a most exotic and enticing fruit in a Britain emaciated by wartime rationing, and ripe for the plucking.

Dick White was as polite as before, but more pointed. He invited Philby to describe once again, but in more detail, exactly when he had met Burgess, what he knew of his politics, and how they had become friends. Philby was told to take his time. "I'm in no particular hurry," said White with a flicker of impatience. A short lie is easy. An extended lie is far harder, as earlier falsehoods overlap, constrain, and contradict the lies that follow. Philby admitted that his first wife had been a communist but insisted that he had "subsequently converted her" and that "he himself had never been a communist." When asked how Maclean might have discovered he was facing arrest, Philby "denied emphatically that he had ever discussed Maclean with Burgess."

In the midst of a long, rambling answer, White realized, with perfect certainty, that Philby was lying.

White now switched focus to 1936 and Philby's first trip to Spain as a correspondent for the *Times*. Philby was quick to correct him: he had initially gone to Spain as a *freelancer* and only later taken a staff job with the newspaper. White's face grew redder and his collar tighter. How, then, as an impoverished young man, had Philby found the money to travel to Spain and set himself up as a correspondent? It was, Philby later wrote, a "nasty little question" because, as White plainly suspected, the order to go to Spain, and the money to do so, had been provided by Soviet intelligence. Philby blustered that he had sold his books and gramophone records to finance the trip. This was White's opportunity to pounce, because just a little more probing would have unpicked that answer: How many books? How many records? Did he sell them for cash? Where were the bank records? Instead, White simply logged Philby's response as another lie. After several more hours, White rose to his feet, indicating that the session was over. This time they did not shake hands. Philby left the second interview knowing that he was now a prime suspect in White's eyes. He remained convinced that MI5 had little hard evidence, probably not enough to prosecute and almost certainly not enough to convict him. But there was more than enough to make him intolerable to MI5 and unemployable by MI6. White sent a memo to Stewart Menzies laying out the grounds for suspicion against Philby and suggesting that MI6 take action as a matter of urgency.

Philby was in deep danger. The middle-class hounds of MI5 were baying for his upper-class blood. He was cornered, compromised, and running out of ammunition. But he still had allies ready to support him, and one in particular whose loyalty remained as solid and unquestioning as it had ever been.

Nicholas Elliott returned to Britain at the very moment the Philby inquisition was reaching a climax. He now leaped to his friend's defense with ferocity, alacrity, and absolute conviction.

The timing of Elliott's recall was probably coincidental. After six successful years as station chief in Switzerland, he was due for a promotion and accepted a new post in London liaising with the intelligence services of friendly foreign powers. It was a job that required plenty of foreign travel and fed what Elliott called his "insatiable appetite for new places and faces." But it also gave him the opportunity to devote himself to a task closer to home and closer to his heart: defending Philby against the accusations swirling around Whitehall. Elliott was wholeheartedly, unwaveringly convinced of Philby's innocence. They had joined MI6 together, watched cricket together, dined and drunk together. It was simply inconceivable to Elliott that Philby could be a Soviet spy. The Philby he knew never discussed politics. In more than a decade of close friendship, he had never heard Philby utter a word that might be considered left wing, let alone communist. Philby might have made a mistake associating with a man like Burgess; he might have dabbled in radical politics at university; he might even have married a communist and concealed the fact. But these were errors, not crimes. The rest of the so-called evidence was mere hearsay, gossip of the most vicious sort. The anticommunist campaign led by Senator Joe McCarthy was at its height in the United States, and in Elliott's firm opinion Philby was the victim of a McCarthyite witch hunt led by a cabal of lower-class, anticommunist fanatics in MI5.

The Elliotts moved into a house in Wilton Street in Belgravia, just a few minutes from where Philby was lodging in his mother's flat in Drayton Gardens. Within MI6 Elliott swiftly emerged as Philby's most doughty champion, defending him against all accusers and loudly declaring his innocence. Philby was his friend, his mentor, his ally, and in the world inhabited by Nicholas Elliott, that meant he simply could not be a Soviet spy. This was a friendship Elliott prized above all others; he saw MI5's accusations not just as a test of that bond but as an assault on the very values of the secret club they had joined in the heat of war. Elliott was standing up for an innocent man "guilty only of an unwise friendship"; and in his own mind, he was also defending his tribe, his culture, and his class.

But Elliott's resolute defense, and the widespread belief within MI6 that Philby was "the victim of unsubstantiated conjecture," could not save his job. With both MI5 and the Americans demanding action, Menzies was left with little choice. C summoned his former protégé. Philby knew what was coming. According to some accounts, he may have offered to quit: "I'm no good to you now. . . . I think you'd better let me go." In Philby's version of events, C told him, with "obvious distress," that he would have to ask for his resignation. His friendship with Burgess, a Soviet spy, had rendered him useless for further work as an MI6 officer. The mere size of his payoff—£4,000, equivalent to more than £32,000 today—was proof that he was leaving with honor and the support of his service. Philby could "not possibly be a traitor," Menzies told White. Philby pretended to be sanguine, accepting his role as a scapegoat. But Elliott was furious and did nothing to hide his belief that a "dedicated, loyal officer had been treated abominably on the basis of evidence that was no more than paranoid conspiracy theory."

Philby's glittering career as an MI6 officer was over. He was now unemployed, under suspicion of treason, and under a "great black cloud" of uncertainty. The family crammed into a rented gatehouse in Heronsgate, deep in the Hertfordshire countryside. Philby spent most of his time in the village pub. He knew he was being watched. Every week or so, a policeman appeared in the village and stood around looking conspicuous. The telephone was bugged and his mail intercepted as MI5 gathered evidence and watched to see if he would break cover. The eavesdroppers could find no evidence that he was in contact with the Soviets but plenty to indicate the continuing support of his colleagues in MI6. Knowing who was listening in, Philby carefully maintained his pose as a man forced out of a job he loved, but without bitterness. "He said that he had been treated very generously and did not have any recrimination against the old firm." Elliott tried to cheer him up by joking about the telephone intercepts: "Personally I would be delighted if MI5 were to bug my own telephone because that would ensure that whenever it went wrong—as from time to time it does—it would be quickly repaired." Philby may not have found this funny.

Nicholas Elliott called often: his conversations with both Philby and Aileen were carefully logged and transcribed. One of these, intercepted in August, sent a sharp jolt of alarm through MI5, when Aileen was overheard telling Elliott that Philby had gone sailing with a friend, a City businessman with a yacht moored in Chichester on the south coast. "I suppose he is not doing a 'dis'?" Aileen asked Elliott, apparently fearful that her husband might use the boat trip to stage a "disappearing act," like Burgess and Maclean, and slip over to France. Elliott laughingly reassured her that there was no danger whatever of Philby defecting.

Guy Liddell pondered whether to intercept the sailing party but concluded that Aileen had only been speaking "in jest." In any case, "it was already too late to stop Philby getting onto the yacht and it seemed equally unjustifiable to issue any warning to the French." Philby returned home that evening, oblivious to the flap he had caused. But as the evidence mounted, so did MI5's fear that Philby might be planning to make a run for it. In December the hunters attacked again.

The trees were bare beside the road into London as Philby drove south in answer to another summons from C. The inquiry was entering a new season. "The case against Philby seems somewhat blacker," wrote Liddell. As Philby headed toward the office, he imagined that MI5 must have found more evidence and that the next few hours might be "sticky." He was right on both counts. Menzies explained apologetically that a "judicial inquiry" had now been launched into the disappearance of Burgess and Maclean. Would Philby mind terribly going to MI5 headquarters to answer some more questions? It was an order disguised as an invitation. Prime Minister Winston Churchill had personally approved the decision to bring him in for questioning again. Philby's apprehensions were fully realized when he was ushered into a fifth-floor office of Leconfield House to find a familiar, hefty, and distinctly alarming figure awaiting him.

"Hello Buster," said Philby.

Helenus Patrick Joseph Milmo, universally known as "Buster," was a barrister of the old school, aggressive, precise, pompous, and ruthless. He had not come by his nickname lightly. He liked to flatten his opponents with a barrage of accusation delivered in a booming baritone with an air of legal omniscience. Philby had witnessed these demolition tactics at first hand during the war when, as MI5's legal adviser, Buster Milmo had joined him in breaking down suspected spies held at Camp 020, the secret interrogation center in Richmond. After the war, Milmo played a starring role for the prosecution in the Nuremberg trials of Nazi war criminals. He would go on to become a High Court judge. Armed with MI5's dossier, Milmo intended to break Philby and coerce him, by sheer force of argument, into a confession.

Philby sat down and, partly to cover his nerves, took out his pipe and lit it. Milmo instantly told him to put it out, with a sharp reminder that this was a formal judicial inquiry, equivalent to a court of law. This was untrue—the interview had no legal standing—but the exchange set the tone for what followed. Milmo came out with all guns blazing. He accused Philby of spying for the Soviets since the 1930s, sending hundreds to their deaths, betraying Volkov, and tipping off Burgess and Maclean. Philby parried, deflecting and ducking. Milmo then fired his best shot: he revealed that the volume of radio traffic between London and Moscow had jumped dramatically after Volkov's offer to defect, suggesting a tip-off to Moscow Center, followed by a similar leap in traffic between Moscow and Istanbul. How did Philby account for this?

Philby shrugged. "How would I know?"

Milmo moved on to Krivitsky's report of the mysterious Soviet spy sent under journalistic cover to civil-war Spain with a mission to assassinate Franco.

"Who was that young journalist?" Milmo demanded. "Was it you?"

Philby replied that if the Soviets had really wanted to kill Franco, they would surely have used a professional hit man, not a Cambridge graduate who had never fired a gun. Frustrated, Milmo now overplayed his hand, accusing Philby of handing sensitive papers to Burgess, a charge Philby could refute without even lying.

Milmo next accused Philby of marrying a communist and smuggling her into Britain. Philby countered that if he had left his Jewish girlfriend in Vienna she would have wound up in a Nazi concentration camp. "How could I not help her?"

The lawyer was running out of ammunition. At each evasion Milmo's voice grew louder, his face redder, his manner more bellicose. He banged the table. He snorted in disbelief. He flapped and thrashed.

A stenographer took down every word. In the next room a posse of senior intelligence officers, including Dick White, Guy Liddell, and Stewart Menzies, listened glumly as Milmo grew more enraged and more ineffectual. "So far, he has admitted nothing," Liddell recorded in his diary. "Milmo is bearing down on him pretty heavily."

"It all became a shouting match," said White.

After four hours, Milmo was hoarse, Philby was exhausted, and the interrogation had ended in stalemate. Milmo knew Philby was guilty. Philby knew he knew, but he also knew that without a confession the accusations were legally toothless. "The interrogation of Philby has been completed without admission," wrote Liddell that evening, "although Milmo is firmly of the opinion that he is or has been a Russian agent, and that he was responsible for the leakage about Maclean and Burgess." Before leaving MI5 headquarters, Philby was asked to surrender his passport, which he happily did, reflecting that if he needed to flee he would be traveling on false papers provided by his Soviet friends.

"I find myself unable to avoid the conclusion that Philby is and has been for many years a Soviet agent," Milmo wrote. To White he was even blunter. "There's no hope of a confession, but he's as guilty as hell." Reviewing the tapes and the transcript of the Milmo interview, Guy Liddell conceded that Philby, his esteemed former colleague and friend, had failed to behave like a man unjustly accused. "Philby's attitude throughout was quite extraordinary. He never made any violent protestation of innocence, nor did he make any attempt to prove his case." But without new, firm evidence, Liddell wrote, Philby "had all the cards in his hands." And if Philby was guilty, what of the other friends they shared? What of his good friend Anthony Blunt, who had known both Burgess and Philby? What of Tomás Harris, another former MI5 man, whose home had been the scene of so many well-oiled get-togethers? Fissures of doubt began to creep through the intelligence establishment as its senior figures eyed one another and wondered.

Philby described his four-hour grilling to Elliott, angrily insisting that he had been lured into a legal trap. Outraged on his friend's behalf, Elliott complained to Malcolm Cumming, a senior MI5 officer and one of the few Etonians in the Security Service.

Nicholas Elliott again referred to PEACH's intense anger with MI5 over the Milmo interrogation. He said that PEACH did not in any way object to such an independent interrogation being carried out but he did resent the fact that after his friendly conversations with Dick White, he should be virtually enticed to London under false pretences and then thrown straight into what proved to be a formal inquiry at which even his request to smoke was refused.

As Philby's advocate, Elliott was determined to extract an apology for the way the interrogation had been handled. MI6 was "counter-attacking," Liddell recorded gloomily, and Elliott was leading the charge.

MI5 was still determined to extract an admission of guilt from Philby and now turned to a man who was, in almost every conceivable way, the polar opposite of Buster Milmo. William "Jim" Skardon, a former detective inspector in the Metropolitan Police, was Watcher in chief, head of the surveillance section A4, and by repute the "foremost exponent in the country" in the art of interrogation. Skardon was mild and unassuming in manner; he wore a trilby, a raincoat, an apologetic expression, and a damp mustache. He spoke in a sibilant, self-effacing whisper and seldom made eye contact. Where Milmo relied on intimidation and noise, Skardon wormed his way into a man's mind by guile and insinuation. He had successfully extracted a confession in January 1950 from Klaus Fuchs, the atomic spy, winning his confidence during long walks in the country and quiet chats in rural pubs. Skardon uncovered truth by increments, asking what seemed to be the same questions, subtly varied, again and again, until his target tripped and became enmeshed in his own lies. Philby knew a great deal about Skardon and his reputation. So when this stooped, unctuous, bland-seeming man knocked on his door in Heronsgate and asked if he might come in for a cup of tea, Philby knew he was still in the deepest water.

As both men sucked on their pipes, Skardon seemed to wander, rather vaguely, from one subject to another, with a "manner verging on the exquisite." Afterward, Philby thought he had spotted, and sidestepped, "two little traps" but wondered anxiously if there had been others he had failed to detect. "Nothing could have been more flattering than the cozy warmth of his interest in my views and actions." Skardon reported back to Guy Liddell that his mind "remained open" on the issue of Philby's guilt. This was the first of several visits Skardon would pay to Kim Philby over the coming months as he probed and prodded, humble, polite, ingenious, and relentless. Then, in January 1952, as abruptly as they had started, Skardon's interviews ceased, leaving Philby "hanging," wondering just how much the detective had detected. "I would have given a great deal to have glimpsed his summing up," he wrote. In fact, Skardon's final report proved that the Philby charm had outlasted Skardon's bogus bonhomie. The interrogator admitted that the hours with Philby had left him with "a much more favourable impression than I would have expected." The charges against Philby were "unproven," Skardon concluded. His passport was returned.

"Investigation will continue and one day final proof of guilt . . . may be obtained," MI5 reported. "For all practical purposes it should be assumed that Philby was a Soviet spy throughout his service with SIS." MI6 sharply disagreed: "We feel that the case against Philby is not proven, and moreover is capable of a less sinister interpretation than is implied by the bare evidence." And that is how the strange case of Kim Philby remained, for months and then years, a bubbling unsolved mystery, still entirely unknown to the public but the source of poisonous discord between the intelligence services. Philby was left in limbo, suspended between the suspicions of his detractors and the loyalty of his friends. Most of the senior officers in MI5 were now convinced that he was guilty but could not prove it; most of his former colleagues in MI6 remained equally certain of his innocence but, again, unable to find the evidence to exonerate him. There were some in MI5, like Guy Liddell, who clung to the hope that it might all turn out to be a ghastly mistake and that Philby would eventually be cleared of suspicion, just as there were some in MI6 who harbored doubts about their former colleague, albeit silently for the sake of the service.

But among those convinced of Philby's guilt was one who knew him better than anyone else and who was finding it ever harder to remain silent, and that was his wife.

Chapter Twelve

The Robber Barons

WHEN DID AILEEN PHILBY, THE FORMER STORE DETECTIVE, UN-cover the clues that proved her husband, the Foreign Office high-flier, the doting father, the establishment paragon, was a Soviet spy? Was it when he was summoned home and lost his job? Or did the appalling realization come earlier? Did she always suspect there was something fishy about Guy Burgess, her bête noire, who trailed after her husband first to Istanbul and then Washington? Did the penny drop after Philby locked himself in the basement the day after Burgess's defection and then drove away with a mysterious bundle and the garden trowel? Or did doubt dawn earlier still, when Philby refused to divorce his first wife, an Austrian communist?

By 1952 Aileen knew that her husband had lied to her, consistently and coldly, from the moment they first met and throughout their marriage. The knowledge of his duplicity tipped her into a psychological abyss from which she would never fully emerge. She confronted Kim, who denied everything. The ensuing row, far from dissipating her fears, merely confirmed her conviction that he was lying. To others she began to hint obliquely at her inner turmoil: "To whom should a wife's allegiance belong?" she asked a friend. "Her country or her husband?" Questioned by a drunken Tommy Harris at a dinner party, she admitted she was "suspicious" of her husband but then backtracked and proclaimed him "entirely innocent."

She probably confided in her friend Flora Solomon, who cannot have been wholly surprised, since Philby had attempted to recruit her as a Soviet agent back in 1936. Aileen certainly shared her fears with Nicholas Elliott, who blithely laughed off her suspicions. MI5 had assumed that Aileen was joking when she told Elliott that Philby might "do a 'dis.'" She wasn't. She lived in fear that he would defect and join his horrible friend Burgess in Moscow, leaving her with five young children and the perpetual shame of having married a traitor. Each time he left the house, she wondered if he would ever return. She threatened to start legal proceedings to gain custody of the children. She began drinking heavily again. Her grip on reality began to slip.

One day Elliott received a telephone call from Aileen, tearful and slurring.

"Kim's gone."

"Where?" asked Elliott.

"I think to Russia."

"How do you know?"

"I got a telegram from Kim."

At this even Elliott's granite loyalty wavered for a moment.

"What does the telegram say?" he asked, staggered.

"It says: 'Farewell forever. Love to the Children.'"

Reeling, Elliott called the duty officer at MI5. An alert was immediately sent out to seaports and airports with instructions to intercept Philby if he attempted to leave the country.

Oddly, when asked to produce the telegram, Aileen said she could not, saying it had been read to her over the telephone. Puzzled, Elliott made an inquiry at the post office but could find no trace of a telegram sent to Aileen Philby. Once again he rang the house in Hertfordshire. It was now late evening. This time Philby answered. At the sound of his familiar voice, Elliott felt a flood of relief.

"Thank God it's you at last."

"Who were you expecting it to be?" said Philby.

"I'm glad you're home."

"Where else would I be at night?"

"The next time I see you I'll tell you where else you could have been tonight," said Elliott, with a brittle laugh, and hung up.

Aileen had fabricated the entire episode, just as she had invented the story of being attacked in Istanbul and staged her various maladies and injuries over the years. Elliott was fond and protective of Aileen, but he had become only too familiar with her mental illness. She suffered another series of "accidents," and drove her car into the front of a shop. Her doctor sent her for psychiatric treatment. Philby told his friends that Aileen was "insane." Far from alerting Elliott to the truth, Aileen's behavior redoubled his sympathy for his beleaguered friend, not only unjustly accused and deprived of his job but now under attack from a wife who was plainly imagining things. Within MI6 Aileen's suspicions were dismissed as the paranoid ravings of a madwoman.

With five children, one unstable wife, and two major drinking habits to support, Philby needed money, but employment was hard to find for a man of forty who had ostensibly worked for the Foreign Office but could not explain why he had left. He toyed with resuming his career in journalism and submitted a number of articles to newspapers but could find no permanent position. The telephone intercepts "disclosed very definitely that Philby was very active in looking for a job" and was failing. Finally, Jack Ivens, a "loyal ex-colleague" from Section V, found him a job in his import-export firm. The salary was a meager six hundred pounds a year. Aileen's mother provided funds for the family to move into a large and ugly Edwardian house in Crowborough, "the poor man's Surrey," in Graham Greene's words. Philby commuted, miserably, to an office in London, where he filled out paperwork, importing Spanish oranges and exporting castor oil to the United States. He did not dare try to reestablish contact with his Soviet controllers. "Philby was under constant watch," wrote Yuri Modin. "Several times our counter-surveillance teams reported the presence of MI5 agents hovering in his vicinity." He was out in the cold as never before.

Philby had always been a high-functioning, sociable alcoholic. He was fast becoming an ill-functioning one with a vile temper. MI5, listening in on his telephone line, noted that "Peach is apt to get blind drunk and behave abominably to his best friends." Long suffering and loyal, Elliott put up with Philby's outbursts. Philby leaned heavily on his old friend. In his strange double world, there was no contradiction here: he genuinely valued Elliott's friendship, needed his support, and relied on his advice while lying to him. Philby did not disguise from Elliott his collapsing marriage, but the subject was only ever tackled obliquely. Like most Englishmen of their class, they tended to steer around embarrassing emotional topics. Elliott lent Philby money when funds ran low, paid his club bills, and took him to watch cricket at Lord's. He urged Philby to go on the offensive: "You must fight like hell. If I was accused of spying, I would go to the Prime Minister and complain," he told him. Philby "smiled wanly" at this suggestion. "The whole family went through a bad time," wrote Elliott, who tried to buoy his friend by insisting that his exile from MI6 was strictly temporary; Philby would soon be back in the club and resuming his career where he had left off.

Sir Stewart Menzies was also firm in his support. On April 1, 1952, he took Philby to dinner at the Travellers Club and asked him "whether he wished for any advance of the bonus that was given to him at the time of his resignation." C later discussed this lunch with Guy Liddell of MI5, who reported:

> C seemed to have reached the conclusion that Kim was innocent. I said that I had come to the conclusion that the only thing to do in cases of this kind, where one knew an individual fairly intimately, was to sink one's personal view and allow those concerned to get on with the job, purely on the basis of ascertainment of facts. Otherwise one was liable to get misled. . . . Kim does not, apparently, bear any particular resentment against this department. If he had been in our position he would have reacted in the same way, even down to the question of withholding his passport.

Elliott's conviction that his friend would soon return to the MI6 fold was echoed by Philby's main ally in the United States.

James Angleton assured a colleague in 1952 that "Philby would recover from his present predicament and would yet become chief of the British Secret Service."

Philby knew that would never be. Cut off from his Soviet handlers, stuck in an ill-paid job he loathed, expecting MI5 to pounce at any moment, living with a wife who knew his secret, Philby's life was spiraling downward.

Elliott did what he could to bolster Philby's flagging spirits, dispensing encouragement and support. MI5, combing through the transcripts of Philby's bugged telephone conversations, expressed surprise and irritation at "the extent to which Peach is still in touch with, and subsidised by, MI6." Philby's oldest son, John, was now eleven, and though Philby himself might be committed to destroying the British establishment he was nonetheless anxious to get his sons into a good public school. Eton and Westminster were beyond his budget, but Elliott came up with the solution. He approached his father, Claude (now Provost of Eton), who agreed to get John Philby (and later his brother Tommy) into Lord Wandsworth College in Hampshire, "of which he was governor and which, being heavily endowed, was not too expensive." The old school tie was still pulling Philby along.

Elliott closely monitored the progress of the Philby case—or rather the lack of it, for the tussle between MI5 and MI6 had settled into acrimonious stalemate. Ronnie Reed, an MI5 officer who had known Philby from the war, noted "the intense disagreement between our two services on Philby." In June 1952 Stewart Menzies retired, to be replaced by his deputy, Major General Sir John "Sinbad" Sinclair, a tall military traditionalist set in his ways. (His lunch never varied: one grilled herring and a glass of water.) Sinclair was just as determined as his predecessor to stand by Philby: the new C "refused to let one of his chaps down." He did, however, agree that serving MI6 officers should be discouraged from socializing with Philby, a directive that Elliott and others simply ignored. MI5, meanwhile, continued to dig for evidence, convinced that other moles must be lurking inside the establishment and enraged at the way MI6 had closed ranks. The Watchers listened and observed, waiting for Philby to make a slip.

MI5's telephone intercepts would eventually fill thirty-three volumes: they revealed no espionage on Philby's part but laid bare the rapidly worsening state of his marriage. He had started an affair with a woman in London, a civil servant, and frequently did not return home for days at a time. When he did, the couple fought bitterly. Philby took to sleeping in a tent in the garden. He told friends that Aileen had denounced him to the Foreign Office, and this had prevented him from getting a decent job. He even claimed she had tried to kill him. Aileen likewise suspected Philby of harboring murderous designs. Secretly and unethically, her psychiatrist was passing information to MI5. One report noted: "In [Aileen's] opinion, and that of her psychiatrist, Philby had by a kind of mental cruelty to her 'done his best to make her commit suicide.'" The same psychiatrist suggested that Philby might be homosexual, despite copious evidence to the contrary. With little money coming in from her estranged husband, Aileen was reduced to working in the kitchen of a grand house on Eaton Square, simply to pay the bills. Nicholas Elliott tried to shore her up with financial and moral support. Her workplace, he wrote, "was close enough to our house in Wilton Street to spend her off duty hours with us."

After eighteen unhappy months selling castor oil and oranges, Philby found himself jobless again after Jack Ivens's import-export firm went bust. He scratched around, trying to make a living from freelance journalism, but with scant success. He was now virtually dependent on friends and family. His father, living in Saudi Arabia as an adviser to Ibn Saud, sent what money he could spare. Elliott paid the school fees of the Philby children. Tommy Harris arranged for Philby to write a book about the Spanish civil war for a London publisher, with a six-hundred-pound advance. The book was never written, and the deal appears to have been a ruse by the wealthy Harris to funnel money to his friend without Philby discovering the source.

Philby continued to socialize with his friends in intelligence, but tensely. One evening Guy Liddell went to dinner with Tommy Harris and discovered that Philby had been invited too. He greeted Philby "in the normal way," although both knew the situation could hardly have been stranger. MI5 was convinced of Philby's treachery; Harris himself was now under suspicion, his telephone bugged in case some clue emerged during his conversations with Philby. The dinner guests all tried to pretend that the occasion was no different from the many that had preceded it. Philby seemed "somewhat worried," Liddell wrote in his diary, and left early.

In his darkest moments Philby considered whether to reactivate his escape plan and defect to Moscow, but there was no way to contact Soviet intelligence without alerting MI5, and he knew it. He was trapped and isolated, aware that he was still just one Soviet defector away from exposure.

VLADIMIR PETROV WAS a Siberian peasant who, through hard work and docile obedience, had survived Stalin's Purges to rise steadily through the ranks of Soviet intelligence. After three decades of service to communism, he was a KGB colonel and the *rezident* at the Soviet embassy in Canberra. Publicly Petrov was a timeserver; privately he was a rebel. He had seen his Siberian village destroyed by famine and forced collectivization. From his work as a cypher clerk he had learned the full extent of Stalin's crimes. In August 1954 he defected in Australia. His wife, Evdokia, was picked up by a KGB snatch squad before she could do the same and then rescued, as her captors tried to manhandle her, missing one shoe, aboard a plane in Darwin.

As the highest-ranking defector since the war, Petrov brought a mass of information on cyphers, agent networks, and the names of some six hundred KGB officers working as diplomats around the world. He also furnished the first hard evidence that Burgess and Maclean were indeed in the Soviet Union (hitherto this had been assumed but unverified) and living in Kuibyshev. Even more explosively, he confirmed that they had been tipped off to escape by another British official, a third man. In Whitehall, Fleet Street, and beyond, the identity of this shadowy third man became the subject of rumor, innuendo, and some highly informed speculation.

Philby heard of Petrov's defection and waited anxiously for Jim Skardon to reappear on his doorstep, this time with a police posse and arrest warrant. As the weeks passed without a knock on his door, he assumed, rightly, that the defector had not identified him by name. But he was haunted by the "worry that Petrov had brought in something substantial that I did not know about" that might be used to trip him up if he was interrogated again.

Dick White, Philby's old adversary, was planning precisely such an entrapment, having now taken over as director general of MI5. Guy Liddell had expected to get the post, but his friendships had damaged his reputation beyond repair. MI6 even hinted that Liddell himself might be a gay Soviet spy, pointing out that he "had parted from his wife, had a faintly homosexual air about him and, during the war, had been a close friend of Burgess, Philby and Blunt." Bitterly disappointed, Liddell heartily congratulated White on his appointment and resigned.

White saw the Petrov defection as an opportunity to flush out Philby once and for all, and he urged Anthony Eden, the foreign secretary, to put the revelations about a third man out in the open. "It will undermine Philby. It will create uncertainty for Philby. We'll lure him into a new interview and try again to get a confession." Eden refused, in part because Sir John Sinclair at MI6 insisted White was "pursuing a vendetta against Philby that was best ignored." The feud between MI5 and MI6 was as fierce and damaging as ever.

Philby could not know it, but his Soviet masters were observing him and worried. An assessment drawn up by the KGB British section reported that Agent Stanley was "desperately short of cash" and drinking heavily. Yuri Modin asked Moscow what to do, pointing out that Philby had "rendered us immense services [and] might need to be reactivated in the future." The Center ordered that Philby be given "a large sum of money" and a re-assurance that the Soviet Union would stand by him. The KGB was not acting out of generosity, or even loyalty, but hardheaded pragmatism: a drunken and destitute spy was a liability who might confess or demand to be extricated. A lump of cash would keep him stable, it was hoped, and in place. But the handover (like most of Moscow's directives) was easier ordered than done, since Philby was still under close surveillance. Moreover, Modin was instructed not to make direct personal contact; his mission was to pay Philby, under the noses of MI5, without actually seeing him. The KGB officer had managed to spirit Burgess and Maclean out of England; but getting Philby to stay put would be rather harder.

ON THE EVENING of June 16, 1954, Professor Anthony Blunt, former MI5 officer, Soviet spy, and distinguished art historian, prepared to give a lecture at the Courtauld Institute of Art, of which he was a director. The subject was the Arch of Gallienus, a Roman triumphal arch in danger of demolition to make way for a modern housing project. The audience was composed of eager classicists, art students, and learned members of the public who had read about the lecture in the *Times* and wanted to support the worthy cause of protecting Rome's classical heritage. In the front row, facing the lectern, sat a squarely built, fair-haired young man who had signed the visitors' book in the name "Greenglass" and identified himself as Norwegian.

Blunt's long, baggy face wore an expression of scholarly concern as he distributed photographs of the threatened arch before launching into an attack on the "villainous Italian authorities" who wanted to do away with it. At the end, everyone clapped, and none more enthusiastically than Greenglass—although he had never been to Italy, knew nothing about classical architecture, and could not have cared less if every arch in Rome was bulldozed and covered over in concrete. At the end of the lecture, Professor Blunt was mobbed, as he often was, by a bevy of enthusiastic, upholstered ladies keen to talk about art, who "vied with one another in showing off their knowledge." Greenglass hung back on the fringes and then, rather abruptly, barged through the throng, elbowing one of the professor's admirers in the ribs as he did so, and thrust a postcard of a Renaissance painting into Blunt's hand.

"Excuse me," asked the rude Norwegian. "Do you know where I can find this picture?"

Blunt turned the postcard over while the artistic ladies looked on frostily. On the back was written: "Tomorrow. 8pm. Angel." The distinctive handwriting, Blunt knew at once, was that of Guy Burgess.

Blunt gave his questioner "a long stare" and recognized him as Yuri Modin, the Soviet spy handler he had last seen in 1951, just before Burgess and Maclean fled. Then he looked back at the postcard and its message. "Yes," he said. "Yes. Yes."

The next evening Blunt and Modin met in the Angel pub in Islington off the Caledonian Road, a nondescript drinking hole they had used for clandestine meetings in the past. They spoke first about Blunt's situation—he had been interviewed by MI5 but did not yet seem to be a suspect—before moving on to Philby. Blunt reported that his fellow spy was in poor shape, jobless and penniless, and had already been subjected to a number of hostile interviews by MI5. Modin asked Blunt to pass on some cash to Philby. Reluctantly—for he had long ago forsaken espionage in favor of protecting Roman arches—Blunt agreed.

A few days later, Philby drove from Crowborough to Tonbridge and bought a ticket for the first train to London. He waited until all the other passengers were aboard and the platform was deserted before boarding. At Vauxhall he took the Underground to Tottenham Court Road, where he purchased a large coat and hat. For an hour he wandered around, looking in shop windows to see if he was being followed, then had a drink in a bar before buying a cinema ticket. He took a seat in the back row. Halfway through the performance, he slipped out. No one seemed to follow him. But for two more hours he walked aimlessly, then hopped on a bus, then jumped off again. By evening he was in North London: "I was virtually certain I was clean."

At dusk three spies converged on a small square off the Caledonian Road. It appears that Modin, following orders, made no direct contact with Philby that night and spoke only to Blunt as he passed over the package, while Philby kept his distance, ready to run. In Modin's melodramatic recollection, "the dark silhouette kept pace with us along the tree-lined path; a solid, foursquare figure, shrouded in an overcoat." Philby returned to Crowborough with five thousand pounds in cash and a "refreshed spirit," buoyed by the knowledge that he was back in contact with Soviet intelligence after a four-year hiatus. Modin had also passed on a reassurance, through Blunt, that the defector "Petrov knew nothing about his career as a Soviet agent." The handover in the dark London park transformed both Philby's finances and his state of mind. "I was no longer alone."

Philby's Soviet friends had rallied to him; his British friends would now do the same. At around the time of the Petrov defection, a group of officers within MI6, led by Nicholas Elliott, launched a concerted campaign to clear his name.

Elliott had by now taken up a new post as head of MI6's London station. Code-named "BIN" and based in Londonderry House, Victoria, the London station acted, in effect, like any other MI6 outpost, but on British soil, with a staff of twenty officers running intelligence operations against diplomats, businessmen, and spies, recruiting agents in foreign embassies, and monitoring the activities of visiting dignitaries. Elliott's new role enabled him to behave like a spy abroad, but within easy reach of his club.

By 1954 a distinct faction had emerged within MI6, with considerable influence over the chief, Sir John Sinclair: these were the Young Turks of the intelligence service, men like Elliott who had learned the spy game in the heady days of war when, with sufficient grit and imagination, anything had seemed possible. Inside the service Elliott and his like were known as the "Robber Barons," swashbuckling types with an acute sense of their own importance and little respect for civilian authority. They believed in covert action, taking risks, and, whenever necessary, breaking the rules. Above all they believed in intelligence as a sort of patriotic religion, a British bulwark against barbarism. George Kennedy Young, a good friend of both Elliott and Philby who would rise to become deputy director of MI6, put into words the creed of this increasingly influential and ambitious group. "It is the spy who has been called on to remedy the situation created by the deficiencies of ministers, diplomats, generals and priests," Young insisted, with an arrogance that did not bode well.

> Men's minds are shaped of course by their environments and we spies, although we have our professional mystique, do perhaps live closer to the realities and hard facts of international relations than other practitioners of government. We are relatively free of the problems of status, of precedence, departmental attitudes and evasions of personal responsibility, which create the official cast of mind. We do not have to develop, like Parliamentarians conditioned by a lifetime, the ability to produce the ready phrase, the smart reply and the flashing smile. And so it is not surprising these days that the spy finds himself the main guardian of intellectual integrity.

Men like Young and Elliott saw themselves as Britain's secret guardians, members of a chosen brotherhood unconstrained by normal conventions. Kim Philby had been a role model for many of the Robber Barons; his worldly savoir faire and wartime successes affirmed their sense of collective identity. They now set out to rescue him.

On July 20, 1955, "Sinbad" Sinclair wrote to Dick White, his counterpart in MI5, claiming that Buster Milmo's interrogation of Kim Philby had been "biased" and that the former MI6 officer had been the "victim of a miscarriage of justice."

In a later memo to Sir Ivone Kirkpatrick, the permanent undersecretary of state for foreign affairs, C summed up the case for Philby's defense.

The Milmo Report, which produces no single piece of direct evidence to show that Philby was a Soviet agent or that he was the "Third Man," is therefore a case for the prosecution inadmissible at law and unsuccessful in security intelligence. It is constructed of suppositious and circumstantial evidence, summing up in a circular argument everything the ingenuity of a prosecutor could devise against a suspect. It seems likely to remain as a permanently accusing finger pointed at Philby [who] was in fact convicted of nothing by the investigation in 1951 and despite four years of subsequent investigation is still convicted of nothing. It is entirely contrary to the English tradition for a man to have to prove his innocence . . . in a case where the prosecution has nothing but suspicion to go upon.

The case should be reexamined, he said, and Philby given an opportunity to defend himself. "Produce the evidence, and there'll be no further dispute," Sinclair told White. White reluctantly agreed that Philby should be interviewed once more, knowing that the case against him was not much stronger than it had been in 1951. The stage was now set for a final showdown, and Elliott, Philby's "greatest defender," would be waiting in the wings to stage-manage the drama.

On September 18, the *People* newspaper broke the story of Vladimir Petrov's defection with a series of dramatic revelations: Burgess and Maclean had both been recruited as Soviet agents while students at Cambridge; their flight to Moscow, just as Maclean was about to be arrested, had been orchestrated by the Soviet intelligence service; these were not "missing diplomats," as the government had maintained for so long, but spies on the run. British secrecy laws had been used to hide the truth and shield the government from embarrassment.

Harold Macmillan, the new foreign secretary, faced a major crisis: "We are going to have to say something," he said gloomily. Five days later the government issued an eight-page white paper, or policy document, purporting to explain the Burgess and Maclean affair. It was a peculiar mixture of half-truth and evasion that played down the scandal and made no mention of Kim Philby, whose name was now being widely whispered and in some cases shouted. At a dinner party Aileen Philby rose unsteadily to her feet and upbraided her husband: "I know you are the Third Man." Even Philby's wife was denouncing him in public; the press would not be far behind. The white paper was dismissed as a cover-up.

On the other side of the Atlantic, J. Edgar Hoover was as convinced of Philby's guilt as James Angleton was sure of his innocence and enraged at Britain's failure to arrest him. The FBI chief decided to bring matters to a head with a characteristic act of subterfuge. But first Philby prepared for one last interrogation.

On October 7, two weeks after the publication of the white paper, Philby presented himself at an MI6 safe house near Sloane Square, where he was ushered into a room furnished with a patterned sofa and chairs arranged around a small table; on one wall stood an ancient sideboard with a telephone on top. Inside the telephone was a high-quality microphone. An amplifier, placed under the floorboards beneath Philby's chair, fed sound to the microphone, which was then relayed to Leconfield House, MI5 headquarters. Here the conversation would be recorded on acetate gramophone records and then handed to typists who would transcribe every word.

Philby was nervous. This would be his fourth formal interrogation. Despite Modin's reassurances, he feared Petrov might have armed the investigators with some damning new clue. Philby had told MI6 he "welcomed the chance to clear his name," but in truth he was tired and worried. He braced himself for another flaying.

Instead, what he experienced was closer to a fireside chat than an inquisition, an interview utterly different from any that had come before. A committee of inquiry, set up by Macmillan, had formally ruled that this round of questioning should be the responsibility of MI6, not MI5. This would not be an inquisition, in the manner of Buster Milmo, but an internal review of the situation carried out by two of Philby's former colleagues "who knew him well." It seems probable that one of them was Nick Elliott.

As the conversation started and the recording machines began to spin, MI5 officers listened with mounting fury as Philby was given the lightest possible grilling by his friends. "To call it an interrogation would be a travesty," one MI5 officer later wrote.

> It was an in-house MI6 interview. . . . They took him gently over familiar ground. First his communist past, then his MI6 career and his friendship with Guy Burgess. Philby stuttered and stammered and protested his innocence. But listening to the disembodied voices, the lies seemed so clear. Whenever Philby floundered, one or other of his questioners guided him to an acceptable answer. "Well, I suppose such and such could be an explanation." Philby would gratefully agree and the interview would move on.

Philby was sent home with a friendly handshake and a not-guilty verdict: "You may be pleased to know that we have come to a unanimous decision about your innocence." Philby was jubilant: "The trail had become stale and muddy," he wrote. "The fact that I had made no attempt to escape over a long period was beginning to tell heavily in my favor." When Dick White read the transcripts, he was "livid"; the MI5 transcribers formally put on record their "belief that one of the questioners was prejudiced in Philby's favor, repeatedly helping him find answers to awkward questions and never pressing questions which he failed to answer." The Robber Barons had launched a highly effective counterattack. But Philby was not yet safe.

Just over a week later, on Sunday, October 23, the Philby family awoke to find their home surrounded by a pack of journalists in full hue and cry. That morning in New York, the *Sunday News* had run a story naming Philby as the "Third Man," the "tipster" who had helped the defectors to flee. This was the work of Hoover, who had leaked Philby's name to a tame journalist to force the British into launching a full judicial investigation. For more than four years Philby's name had been kept out of the newspapers, despite being common knowledge on Fleet Street. Now the hunt was on. "The house at Crowborough was besieged," reported Elliott, who advised Philby to hold off the press as long as possible. If British newspapers repeated what the *Sunday News* had reported, they could be sued for libel. But Philby's name was now in print, and everyone was talking about the third man. It took two days more before the dam burst.

Chapter Thirteen

The Third Man

COLONEL MARCUS LIPTON, MP, THE LABOR MEMBER FOR BRIXton, was a stuffy, old-fashioned troublemaker who distrusted government and loathed modern music, which he believed would bring down the monarchy. "If pop music is going to be used to destroy our established institutions, then it must be destroyed first," he once declared. He specialized in asking awkward questions. No one ever accused Lipton of being subtle, but he had a firm grip on political procedure and in particular "parliamentary privilege," the ancient right of MPs to make statements in Westminster without danger of prosecution.

On Tuesday, October 25, he rose to his feet during Prime Minister's Questions and dropped a bombshell:

Has the Prime Minister made up his mind to cover up at all costs the dubious third man activities of Mr Harold Philby who was first secretary at the Washington embassy a little time ago, and is he determined to stifle all discussions on the very great matters which were evaded in the White Paper, which is an insult to the intelligence of the country?

This was raw meat for the press: a feeding frenzy erupted.

That afternoon, on a London Underground train heading home, Kim Philby's eyes idly wandered to the newspaper headline on the front page of his neighbor's copy of the *Evening Standard*: MP TALKS OF "DUBIOUS THIRD MAN ACTIVITIES OF MR. HAROLD

PHILBY." The newspaper reported Lipton's words verbatim. After more than two decades in hiding, Philby had been flushed into the open.

Back in Crowborough, Philby immediately called Nicholas Elliott.

"My name is in the newspapers. I have to do something."

Elliott was calm. "I agree with you. Certainly. But let's think about it for a day, at least. Don't do anything for a day, all right? I'll call you tomorrow."

Making a statement at this stage would only add fuel to an already raging fire and "might prejudice the case." If Marcus Lipton had new evidence implicating Philby, he would surely have passed it on to the authorities and MI5 would have acted on it. The MP was simply repeating what had already appeared in the American press, under cover of parliamentary privilege. Harold Macmillan, as the minister in charge of the Foreign Office and MI6, would have to make a statement, either supporting Philby or damning him: since MI5 plainly lacked the evidence to prosecute, there was a good chance Philby might be exonerated. Elliott's advice was to stand firm, say nothing, ride out the storm, and allow his friends in MI6 to go to work on his behalf.

"We've decided that you naturally must respond," Elliott told him the next day. "But it should be done only when the Parliamentary debates begin. Please bear up for two weeks."

The Crowborough house presented a bizarre spectacle, with dozens of journalists camped out on the lawn. They followed Philby to the pub at lunchtime and then trailed him back again, asking questions that he declined, most politely, to answer. The telephone rang incessantly. The *Sunday Express* posted a letter through the front door, offering one hundred pounds if Philby would take part in a public debate with Marcus Lipton. Elliott worried about the "additional stress for Aileen and the children" and helped to spirit them away to stay with a relative. Philby himself took refuge with his mother in her South Kensington flat, where he disconnected the doorbell and stuffed the telephone under a pile of cushions. The press tore off the door knocker in their efforts to gain access. A journalist tried to climb in through the fire escape, terrifying the cook.

The government had promised to make a statement and hold a debate on November 7. Elliott now set to work ensuring that when Macmillan came to speak, he would say the right thing. The man selected to brief the foreign secretary on this tricky issue was none other than Richard Brooman-White, Elliott's old friend from Eton and Trinity, who had helped to recruit Philby into MI6 during the war. Brooman-White had left the secret service for a career in politics and in 1951 been elected Conservative MP for Rutherglen. Philby, Elliott, and Brooman-White had been friends since 1939. When Parliament was sitting, Brooman-White lived in the top floor of Elliott's house in Wilton Street; Elizabeth Elliott worked as his secretary; Claudia Elliott was his goddaughter; Elliott and Brooman-White even shared ownership of a racehorse. Brooman-White was the parliamentary voice of the Robber Barons and Philby's most vigorous defender in the House of Commons. In Philby's words, Elliott, Brooman-White, and his other allies remained "absolutely convinced I had been accused unfairly [and] simply could not imagine their friend could be a communist. They sincerely believed me and supported me."

The brief Brooman-White drew up for Macmillan purported to be unbiased but "leaned heavily in favour of Philby's innocence." There was no hard evidence, Brooman-White insisted; his former colleague had lost his job simply because of a youthful dalliance with communism and an ill-advised friendship with Guy Burgess. These views chimed with Macmillan's own instincts. An aristocratic Old Etonian, Macmillan regarded intelligence work as faintly dirty and the row over Philby as an unnecessary spat between MI5 and MI6. He dearly wished to avoid a scandal, let alone a trial. "Nothing would be worse than a lot of muckraking and innuendo," Macmillan told the cabinet, just five days before Lipton launched his attack. The foreign secretary simply wanted this embarrassing, unseemly mess to go away.

On November 7, Macmillan rose in the House of Commons

and made a statement that might have been written by Nicholas Elliott and Richard Brooman-White—and probably was.

> Mr Philby had Communist associates during and after his university days [but] no evidence has been found to show that he was responsible for warning Burgess or Maclean. While in Government service he carried out his duties ably and conscientiously. I have no reason to conclude that Mr Philby has at any time betrayed the interests of this country, or to identify him with the so-called "third man" if, indeed, there was one.

Richard Brooman-White followed up with a rousing defense of Philby—"a man whose name has been smeared"—and a ferocious attack on Marcus Lipton as a McCarthyite witch-hunter too cowardly to repeat his allegations outside the House of Commons and face the legal consequences.

> He [Lipton] is in favour of acting on suspicion, of smearing on suspicion, by directing public suspicion on to an individual against whom nothing at all has been proved. We must leave it to his own conscience to straighten out what that may cost in personal suffering to the wife, children and friends of the person involved. The only thing that has been proved against Mr Philby is that he had Burgess staying with him and he had certain Communist friends. He may not have been very wise in his choice of friends, but what honourable member of this House could say that all his friends were people against whom no shadow of suspicion could ever be cast?

From the Labor benches came grumbling claims of another whitewash. "Whoever is covering up whom and on what pretext, whether because of the membership of a circle or a club, or because of good fellowship or whatever it may be, they must think again and think quickly," declared Frank Tomney, MP, a tough northerner.

Lipton tried to fight back. "I will not be gagged by anybody in this House or outside in the performance of my duty," he blustered. "Say it outside!" chorused the Tories. Lipton limply responded: "Even Mr Philby has not asked for it to be repeated outside." He then sat down, visibly sagging.

Philby now went in for the kill. Elliott had tipped him off that he would be cleared by Macmillan, but mere exoneration was not enough: he needed Lipton to retract his allegations, publicly, humiliatingly, and quickly. After a telephone consultation with Elliott, he instructed his mother to inform all callers that he would be holding a press conference in Dora's Drayton Gardens flat the next morning.

When Philby opened the door a few minutes before 11:00 a.m. on November 8, he was greeted with gratifying proof of his new celebrity. The stairwell was packed with journalists from the world's press. "Jesus Christ!" he said. "Do come in." Philby had prepared carefully. Freshly shaved and neatly barbered, he wore a well-cut pinstriped suit, a sober and authoritative tie, and his most charming smile. The journalists trooped into his mother's sitting room, where they packed themselves around the walls. Camera flashes popped. In a conspicuous (and calculated) act of old-world gallantry, Philby asked a journalist sitting in an armchair if he would mind giving up his seat to a lady journalist forced to stand in the doorway. The man leaped to his feet. The television cameras rolled.

What followed was a dramatic tour de force, a display of cool public dishonesty that few politicians or lawyers could match. There was no trace of a stammer, no hint of nerves or embarrassment. Philby looked the world in the eye with a steady gaze and lied his head off. Footage of Philby's famous press conference is still used as a training tool by MI6, a master class in mendacity.

Philby first read a prepared statement, explaining that he had not spoken out before because, having signed the Official Secrets Act, he could not legally disclose information derived from his position as a government official. "The efficiency of our security services can only be reduced by publicity given to their organisation, personnel and techniques," he intoned, sounding exactly like a Whitehall mandarin upholding the ancient rules of British secrecy. Edwin Newman, an American journalist with NBC, was delegated to ask the questions.

If there was a third man, were you in fact the third man?
No, I was not.
Do you think there was one?
No comment.
Mr Philby, you yourself were asked to resign from the Foreign Office a few months after Burgess and Maclean disappeared. The Foreign Secretary said in the past you had communist associations. That is why you were asked to resign?
I was asked to resign because of an imprudent association.
That is your association with Burgess?
Correct.
What about the alleged communist associations? Can you say anything about them?
The last time I spoke to a communist, knowing him to be a communist, was some time in 1934.
That implies that you have spoken to communists unknowingly and not known about it.
Well, I spoke to Burgess last in April or May, 1951.
He gave you no idea that he was a communist at all?
Never.
Would you still regard Burgess, who lived with you for a while in Washington, as a friend of yours? How do you feel about him now?
I consider his action deplorable. . . .

And here Philby paused, for just a beat, a man, it seemed, wrestling with his own conflicted feelings, his duty, conscience and personal loyalty, and the pain of betrayal by a dear friend.

> *. . . On the subject of friendship, I'd prefer to say as little as possible, because it's very complicated.*

As for Lipton, Philby invited his accuser to repeat his allegations outside the House of Commons or else hand over whatever information he had to the proper authorities.

The press conference came to an end. Philby, ever the generous host, served the assembled journalists beer and sherry in his mother's dining room. "I see you understand the habits of the press very well," joked an American reporter. The resulting press coverage contained no suggestion that Philby was anything other than an honest, upright government official, brought down by his friendship with a secret communist and now definitively absolved. The Soviet intelligence officer Yuri Modin watched the press conference on the evening news and marveled at Philby's "breathtaking" performance: "Kim played his cards with consummate cunning. We concluded, just as he had, that the British government had no serious evidence against him."

Marcus Lipton had no choice but to retreat in ignominy, formally withdrawing his accusations, which he "deeply regretted."

"My evidence was insubstantial," the MP admitted. "When it came to a showdown my legal advisers counselled me to retract." Philby issued a clipped and gracious statement: "Colonel Lipton has done the right thing. So far as I am concerned, the incident is now closed."

Philby's triumph was complete. Elliott was "overjoyed" at Philby's victory and the prospect of bringing him back into the firm. The Robber Barons would now actively "seek his reemployment by his old service," which in turn raised the prospect of Philby's "further service to the Soviet cause."

Elliott had rehabilitated his old friend just as his own career was about to take a most almighty dive.

IN THE DAWN light of April 19, 1956, a peculiar figure in a rubber diving suit and flippers waddled sideways down the King's Stairs at Portsmouth Harbor and clambered into a waiting dinghy. The man was no more than five feet five inches tall. On his head he wore a woolly balaclava with a diving cap on top and on his back a tank with enough oxygen for a ninety-minute dive. He was a decorated war hero, Britain's most famous frogman, and his name was Commander Lionel "Buster" Crabb.

In the distance, through the drifting mist, loomed the faint shapes of three Soviet warships, newly arrived in Britain on a goodwill mission and berthed alongside the Southern Railway Jetty. An oarsman rowed the boat out some eighty yards offshore. Crabb adjusted his air tank, picked up a new experimental camera issued by the Admiralty Research Department, and extinguished the last of the cigarettes he had smoked continuously since waking. His task was to swim underneath the Soviet cruiser *Ordzhonikidze*, explore and photograph her keel, propellers, and rudder, and then return. It would be a long, cold swim, alone, in extremely cold and dirty water, with almost zero visibility at a depth of about thirty feet. The job might have daunted a much younger and healthier man. For a forty-seven-year-old, unfit, chain-smoking depressive who had been extremely drunk a few hours earlier, it was close to suicidal.

The mission, code-named "Operation Claret," bore all the hallmarks of a Nicholas Elliott escapade: it was daring, imaginative, unconventional, and completely unauthorized.

Seven months earlier, Nikita Khrushchev had announced that he would visit Britain for the first time, accompanied by his premier, Nikolai Bulganin. The first secretary of the Soviet Communist Party would travel aboard the latest Russian cruiser, the *Ordzhonikidze*, escorted by two destroyers. The Soviet leader would then be taken by special train to London and dine at Number 10 with the prime minister, Anthony Eden. The visit was hailed by diplomats as an important thaw in the cold war. The spies saw other opportunities.

The Soviets were rumored to have developed a new type of propeller, as well as enhanced underwater sonar technology to evade submarines. With the arms race running at full tilt, MI6 and Naval Intelligence wanted to find out more. There was also an element of tit for tat. British warships had recently docked in Leningrad, and "frogmen had popped up all over the place," in Elliott's words. Anything the Soviets could do MI6 could do better, and more secretly.

The intelligence services sprang into action. MI5 set about bugging the Soviet leader's suite at Claridge's Hotel and installed a listening device in the telephone. The Naval Intelligence Department urged that the investigation of the undersides of the Soviet vessels be undertaken as "a matter of high intelligence priority." Elliott, the London station chief for MI6, was charged with exploiting this golden opportunity for espionage. As he put it, with typical ribaldry: "We wanted a closer look at those Russian ladies' bottoms." He knew just the man for the job.

Lionel Crabb earned his nickname from the American actor, athlete, and pin-up Buster Crabbe, who had played Flash Gordon in the film series and won a gold medal in swimming at the 1932 Olympics. In almost every way, the English Buster Crabb was entirely unlike his namesake, being English, tiny, and a poor swimmer (without flippers he could barely complete three lengths of a swimming pool). With his long nose, bright eyes, and miniature frame, he might have been an aquatic garden gnome. He was, however, spectacularly brave and supremely resilient. Born to a poor family in South London, he first served in the merchant navy and then joined the Royal Navy after the outbreak of war, training as a diver. In 1942 he was dispatched to Gibraltar to take part in the escalating underwater battle around the rock, where Italian frogmen, using manned torpedoes and limpet mines, were sinking thousands of tons of Allied shipping. Crabb and his fellow divers set out to stop them with remarkable success, blowing up enemy divers with depth charges, intercepting torpedoes, and peeling mines off the hulls of ships. When the war ended, Crabb cleared mines from the ports of Venice and Livorno, and when the militant Zionist group Irgun began attacking British ships with underwater explosives, he was called in to defuse them. The risks were staggering, but Crabb survived and was duly awarded the George Medal for "undaunted devotion to duty." He became, briefly, a celebrity. Small boys mobbed him, and he frequently appeared in the newspapers. Long after demobilization, Crabb continued to do odd, secret, or particularly dangerous underwater jobs for the navy.

Elliott had gotten to know Crabb during the war and considered him "a most engaging man of the highest integrity . . . as well as being the best frogman in the country, probably in the world." He cut a remarkable figure in civilian life, wearing beige tweeds, a monocle, and a porkpie hat and carrying a Spanish sword stick with a silver knob carved into the shape of a crab. But there was another, darker side to this "kindly bantam cock." Crabb suffered from deep depressions and had a weakness for gambling, alcohol, and barmaids. When taking a woman out to dinner, he liked to dress up in his frogman outfit; unsurprisingly, this seldom had the desired effect, and his emotional life was a mess. In 1956 he was in the process of getting divorced after a marriage that had lasted only a few months. He worked variously as a model, undertaker, and art salesman, but like many men who had seen vivid wartime action, he found peace a pallid disappointment. He was also feeling his age. When Elliott contacted him, Buster Crabb was working at Espresso Furnishings in Seymour Place, selling tables to cafés. Crabb accepted the mission without hesitation. He wanted, he said, "to get m' feet wet again, get m' gills back." Money was not discussed. Instead, Elliott joked that if the investigation of the *Ordzhonikidze* proved successful, Crabb could be assured of "supplies of whisky for many years." Others were doubtful that Crabb was up to the task. John Henry, the MI6 technical officer, pointed out that the diver seemed to be "heading for a heart attack." But Elliott insisted that "Crabb was still the most experienced frogman in England, and totally trustworthy. . . . He begged to do the job for patriotic as well as personal motives." Ted Davies, a former sailor who headed MI6's naval liaison unit, was assigned as his case officer.

Operation Claret proceeded with the sort of smoothness that suggested no one in authority was paying adequate attention.

Michael Williams, a Foreign Office official recently posted to oversee MI6, was handed a list of possible operations for the Soviet visit.
"The dicey operations [are] at the beginning of the file and the
safer ones at the back," he was told. Williams was distracted by the
death of his father that morning. A short while later he handed
the file back without comment. MI6 assumed this amounted to
Foreign Office approval; Williams assumed someone senior to
him must already have given the go-ahead; the admiralty assumed
that MI6 was responsible, since it was carrying out the mission;
and MI6 assumed the admiralty was in the driver's seat, since it
had asked for the information in the first place. And the prime
minister assumed that no spies were doing anything, because that
was exactly what he had ordered them to do.

Back in September, when the Khrushchev trip had first been
mooted, Anthony Eden had stated categorically: "These ships are
our guests and, however we think others would behave, we should
take no action which involves the slightest risk of detection." Eden
shared Macmillan's distaste for spying and was not about to have
the adventurers of MI6 spoiling this moment of delicate international diplomacy. When Elliott was later quizzed about who had
signed off on the operation and in what capacity, his shrugging
reply was most revealing. "We don't have a chain of command. We
work like a club."

A week before the Soviet delegation arrived, Anthony Eden
learned that plans were being hatched for underwater surveillance of the *Ordzhonikidze* and put his foot down even more firmly.
"I am sorry, but we cannot do anything of this kind on this occasion," he wrote. Elliott would later insist that the "operation was
mounted after receiving a written assurance of the Navy's interest
and in the firm belief that government clearance had been given."
He either did not know about the prime minister's veto or, more
likely, didn't care.

Kim Philby, meanwhile, was in Ireland. Immediately after the
triumphant press conference, William Allen, a friend who had
been press counselor at the British embassy in Turkey, offered
him a job writing a centenary history of his family firm, David

Allen & Sons, a large printing and poster company. Allen was an Old Etonian, and it is possible that Elliott had a hand in arranging what was, in effect, a "working holiday." Allen was also a fascist sympathizer, a close friend of Oswald Mosley, and as politically far removed from his guest as it was possible to be. This did not stop Philby from spending several months living at Allen's expense in the family home in County Waterford, writing a very boring book about printing, ink, and paper. He returned to Britain just as Operation Claret was being uncorked. Philby knew "Crabbie" well. As head of the Iberian section of Section V, he had been involved in Crabb's wartime exploits off Gibraltar. Elliott would surely have been unable to resist telling Philby that he had brought the great frogman, their old comrade in arms, out of retirement in order to pay an underwater call on the visiting Soviet delegation.

The day before the Soviet mini-flotilla was due to arrive, Buster Crabb and Ted Davies took the train to Portsmouth and checked in to the Sally Port Hotel. Davies, somewhat unimaginatively, signed in as "Smith" but added "attached Foreign Office"; Crabb signed the hotel register in his own name. He then contacted an old friend, Lieutenant George Franklin, the diving instructor from the training ship HMS *Vernon*, who had agreed, unofficially, to help him prepare for the dive and supply additional equipment. The next day Crabb watched through powerful binoculars as the Soviet warships cruised into port. Then he went on a bender. Crabb had many friends in Portsmouth, and they all wanted to buy him a drink. During his prolonged pub crawl, Crabb was heard to boast that he was being paid sixty guineas to go "down to take a dekko at the Russian bottoms." The night before the dive, Crabb drank five double whiskies with a similar number of beer "chasers."

The next morning Franklin helped him into his two-piece Pirelli diving suit, purchased from Heinke of Chichester, handed him his flippers, and adjusted the valves on his air tank. Two uniformed policemen escorted them through the docks and down the King's Stairs. Franklin rowed the boat, while Crabb sat smoking in the stern. At around 7:00 a.m. Crabb checked his gear for the last time and slipped backward over the gunwale with a gentle splash, leaving behind a trail of bubbles in the murky water. Twenty minutes later he reappeared, a little breathless, and asked Franklin to attach "an extra pound of weight." Then he was gone.

Aboard the *Ordzhonikidze* the Soviets were waiting.

What happened next has been a matter of conjecture, imaginative guesswork, and a great deal of pure fantasy ever since.

In 2007 a seventy-four-year-old retired Soviet sailor named Eduard Koltsov came forward with this account. Koltsov claimed to have been trained as a combat frogman by the Soviet navy, as part of a team known as the "Barracudas." In 1956 he was twenty-two and stationed aboard the *Ordzhonikidze*. On the morning of April 19 he was ordered to dive beneath the ship and patrol for any spying frogmen: at around 8:00 a.m., on the starboard side of the hull, he spotted a diver carrying what he took to be a limpet mine. At first the swimmer seemed so small that Koltsov thought it was a boy. Swimming up behind him, and believing the ship was in imminent danger, Koltsov says he drew a knife, severed the frogman's air tubes, and then cut his throat. The body then floated to the harbor bottom. Koltsov said he had been awarded a Soviet medal for this action and even produced the knife with which he claimed to have killed Lionel Crabb.

Koltsov's claim is no more, or less, plausible than the myriad other theories that still cluster around the strange case of Commander Crabb, a story so encrusted with myth it will never be fully solved. But one part of Koltsov's story has a clear ring of truth: "A tip-off from a British spy meant that he had been lying in wait." There now seems little doubt that the Soviet delegation was fully prepared for Crabb's underwater visit. Three Soviet sailors saw the frogman pop up between two of the ships before diving again. That was the last time Buster Crabb was seen alive.

As the sun came up over Portsmouth harbor with no sign of Crabb, George Franklin came to the appalled realization that something terrible had happened. He rowed back to the steps and told Ted Davies that Crabb had vanished. Under normal circumstances, rescue teams would have been sent to scour the harbor at once in the hope of finding the missing frogman alive, but to do so would have alerted the Soviets to what was going on. Davies hurtled back to the Sally Port Hotel, packed up his own belongings and those of Crabb, and rushed back to London. The news of Crabb's disappearance sent a flood of panic through the upper reaches of British intelligence. "There will be blood all over the floor," predicted one MI5 officer before resorting to a cricketing metaphor, as Englishmen do in times of stress: "We'll all be for the pavilion."

A classic cover-up ensued, as MI5, MI6, and Naval Intelligence conspired to conceal the truth from their political bosses, the visiting Soviet delegation, and the public. An official lie was prepared stating that Crabb had been "specially employed in connection with trials of certain underwater apparatus" and had not returned from a test dive in Stokes Bay, about three miles from Portsmouth; he was now missing and "presumed drowned." A police officer was dispatched to the Sally Port Hotel, where he tore out the incriminating pages from the hotel register. The hotel owner was told it was all hush-hush and warned to keep his mouth shut. But Dick White of MI5 knew what was coming. "I'm afraid it rather looks to me as if the lid will come off before too long," he predicted grimly. Crabb's family and friends were becoming alarmed; the press was sniffing around, and the Soviets were determined to extract maximum diplomatic capital from the situation.

The evening after Crabb's disappearance, Anthony Eden hosted a dinner in London for the Soviet leader, attended by ministers and members of the royal family. In the course of the banquet Nikita Khrushchev mentioned the *Ordzhonikidze* and made an apparently jocular reference to "missing or lost property." Khrushchev was given to obscure utterances: everyone smiled, and no one had a clue what he was talking about. The next night Rear Admiral V. F. Kotov, the commander of the Soviet ship, attended a formal dinner hosted by the Portsmouth naval authorities. Over coffee he told his British counterpart that three days earlier, sailors aboard the destroyer *Sovershenny*, moored alongside the cruiser, had spotted a diver on the surface. With disingenuous concern the Soviet admiral noted that the frogman seemed to be "in trouble" and "he hoped he was all right." The British admiral categorically denied that any diving operations had taken place that day.

The carefully timed Soviet inquiry made it impossible to keep the truth from the prime minister any longer. When Anthony Eden discovered that his direct orders had been ignored, a covert operation had been launched, a famous frogman was missing and probably dead, and the Soviets knew all about it, he hit the roof. The prime minister demanded to know who had authorized the dive and why its failure had been concealed from him for four days. The press was now in frothing pursuit, Crabb's family wanted answers, and the discovery that the hotel register had been doctored added momentum to what was already a galloping news story. On May 5 the Soviets weighed in again with a formal diplomatic protest, demanding a full explanation for "such an unusual occurrence as the carrying out of secret diving operations alongside Soviet warships visiting the British Naval Base at Portsmouth." The squirming diplomatic reply expressed "regret about this incident" but continued to insist that Crabb's approach to the destroyers was "completely unauthorized." Disgracefully, a draft response drawn up by the Foreign Office, but never issued, tried to blame Crabb for his own death, claiming he had "paid no attention when recalled by his assistant" and concluding "it can only be assumed that in a spirit of adventure he was determined on his own initiative to inspect the Russian ships. . . . He died while diving on his unauthorised expedition."

On May 9 Eden made a statement in the House of Commons, through gritted teeth, in which he refused to provide details of the operation while making it quite clear that he was not to blame.

> It would not be in the public interest to disclose the circumstances in which Commander Crabb is presumed to have met his death. While it is the practice for ministers to accept responsibility, I think it is necessary in the special circumstances of this case to make it clear that what

was done was done without the authority or knowledge of Her Majesty's ministers. Appropriate disciplinary steps are being taken.

With unconcealed glee the Soviet newspaper *Pravda* denounced what it called "a shameful operation of underwater espionage directed against those who come to the country on a friendly visit."

Operation Claret was an unmitigated, gale-force cock-up: it embarrassed the government, offered the Soviets an open target, deepened cold-war suspicion, produced no useful intelligence, turned Eden's diplomatic triumph to disaster, provoked renewed infighting between the secret services, and led to the death of a certified war hero. A month later Eden was still fuming and demanding that heads should roll for this "misconceived and inept operation." A twenty-three-page report on the incident, filled with bureaucratic obfuscation, was festooned with the prime minister's furious jottings: "Ridiculous . . . Against Orders . . . This proves nothing." The first lord of the Admiralty offered his resignation. MI5 blamed what one officer called "a typical piece of MI6 adventurism, ill-conceived and badly-executed." The most prominent victim of the fallout was Sir John "Sinbad" Sinclair, the head of MI6. Eden ordered that his retirement be swiftly advanced, and by July 1956 he was gone, replaced by Dick White, who was moved from MI5 to take over the sister service. On arrival at MI6 headquarters, White's new deputy, Jack Easton, warned him: "We're still cloak and dagger. Fisticuffs. Too many swashbuckling green thumbs thinking we're about to fight another second world war." There is no doubt whom he was referring to.

Nicholas Elliott should have been fired for what one colleague called a "one man Bay of Pigs." Astonishingly, he survived—if not unscathed, then at least unsacked, an outcome that would have been highly unlikely in any other organization. As Elliott had himself demonstrated, this was a club that looked after its members. With typical insouciance he wrote: "A storm in a teacup was blown up by ineptitude into a major diplomatic incident which reflected unjustifiable discredit on MI6. The incompetence lay on the shoulders of the politicians, most notably Eden, in the way the matter was handled." Elliott remained in post as London station chief, flatly denying that he, or anyone else in the intelligence services, was to blame. For the rest of his life Elliott defended the memory of Buster Crabb, insisting that his friend had perished in the line of duty. "Crabb was both brave and patriotic," wrote Elliott. "Qualities which inspired him to volunteer to do what he did." Crabb had proven his loyalty and that, in Elliott's world, was all that mattered.

More than a year after Crabb's disappearance, a fisherman spotted a decomposing body floating in the water off Pilsey Island in Chichester Harbor. The head and hands had rotted away completely, but a postmortem concluded, from distinguishing marks on the remains preserved inside the Pirelli diving suit, that the small corpse was that of Lionel Crabb. The coroner's open verdict on the cause of death, and the absence of head and hands, left the way clear for a flood of conspiracy theory that has continued, virtually unabated, ever since: Crabb defected to the USSR; he was shot by a Soviet sniper; he had been captured and brainwashed and was working as a diving instructor for the Soviet navy; he had been deliberately planted on the Soviets as an MI6 double agent. A South African clairvoyant insisted Crabb had been sucked into a secret underwater compartment on the *Ordzhonikidze*, chained up, and then dumped at sea. And so on. Eight years later Marcus Lipton, the indefatigable MP, was still calling for the case to be reopened, without success. The Crabb mystery has never been fully explained, but the diminutive frogman did achieve a sort of immortality. Crabb has been cited as one of the models for James Bond. As an officer in Naval Intelligence, Ian Fleming had known him well, and the Crabb affair inspired the plot of *Thunderball*, in which Bond sets out to investigate the hull of the *Disco Volante*.

Elliott's verdict on Crabb's death still seems the most likely. "He almost certainly died of respiratory trouble, being a heavy smoker and not in the best of health, or conceivably because some fault had developed in his equipment." Elliott dismissed out of hand the theory that the Soviets might have killed Crabb, and the idea of betrayal never crossed his mind. But more than half a century later a Russian frogman popped up out of the murk to claim that he had killed Crabb with his own hands, following a tip-off from a British spy.

If the Soviets *were* forewarned of the underwater operation (which now seems probable), and if Crabb *did* die as a result (which seems at least possible), then there was only one person who could have passed on that information.

Kim Philby's heart sank when Nicholas Elliott called him in July and asked him to "come down to the firm." It was barely seven months since Macmillan had cleared him of suspicion. Could it be that MI5 had already found fresh evidence? Had another defector emerged?

"Something unpleasant again?" asked Philby warily.

"Maybe just the opposite," Elliott replied.

Despite the storm raging around him over the Crabb affair, Elliott had found time to demonstrate his own peculiarly durable brand of loyalty. He had done what he promised to do and what no one (including Philby) had believed was possible: he had engineered Philby's return to MI6.

Chapter Fourteen

Our Man in Beirut

KIM PHILBY'S RETURN TO BRITISH INTELLIGENCE DISPLAYED THE old boys' network running at its smoothest: a word in an ear, a nod, a drink with one of the chaps at the club, and the machinery kicked in.

Nicholas Elliott made a point of cultivating journalists and maintained close relations with several highly placed editors. He would host regular dinners at White's to introduce senior journalists to C. His old friend from wartime Naval Intelligence, Ian Fleming, had become foreign manager of the Kemsley newspaper group, which included the *Sunday Times*. "In those days SIS kept in touch with useful persons," Elliott later recalled. "And Ian was quite useful: he had important contacts in certain places, and every now and then he got hold of a useful piece of information. I would ask him if I needed someone in the City and, very occasionally, someone out in the field." Fleming was perfectly willing to oil the wheels of British intelligence. "Kemsley Press allowed many of their foreign correspondents to cooperate with MI6, and even took on MI6 operatives as foreign correspondents." Another helpful journalist was David Astor, the editor of the *Observer*. Astor later tried to play down his links with British intelligence, but he and Elliott went back a long way: a fellow Etonian, Astor had been in The Hague in 1939 "doing secret service stuff," according to his cousin, the actress Joyce Grenfell, at the same time as Elliott.

In the summer of 1956 Elliott asked Astor for a favor: would he take on Philby as a freelance correspondent in Beirut? The newspaper editor was happy to help. With the Suez crisis building, journalists were flocking to the Middle East. Philby had a proven track record, and he had written for the *Observer* before. Through his father, who was now living outside the Lebanese capital, he would have access to important people in the region. Astor contacted Donald Tyerman, the editor of the *Economist*, who was also looking for a Beirut stringer, and a deal was struck: the *Observer* and the *Economist* would share Philby's services and pay him three thousand pounds a year plus travel and expenses. At the same time Elliott arranged that Philby would resume working for MI6, no longer as an officer but as an agent, gathering information for British intelligence in one of the world's most sensitive areas. He would be paid a retainer through Godfrey "Paul" Paulson, chief of the Beirut MI6 station and a close friend of Nick Elliott who had been at Westminster with Philby. Elliott insisted that Philby was "being re-engaged for reasons of simple justice" but also because he would be a useful asset with long experience of the game: "The country could ill afford to be without Philby's abilities." Astor later claimed, implausibly, that he had no idea Philby would be working for MI6 while reporting for his newspaper. The gray area between implicit and explicit was Elliott's natural terrain. George Kennedy Young, by now chief of Middle East operations, waved the deal through. "Nick did all the negotiations," said Young. "I simply approved them."

Philby accepted the double job offer without hesitation. Here was an arrangement that suited everyone: the *Observer* and the *Economist* got an experienced reporter with good local contacts; MI6 got a veteran agent in a volatile part of the world whose cover as a journalist would enable him to travel freely; Elliott got his friend back in the saddle; and Philby got paid and an opportunity to start a new life in sunny Beirut.

Dick White, the new head of MI6, had led the hunt for the third man, but he did not try to prevent the rehiring of Philby. Indeed, at this stage he may have been unaware of it. After Macmillan's statement, the case against Philby had gone cold and, according to White's biographer, there was "no appetite for reopening old wounds." Though still convinced of Philby's guilt, and "irritated that Elliott should number himself among Philby's staunchest supporters," White is said to have shown "no emotion" when the subject of Philby was raised. But it is also possible that Elliott chose not to explain that Philby was back on the payroll. Senior MI6 officers enjoyed considerable latitude, and in the more remote stations they carried on their business with little supervision. Officers in Beirut believed that the new C was "unaware" of their activities and would have been "horrified if he knew." Some historians have speculated that White sent Philby to Beirut as part of a clever trap to lure him into making contact with Soviet intelligence. More likely, White did not know (and perhaps did not want to know) the full story, and Elliott did not want to tell him. The responsibility for bringing Philby in from the cold was down to one man. As Phillip Knightley writes: "It was Nicholas Elliott, his old friend, his most ardent defender in SIS who was giving him this chance to work his way back into the club."

Once again Elliott's and Philby's lives seemed to move in parallel: while Philby headed to the Middle East, Elliott took up a new job as MI6 station chief in Vienna. Usually so ebullient, Elliott could summon little enthusiasm for his new posting. Vienna, he wrote, "had an ersatz gaiety and smelled of corruption." The city seemed dowdy and drab, with few opportunities for high-grade espionage. His former school friend Peter Lunn preceded him in the post and bequeathed him a comfortable apartment overlooking the Belvedere Palace gardens, with room for his growing family. Lunn also left him a bad-tempered Slovene cook called Irene and a red Wolseley (a conspicuous vehicle for a spy since it was the only one of its kind in the city). He went skiing on weekends, enjoyed poking fun at his stodgy Viennese counterparts, and set about establishing a network of spies. But he was bored in Austria. "The climate of Vienna is not conducive to energy," he wrote.

The Beirut job finally put paid to the Philbys' marriage. "Haunted by Kim's life of treason" and agonized by the stress of his public acquittal, the discovery that her husband was leaving the country sent Aileen into terminal alcoholic decline. There was never any question that she and the children would accompany him to Beirut; she did not try to stop him, and if she had, it would have made no difference. Her psychiatrist became so alarmed by her disintegration that he had her briefly committed to a mental hospital. With the children at boarding school, Aileen shut herself up in the gloomy house in Crowborough, which, according to Flora Solomon, "she maintained in the hope of a reconciliation with her errant Kim." Philby told Aileen he would refund her household bills and left.

Beirut was exotic, tense, and dangerous, a salmagundi of races, religions, and politics rendered even more febrile by the rising tide of Arab nationalism and cold-war conflict. It was fertile ground for journalism in 1956 and an even better place for espionage. "Lebanon was the only Arab country without censorship and with good communications," wrote the newspaper correspondent Richard Beeston, who arrived in the city shortly before Philby. "So inevitably Beirut became the listening post for the region, with the St Georges [Hotel] and its bar its epicentre—a bazaar for the trading of information between diplomats, politicians, journalists and spies." Philby landed at the Beirut airport in August and made straight for the bar of the St. Georges.

The Beirut beat was a demanding one. Middle Eastern politics were as complex and volatile in 1956 as they are today. But as Philby knew from his years as a correspondent in civil-war Spain, there is no better cover job for a spy than that of journalist, a profession that enables the asking of direct, unsubtle, and impertinent questions about the most sensitive subjects without arousing suspicion. A topic of interest to readers of the *Observer* could, when explored in greater depth, be passed on to British intelligence. Philby began cultivating people—politicians, military officers, diplomats, and other journalists—who might prove useful as sources for journalism or espionage or both. The line between Philby's two occupations was blurred from the outset. At first he lived in a house rented by his father outside Beirut, where the elder Philby had been exiled after criticizing Ibn Saud's successor. When St John Philby returned to Saudi Arabia, Philby took a flat in the Muslim quarter of the city. Richard Beeston met Philby soon after his arrival in the Lebanese capital: "He was quintessentially English, relaxed and courteous, amusing—and this, combined with a rather painful stammer, made him pretty well irresistible to women. He could charm the birds out of the trees." But beneath the bonhomie Beeston sensed Philby's inner solitude. "He seemed a rather lonely, rumpled figure." He was not alone for long.

Eleanor Brewer was a sometime architect, amateur sculptor, and former Red Cross worker from Seattle, married to Sam Pope Brewer, the *New York Times* correspondent in Beirut. She was tall and slim, sweet natured, and restless. She had met her husband in wartime Istanbul, where he was reporting for the *New York Times* and she was working in the overseas branch of the Office of War Information. Nicholas Elliott had known them both in those years as another glamorous couple in the Istanbul throng. By 1956 Eleanor was forty-two, unhappily married, and bored. Beeston recalled her as a "rangy, steady-drinking American, who looked tough and sophisticated. Underneath she was a romantic, and politically naïve." Like most people who proclaim themselves free spirits, she was fiercely conventional. Sam Brewer had first encountered Philby while covering the Spanish civil war, so when the American newspaperman learned that his former colleague had arrived in Beirut, he was eager to extend a welcome. In early September Brewer left Beirut on an extended reporting trip and told his wife to keep an eye out for Philby: "If I should meet Kim I was to introduce him to our friends, and do what I could to help him," she later recalled. Eleanor's welcome to Philby would prove rather warmer than her husband had intended.

On September 12, 1956, Eleanor Brewer was drinking with some friends at the St. Georges when someone pointed out Kim Philby sitting at the bar. She sent a message via the waiter inviting him to join their party.

> What touched me first about Kim Philby was his loneliness. A certain old-fashioned reserve set him apart from the easy familiarity of the other journalists. He was then

forty-four, of medium height, very lean with a handsome heavily lined face. His eyes were an intense blue. . . . He had a gift of such intimacy that I found myself talking freely to him. I was very impressed by his beautiful manners. We took him under our wing. He soon became one of our closest friends.

Philby spent Christmas with the Brewers. Sam Brewer enjoyed discussing Middle Eastern politics with Philby; Philby enjoyed sleeping with his wife. The secret lovers met at a little café they called the Shaky Floor, although the shakiness of the floor may have been due to the amount they drank there. They shared picnics in the hills, smoked hubble-bubble pipes in the Arab coffeehouses, and exchanged love notes written in gushing teenage prose. "Kim was a delightful companion," Eleanor wrote. "I had never met a kinder, more interesting person in my entire life." Eleanor was besotted and blamed her husband for their deteriorating marriage. Sam was only interested in politics, she complained, and criticized her cooking: "My soufflés were never quite right." As in his other life, Philby reveled in the subterfuge, the secret messages and surreptitious meetings, the thrill of deception. While conducting his clandestine love affair, Philby discreetly checked for any signs of surveillance. No one was following him.

Philby's journalism from Beirut was solid, if unspectacular. When asked to write on a subject he considered too fluffy—such as Arabian slave girls—he used the pseudonym "Charles Garner." Even in journalism he embraced a double existence. He also began to collect information for his MI6 handlers. He possessed a "sound knowledge of their requirements." Much of his early intelligence work in Beirut involved chatting informally to senior Arab politicians and then "telling the British government what they really thought." MI6 was evidently satisfied: a year after Philby's arrival in Beirut, the visiting head of MI6's Middle East desk took him to lunch at an expensive restaurant overlooking the sea and told him his status was being confirmed and his retainer increased. "Anxious to be in their good books," Philby resolved to work "as conscientiously as possible" for MI6 while awaiting the inevitable call from the KGB.

Philby's Beirut habits were regular. At midday he would repair to the Normandie Hotel, less conspicuous and cheaper than the St. Georges, to down his first drink of the day, vodka with V8, open his post, and read the newspapers. One afternoon a chunky young man in his thirties, evidently a foreigner, approached Philby at his corner table and presented him with his card: "Petukhov, Soviet Trade Mission."

"I read your articles in the *Observer* and in *The Economist*, Mr Philby," he said. "I find them very deep. I sought you out to ask you for the favor of your time for a conversation. I am particularly interested in the prospects for a Common Market of the Arab countries."

Philby could have put an end to his double life at that moment. He could have explained to Petukhov that he had no interest in discussing Arab economics with him and so conveyed a message to the KGB that he was no longer in the game. Other agents recruited in the 1930s, including Anthony Blunt, had successfully disengaged from Soviet intelligence. He had a new life, a new lover, and two interesting, compatible, and remunerative jobs; with the protection of Nicholas Elliott, he was safe from further investigation by MI5; his reputation as a journalist and Middle East expert was growing. He could have rejected the approach from the KGB with impunity. Instead, he invited Petukhov to tea at his flat.

Philby would later frame his decision as one of ideological purity, consistent with the "total commitment to the Soviet Union" he had made at the age of twenty-one. He did what he did, in his own estimation, out of pure political conviction, the guiding principle of his life. He looked with disdain on others who had seen the horrors of Stalinism and abandoned ship. "I stayed the course," he wrote, "in the confident faith that the principles of the Revolution would outlive the aberration of individuals." Philby later claimed that he had experienced moments of doubt and that his views had been "influenced and modified, sometimes rudely, by the appalling events of my lifetime." But there is no evidence that he ever questioned the ideology he had discovered at Cambridge, changed his opinions, or seriously acknowledged the iniquities of practical communism. Philby never shared or discussed his views, either with friend or foe. Instead, he retained and sustained his faith, without the need for priests or fellow believers, in perfect isolation. Philby regarded himself as an ideologue and a loyalist; in truth, he was a dogmatist, valuing only one opinion, his own.

But there was more than politics in Philby's eager return to the embrace of the KGB. Philby *enjoyed* deception. Like secrecy, the erotic charge of infidelity can be hard to renounce. Some men like to parade their knowledge. Others revel in the possession of information that they decline to share, and the private sense of superiority that this brings. Philby was a faithless husband, but a kind lover, a good friend, a gentle father, and a generous host. He had a talent for tenderness. But he also relished withholding the truth from those he was closest to; there was the Philby they knew, and then there was the Philby only he knew. The alcohol helped maintain the double life, for an alcoholic has already become divorced from his or her real self, hooked on an artificial reality. Philby did not want to give up spying, and he probably could not have stopped if he had wanted to: he was addicted.

The day after their encounter at the Normandie, Petukhov arrived promptly at Philby's flat at three o'clock—it was a dangerous place for a rendezvous and one that would not be repeated. The ground rules were established. If Philby wanted a meeting, he would stand on his balcony holding a newspaper at a given hour; if he needed to see Petukhov urgently, he would be holding a book. Henceforth, Philby and his new case officer would meet at regular intervals, always after sunset, always in Beirut, always in some discreet corner of the city. The KGB residence in Beirut was "a hive of activity," according to Yuri Modin, with agents deployed throughout the Middle East. Philby was told that his first priority was to ascertain "the intentions of the United States and British governments in the area." He happily set to work.

In the autumn of 1956, Eleanor Brewer told her husband that she was leaving him. Sam Brewer, who had finally caught on to his wife's torrid affair, raised no objection, and Eleanor returned to Seattle with her daughter, telling Philby she would get a "Mexican Divorce," which was quicker and cheaper than the American variety since the spouse did not need to be present. The only remaining obstacle was Aileen Philby.

Since Philby's departure, Aileen had hurtled downhill. She was virtually penniless, deeply unhappy, and usually drunk. Philby complained of Aileen's "idleness" and claimed she spent most of her time going to point-to-point races. He refused to send her more cash until she explained what she was spending it on: "No receipts, no money," he said. She spent longer and longer periods in psychiatric hospitals. Her old friend Flora Solomon dispatched Stuart Lisbona, of the Marks & Spencer pensions department, to keep a "helpful eye" on "poor Aileen . . . abandoned by her husband."

On December 12, 1957, Aileen Philby was discovered dead in the bedroom of the house in Crowborough. Her friends believed she had killed herself with drink and pills. Her psychiatrist suspected, fantastically, that she "might have been murdered" by Philby because she knew too much. The coroner ruled she had died from heart failure, myocardial degeneration, tuberculosis, and a respiratory infection, having contracted influenza. Her alcoholism undoubtedly accelerated her death. She was forty-seven.

Elliott was deeply upset when news of Aileen's tragic end reached him in Vienna. She had shown "considerable strength of character" throughout her suffering, and he would always remember her as she had once been, "a charming woman, and a loving wife and mother." But he could not bring himself to blame Philby for her death, which he ascribed to Aileen's "grave mental problem." Not so Flora Solomon, who held Philby directly and personally responsible. "I endeavoured to strike him from my memory," she wrote. "This, however, was not to be."

Richard Beeston and his wife, Moyra, were Christmas shopping in Beirut's Bab Idriss when they were spotted by Kim Philby, who rushed across the road: "I have wonderful news darlings," he said excitedly. "I want you to come and celebrate." Philby dragged the Beestons off to the Normandie, plied them with drink, and then produced a telegram from England informing him of Aileen's death. It was, he said, a "wonderful escape," as he was now free to marry "a wonderful American girl." The Beestons were "stunned."

The Furse family took over all the arrangements for her funeral back in England, which Philby did not attend. The five Philby children never knew where their mother was buried.

It took another seven months for Eleanor to obtain her divorce. When it was finalized, she at once sent a telegram to Philby, who cabled back: "Clever wonderful you fly back happily song in heart life is miraculous greatest love kim." The same morning, Philby rushed to the St. Georges to find Sam Brewer. Their conversation, as described by Eleanor herself, is one of the classic exchanges between a cuckold and an adulterer.

PHILBY: "I've come to tell you that I've had a cable from Eleanor. She has got her divorce and I want you to be the first person to know that I'm going to marry her."
BREWER: "That sounds like the best possible solution. What do you make of the situation in Iraq?"

Kim Philby and Eleanor Brewer were married in the Holborn registry office in London on January 24, 1959, just over a year after Aileen's death. Nicholas and Elizabeth Elliott returned from Vienna to attend the ceremony, along with other MI6 colleagues past and present. Elliott had not forgotten Aileen, but he swiftly took Philby's new wife to his heart: "Eleanor was in many ways not dissimilar to Aileen," he wrote. "She had integrity, courage and humour. Like Aileen, she could not be described as intellectual but she was certainly intelligent." The couple spent their honeymoon in Rome, where Philby wrote: "We shall take a house in the

mountains: she will paint; I will write; peace and stability at last."
Eleanor was his third wife, and the second to know nothing of his
true allegiance.

Back in Beirut, the newlyweds moved into a fifth-floor flat on
the rue Kantari with a large balcony overlooking the mountains
and sea that offered a "ringside view" of the civil war now engulf-
ing Lebanon. "He would sit in his terrace at night and listen to the
guns going off," Eleanor recalled. The flat was spacious enough
to accommodate all their children during holidays from boarding
school. Despite the grim circumstances of Aileen's death and Philby's swift remarriage, his children adored him, and he remained
an attentive and caring father.

And so began a period of domestic harmony, unchallenging
journalism, and discreet international espionage. There were parties and picnics and much alcohol. Eleanor described a "leisurely
daily circuit of shopping and gossip," starting at the Normandie
("Kim treated the place like a club") before moving on to the
St. Georges "to see what the other journalists were up to." Philby
hinted to his new wife that he was "connected with British intelligence" but naturally provided no details. He would disappear
from time to time. It never occurred to Eleanor to ask where he
had been. Compared to her first husband, Philby took a relaxed,
even casual, approach to journalism. "He seemed to write his
weekly articles fast and painlessly—often dictating them to me."
Philby's fellow hacks considered him lazy yet "compelling a certain respect," in part because he appeared to wear his responsibilities so lightly.

Philby devoted more energy (though not much more) to intelligence gathering. A fellow journalist noticed that he was often
to be seen in the company of "men whose ostensible jobs as businessmen, bankers, university professors, consultants for foreign
companies, and so forth, did not wholly account for their insid-
ers' preoccupation with Arab politics." Whatever information of
value he gleaned was handed over to Paulson of MI6; then Philby
passed the same information to Petukhov of the KGB, with whatever additional intelligence might be helpful to the Soviet cause.

On both sides of the iron curtain, opinion in intelligence circles was divided over Philby's usefulness. Yuri Modin, still monitoring Agent Stanley, was enthusiastic. "The information he supplied on British policies in the region proved invaluable to our government in our relations with Arab countries. . . . I myself read several of his reports, noting with satisfaction that he had not lost his brilliant touch." Philby's information "attracted much attention at the top." Yet some in Moscow complained that Philby was simply peddling recycled journalism. "There was criticism," Modin noted, "concerning his tendency to send us hard news wrapped up in beautifully-written political evaluations. We did not need this because we had our own people to make evaluations. . . . The KGB had its own experts here in Moscow and in the capitals, highly trained Arabists all." This is an old trick of espionage: when spies obtain knowledge but not secrets, they tend to dress up mere information to make it look like intelligence; and when they do not have solid information, they fabricate it. Similar grumbling could be heard in parts of Broadway, particularly among the Arabists of MI6. "You could have read it all in the *Economist* last week," said one London analyst after looking through Philby's latest submission. "He's got a lot of it wrong as well. It's invented. He's taking us to the cleaners." Philby's supporters, notably Elliott and Young, ignored the carping and circulated Philby's reports as the latest penetrating insights from Our Man in Beirut.

In truth, Philby was going soft and drinking hard, content to do a little journalism, a little espionage on the side for both sides, but nothing too strenuous. He was coasting, it seemed, toward quiet and comfortable irrelevance as a second-rate journalist and a minor spy.

Then Nicholas Elliott arrived in Beirut as the new station chief of MI6, and the wheel of their friendship turned again.

Chapter Fifteen

The Fox Who Came to Stay

BEIRUT WAS ANOTHER PLUM POSTING. THE CRABB AFFAIR HAD done Nicholas Elliott's career no lasting damage, and he had performed well during his brief stint in Vienna. Indeed, within MI6 he was still considered a highflier, the leader of the Robber Barons. It was said that, "but for his preference for operations, not administration, he might well have been appointed C." Elliott was pleased to be moving on from Austria. "I have no wish to be churlish about our time in Vienna," he wrote (Elliott's politeness even extended to cities), "nevertheless we were not unhappy" to leave. With the Middle East heating up, Beirut was an important step up the intelligence ladder. The Elliotts traveled by boat from Genoa, and as they pulled into port, Elliott marveled at how little Beirut had changed since their last visit in 1944. Elizabeth had been his secretary then, and he had courted her over lunch at the Hotel Lucullus, whose restaurant was famed for its French-Lebanese cuisine. As soon as they landed, Elliott announced with romantic fanfare, they would be lunching at the Lucullus again. No sooner were they seated than a beaming Kim Philby appeared and wrapped Elliott in a welcoming hug. "It was a most agreeable reunion," recalled Elliott, who pretended that the meeting had been accidental. He was taking over as station chief from Paul Paulson, but Philby was the person he wanted to see on his first day in Beirut. They were joined by Eleanor, an "excellent bouillabaisse" was served, more bottles were opened, glasses were raised and drained. Elliott happily turned to Philby: "Fill me in, old boy."

The Elliotts moved into a flat on the top floor of the Immeu-
ble Tabet on the rue Verdun, on the border between the Christian
and Muslim quarters, not far from the Philbys. The apartment
had "cool, high rooms, wide balconies and marble floors" and was
"perfect in every way." That evening, as they listened to the muezzin's call wafting over the city, Elliott "thought nostalgically of the
gentle sound of the Mullahs calling the faithful to prayer from
the minarets of Istanbul many years before." He was as happy as
he had ever been and back in his element, in a foreign city seeth-
ing with espionage possibilities, fighting communist aggression
alongside his oldest friend, his most trusted colleague, and the
man who would explain to him the mysteries of the Middle East.
Once more they would be "two old friends in crown service on the
frontiers."

As Eleanor Philby observed, Elliott had hitherto been a "European specialist and knew little of Arab politics. He came green to
the Middle East." He had much to learn, as he admitted: "Apart
from all the political complexities and the plotting—almost any
major financial or political intrigue in the Middle East at that time
had its roots in Beirut—you had to get to grips with the Lebanese
character. The labyrinths of Lebanese politics were of daunting
complexity." Philby would be his guide, "his personal adviser."

The arrival of a new spy chief did not go unnoticed among
Beirut's journalists. One left this portrait of Elliott:

> He was a thin, spare man with a reputation as a shrewd
> operator whose quick humorous glance behind round
> glasses gave a clue to his sardonic mind. In manner and
> dress he suggested an Oxbridge don at one of the smarter
> colleges, but with a touch of worldly ruthlessness not al-
> ways evident in academic life. Foreigners liked him, ap-
> preciating his bonhomie and his fund of risqué stories.
> He got on particularly well with Americans. The formal,
> ladylike figure of his wife in the background contributed
> to the feeling that British intelligence in Beirut was being
> directed by a gentleman.

Elliott and Philby were once again inseparable, professionally and socially. The pace of Philby's intelligence gathering, hitherto leisurely, even lackadaisical, suddenly became frenetic, as Elliott "put Kim to work, setting him targets, sending him on trips, requesting reports which were then combed over in conversation." During his first four years in Beirut, Philby had ventured outside Lebanon only as far as Syria, and once to visit his father in Saudi Arabia. Now, at Elliott's behest, he scrambled all over the Middle East, ostensibly on newspaper assignments, to Jordan, Iraq, Egypt, Kuwait, and Yemen. The hitherto indolent journalist was a reporting whirlwind. But a careful observer might have spotted that his output fell far short of his industriousness; he was visiting many more places and people than he was writing about, at least publicly. In the first nine months of 1960, he filed just six stories for the *Observer*. One editor from the *Economist* paid him a visit, noted how seldom he seemed to write for the magazine, and casually asked him if he found it difficult "serving two masters." Philby was momentarily speechless, until he realized she was referring to his newspaper employers, not his espionage.

Philby delivered a torrent of information to Elliott, "mainly political and personality reporting" and "reports about political developments in most Arab states." The two men would huddle together for long debriefing sessions. "They used to meet once or twice a week," wrote Eleanor. "Vanishing into another room and leaving me to gossip with Elizabeth." Elliott's support and confidence was demonstrated in other, more practical ways. Toward the end of 1960, Philby returned home late one night, clutching a sheaf of hundred-dollar bills. "Oh boy," he said, happily scattering them around the room. "This is going to make our Christmas!" Eleanor had no doubt the money came from Elliott, an early Christmas present for his best friend and most industrious agent.

Some have claimed that Elliott's energetic deployment of Philby was merely a ruse to see if "greater participation in the British intelligence effort" would reveal contact with the Soviets. There is little evidence to support this theory. If Elliott had

suspected Philby, he would have put a tail on him and easily discovered his meetings with Petukhov. He did not. Dick White's
instructions were to "keep an eye on Philby," but there was no suggestion that he should be investigated, probed, or put under surveillance. White seems to have accepted, at least outwardly, that
the Philby case was closed. Far from doubting him, Elliott trusted
Philby completely, and his determination to employ him to the
fullest reflected only "Elliott's overt and innocent friendship" and
an admiration stretching back twenty years.

Philby, in turn, was buoyed by his return to active intelligence
work and "seemed to relish the confidence reposed in him" by
his old friend. Eleanor noticed the change in her husband's demeanor following Elliott's arrival: "I had begun to feel that Kim
was bored with journalism, and that writing articles for newspapers did not wholly satisfy him. His meetings with [Elliott] were
more like *real* work." What Philby considered his real work, of
course, consisted of passing to Soviet intelligence every scrap of
information he could gather, both on his travels and from Elliott.
Their relationship was running along the old tracks in more ways
than Elliott knew.

Philby's value as a Soviet agent increased in direct proportion
to his activities as a British agent, and as Elliott's informant he
was privy to important information, including the identities of
MI6 contacts in the region, as well as sympathetic Arab politicians
and officials on the payroll. Elliott achieved a remarkable coup by
being able to "broker a deal with the director of Mossad [the Israeli intelligence agency] for the exchange of intelligence on the
Middle East." Philby did not know everything that Elliott knew;
but from the instructions issued by Elliott he at least knew what
MI6 wanted to know, and that, in the negative world of spying, is
almost as valuable. Yuri Modin was pleased with Agent Stanley:
"In all he served us well."

Elliott and Philby spied, plotted, and socialized together in a
family friendship that intensified over time. Eleanor and Elizabeth
became as close as their husbands. On weekends the two families
shared a bathing cabin named "Acapulco" on Khalde Beach with

Colonel Alec Brodie, a much-wounded, one-eyed, pipe-smoking war veteran who was the military attaché at the embassy. During school holidays, the Elliott and Philby children mixed happily together. Elliott's teenagers, Mark and Claudia, both liked Philby, an avuncular, amusing presence. "He was one of the few adults to take me seriously," Mark Elliott recalled.

Despite the rising political tension, Beirut was still a happy playground for expatriates and tourists, a place where, in Elliott's words, one could "ski in the mornings and swim in the afternoons" and enjoy hillside picnics in between. The fun did not stop at nightfall but extended long into the night with an endless round of cocktails and dinners. As they had in Switzerland, the Elliotts played host to a stream of visitors. One of the earliest was Ian Fleming, who called unannounced from the airport in November 1960 and invited himself to stay. Fleming was en route to Kuwait, on a lucrative assignment from the Kuwait Oil Company to write about the country. By now a hugely successful writer, Fleming continued his freelance intelligence activities and explained to Elliott that Naval Intelligence was keen to learn more about the defenses of the Iraqi port at Basra. Elliott "promised to look after it." Elliott asked for a favor in return: A rare fall of rain in Kuwait had brought out a crop of delicious white truffles. Would Fleming send back a box? Here was a perfect example of Elliott-style espionage: a little spying in return for truffles. That evening Fleming announced he was meeting "an Armenian" in the Place des Canons; Elliott got the distinct impression that the creator of 007 had in fact "arranged to see a pornographic film in full color and sound."

As the months passed, Elliott and Philby socialized together more and more, meeting regularly "at parties for British diplomats and journalists." The Elliott family photographs from the summer of 1960 are filled with images of the intermingled Philby and Elliott clans, enjoying Beirut's beach life and nightlife: Philby is in most pictures, in bathing trunks, T-shirt, or suit, smiling, tanned, and frequently very obviously drunk.

Philby's behavior was becoming increasingly outrageous, in

ways reminiscent of the antics of Guy Burgess. "Out of fun rather than malice," wrote Elliott, he "would make some remark well calculated to stop the conversation dead in its tracks. Such remarks served to lighten the atmosphere of a dreary party but were often the cause of severe umbrage." Elliott egged him on and recalled one particularly spectacular episode of Philby devilry that "caused a chain reaction of offense unparalleled in my experience." In social fallout the Cocktail Party from Hell came close to the Dinner Party from Hell.

> It was at a cocktail party given in our flat by Elizabeth and myself when my parents, then pretty elderly, had come out to stay. We had invited some forty people, including the Philbys and our ambassador, Sir Moore Crosthwaite. There was an unusual pause in the babble of conversation during which Philby was heard to remark to Moore: "Don't you think Anne [the wife of a member of the embassy staff who was standing next to him] has the finest breasts in Beirut?" Moore was undoubtedly annoyed because he thought that the breasts of the wife of a member of his staff were not an appropriate subject of conversation at a cocktail party. Anne, while doubtless justifiably proud of that part of her anatomy, was annoyed at having it discussed in public and in particular with the ambassador. Her husband was annoyed as he agreed with the ambassador that his wife's breasts were an off-target subject for cocktail party gossip. Jane, the wife of another member of the embassy staff, was annoyed because she thought she had better breasts than Anne. Jane's husband was annoyed possibly because he thought his wife had been slighted. Eleanor Philby was more than just annoyed because she was not particularly well endowed in that respect and comparisons are odious. And, finally, Elizabeth was annoyed because she felt the whole party was getting out of hand. In fact the only person who thought the whole episode was a huge joke was Kim Philby himself.

And Nicholas Elliott, who regaled listeners with it for the rest of his life.

Privately, Elliott worried about Philby's alcohol intake. He had seen Aileen drink herself into the grave. Philby's mother, Dora, was drinking a bottle of gin a day by the time of her death in 1957. Elliott feared the effect Philby's boozing might be having on his health, and on his children. "He had no inhibitions about getting drunk in front of them," Elliott noted. Philby even trained his young son Harry to mix a "fierce martini."

Philby and Elliott both worked assiduously to cultivate Americans, particularly those involved in intelligence, with which Beirut, as a cold-war battleground, was plentifully supplied. Relations between the CIA and MI6 had come under intense strain after the Burgess and Maclean defections and the accusations against Philby, but by 1960 the relationship was back on an even keel. In some quarters of Washington, suspicion of Philby still lingered: at the FBI J. Edgar Hoover remained convinced of his guilt, as did Bill Harvey. But within the CIA it was generally agreed that if MI6 considered him trustworthy, and Harold Macmillan had said he was innocent, then Philby must be clean. Angleton had risen to new heights in the CIA. In 1954 he was named chief of the counterintelligence staff, a position he would retain for the next two decades. As America's premier spy catcher, he was becoming "recognized as the dominant counterintelligence figure in the non-communist world." More gaunt and aloof than ever, Angleton trusted few and mistrusted most, inspiring a peculiar mixture of awe and fear among his colleagues. He later claimed to have uncovered what Philby was up to, but his actions clearly indicate otherwise. According to one historian, Philby was still in amicable contact with Angleton from time to time, "and used those opportunities to reassure his American friend of his innocence." If the CIA had suspected Philby of being a Soviet spy, then Angleton's operatives in Beirut would have been under instructions to avoid him, watch him, and, if possible, catch him. Instead, Philby mixed freely among the throngs of American spies.

One of the most flamboyant of these was Wilbur Crane Eveland, a boisterous intelligence veteran from the West Coast who favored full morning dress and arrived in Beirut at around the same time as Philby as a special agent for Allen Dulles, the CIA chief. Working independently of the CIA station, Eveland's role appears to have been that of anticommunist paymaster in the Middle East: he bankrolled CIA efforts to overthrow the Soviet-sponsored government in Syria, provided support to the Saud dynasty in Riyadh, and propped up Lebanon's pro-Western president, Camille Chamoun. "He travelled regularly to the presidential palace with his briefcase stuffed with Lebanese pounds," according to Richard Beeston, "returning late at night to the American embassy to replenish the slush fund." Eveland had met Philby through the Brewers (Eveland and Eleanor were both from Spokane), and they immediately struck up a friendship. He knew Philby had links with British intelligence and saw him as someone "whose brain was there to be picked," an attitude that was entirely reciprocated by Philby. Eleanor later told the CIA that Philby had once remarked that "all he had to do was to have one evening with Bill Eveland in Beirut and before it was over he would know of all his operations."

Philby established a similarly cozy relationship with Edgar J. Applewhite, the clever, sharp-suited, Yale-educated CIA station chief sent to Lebanon in 1958. Applewhite knew of the earlier suspicions surrounding Philby but cultivated him nonetheless, at first guardedly, later wholeheartedly. The American concluded Philby was "much too sophisticated to give his allegiance to such a doctrinaire business as Marxism," and besides, the Anglophile Applewhite "liked to talk to Philby about Arab problems" and enjoyed the Englishman's erudite company. The American intelligence community was, if anything, even more welcoming to Philby than the British one, for this charming, openhanded Englishman seemed trustworthy, the sort of Englishman who had helped America to win the Second World War and was now helping her to win the cold war. "Philby was friendly with all the Yanks in Beirut," George Young later noted. "A lot of them babbled. He was pretty good at getting them to talk."

One American spy talked more than any of the others and would be drawn into the heart of the Philby-Elliott circle. Miles Copeland Jr. was a drawling jazz musician from the Deep South, a wartime spy, a former CIA agent, and now a public relations executive and espionage fixer. The son of a doctor from Birmingham, Alabama, Copeland had spent his teenage years gambling on the riverboats before dramatically changing tack and heading to the University of Alabama to study advanced mathematics. A gifted trumpeter, he played in an otherwise all-black radio band and ended up in the Glenn Miller Orchestra. Copeland joined the OSS soon after Pearl Harbor and headed to London with the other young Americans eager to learn the spying game. There he became a close friend of James Angleton (who left him a bequest in his will) and went on to become one of the most effective (and dubious) operatives in the CIA: he helped to organize a coup against Iran's democratically elected prime minister in 1953 and tried to steer his friend Colonel Nasser of Egypt away from Moscow. Copeland shared Angleton's views of America's role in the world, believing that the CIA had a right and a duty to steer political and economic events in the Middle East: "The United States had to face and define its policy in all three sectors that provided the root causes of American interests in the region: the Soviet threat, the birth of Israel, and petroleum." By 1956 he was living in Beirut, a partner in the industrial consultancy and PR firm Copeland and Eichelberger, no longer officially in the CIA but alert to every aspect of agency activities and with access to the daily cables passing through Applewhite's office. Far from hiding his intelligence links, Copeland paraded them as part of his business pitch.

Copeland had "known and liked" Philby since 1944 when, alongside Angleton, he had studied the art of counterespionage under Philby's tutelage on Ryder Street in London. Their friendship was renewed in Beirut, and Copeland would later claim to have known Philby "better than anyone else, excepting two or three British intelligence officers." Elliott also relished the piratical Copeland, "a humorous and highly intelligent extrovert [and] a most colourful and entertaining friend." The three families formed an intense triangular bond: Eleanor Philby, Elizabeth Elliott, and Lorraine Copeland, Miles's outspoken Scottish wife, studied archaeology in the same class at the American University in Beirut and went on digs; their husbands plotted and drank together; their children played tennis, swam, and went skiing together. The Copelands lived in a large hilltop house (known to the local Lebanese, with blunt precision, as the "CIA House"), which they filled with their friends and their children (one of whom, Stewart Copeland, would go on to become the drummer in the band the Police). As Beeston recalled, Copeland was the life and soul: "Generous, outrageous, always fun, he never took himself too seriously and had a thoroughly irreverent approach to the intelligence profession." He was also, in Elliott's estimation, "one of the most indiscreet men I have ever met"—which endeared him even more to Elliott and Philby, for different reasons.

Copeland was an incurable gossip and an unstoppable show-off. "I could trust him with any secret that had no entertainment value," wrote Elliott. What neither Philby nor Elliott knew was that Copeland was also a paid spy for James Angleton, their friend. As the chief of CIA counterintelligence, Angleton maintained his own network of informers, and Copeland was one of them, though he appeared nowhere on CIA accounts. Their arrangement was simple: Copeland would forward his (very large) entertainment bills to Angleton for payment; in return, Copeland kept Angleton abreast of what was going on in Beirut.

Many years later Copeland claimed that Angleton had specifically instructed him to "keep an eye on Philby" and "report signs that he might be spying for the Soviets"; he even claimed to have sent a Lebanese security officer to follow Philby but found that the Englishman was "still practising his old tradecraft [and] invariably shook off his tail." Like Angleton's later assertions, Copeland's claim to have monitored Philby at Angleton's behest is almost certainly untrue. He was a practiced fabulist, given to "entertaining and colourful invention," in Elliott's words. If he had really put Philby under surveillance, then he would easily have caught him. But he didn't, for the very obvious (and very embarrassing) reason that he did not believe Philby *was* a Soviet spy, and neither did Angleton.

The major players in the Philby story were invariably wise after the event. Spies, even more than most people, invent the past to cover up mistakes. The Philby case has probably attracted more retrospective conspiracy theories than any other in the history of espionage: Dick White of MI6 was running a ruse to trap him; Nicholas Elliott was secretly jousting with him; James Angleton suspected him and set Miles Copeland to spy on him; Philby's fellow journalists (another tribe adept at misremembering the past) later claimed that they had always seen something fishy in his behavior. Even Eleanor, his wife, would later look back and claim to have discovered clues to his real nature. No one likes to admit they have been utterly conned. The truth was simpler, as it almost always is: Philby was spying on everyone, and no one was spying on him, because he fooled them all.

Every few weeks, on a Wednesday evening, Philby would stand with a newspaper on his balcony; later the same night, he would slip away to a nondescript backstreet restaurant in the Armenian quarter called Vrej (Armenian for "revenge"), where Petukhov would be waiting.

For Kim Philby these were days of professional satisfaction and domestic tranquillity. Not since 1949 had his double lives coexisted so comfortably and invisibly: admired and feted by American and British intelligence officials, protected by Elliott and Angleton, paid regularly by the *Observer* and the *Economist* and secretly by MI6 and the KGB. Evenings were spent in a social whirl on the Anglo-American diplomatic circuit. On the rare occasions they stayed in, Philby would cook and then read German poetry to his wife in "a melodious voice" without a stutter. The happy household was completed by the addition of an exotic and unlikely pet, after some friends bought a baby fox cub from a Bedouin in the Jordan Valley and presented it to the Philbys. They called it Jackie and reared it by hand. The animal slept on the sofa and obeyed commands, like a dog. Jackie also shared Philby's taste for alcohol, "lapping up" whiskey from a saucer. "She was affectionate and playful, cantering round the top of the parapet of our balcony." Philby found the animal "hopelessly endearing" and wrote a sentimental article for *Country Life* entitled "The Fox Who Came to Stay."

These were the "happiest years," wrote Eleanor.

Philby's world of contented marriage and secret duplicity was about to fall apart, with two deaths, one defection, and the unmasking of a Soviet spy within British intelligence who had nothing whatsoever to do with Kim Philby.

Chapter Sixteen

A Most Promising Officer

ST JOHN PHILBY, THAT REBEL TRADITIONALIST, ATTENDED AN Orientalists' conference in Moscow in the summer of 1960, then the Lord's cricket test match in London. On his way back to Saudi Arabia, he stopped off to visit his son in Beirut. At seventy-five the older Philby was as cantankerous and complicated as ever. He checked in to the Normandie Hotel, where he was "treated with the deference due to an Eastern potentate." Nicholas Elliott threw a lunch party for him, not without trepidation, knowing the elder Philby's capacity for extreme and unprovoked rudeness. "Elizabeth and I were among the few English people to whom St John Philby was prepared to be civil." To Elliott's surprise, the lunch was a social and diplomatic success. Humphrey Trevelyan, the British ambassador to Iraq, who was staying with the Elliotts, "drew the old man out into telling us the story of his relationship with Ibn Saud." The Philbys, the Copelands, and several other friends attended this "memorable occasion" lubricated by a small river of Lebanese wine. Elliott described the ensuing events: St John Philby "left at tea time, had a nap, made a pass at the wife of a member of the embassy staff in a night club, had a heart attack, and died." The last words of this brilliant and impossible man were "God, I'm bored." He left behind a shelf of scholarly works, two families, a black-throated partridge named after him (*Alectoris philbyi*), and an enduring trail of notoriety.

The relationship between father and son, Elliott reflected, had been "a mixture of love and hate." Philby admired and feared his father, whose domination, he felt, had caused his stammer. Back in the 1930s, he had spied on St John while reporting to Soviet intelligence that his father was "not completely well in the head." But they had grown closer in later life, particularly after Kim's move to the Middle East. Philby told Elliott that his father had once advised him: "If you feel strongly enough about anything you must have the guts to go through with it no matter what any-one might think." Both Philbys had certainly done that. Kim later wrote that had his father lived to learn the truth about him, he would have been "thunderstruck, but by no means disapproving." That verdict is questionable. The elder Philby was a contrarian, a rule breaker, and something of an intellectual thug, but he was no traitor. Even so, he had always supported his son, driven his ambi-tion, and undoubtedly planted the seeds of his sedition.

Kim buried St John Philby, with full Islamic rites under his Muslim name, and then disappeared into the bars of Beirut. El-liott noted that Philby "went out of circulation for days." Eleanor was more specific: "He drank himself senseless" and emerged from this ferocious drinking bout a changed man, frailer in both body and spirit. Philby's mother, Dora, had always doted on him, while his relationship with St John was often tense; yet St John's death affected him far more. "Kim seemed overwhelmed by his fa-ther's death," wrote Richard Beeston. His moorings began to slip.

A few months earlier, the British intelligence community in Beirut had been enlivened by the arrival of a new and glamor-ous addition to their ranks. At thirty-eight the man born George Behar had lived several lives already. Born in Rotterdam in 1922 to a Dutch mother and Egyptian-Jewish father, as a teenager he had joined the anti-Nazi resistance in the Netherlands, endured internment, and then disguised himself as a monk and fled to London, where he joined MI6, trained as an interrogator in multiple languages, and changed his name to the more English-sounding George Blake. After the war he was posted to Korea to set up an MI6 intelligence network but was captured by the advancing communist forces of North Korea soon after his arrival and held in captivity for three years. Finally emerging in 1953, Blake was welcomed back by MI6 as a returning hero and sent to Berlin as a case officer working under Elliott's friend Peter Lunn, tasked with recruiting Soviet intelligence officers as double agents. With his Egyptian blood and gift for languages, Blake was considered ideal material for a Middle East posting, and in 1960 he was enrolled in the Middle Eastern Centre for Arabic Studies, the language school in the hills outside Beirut run by the Foreign Office. The center offered intensive eighteen-month courses in Arabic for diplomats, international businessmen, graduates, and intelligence officers. The Lebanese regarded it as a spy school. With his sterling war record and his experience as a prisoner in North Korea, Blake was a minor celebrity in intelligence circles, and when the handsome young MI6 officer arrived in Beirut with his two sons and a pregnant wife, he was eagerly embraced by Anglo-American spy society.

Elliott considered George Blake "a most promising officer" and a credit to the service, "a good-looking fellow, tall and with excellent manners and universally popular." He was stunned, therefore, to receive a message from London in April informing him that Blake was a Soviet spy who must be tricked into returning to Britain, where he would be interrogated, arrested, and tried for treason.

Blake had been "turned" during his North Korean captivity. In detention he had read the works of Karl Marx and found what he thought was truth. But "it was the relentless bombing of small Korean villages by enormous American flying fortresses" that triggered his wholehearted conversion to communism. "I felt I was on the wrong side." British snobbery and prejudice may have played a part in his embrace of revolution, for as a foreign-born Jew, Blake was never fully admitted to the MI6 club. "He doesn't belong in the service," sniffed one colleague. Blake considered himself a "man of no class," but in the long intelligence tradition he had wanted to marry his secretary, Iris Peake, the upper-crust daughter of an Old Etonian Conservative MP. The relationship ran aground on the immovable British class system. "He was in love with her, but could not possibly marry her because of his circumstances," wrote his wife, Gillian, who believed the breakup had sharpened his resentment of the British establishment. In Berlin Blake contacted the KGB, under the guise of recruiting spies within the Soviet service, and began passing over reams of top secret and highly damaging information, including details of numerous covert operations such as the Berlin tunnel, a plot to eavesdrop on the Soviets from underground. At night he copied out Peter Lunn's index cards, listing and identifying every MI6 spy in Germany. Blake betrayed an estimated four hundred agents, sending an untold number to their deaths. Soon after his arrival in Beirut, Blake established contact with Pavel Yefimovich Nedosekin, the KGB head of station, who gave him a telephone number to call in case of an emergency—a moment that was, though neither knew it, imminent.

Early in 1961 a Polish spy with a large mustache and an extravagant ego defected in Berlin. Lieutenant Colonel Michael Goleniewski had been deputy head of military counterintelligence and chief of the technical and scientific section of the Polish intelligence service. In the 1950s he passed Polish secrets to the Soviets. Then, in 1959, he began anonymously passing Polish and Soviet secrets to the CIA, which passed them on to MI6. Goleniewski was a fantasist (he would later claim to be the tsarevich Alexei of Russia), but some of his intelligence was first rate, including the revelation that a Soviet spy code-named "Lambda" was operating within British intelligence. And he had proof: copies of three MI6 documents that this spy had handed to his Soviet handlers. MI6 worked out that only ten people, in Warsaw and Berlin, could have had access to all three pieces of paper: one of them was George Blake. By the spring of 1961, MI6 was "90 per cent sure" that Blake was "Lambda." Dick White sent a cable to Elliott instructing him that Blake should be lured "to London immediately, on the pretext of discussing a future posting." For once, Elliott did not tell his friend Kim Philby what was going on. The trap for George Blake was baited and set for Saturday, March 25.

A direct summons to London would have alerted Blake to the danger. Instead, Elliott contrived a chance meeting. On the morning of the twenty-fifth, Elliott's secretary called on the Blakes and told them that she had a spare ticket to an amateur production of *Charley's Aunt*. Blake's wife was busy looking after a sick child, and the secretary wondered "whether Blake would like to accompany her." Blake reluctantly agreed to take a break from his studies and spend a few hours watching British people performing this most English of plays. During the interval, Blake and the secretary repaired to the bar with the other thirsty expats and found Elliott and Elizabeth. "In the course of conversation, Elliott drew me aside and said he was glad I happened to be there as this had saved him a trip up the mountain to see me. He had received a letter from Head Office with instructions for me to return to London for a few days' consultation in connection with a new appointment. It suggested that I should travel on Easter Monday so as to be available in London on Tuesday morning."

The encounter was staged to allay suspicion: an unplanned meeting at a bar, not a directive; a leisurely letter, not an urgent telegram; a suggestion of when he might like to come to London, not an order. Yet Blake was alarmed. He was in the middle of his language course (for which MI6 was paying) and about to take some important exams. He would be returning to London on holiday in July. What was the urgency? Blake called the emergency number Nedosekin had given him. They met later that evening on a beach near Beirut. Nedosekin said he would consult Moscow Center: Blake held a valid Syrian visa, and if necessary he could be across the border in a few hours and then whisked to Moscow. But when they met again the next day, Nedosekin was reassuring: "Moscow saw no cause for concern. The KGB's enquiries had failed to reveal a leak: Blake should return to London, as requested."

Before heading to England, Blake paid a last visit to Elliott, to say good-bye and collect some money for his airfare. Elliott was as jovial as ever, but as Blake was leaving, the MI6 station chief asked him whether he would like to be booked into St Ermin's Hotel, just a few yards from MI6 headquarters, for the duration of his London visit. Blake politely declined, explaining that he planned to stay with his mother in Radlett, north of London. Elliott pressed the point, insisting it "would be more convenient to stay at the hotel." St Ermin's is the spy hotel: it was where Krivitsky was debriefed and Philby was recruited; it was just yards from MI6 headquarters, bristling with intelligence officers, and probably the easiest place in London to keep tabs on a suspected traitor. Why was Elliott so insistent he should stay there, rather than with his mother in rural Herefordshire? "For a moment a shadow of a doubt passed my mind but it passed away again," Blake wrote. Elliott was probably just being helpful.

Dick White had seen Philby slip through his fingers in 1951; a decade later, he was not going to make the same mistake with Blake. On arriving in London, Blake was escorted to the MI6 house in Carlton Gardens, ushered into an upstairs room (which was bugged), and told that "a few matters had cropped up about his time in Berlin that needed to be ironed out." Elliott had told him he was coming back to discuss a future appointment; there had been no mention of the past. Blake now realized, with grim certainty, what was at hand: "I was in deep trouble." On the first day of interrogation he stonewalled as a trio of MI6 officers chipped away at his explanations; on the second, as the pressure mounted and he was shown evidence of his own espionage, he began to wobble. "It wasn't hostile, but it was persistent." Blake was now in no doubt that MI6 knew he was guilty. On day three one of the interrogators remarked, in a friendly manner, that Blake must have been tortured by the North Koreans into confessing he was a British intelligence officer and then blackmailed into working as a communist spy. It was all perfectly understandable. Then Blake snapped.

"No, nobody tortured me! No, nobody blackmailed me! I myself approached the Soviets and offered my services to them of my own accord."

Blake's pride could simply not allow him to accept the suggestion that he was spying for anything other than the loftiest ideological motives. Perhaps the same tactic might have flushed out Philby a decade earlier; then again, Blake lacked Philby's innate duality. "The game was up," he wrote. Over the ensuing days, his confession tumbled out in a cathartic affirmation of his own guilt, delivered with some pride. But if Blake imagined that candor would win him clemency, he was mistaken. The British authorities hit him with "the biggest hammer possible."

The Blake case was the worst spy scandal since the defection of Burgess and Maclean and, in terms of raw intelligence losses, far more damaging. Blake had exposed scores of agents, though he would always maintain, implausibly, that there was no blood on his hands. He was charged under the Official Secrets Act, remanded in custody at a closed hearing, and incarcerated in Brixton Prison to await trial. A telegram flew around the world, in two sections, to every MI6 station: the first part read: "The following name is a traitor"; the second, when decoded, spelled out the letters G-E-O-R-G-E-B-L-A-K-E.

The discovery of another spy in MI6 provoked a mixed reaction in the United States. For some CIA veterans (including Bill Harvey, Philby's first and most vehement accuser) it was yet more evidence of British incompetence and treachery, but James Angleton was reassuring, telling Dick White: "It can happen to anyone."

The news of Blake's arrest and impending trial caused consternation in Beirut's intelligence community; no one was more genuinely shocked and alarmed than Kim Philby.

In accordance with established intelligence rules, the KGB had maintained total separation between the Blake and Philby cases. The two spies had never met, and Blake had been recruited quite independently of the Cambridge network. But Blake's capture suggested, rightly, that MI6 must have new sources within Soviet intelligence, and if one mole had been dug out, then Philby might well be next.

Less than a month after confessing, Blake was in the dock at the Old Bailey. The maximum penalty for violation of the Official Secrets Act was fourteen years. The prosecutors, however, brought five separate charges against him, relating to five distinct time periods. The verdict was never in doubt, but the sentence drew gasps from the court. "Your case is one of the worst that can be envisaged," the judge declared, then handed down a fourteen-year jail term for each of the charges; he further ordered that three of the terms should run consecutively—a total of forty-two years' imprisonment. The conviction was front-page news in every newspaper. It was the longest prison sentence ever handed down by a British court. Reporters suggested, fancifully, that Blake had been given a year for every agent he had betrayed and killed. By that arithmetic he would have been sentenced to some four centuries behind bars.

The news of Blake's harsh sentence left Philby stunned. He had spied for longer than Blake, at a far higher level, and at greater human cost. In the 1950s the government had quailed at the prospect of a public trial for espionage; now the authorities seemed prepared to prosecute, and ruthlessly. If Philby were to be caught, tried, and convicted in the same way as Blake, he would never get out of prison. For perhaps the first time Philby realized the full extent of the peril he was in.

The journalist Richard Beeston visited Philby a few days later to see what he made of the Blake story.

> I went round to his flat late in the morning to find it in chaos after a party with furniture overturned and bottles and glasses everywhere. Kim was looking terrible, nursing a hangover which made him even more incoherent. "Never met Blake, never even heard of the chap until I read of his arrest," Kim told me. . . . Kim's appearance had strikingly deteriorated since I had last seen him. And there is little doubt that Blake's arrest and his savage 42-year prison sentence precipitated Kim's further decline.

For decades Philby had drunk heavily, but never uncontrollably; henceforth, he became increasingly volatile and unpredictable. As an evening progressed, "Kim would become insulting, abusive, make lunges at women and not infrequently goose the hostess." Even Eleanor, a prodigious boozer herself, noticed that her husband was "not light-hearted about drink any longer." They argued publicly and sometimes fought physically: one dinner party ended with the Philbys hurling mantelpiece ornaments at each other while their appalled hosts looked on. Once a voluble drunk, he now drank himself incoherent, then silent, and finally unconscious. Parties ended with Philby slumped insensible on a sofa, or even under a blanket on the floor, while the party continued around him. After sobering up, he would send a charming note of apology and frequently flowers. "By the next day he was usually forgiven."

Philby had always prided himself on maintaining his spy craft no matter how much alcohol he consumed. Now he began to make mistakes. A first rule of espionage is to avoid consistency of behavior, but friends noticed that Philby was frequently absent on Wednesday nights. One teased him: "I know all about your Wednesday nights." Philby looked aghast. Wednesday was his night for meeting Petukhov. He dropped remarks suggestive of a man in fear. One night at Joe's Bar, Moyra Beeston asked Philby, half in jest, if he really was the "third man." Instead of denying it, or even replying directly, he seized her by the wrist so hard he left a bruise. "You know Moyra, I always believe that loyalty to your friends is more important than anything else"—a self-revealing remark for a man who had repeatedly betrayed his own friends in obedience to what he claimed was a higher loyalty. "What would you do if you knew something awful was going to happen to a friend and only you could do something about it?" he asked her. He was plainly referring to his own decision to tip off Maclean so many years earlier, but also to his current predicament, as he awaited "something awful."

In late August 1962 Kim and Eleanor headed to Jordan for a long-planned family holiday. A few days before they were due to come home, Philby announced that he had to return to Beirut at once, offering no explanation for his sudden departure. When Eleanor got back to the flat, she found the lights off and Philby sitting in the dark on the terrace, sodden with drink and inconsolable with grief.

"What's the matter? What's wrong?"

"Jackie's dead," said Philby.

The pet fox had fallen from the balcony, dropping five floors to the street below. Eleanor suspected that the Lebanese maid, who had long disapproved of keeping a smelly wild animal in a city flat, had pushed the fox over the parapet.

"Kim seemed to give himself up to grief," wrote Eleanor, who thought his mourning for the pet, while understandable, "seemed out of all proportion." Nicholas Elliott too was surprised and worried that Philby seemed "shattered" by the death of the fox, anguished and tearful: "Apart from when his father died, this was the only occasion, in all the times I spent with Philby, that I knew him to display visible emotion." Philby was cracking up, partly through grief and partly through fear.

In Helsinki some seven months earlier, a short, stout Russian wrapped in a fur coat had knocked on the door of Frank Freiberg, the CIA representative in Finland, and announced, in very bad English, that he wanted to defect to the West. Major Anatoliy Golitsyn of the KGB had been planning his move for some time. As a senior officer in the KGB's strategic planning department and a fifteen-year veteran of Soviet intelligence, he had accumulated a vast trove of secrets, most of them memorized or half-memorized or almost remembered. The problem with Golitsyn was that while he knew a great deal about some aspects of Soviet intelligence, he also knew a little about a lot. Much of the information he carried, in his head and in the package of documents he had hidden in the snow before knocking on Freiberg's door, was reliable and accurate; but much was fragmentary, and some was wrong. Golitsyn was whisked to the United States to begin a debriefing process that would continue for many years. James Angleton was delighted, insisting that Golitsyn was "the most valuable defector ever to reach the West." Others considered him unreliable. Some thought he was a fruitcake. In the spring of 1962 the CIA allowed Golitsyn to travel to London to be interviewed by British intelligence. There Golitsyn described how, in Moscow, he had heard tell of a "very important spy network in the United Kingdom called the Ring of Five," a quintet of British spies who had met at university and over many years had furnished Soviet intelligence with the most valuable information. Although Golitsyn could not identify Philby by name, or even code name, that information alone was enough to revive the long-dormant investigation and put MI5's mole hunters firmly back on Philby's trail.

The defection sent shock waves through the KGB. Some fifty-four KGB stations around the world were instructed to report whatever Golitsyn might know about their operations. Meetings with important KGB agents were suspended, and plans were approved for the assassination, at the earliest opportunity, of Anatoliy Golitsyn.

Yuri Modin had left Britain in 1958. But in the summer of 1962, according to CIA records, he traveled to the Middle East via Pakistan. Not until much later did MI5 investigators work out that Modin's trip coincided with the moment that Philby had suddenly returned early from the family holiday in Jordan, from which point on he had "exhibited increasing signs of alcoholism and stress." MI5 concluded that "Modin had gone to Beirut to alert Philby" and tell him that another well-informed defector was spilling secrets. If Modin made contact with Philby in Beirut, the location has never been revealed. He later described the once-irrepressible Agent Stanley as "a shadow of his former self." The purpose of his visit was clear: "to warn Philby not to return to Britain because of the danger of arrest, and to make contingency plans for his escape." The warning, however, seems to have sent Philby into a tailspin of fear. When Eleanor found Philby sitting in the dark, his tears were not only for his dead fox.

In October 1962 Nicholas Elliott was offered a new post as the MI6 director for Africa based in London. It was another major promotion covering another important cold-war arena. His two years in Lebanon had been fascinating, fruitful, and fun, with plenty of the "belly laughs" for which Elliott lived. He would be leaving Beirut with regrets, not least over Philby's deteriorated state. Peter Lunn, his predecessor in Vienna, would replace him as MI6 station chief. Before heading to Beirut to take over from Elliott, Lunn asked Dick White what, if anything, he should do about Kim Philby. White was aware that Philby was back in MI5's

CLOSING CITY PRICES

SHERRY
GONZALEZ
TIO PEPE
PRODUCE OF SPAIN

Evening Standard

FINAL NIGHT EXTRA

ROOTES
CAR HIRE
RING CUNNINGHAM 5141
ABBEY HALL, ABBEY RD., LONDON, N.W.

40,863   TUESDAY, OCTOBER 25, 1955   ●● Twopence

EDEN REJECTS INQUIRY INTO MACLEAN CASE

But early debate is promised

MP TALKS OF 'DUBIOUS THIRD MAN ACTIVITIES OF MR. HAROLD PHILBY'

General Lopes rides to the Palace

Sir Anthony Eden refused in the Commons this afternoon to appoint a select committee to investigate the disappearance of Burgess and Maclean and the efficiency of civil service security arrangements in general.

But he said it was desirable to have an early debate on the subject and he would be glad to take part.

Colonel Marcus Lipton (Soc., Brixton) had asked the Prime Minister whether he would appoint a select committee.

"No, sir," replied Sir Anthony Eden.

Colonel Lipton then asked: "Has he made up his mind to cover up at all costs the dubious 'third man' activities of Mr. Harold Philby, who was First Secretary of the Washington Embassy a little while ago, and is he determined to stifle all discussion on the very grave matters he evaded in the wretched White Paper which was an insult to the intelligence of the country?"

Early debate

The Prime Minister said that his answer referred only to the question of a select committee and to this, reply remained "No."

He went on: "So far as the wider issues raised in the supplementary are concerned, the Government themselves take the view that it is desirable to have a debate and an early debate on this subject.

"I personally, as Prime Minister, would be glad to take part."

Mr. Alfred Robens (Soc., Blyth) asked the Prime Minister whether he had "made any investigation as to the reason why briefs supplied by Foreign Office officials to Ministers answering questions in this House had been as much at variance with the facts of the case?"

Sir Anthony suggested that this might be one of the matters to be raised in the debate.

The Speaker then called the next question.

FOOTNOTE: Mr. Harold Philby lives at Crowborough, Sussex. He joined the Foreign Office after the war with the rank of First Secretary and was posted to Washington.

Mr. Philby, father of five children, is now a free-lance journalist.

Lord Elton asks about Maclean

Earlier in the House of Lords, Lord Elton raised the case of Donald Maclean. He pointed out that a White Paper had now disclosed that Maclean, who had already been guilty of "serious misconduct," and "excessive drinking," had for some time before he disappeared in May, 1951, been under the gravest suspicion of being an enemy agent.

He asked the Government to explain statements in reply to a question on October 28, 1952, that Maclean had performed his official duties satisfactorily up to the date of his disappearance and that they knew his back-

▶ Back Page, Col. Five

GORDON PIRIE TO MARRY SHIRLEY HAMPTON

Evening Standard Reporter

Gordon Pirie, the 24-year-old British runner, who defeated Zatopek, is to marry 20-year-old Miss Shirley Hampton.

She is also an athlete—the only child of Mr. and Mrs. Harold Hampton, of Crofton Road, Orpington.

Gordon Pirie and Shirley lunched together in London today before making a second attempt to get an engagement ring. When they tried yesterday they could not find the one they wanted.

Mrs. Hampton said "There will be no special celebration tonight. Gordon has to continue his training. Shirley plans to go to an old girls' reunion at her Eltham school."

Said Mrs. Pirie "They became engaged during the weekend."

She did not tell

Miss Hampton works in the accounts department of Shell Tankers, White Kennett Street, City.

A colleague said "she came into the office at the usual time this morning, but left about 10 o'clock. She did not tell us where she was going. She did not mention her engagement."

Shirley was runner-up in the 220 yards in the women's championships this year and was in the British team with Gordon Pirie that competed in Moscow and Prague last month.

MISS SHIRLEY HAMPTON Looking for a ring.

CABINET HEARS BUDGET SECRETS

Evening Standard Political Correspondent

The Cabinet met today for a preview of Mr. Butler's supplementary Budget, which he will introduce in the Commons tomorrow.

The Chancellor has now completed his speech. It will last about 75 minutes.

Besides acquainting Ministers with its contents, Mr. Butler briefed them for the socialist attack that will follow.

The Opposition is preparing to censure Mr. Butler's economic policy in the strongest terms. The Budget debate on Thursday and Friday will undoubtedly be the toughest that Sir Anthony Eden's administration has yet experienced.

HOUSING SUBSIDIES

Mr. Duncan Sandys, the Minister of Housing, announced in the House of Commons today that he would make a statement later this week on the housing subsidies.

Missing girl found

Sarah Grubb, 18-year-old daughter of the Rev. Geoffrey Watkin Grubb, rector of Cranfield, Beds who disappeared from her home on Sunday, has been found in Eastbourne, staying with a relative.

TOPFOTO

The *Evening Standard* headline identifying Philby as the Third Man.

Marcus Lipton, MP, defender of parliamentary privilege, enemy of pop music, and Philby's primary accuser.

Philby's second wife, Aileen, besieged by the press in October 1955 at the family home in Crowborough.

She made no comment, despite knowing that Philby was guilty.

Aileen would die inside this house, after Philby's departure for Beirut, alcoholic and alone.

James Angleton would later claim that he had long suspected Philby was a spy. The evidence suggests otherwise.

J. Edgar Hoover, the FBI director, was convinced of Philby's treachery and enraged that he had not been prosecuted.

Helenus "Buster" Milmo, the MI5 barrister who subjected Philby to cross-examination and declared: "He's as guilty as hell."

Jim Skardon, former police detective, head of the surveillance section, and MI5's chief interrogator. He set out to break Philby.

Dick White became director general of MI5 in 1953 and chief of MI6 in 1956. He hunted Philby for over a decade.

Richard Brooman-White, MP. With Elliott's help, the former MI6 officer drew up a brief for Macmillan, stoutly defending Philby.

Sir John "Sinbad" Sinclair, head of MI6, accused MI5 of pursuing a vendetta against Philby.

Harold Macmillan, foreign secretary in 1955, told the House of Commons there was "no reason" to suspect Philby of treachery.

Philby invited the world's press into his mother's flat to hear him clear his name. "Were you in fact the Third Man?" one journalist asked. Philby answered: "No, I was not."

"The last time I spoke to a communist, knowing him to be a communist, was sometime in 1934."

"On the subject of friendship, I'd prefer to say as little as possible."

Philby's moment of triumph. His Soviet handler, Yuri Modin,
described his performance as "breathtaking."

Commander Lionel "Buster" Crabb, the most famous frogman in Britain, is mobbed by a group of young admirers.

Buster Crabb prepares for a dive.

The Soviet cruiser *Ordzhonikidze* and curious crowds in Portsmouth Harbor.

Prime Minister Anthony Eden gave instructions that no covert operations should take place during the Russian visit. Operation Claret went ahead anyway.

Nikita Khrushchev, first secretary of the Soviet Communist Party, and his premier, Nikolai Bulganin, are welcomed to Britain.

Kim and Eleanor Philby, his third wife, relax at the luxury bathing hut they shared with the Elliotts on Beirut's Khalde Beach.

Philby relaxes in a mountain pool. These were the "happiest years," wrote Eleanor.

Nicholas Elliott in casual pose in the family's Beirut apartment.

Kim Philby, drunk, at a picnic in the hills outside Beirut.

A party at the Copelands'. From left to right: Eleanor Philby, Kim Philby, Miles Copeland, Nicholas Elliott, Lorraine Copeland, and Elizabeth Elliott. Three spies serving three intelligence agencies: MI6, the CIA, and the KGB.

The last photograph of Kim Philby together with his father. In 1960, St John visited his son in Beirut, went to a cocktail party, made a pass at a member of the embassy staff, and died. The loss of his father plunged Kim Philby into a deep alcoholic despair.

Philby playing with his pet fox, Jackie. The death of this animal left him "inconsolable."

Soviet intelligence officer Anatoliy Golitsyn, whose defection rekindled the Philby investigation.

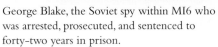

Flora Solomon, Philby's old friend, told MI5 that he had attempted to recruit her for "dangerous" work in the communist cause in 1935.

George Blake, the Soviet spy within MI6 who was arrested, prosecuted, and sentenced to forty-two years in prison.

Philby's disappearance from Beirut, and subsequent reappearance in Moscow, prompted a media frenzy.

Out in the cold: Kim Philby in Moscow. The veteran spy insisted Russia was his "homeland" while describing himself as "wholly and irreversibly English," and was never fully trusted by the KGB.

James Jesus Angleton never recovered from Philby's betrayal, and launched a mole hunt that inflicted huge damage on the CIA.

TOPFOTO

THE TIMES OF LONDON

Nicholas Elliott in 1992. He never stopped wondering how a man who had seemed so similar to him in every way could have been so utterly different.

Kim Philby: "I have always operated on two levels, a personal level and a political one. When the two have come into conflict, I have had to put politics first."

sights: "Of course he's a traitor," he snapped. "Just keep an eye on him. Let's wait and see what happens."

Philby was also waiting, with dread. Bereaved, under threat of exposure, alarmed by the shocking example made of Blake, and now deprived of the companionship and immediate support of the one person who had always defended him, Philby sank ever deeper into the whiskey bottle.

The denouement came not by way of new information from a fresh defector, as Philby feared, but through an old friend recalling a thirty-year-old conversation he had long forgotten.

Chapter Seventeen

I Thought It Would Be You

FLORA SOLOMON HAD LIVED A LIFE THAT STRETCHED, RATHER BI-zarrely, from the Russian Revolution to the British high street: after an early affair with a Bolshevik revolutionary and marriage to a British soldier, she had been widowed young, raised her son Peter alone (who in 1961 founded Amnesty International), and then created the welfare department at Marks & Spencer. A pillar of Anglo-Jewish society, she continued to hold regular salons in her Mayfair home, just as she had in the 1930s. Solomon remained Russian in accent, British in manner, and a committed Zionist in her politics. "Russian soul, Jewish heart, British passport" was how she described herself. By 1962 her main passion in life was the State of Israel, which she defended and supported in word, deed, and funds at every opportunity. It was Flora Solomon's commitment to Israel that brought Kim Philby back into her life. Every week she read the *Observer*, paying particular attention to coverage of the Middle East, and found herself becoming increasingly irritated by Philby's articles. "To anyone with eyes to see they were permeated with anti-Israel bias. They accepted the Soviet view of Middle East politics," she wrote. In the simplistic divisions imposed by the cold war, while Israel was supported by Washington, Moscow curried favor among the Arab states, and in Solomon's subjective opinion Philby was churning out Soviet propaganda designed to weaken her beloved Israel. (This was not actually true: Philby was instinctively pro-Arab, but he was far too canny to reveal any overt pro-Soviet bias in his journalism.) During the 1950s, she had assumed that the accusations against Philby were merely McCarthyite smears. Now she was not so sure. She remembered his remarks about "the cause" back in 1935 and the rather clumsy attempt to recruit her. "The thought occurred to me that Philby had, after all, remained a communist, notwithstanding his clearance by MI5 of possible complicity in the Burgess-Maclean scandal."

In August 1962 Flora Solomon visited Israel, as she had done many times before, to attend a conference at the Chaim Weizmann Institute, the science research center in Rehovot founded by Israel's first president and endowed by Baron Sieff, the chairman of Marks & Spencer. At a party in Weizmann's home she encountered Victor, Lord Rothschild, another patron of the institute. A distinguished scientist himself, Rothschild had headed MI5's sabotage and explosives section during the war and won the George Medal for "dangerous work in hazardous circumstances." A regular at the Harris soirees and a Cambridge contemporary of Burgess and Blunt, Rothschild would later be accused, quite unfairly, of being a Soviet spy himself. In fact, though a left-winger in his youth, like Flora Solomon he had no truck with communism and retained close links with MI5. Rothschild and Solomon had known each other since the 1930s, and their conversation naturally drifted toward their mutual acquaintance Kim Philby.

"How is it the *Observer* uses a man like Kim? Don't they know he's a communist?" observed Solomon.

Rothschild was startled by the certainty in her voice. Solomon went on to describe how, back in 1935, Philby had told her with pride that he was doing a "very dangerous job for peace" and attempted to enlist her as a Soviet spy. Rothschild was now listening intently. He had followed the Philby case closely and knew that despite an array of circumstantial evidence against a man who had once been his friend, no one had come forward to link Philby directly with Soviet intelligence. He began to quiz her about Philby and the wartime circle of friends they had shared. She replied that she had always suspected that Tommy Harris might be a Soviet spy, based on an "intuitive feeling that Harris was more than just a friend" to Kim Philby.

Flora Solomon later maintained that her motives in exposing Philby were strictly political: he was writing anti-Israeli articles, and she wanted him sacked from the *Observer*. But her reasons were also personal. Solomon had introduced Philby to Aileen back in 1939 and felt partly responsible for the saga that had ensued, ending in Aileen's sad and lonely death. Solomon had tried to put the tragedy out of her mind, but she remained furious with Philby for "the terrible way he treated his women." The ghost of Aileen Furse was about to exact revenge.

"You must do something," Flora Solomon told Rothschild in her imperious way.

"I will think about it," he told her.

Victor Rothschild was a veteran string puller. He did more than think. On his return to London, he immediately reported the conversation to MI5, sparking jubilation among the small group of officers still determined to bring Philby to justice. Here at last was a "major breakthrough." With difficulty, Flora Solomon was persuaded to come to an interview with MI5 officers in Rothschild's flat, which was bugged for the occasion. There she repeated her account of the conversation with Philby from three decades earlier. The investigators found her "a strange, rather untrustworthy woman" and suspected she had been more deeply implicated in left-wing radicalism than she was admitting. The interview was recorded by MI5 investigator Peter Wright. Writing many years later in his explosive book *Spycatcher*, Wright wondered if she and Philby had been lovers and whether her belated revelation was motivated by spite: "She clearly had a grudge against him."

Flora Solomon was now getting cold feet, alarmed that if she testified against Philby she might invite the attentions of a KGB assassination squad. "I will never give public evidence," she told MI5. "There is too much risk." The more MI5 pressed her to make a formal legal statement, the more anxious she became: "It will leak, I know it will leak, and then what will my family do?" She did, however, agree to speak to officers from Mossad, although offended by the implication that she would be more forthcoming with Israeli intelligence officials than British ones.

Solomon's revelation finally provided evidence that Philby had been an active Soviet spy, a recruiter for the communist cause who had deliberately covered up his past and lied repeatedly under interrogation. It was the ammunition that Buster Milmo had lacked and the evidence of guilt that Philby's supporters had always demanded. "Why didn't she tell us ten years ago?" said White, when told of Solomon's revelation. She had a ready answer for that question: "I had not volunteered information as every public statement had pointed to his innocence." The fault was not hers, she insisted, but theirs: Philby's escape from justice was proof of "how clubmanship and the old school tie could protect their own."

That protection was now at an end; MI5 prepared to strike. The officer who had worked on the Philby case since 1951, Arthur Martin, would administer the coup de grâce. For more than a decade Martin had tried to pierce Philby's armor. No one knew the case better. With Solomon's evidence and the corroborative testimony from Golitsyn, the other elements of suspicion slotted into place. An intense debate now began over how to bring Philby to account, a task that still presented major problems politically, legally, and practically. Even if Solomon could somehow be persuaded to testify, her evidence was hearsay. George Blake had been convicted by his own testimony, but Philby would probably deny everything, as he always had, and without a confession there was no guarantee of a conviction. Any trial would be embarrassing, particularly if it emerged that Philby was still in the pay of MI6; but a trial that failed to secure a conviction would be disastrous. For Harold Macmillan, now prime minister, the issue was particularly sensitive: as foreign secretary he had personally cleared Philby; another espionage trial could bring down the Conservative government. Philby might be tricked into returning to England, perhaps by a summons from his editors, and then forced into a confession. But Philby knew very well how Blake had been trapped and was adjudged "far too wily" to fall for the same ruse;

a summons to London would merely alert him. There were even more radical alternatives: Philby could be abducted from Beirut, or even killed. But given the rising cold-war tension, the murder or kidnapping of a Soviet spy might set off an ugly retaliation with untold consequences. Besides, since the Crabb affair there had been little appetite for dramatic adventures. Only Philby knew the full extent of his own espionage; alive, he might be persuaded to reveal other Soviet spies lurking inside the British establishment. "We need to discover what damage he caused," Dick White told Macmillan. "A full damage report with all the details of how the Russians had operated and who else was working with Philby is of great importance." Besides, though he might be a traitor, Philby "should be treated as a gentleman." White sketched out a plan of action that would cause the least embarrassment while yielding the maximum benefit: Arthur Martin should fly to Beirut as soon as possible, present Philby with the conclusive evidence against him, and then offer him a way out: immunity from prosecution in return for a full confession and complete cooperation. No such deal had been offered to George Blake; but then Blake, a foreigner, was not a gentleman. Macmillan agreed to the plan but insisted on total secrecy: "Keep a lid on things," he instructed Dick White. The attorney general and the under secretary at the Foreign Office also approved the plan, though they were careful to commit nothing to paper. MI5 compiled a "voluminous brief in preparation for the confrontation," which Martin studied as he prepared for the showdown in Beirut: he would break Philby, extract the truth, and destroy him once and for all. The only obstacle to this happy scenario was Nicholas Elliott.

Within days of his return to London, Elliott was summoned to see Dick White and told, with some relish, that there could no longer be any doubt: Flora Solomon's evidence confirmed that Philby had been a Soviet spy since the early 1930s. He had betrayed his country, his class, and his club; he had lied to MI5 and MI6, the CIA and the FBI, his family, friends, and colleagues; he had deceived everyone, egregiously, brilliantly, for more than thirty years. But no one had been betrayed more comprehensively than Nicholas Elliott.

Elliott had been just twenty-four, grieving over the death of Basil Fisher, when he was befriended and beguiled by Philby, a man he had then trusted, revered, and supported throughout his adult life. Their lives had seemed to run in tandem through public school, Cambridge, and MI6, overlapping professionally, culturally, and geographically. From St Albans to Istanbul, Elliott had modeled himself on Philby: his spy craft, his air of worldly irony, his umbrella with the ebony handle. They seldom discussed their fears or hopes, for theirs was a most English friendship, founded on cricket, alcohol, and jokes, based on a shared set of assumptions about the world and their privileged place in it. They were as close as two heterosexual, upper-class, midcentury Englishmen could be. Elliott's loyalty was of the military type, an unquestioning readiness to stand by a comrade under fire. He had valued this friendship forged in wartime above all else. Now, for the first time, he began to count its cost, to wonder how many people he, James Angleton, and others had unwittingly condemned to death. Some of the victims had names: the German anticommunist Catholics identified by the Vermehrens; the Volkovs in Istanbul; the young Georgians slipped across the Turkish border to their deaths; perhaps even Buster Crabb's strange death could be attributed to Philby. Many casualties remained nameless: the multiple agents infiltrated behind the iron curtain and never seen again; the Albanian "pixies," captured and killed in their hundreds, along with their families; the unknown number of agents exposed in the Middle East. Elliott would never be able to calculate the precise death tally, for who can remember every conversation, every confidence exchanged with a friend stretching back three decades? The weekends at the cricket, the evenings at the club, the nights on the town in Beirut: it had all been a charade, the simulacrum of comradeship, while Philby gathered information for his Soviet masters. Elliott had given away almost every secret he had to Philby; but Philby had never given away his own.

Elliott's emotions on discovering Philby's betrayal can only be surmised, for he preferred not to discuss them. His upper lip remained ramrod stiff. He came from a generation of Englishmen who believed that feelings are a sign of weakness to be suppressed, ignored, or laughed off. A different sort of man might have buckled under the pain, but Elliott was tough and a dissembler in his own way, for British breeding and schooling produce a very distinctive brand of protective dishonesty. As John le Carré once wrote: "The privately educated Englishman is the greatest dissembler on earth. . . . Nobody will charm you so glibly, disguise his feelings from you better, cover his tracks more skilfully or find it harder to confess to you that he's been a damn fool. . . . He can have a Force Twelve nervous breakdown while he stands next to you in the bus queue and you may be his best friend but you'll never be the wiser." Elliott had survived a brutal prep school, the chilliness of his father, the death of his first friend, by pretending that everything was perfectly all right. And he survived Philby's intimate disloyalty in exactly the same way. But those who knew him best saw that beneath the ever-languid manner, the armory of jokes, and the insouciant air, from the moment he finally understood and accepted Philby's treachery Elliott's world changed utterly: inside he was crushed, humiliated, enraged, and saddened. For the rest of his life he would never cease to wonder how a man to whom he had felt so close, and who was so similar in every way, had been, underneath, a fraud. Once he would have died for Philby; now, as he told his son, he would "happily have killed him." Philby had made a first-class fool of him and a mockery of their lifelong friendship; he had broken every canon of clubmanship and fraternity and caused incalculable damage to the service and the country that Elliott loved. Elliott needed to know why. He wanted to look Philby in the eye one last time. He wanted to understand.

Elliott demanded to be allowed to confront Philby himself. He had known him more than half his life, and if anyone could extract a confession from the man, it was surely he. The idea appealed to Dick White. Elliott's righteous anger might lend him additional moral weight, and "there was more chance that Philby could be persuaded to confess by an outraged sympathizer than by a stiff, lower-middle-class MI5 officer." White calculated that since Elliott had been "Philby's greatest supporter in 1951, his anger at having been betrayed would suggest that we had more proof than he realized." In the past, White had been nettled by Elliott's support for Philby, but he considered him "a proficient, clever and determined officer who would stop at nothing if the interests of the Crown required." It was agreed: Elliott would fly out to Beirut and nail Philby. The CIA was not informed about the proof of Philby's guilt or the decision to have Elliott confront him. The Americans could be informed once the case had been resolved. If James Angleton found out what was going on, he would certainly demand some involvement. He had been, after all, almost as close to Philby as Elliott himself. The decision was made to keep him in the dark. Some wondered whether Elliott would be able to restrain his anger if he was allowed in the same room as the friend who had cheated him so thoroughly, but "Elliott swore not to exceed his brief, coldly angry though he now was."

Peter Wright described the reaction inside MI5 to the news that MI6 was sending not the dogged Arthur Martin to confront Philby but one of their own tribe:

> The few of us inside MI5 privy to this decision were appalled. It was not simply a matter of chauvinism, though, not unnaturally, that played a part. We in MI5 had never doubted Philby's guilt from the beginning, and now at last we had the evidence needed to corner him. Philby's friends in MI6, Elliott chief among them, had continually protested his innocence. Now, when the proof was inescapable, they wanted to keep it in-house. The choice of Elliott rankled strongly.

To strengthen Elliott's hand, Dick White told him that new evidence had been obtained from the defector Anatoliy Golitsyn, although exactly what he revealed remains a matter of conjecture and some mystery. Golitsyn had not specifically identified Philby as "Agent Stanley," but White gave Elliott the impression that he had. Was this intentional sleight of hand by White, allowing Elliott to believe that the evidence against Philby was stronger than it really was? Or did Elliott interpret as hard fact something that had only been implied? Either way, he prepared for his trip to Beirut in the certainty that Philby was guilty: "We'd fully penetrated the KGB, so we had confirmation." Elliott's instructions were verbal, and only two men knew what they were: Dick White and Nicholas Elliott himself.

In Beirut Eleanor Philby watched in despair as her once-charming husband fell apart in a miasma of drink and depression. Philby was "vertically intoxicated, horizontally intoxicated," and often intoxicated in solitude. "It was as if our flat was the only place he felt safe." When he did venture out for social events, he invariably ended up insensible. To her deep embarrassment he had to be bodily carried out of an embassy party. "He only had to smell a drink to set him off. His depression never seemed to lift," wrote Eleanor, who "groped to understand his tension and remoteness."

"What is the matter?" she asked him repeatedly. "Why don't you tell me?"

"Oh nothing, nothing," he would reply.

Looking back, she realized that Philby's desperate drinking, his search for alcoholic oblivion, was the mark of a man living in dread.

Philby's journalism dried to a trickle. Peter Lunn, the new MI6 station chief, noticed that Philby's hands shook when they met for the first time. Philby insisted that if they should ever encounter each other at a social event, they should pretend to be strangers—a precaution that Lunn considered bizarre and unnecessary. After Elliott's warmth, Eleanor found Lunn a "very cold fish indeed."

On New Year's Eve Philby refused to go to any of the numerous Beirut parties on offer and instead sat drinking champagne with Eleanor on the balcony of the flat in gloomy silence. The next day was his fifty-first birthday, and Eleanor had planned a small midday drinks party. By two thirty the guests had left. The Philbys intended to spend the day quietly at home, but then Miles Copeland appeared: "He dragged us protesting to an all-day New Year party given by some Americans." Philby had "already had a good deal to drink" and became steadily drunker. As night fell, they staggered home to the rue Kantari. Eleanor was preparing for bed when she heard a loud crash from the bathroom, a cry of pain, and then another crash. Philby had fallen over, smashed his head on the radiator, lurched to his feet, and fallen again. "He was bleeding profusely from two great gashes on the crown of his head. The whole bathroom was spattered with blood." Eleanor wrapped his head in a towel and rushed frantically to the telephone. Philby, dazed and still drunk, refused to leave the flat. Finally, a Lebanese doctor arrived and declared: "If we don't get your husband to the hospital I will not be responsible for his life." Philby was coaxed into the lift and driven to the American University hospital, where he was stitched up and sedated. A doctor took Eleanor aside and told her gravely that with "one more ounce of alcohol in his blood, he would have been dead."

Philby insisted on returning home that night. He cut a pathetic figure in a bloodstained dressing gown, with two livid black eyes and a turban of bandages around his head. "I was a bloody fool," he muttered. "I'm going on the wagon—forever."

A week later Nicholas Elliott broke the journey to Beirut in Athens, where he met Halsey Colchester, the MI6 station chief, and his wife, Rozanne, valued friends from Istanbul days. Elliott had already "prepared himself for a battle of wits he was determined to win," but he needed to unburden himself before heading on to Beirut. "I've got an awful task," he told Halsey and Rozanne. "I've got to beard him." Like Elliott, the Colchesters had long admired and defended Philby, and they were stunned by the proof of his guilt. "It was a terrible shock to hear he was this awful spy. He was always so nice, so affable and intelligent."

Rozanne had known Elliott as a carefree spirit—"he always laughed about things"—but over dinner in Athens he was deadly serious, anxious, and anguished. Rozanne's account of that night is a picture of a man facing the worst moment of his life.

> Nicholas knew he had blood on his hands. He knew Philby so well, and he was horrified by the whole thing. He said he wouldn't mind shooting him. He didn't know what he was going to say, and I remember him coaching himself: "There's no pretending now. We know who you are." Nick was usually a very funny man. Like an actor or entertainer, you never felt he was quite real. One never *really* felt one knew him. Nicholas had that English way of not getting too involved, a sort of façade with endless jokes. But that night he was very highly strung. He was dreading it, and it was quite dangerous. He thought he might have been shot by Philby, or the Soviets. "I hope he doesn't take a pot shot," he said. He talked obsessively about Philby, about how he had known him so well. He didn't have to go through the ordeal, but he wanted to. It was really quite brave. He wanted to make sure for himself.

Elliott arrived in Beirut on January 10, 1963, and checked into a small, discreet hotel far from the usual haunts of the spies and journalists. Only Peter Lunn knew he was in the city. Together they prepared the ground for the confrontation. Lunn's secretary had an apartment in the Christian quarter, near the sea. The sitting room was carefully bugged by an MI6 technician, with a hidden microphone under the sofa and a wire running to a tape recorder in the next-door room. Elliott bought a bottle of brandy. When everything was ready, Lunn telephoned Philby and, "in a casual voice," suggested "a meeting between himself and Philby to discuss future plans." He gave no hint that anything was amiss. Since Philby had himself stressed the need for security, Lunn suggested meeting over tea at his secretary's flat, where they could chat in private. Philby had barely left the rue Kantari since his drunken fall on New Year's Day, but he agreed to meet Lunn at the appointed address the following afternoon. He later told Eleanor: "The minute that call came through, I knew the balloon was up."

At four o'clock on January 12, Philby, his head still swathed in bandages and a little unsteady on his feet, climbed the stairs and knocked on the apartment door.

When it was opened by Nicholas Elliott, Philby seemed strangely unsurprised. "I rather thought it would be you," he said.

Chapter Eighteen

Teatime

Philby's reaction to Elliott's unannounced arrival in Beirut was interpreted, in the more paranoia-prone parts of MI5, as evidence that he had been tipped off in advance. It sparked a hunt for another Soviet spy within British intelligence that lasted two decades and a conspiracy theory that still smolders today. In reality, when Philby said he was not surprised to find Elliott waiting for him at the flat, he was stating a fact. He had feared exposure for years and expected it imminently; he knew how Elliott's mind worked, and he knew that if the truth about his spying had finally emerged, then Elliott would want to confront him with it.

The two men shook hands. Elliott inquired about the bandage on Philby's head. Philby explained that he had fallen over after a party. The embassy secretary poured tea and then discreetly left the apartment. The two men sat down, for all the world as if they were meeting in the club. In the next room Peter Lunn and a stenographer, both wearing headphones, hunched over a turning tape recorder.

The full transcript of the ensuing dialogue has never been released by MI5. Indeed, parts of the recording are almost inaudible. Elliott was no technical expert. Shortly before Philby's arrival, he had opened the apartment windows, and as a result, much of their dialogue is obscured by the sounds wafting up from the busy Beirut street below. One of the most important conversations in the history of the cold war takes place to the accompaniment of car horns, grinding engines, Arabic voices, and the faint clink of china teacups. But enough could be heard to reconstruct what followed: a display of brutal English politeness, civilized and lethal.

Elliott asked after Philby's health.

"Perfectly tolerable," said Philby, adding that he was recovering from a double bout of flu and bronchitis. "They were both against me."

Philby asked after Elliott's family. All well, said Elliott. Mark was starting the new term at Eton.

"Wonderful tea," he said. A pause.

"Don't tell me you flew all the way here to see me?" said Philby.

Elliott took out his Mont Blanc pen, placed it on the table, and began to roll it back and forth under his palm. It was an act of nervous tension but also an old interrogation trick, a distraction.

"Sorry for getting right on with it. Kim, I don't have time to postpone this. And we've known each other for ever, so, if you don't mind, I'll get right to the point," said Elliott, not getting to the point. "Unfortunately it's not very pleasant." Another pause. "I came to tell you that your past has caught up with you."

Philby immediately counterattacked. "Have you all gone mad once again? You want to start all that? After all these years? You've lost your sense of humor. You'll be a laughing stock!"

"No, we haven't lost anything. On the contrary we've found additional information about you. It puts everything in place."

"What information? And what is there to put in place?"

Elliott stood, walked to the window, and stared down into the street.

"Listen Kim, you know I was on your side all the time from the moment there were suspicions about you. But now there is new information. They've shown it to me. And now even I am convinced, absolutely convinced that you worked for the Soviet intelligence services. You worked for them right up until '49."

Philby later expressed bafflement as to why Elliott should identify 1949 as the date he stopped spying for the Russians. The answer was simple: 1949 was the year Philby went to Washington; if he admitted to spying while in America, then James Angleton, the CIA, and the FBI would all want to know what intelligence secrets he had given away and could well demand his extradition to face charges under U.S. law. The offer of immunity would be meaningless. For the purposes of the deal, Elliott needed Philby to admit spying up to, but no later than, 1949. That way the problem could be dealt with "in-house" by MI6, without American involvement.

But Philby was not ready to admit anything.

"Who told you that nonsense? It's totally absurd, and"—appealing to Elliott's sense of fair play—"You know yourself that it's absurd."

But Elliott pressed on: "We have new information that you were indeed working with the Soviet intelligence service. . . ."

"Do you want me to go into all this again?"

"Kim, the game's up. We know what you did. We've penetrated the KGB, Kim. There's no doubt in my mind any more that you were a KGB agent."

Decades of friendship were fracturing around them. But still the atmosphere remained calm, the words polite. More tea was poured.

Elliott rolled his pen back and forth. Philby broke the silence.

"Look how stupid this seems. Astonishing! A man is suspected for a long time of mortal sin, they can't prove a thing, they're embarrassed in front of the whole world. They apologize. Then ten years later, some chief is struck by the old idea again. They decide to send an old friend, a wise and decent man, with only one goal, to persuade an innocent man to confess that he's a Russian spy. . . . Is that why you're here?"

"Kim, if you were in my place, if you knew what I know . . ."

"I wouldn't talk to you the way you're talking to me."

"And how would you talk to me?

"I would offer you a drink instead of this lousy tea." It was meant to be a joke, but Elliott did not laugh. And he did not offer him a drink.

"Do you want me to give you my version of your work for the Russians? Do you want me to tell you what you were thinking?"

"Nicholas, are you serious?"

"I am."

Elliott had spent years believing he knew what was in Philby's mind, only to discover that he had been completely wrong. The speech he now delivered was that of a man struggling to understand the incomprehensible.

"I understand you. I've been in love with two women at the same time. I'm certain that you were in the same situation in politics: you loved England and the Soviet Union at the same time. But you've worked for the Soviet Union long enough, you've helped it enough. Now you must help us. . . . You stopped working for them in 1949. I'm absolutely certain of that. Now it's January 1963. Fourteen years have gone by. In that time your ideas and views have changed. They had to change. I can understand people who worked for the Soviet Union, say, before or during the war. But by 1949, a man of your intellect and spirit had to see that all the rumours about Stalin's monstrous behavior were not rumours, they were the truth. You decided to break with the USSR."

Philby shrugged and shook his head. "You came here to interrogate me. And I keep thinking I'm talking to a friend."

It was the second time Philby had invoked their friendship. Something snapped. Elliott suddenly exploded.

"You took me in for years. Now I'll get the truth out of you even if I have to drag it out. You had to choose between Marxism and your family, and you chose Marxism. I once looked up to you, Kim. My God, how I despise you now. I hope you've enough decency left to understand why."

These were the first angry words he had ever spoken to Philby. The pretense of politeness was gone. Neither man moved or spoke.

Elliott slowly regained his composure and eventually broke the crackling silence. "I'm sure we can work something out."

Elliott laid out the deal. If Philby confessed everything back in London or, if he preferred, in Beirut, then he would not be prosecuted. But he would need to reveal all: every contact with Soviet intelligence, every other mole in Britain, every secret he had passed to Moscow over a lifetime of spying. "I can give you my word, and that of Dick White, that you will get full immunity, you will be pardoned, but only if you tell it yourself. We need your collaboration, your help."

Philby said nothing, and Elliott's voice hardened as he continued. If Kim refused to play ball, if he persisted in denying the truth, he would be left in the cold. His passport would be withdrawn and his residence permit revoked. He would not even be able to open a bank account. He would never work for another British newspaper, let alone MI6. His children would be removed from their expensive schools. He would live the rest of his life as a penniless pariah, a "leper," in Elliott's words. The choice was stark: a gentleman's agreement, safety in return for a full confession; or he could stand by his denials, and "his life would be rendered intolerable." There was, of course, a third option, so obvious to both men that Elliott had no need to mention it. Philby could cut and run.

Philby was now on his feet and making for the door. The tea party was over.

"If you cooperate, we will give you immunity from prosecution. Nothing will be published."

The door was now open.

"You've been a lucky chap so far, Kim. You have exactly 24 hours. Be back here at precisely 4pm tomorrow. If you're as intelligent as I think you are, you'll accept."

Philby's reply, if he made one, was not picked up by the hidden microphone.

"I'm offering you a lifeline, Kim . . ."

The door closed behind him.

Philby's parting silence was itself an admission. "He never once asked what the new evidence was." He was no longer protesting. He would seize the lifeline. "Kim's broken," Elliott told Lunn. "Everything's OK." And that evening he dashed off a reassuring telegram to Dick White in London, as ebullient and confident as ever. Inside, however, he was deeply anxious. Would Philby come back? Would he cooperate, clam up, or try to escape? "The next 24 hours were a testing time."

The next day, on the stroke of 4:00 p.m., Philby reappeared at the apartment. He seemed sober and composed.

"OK, here's the scoop," he said. "But first you owe me a drink. I haven't had one since my birthday on New Year's Day."

Elliott poured two large brandies.

Philby then launched into a prepared speech, a peculiar confection of truth, half-truth, and lies. He said that he had been recruited into the Soviet secret service by his first wife, Litzi (which was not exactly true) and that he had, in turn, recruited Maclean and Burgess (which was). From his pocket he drew two sheets of paper on which he had typed a sanitized, incomplete account of his work for Moscow, with few details and fewer names. He admitted he had been recruited by the Soviet intelligence service in 1934 but claimed that he had stopped working for Moscow immediately after the war, having "seen the error of his ways." Yes, he had tipped off Maclean in 1951, but merely as an act of loyalty to a friend, not as one active spy protecting another. He listed his early NKVD handlers but made no mention of the Soviet intelligence officers he had dealt with in Istanbul, Washington, London, and Beirut.

"Is Nedosekin your contact?" asked Elliott, referring to the KGB station chief who had handled George Blake before his capture and arrest.

"I've got no bloody contact," lied Philby with a show of irritation. "I broke contact with the KGB."

Elliott knew Philby was withholding. The two-page summary was a "very bland document" that admitted spying within a narrow time frame. It was, Elliott knew, a "limited confession," but it was nonetheless a signed admission of guilt, admissible in a court of law, and a document that transformed the game. Philby had acknowledged being a Soviet spy, and more disclosures would surely follow. By implication he had accepted the deal in principle, and a negotiation was under way: his liberty in exchange for information. MI6 now held a signed confession, however partial.

He would never be able to row back from here. Elliott had the upper hand.

But what was Philby up to? The question is hard to answer, because Philby himself never told the whole truth about his own intentions. He would later claim he had been merely playing for time, toying with Elliott, controlling the situation with "just a little stalling, just a little drinking" while he made his plans. His behavior suggests otherwise. Philby was in turmoil, trapped, tempted by Elliott's offer, and acutely conscious that his future depended on how he played the game. How much could he get away with concealing? Would MI6 honor the deal? If he said too much, would he end up hanging himself? Was Elliott his friend still, or his nemesis?

Elliott demanded answers. With Philby's confession in hand, he began to increase the pressure. "Our promise of immunity and pardon depends wholly on whether you give us all the information that you have. First of all we need information on people who worked with Moscow. By the way, we know them." This was partly bluff, of course, but Philby could not know that. How much did Elliott know? Had Anthony Blunt cracked? Was he deploying the old interrogator's trick, asking questions to which he already had answers? For two hours they drank and dueled, until the sun was setting and the sound of the muezzin drifted over Beirut. In the language of the sport they both loved, Elliott bowled and Philby batted, padding up, leaving the ball, trying to stay at the crease, and knowing that the next delivery could end his long, long innings. Listening to the tape recording many months later, Peter Wright heard Elliott "trying his manful best to corner a man for whom deception had been a second skin for 30 years." The game was finely balanced, a brutal fight to the death conducted in tones of perfect English civility, played out to a gently drunken tempo. "By the end, they sounded like two rather tipsy radio announcers, their warm, classical public school accents discussing the greatest treachery of the 20th century."

Rising to leave, Philby suggested dinner at his flat that evening. Eleanor knew Elliott was in Beirut, and if he failed to pay a visit she would wonder why. Elliott agreed to come after he had sent another report to Dick White in London. White's response was encouraging; Philby was "finally broken," and Elliott should continue the interrogation. When Elliott arrived at the rue Kantari a few hours later, he found Philby passed out on the floor, having consumed an entire bottle of whiskey. Not for the first time, Elliott and Eleanor carried him to bed. They chatted for a while afterward. Elliott did his best to act normally, but Eleanor was no fool. Why, she asked, was he staying in an "obscure hotel"? Elliott replied that "he did not want too many people to know he was around." Eleanor had come to like Elliott, and "this furtiveness was not characteristic."

Elliott called the next morning and invited the Philbys to dinner at Chez Temporel, one of Beirut's most fashionable and expensive restaurants. He would be bringing his former secretary to make up a foursome. The charade of normality would be maintained. Elliott chose a quiet, candlelit corner table. The food was good—steak *au poivre vert* and Syrian truffle salad—the view through the white arches over the sea enchanting, and the conversation unmemorable. Both Philby and Elliott tried to act "as if nothing had intervened to destroy an old and treasured friendship." It was almost like old times. Yet Eleanor was uneasy. Philby was visibly anxious, and Elliott's behavior was distinctly odd.

> His greatest passion was telling naughty stories. He always had one up his sleeve. This was the way he loosened up at parties. But behind the jokes was a keen professional mind. As usual one doubtful joke followed another, but I had a clear feeling the gaiety was false. Something was going on between them that was escaping me. . . . Here was a man, a very old friend from Kim's past, whom I thought I could confide in. Kim got up to go to the lavatory, and I was on the verge of saying to Elliott: "Something is worrying Kim terribly. What the hell is going on?"

But before she could do so, Elliott also excused himself and followed Philby into the restaurant toilets. Over the urinals Philby handed over a sheaf of typewritten pages, perhaps eight or nine in all, the second installment of his confession and much fuller than the first. Philby was producing the goods.

The following day Philby and Elliott met once more. This time Elliott brought his own paperwork: a single sheet of paper on which was written a list of names, perhaps a dozen in all. Elliott passed it over. Which of these individuals were Soviet spies? Two of those named were Anthony Blunt and John Cairncross, the fourth and fifth men in the Cambridge network; both had been under investigation ever since the defection of Burgess and Maclean. Another on the list was Tim Milne (Philby's old school friend and the witness at his wedding to Eleanor), who was now an MI6 officer in the Far East. The other names are unknown, but Philby's friend Tomás Harris was surely on the list, along with Guy Liddell, who had left MI5 under a cloud because of his association with Burgess and Blunt.

Elliott was fishing: naming everybody he could think of who might have been in league with Philby, Burgess, and Maclean. As Philby later noted, the list included "several names which alarmed me," and his instinctive response was to mislead, to muddy the waters, to present black as white or gray. According to Philby, "Blunt was in the clear but Tim Milne, who had loyally defended him for years, was not." Milne, of course, was entirely innocent and Blunt entirely guilty. Elliott pressed him for more names, but Philby "claimed to know nothing" about any other spies in the UK and repeatedly insisted he had not been in contact with Soviet intelligence for fourteen years.

The exchange threw Philby's predicament into sharp relief. MI6 would continue to squeeze him until every ounce of information had been extracted. He could never hope to hold them off with a partial confession. Blunt might already have admitted his guilt, in which case Elliott would know Philby's insistence on his innocence was another lie. This time MI6 would not let up. Elliott had told him "the debriefing would be a long affair," with the clear implication that Philby should expect to be wrung dry, forced into revealing everything he "knew about the KGB and naming names in Britain." Whether he returned to London or stayed in Beirut, he would effectively be a prisoner of MI6; if he ever refused to cooperate or was found to be lying, then the confession he had already signed could be used against him. "It became clear to me that my immunity could be withdrawn at any time," he later wrote. Elliott had told Philby that his signed confession "might stand him in good stead" with the authorities in London; in fact, it gave Elliott the hold he needed. The "lifeline" offered by Elliott was effectively a noose; the man who had been Philby's protector for so long would now be his jailer. His options were running out, and both of them knew it.

The confrontation had lasted four days. Elliott told Philby that he would be leaving Beirut the next day and traveling on to the Congo. Peter Lunn would take over the debriefing process in Beirut; London would send more questions; the Americans would want to talk to him; the process of interrogation was only just beginning. Back in London the mood was jubilant. Dick White was "effusive in his gratitude" to Elliott, convinced that Philby was playing ball. "He could have rejected the offer of immunity," White said, "but since he has accepted, he'll stay and cooperate." The head of MI5, Sir Roger Hollis, decided to bring the FBI into the picture and wrote a soothing memo to J. Edgar Hoover:

> In our judgment [Philby's] statement of the association with the RIS [Russian Intelligence Service] is substantially true. It accords with all the available evidence in our possession and we have no evidence pointing to a continuation of his activities on behalf of the RIS after 1946, save in the isolated instance of Maclean. If this is so, it follows that damage to United States interests will have been confined to the period of the Second World War.

The chief FBI officer in London was invited to draw up a list of questions that Lunn should ask Philby when the debriefing resumed. "What makes you think he will still be there?" the officer asked. "He will be," he was told. "He isn't going anywhere." The CIA was not informed of developments in the Philby case. There would be plenty of time to fill in James Angleton later. As Elliott prepared to leave Beirut and hand over to Lunn, he reported that Philby was still unpredictable, in a nervous, drunken, and depressed state: "He might, I suppose, commit suicide," he warned. Elliott no longer cared if his former friend lived or died. That, at least, was the impression he gave.

Kim Philby and Nicholas Elliott shook hands and parted with one last display of their old amity. Ostensibly, they were back on the same side, working together after an unpleasant interlude, and friends once more. Both knew this was untrue.

Elliott's decision to fly to Africa, leaving Philby unguarded in Beirut, was later condemned as a critical mistake, an act of egregious complacency that enabled Philby to pull off one last espionage coup. That is certainly how Philby and his KGB handlers chose to portray the ensuing events. But there is another, very different way to read Elliott's actions.

The prospect of prosecuting Philby in Britain was anathema to the intelligence services: another trial, so soon after the Blake fiasco, would be politically damaging and profoundly embarrassing. Blake was foreign and flaky, whereas Philby was an insider and, until very recently, a paid MI6 agent. He had already demonstrated his skill at handling the press. He knew far too much. Elliott was emphatic: "Nobody wanted him in London." But keeping him in Beirut indefinitely was almost equally unpalatable. Once Philby was fully interrogated, what would be done with him? He plainly could no longer work for British newspapers, so would MI6 have to continue paying him? The prospect of subsidizing a known traitor to prop up the bar of the Normandie Hotel did not appeal.

Elliott later claimed that the idea Philby might defect to the USSR had never occurred to him or anyone else. "It just didn't dawn on us." This defies belief. Burgess and Maclean had both defected; Blake would escape from Wormwood Scrubs Prison in

1966 and make his way to Moscow. Elliott must have suspected that Philby would have a backup escape plan. Moreover, Elliott had deliberately forced him into a corner: Philby knew he now faced sustained interrogation, over a long period, at the hands of Peter Lunn, a man he found "unsympathetic." Elliott had made it quite clear that if he failed to cooperate fully, the immunity deal was off and the confession he had already signed would be used against him. Burgess and Maclean had vanished into the Soviet Union and barely been heard of again. Allowing Philby to join his friends in Moscow—to "do a fade," in intelligence jargon—might be the tidiest solution all around.

Elliott could not have made it easier for Philby to flee, whether intentionally or otherwise. In defiance of every rule of intelligence, he left Beirut without making any provision for monitoring a man who had just confessed to being a double agent: Philby was not followed or watched; his flat was not placed under surveillance; his phone was not tapped; and MI6's allies in the Lebanese security service were not alerted. He was left to his own devices and told that Peter Lunn would be in touch in due course. Elliott simply walked away from Beirut and left the door to Moscow wide open.

That was either monumentally stupid or exceptionally clever.

The very next evening, on the stroke of six o'clock, Philby stood on the balcony of his flat on rue Kantari with a book in his hand.

Chapter Nineteen

The Fade

PHILBY AND PETUKHOV MET A FEW HOURS LATER IN VREJ, THE backstreet Armenian restaurant. It took Philby only a few rushed minutes to explain the situation: MI6 had new and damning information from Golitsyn and had offered him immunity in exchange for information. He did not tell his KGB handler that he had already confessed; instead, he allowed Petukhov to believe that he was holding out under questioning (as he had so often before) but would soon face another round of interrogation. Petukhov hurried back to the Soviet embassy and sent a cable to Vassili Dozhdalev, the head of the British desk at Moscow Center, requesting instructions. Dozhdalev asked whether Philby could withstand another cross-examination. "Philby does not think he can escape again," Petukhov told him. Dozhdalev gave the order: Philby should be extracted from Beirut as soon as possible.

"Your time has come," Petukhov told Philby at another hurriedly arranged meeting. "They won't leave you alone now. You have to disappear. There's no other way. There's room for you in Moscow." This was probably what Philby had hoped to hear, though he had not yet fully made up his mind to flee. Elliott's words, he later hinted, "had planted doubts in me and made me think about arguments he had used." He had mentally rehearsed the drama of defection many times, but still he hesitated.

"Arrangements will take some time," said Petukhov. But when the time came, Philby would have to move swiftly. As before, Petukhov would walk past the rue Kantari flat at prearranged times:

"If you see me carrying a newspaper, that means I have to meet you. If I'm carrying a book, that means everything is prepared for your departure, and you have to get moving."

Philby waited. A few days later Peter Lunn called the apartment to ask if he was ready to discuss "the question that interests us." Philby said he needed more time. Lunn did not put him under pressure; he did not offer to come to the flat and help to jog Philby's memory. Instead, he announced he was going skiing. Philby learned from a friend at the embassy that a fresh fall of snow in the mountains had created ideal conditions and Lunn, the Olympic skier, would be gone for the next four days. That, at least, is what Philby was told. But Lunn did not go skiing.

On January 23, 1963, Glen Balfour-Paul, the first secretary at the British embassy, and his wife, Marnie, threw a dinner party. Several journalists were invited, including Clare Hollingworth of the *Guardian* and Kim Philby of the *Observer*. Philby had "proved a helpful and friendly contact" since Balfour-Paul's arrival in Beirut two years earlier, and the couples had grown close. Eleanor Philby was looking forward to dinner; for the first time in weeks, Philby had agreed to leave the flat for a social occasion. Glen Balfour-Paul was an expert Arabist, and Eleanor wanted to pick his brain about Middle Eastern archaeology, her new hobby. Marnie's cook was making sherry trifle.

Philby spent the morning drinking coffee on the balcony, despite the lashing rain. Beirut was braced for one of the winter storms that batter the city with unpredictable ferocity. A figure carrying a book walked slowly past in the wet street without looking up. In the late afternoon Philby grabbed his raincoat and scarf and announced he was going to meet a contact but would be home by six, leaving plenty of time to dress for dinner. He was seen at the bar of the St. Georges Hotel, apparently deep in thought. After downing several drinks, Philby asked the barman if he could use the telephone. Eleanor was making supper for her daughter Annie and Philby's youngest son, Harry, who were staying for the holiday, when the telephone rang. Thirteen-year-old

Harry answered it and shouted to Eleanor in the kitchen: "Daddy's going to be late. He says he'll meet you at the Balfour-Pauls' at eight."

But eight o'clock came and went at the Balfour-Pauls' with no sign of Kim Philby. Eleanor apologized for her husband's tardiness and said she thought he might be sending a story to the *Economist*. By nine thirty what had been a "cosy gathering" was becoming fractious and hungry. Marnie announced that they should eat anyway. The storm outside was building. When the food was cleared away, fresh drinks were served, and Eleanor, now quite drunk, was becoming worried. "God, what a horrible night! Perhaps he's been hit by a car, or stumbled into the sea."

Marnie tried to reassure her: "Don't be silly, Kim's obviously been held up." Clare Hollingworth noticed that her host, the diplomat Glen Balfour-Paul, "had nothing to say about his missing guest," which struck her as strange.

While the Balfour-Pauls' guests were eating trifle, a car with diplomatic plates drove toward the harbor in the sheeting rain. In the back sat Philby, with Pavel Nedosekin alongside him; Petukhov sat in front beside the driver. "Everything is fine, everything is going the way it should," said Nedosekin. Philby wondered, with a flicker of malice, just how much trouble Peter Lunn would get into for his ill-timed skiing break. At that moment a Latvian sailor was getting hopelessly drunk, with the generous encouragement of a Soviet intelligence officer, in one of the harbor bars. The car entered the port, drove along the quay, and pulled up alongside the *Dolmatova*, a Soviet freighter taking on cargo and bound for Odessa. The Russian captain shook hands with Philby on the gangplank and led him to a cabin. A bottle of cognac stood on the table. Philby, his minders, and the captain raised their glasses and drank. In a few minutes the bottle was empty. Petukhov handed him an identity card in the name of "Villi Maris," a merchant seaman from Riga. New clothes were laid out on the bed, including warm underwear. It would be cold in Moscow.

Eleanor left the Balfour-Pauls' dinner party before midnight and returned home through the rain. There was no sign of her husband at the rue Kantari and no message. She was now seriously alarmed. Soon after midnight she telephoned Peter Lunn at home. Lunn's wife Antoinette picked up and explained that Peter was out. She agreed to pass on a message that he should contact Eleanor as soon as possible. In fact, Lunn was already at the British embassy, attending "a hastily summoned meeting about Kim." The speed with which Lunn swung into action that night suggests that he was primed and waiting: perhaps the news of Philby's failure to appear for dinner reached him from Balfour-Paul, but it is also possible that he was tracking Philby's movements by other means. Within minutes Lunn was on the telephone to Eleanor:

"Would you like me to come round?" he asked.

"I would be most grateful," she said.

When Lunn duly appeared, Eleanor explained that Philby had left the flat earlier that afternoon, telephoned in the afternoon, and then vanished. Lunn asked if anything was missing, such as clothes, documents, or Philby's typewriter, but all was in place, including his British passport. Lunn surely knew that Philby was doing a "fade" and already on his way to Moscow. The most important Soviet spy in history was on the run. But instead of behaving as one might expect in such a crisis, Lunn was calm; he did not conduct a full search of the flat, alert the Lebanese police, or put a watch on the borders, the ports, or the airports. Fearing her husband had suffered some sort of accident, Eleanor wanted to call the hospitals or search some of his favorite bars, but Lunn was almost nonchalant: "His advice was to do nothing until morning." Lunn left the flat at around 2:00 a.m. and immediately telephoned the British ambassador. Then he wrote a twenty-six-paragraph cable to Dick White in London.

Eleanor spent a sleepless night, waiting and wondering, struggling with the "terrible fear" that her life had changed forever. Before dawn the *Dolmatova* weighed anchor and headed out to sea. The Russian freighter had obviously departed in haste, because some of her cargo was left lying on the quayside. She also left behind a member of her crew, a very drunk Latvian seaman called Villi Maris, who would discover, when he finally woke up, that he had lost both his identity card and his ship. Philby stood at the rail of the *Dolmatova*, wrapped up against the cold in his Westminster scarf, and watched the dawn break over the receding bay, knowing that the "last link with England had been severed forever."

Three years after independence, the former French Congo was in turmoil, a cold-war battleground riven by civil war. It was certainly a logical place for Elliott to be. He always claimed he was in Brazzaville, preparing to cross the Congo River, when he received a coded message informing him of Philby's disappearance and instructing him to return at once to Beirut. But the speed with which he reappeared in Beirut suggests he may have been somewhere nearer at hand. Elliott concluded at once that "Philby had vanished into the blue (or rather the red)." He found Eleanor close to hysteria, fearing that her husband had been abducted, or worse. Within days she received a mysterious letter, purporting to come from Philby (several more would follow), hinting that he was on a secret journalistic assignment: "Tell my colleagues I'm on a long tour of the area." The letter was so peculiar in tone that Eleanor thought it might have been written under duress. Among Beirut's journalists it was generally assumed that if Philby was not chasing a story, he must be off on a bender or bedded down somewhere with a mistress. MI6 knew better. The hasty departure of the *Dolmatova* clearly indicated where Philby had gone, and how. The Russian link was confirmed by the discovery of banknotes in Philby's safe with serial numbers matching those recently issued to a Soviet diplomat by a Beirut bank.

Elliott did his best to calm Eleanor without giving away what he knew. "There is no question that she was deeply in love with him and had no suspicion that he was a traitor to his country," Elliott wrote. Philby had disappeared "in circumstances calculated to do her maximum hurt," but Elliott could not yet bring himself to reveal to Eleanor that Philby was a Soviet spy who had lied to her throughout their marriage, just as he had lied to Aileen throughout his previous marriage and to Elliott himself throughout their friendship. Yet he hinted at the truth: "You do realise that your husband was not an ordinary man?" he told her. She would find out just how extraordinary soon enough.

A few weeks later, a scruffy stranger knocked on the door of the apartment on the rue Kantari, thrust an envelope into Eleanor's hand, and disappeared back down the stairwell. The envelope contained a three-page typewritten letter, signed with love from Kim, instructing her to buy a plane ticket for London, to throw any watchers off the scent, and then secretly go to the Czech airlines office and buy another ticket for Prague. Then she should go to the alleyway opposite the house, leading to the sea, "choose a spot high up on the wall, towards the right," and write, in white chalk, the exact date and time of the flight to Prague. Philby instructed her to burn the letter after reading. Eleanor was deeply suspicious and distraught, "convinced that Kim had been kidnapped" and that she was being lured into a trap. In fact, Philby's plan to get Eleanor to join him was genuine, if unworkable: the press had by now picked up the story of his mysterious disappearance, her movements were being watched, and the idea that Eleanor could blithely walk onto a plane and fly to Czechoslovakia was ludicrously impractical. After some indecision, she told Elliott about the letter, and he instructed her "on no account to meet any strangers outside the house." Elliott then crept up the alleyway and chalked a date and flight time on the wall, "to test the system and cause confusion in the enemy ranks." It was the first thrust in a peculiar duel across the iron curtain.

The news of Philby's defection tore like brushfire through the intelligence communities on both sides of the Atlantic, provoking shock, embarrassment, and furious recrimination. Philby's defenders in MI6 were stunned and his detractors in MI5 enraged that he had been allowed to escape. In the CIA there was baffled dismay at what was seen as yet another British intelligence disaster. Hoover was livid. "Many people in the secret world aged the night they heard," wrote one MI5 officer. "To find that a man like Philby, a man you might like, or drink with, or admire, had betrayed everything; to think of the agents and operations wasted: youth and innocence passed away, and the dark ages began." Arthur Martin, the officer originally slated to confront Philby in Beirut, was apoplectic: "We should have sent a team out there and grilled him while we had the chance." The belief that Philby must have been tipped off by another Soviet spy within British intelligence took root within MI5, prompting a mole hunt that would continue for years, sowing paranoia and distrust into every corner of the organization. Even Elliott came under investigation. Arthur Martin was detailed to grill him: "But after lengthy interrogation Elliott just convinced his interrogator that he was in the clear."

Desmond Bristow, Philby's protégé back in St Albans, who had risen steadily through MI6 ranks, was stunned by the news: "He had been my boss and in many ways my teacher on the ways of espionage. I could not bring myself to think of him as a Soviet agent. Philby's defection turned into a perennial cloud of doubt hanging over the present, the past, and the future." Dick White was said to have reacted with "horror" to the news. "I never thought he would accept the offer of immunity and then skip the country," he said. To Elliott he confided: "What a shame we reopened it all. Just trouble." The head of MI6 may have been genuinely astounded by events, or he may simply have been playing a part. Philby's defection might be embarrassing, but it had also solved a problem. C's colleagues noted that while he professed surprise at Philby's vanishing act, White did not seem unduly "disappointed."

To Elliott fell the delicate and exceedingly unpleasant task of breaking the news to James Angleton. The FBI knew about the confrontation in Beirut and Philby's confession, but the CIA had been kept entirely in the dark. "I tried to repair the damage by telephoning Jim Angleton," Elliott later said, "but it was too late." Angleton was publicly incensed and privately mortified. Like Elliott, he now had to "face the awful truth and acknowledge that his British friend, hero, and mentor had been a senior KGB agent." This master spy had been taken in by a spy far more adept than he. The long liquid lunches, the secrets spilled so easily more than a decade earlier, the deaths and disappearances of so many agents sent to make secret war in the Soviet bloc; it had all been part of a brutal game, which Philby had won hands down. The impact of that traumatic discovery would have far-reaching consequences for America and the world. In the short term Angleton set about doctoring the record, putting it about that he had always suspected Philby, had kept him under surveillance, and would have trapped him but for British incompetence—fictions that he would propagate and cling to obsessively for the rest of his life. But the truth was in the files. Each of the thirty-six meetings Philby attended at CIA headquarters between 1949 and 1951 had been typed up in a separate memo by Angleton's secretary Gloria Loomis; every one of the discussions at Harvey's restaurant was carefully recorded. Everything that Angleton had ever told Philby, and thus the precise human and political cost of their friendship, was on paper, stored in an archive under the direct control of the chief of CIA counterintelligence, James Angleton. Years later the CIA conducted an internal search for these files: every single one has vanished. "I had them burned," Angleton told MI5 officer Peter Wright. "It was all very embarrassing."

Philby's former friends and colleagues found themselves combing back over the years they had known him, searching for clues. The more candid among them acknowledged they had never suspected him. Others claimed that they had doubted his loyalty since the defection of Burgess and Maclean in 1951. Still others now claimed that they had *always* seen through him, proving that the least trustworthy people are those who claim to have seen it all coming, after it has all come. The most honest admitted that Philby's ruthless charm had seduced them utterly. Glen Balfour-Paul, whose dinner party Philby skipped on the night he vanished, wrote: "He was an unforgivable traitor to his country, responsible among much else for the assassination by his Soviet associates of many brave men. All I can say is that in the half of him that I knew (the deceitful half, of course) he was a most enjoyable friend."

Miles Copeland was "dumbfounded" by Philby's "unbelievable" defection, concluding: "He was the best actor in the world."

Copeland's astonishment rather undermines his later claim to have kept Philby under surveillance, on Angleton's orders, during the Beirut years. Copeland had been duped like everyone else and offered a clear-eyed assessment of the damage inflicted by the KGB's most effective spy: "What Philby provided was feedback about the CIA's reactions. They [the KGB] could accurately determine whether or not reports fed to the CIA were believed or not. . . . What it comes to, is that when you look at the whole period from 1944 to 1951, the entire Western intelligence effort, which was pretty big, was what you might call minus advantage. We'd have been better off doing nothing."

In March 1963, under intense pressure from the media, the British government was forced to acknowledge that Philby was missing. Three months later Edward Heath, the Lord Privy Seal, issued a statement declaring: "Since Mr Philby resigned from the Foreign Service in 1951, twelve years ago, he has had no access of any kind to any official information." That same month, Philby was granted Soviet citizenship. HELLO, MR PHILBY, ran the headline in *Izvestia*, the official Soviet newspaper, accompanied by a sketch of the defector in Pushkin Square. And so began the Great Philby Myth: the superspy who had bamboozled Britain, divulged her secrets and those of her allies for thirty years, and then escaped to Moscow in a final triumphant coup de théâtre, leaving the wrong-footed dupes of MI6 wringing their hands in dismay. That myth, occasionally spruced up by Russian propaganda and eagerly propagated by Philby himself, has held firm ever since.

But there were some to whom the story of Philby's daring nighttime getaway did not quite ring true. "Philby was allowed to escape," wrote Desmond Bristow. "Perhaps he was even encouraged. To have brought him back to England and convicted him as a traitor would have been even more embarrassing; and when they convicted him, could they really have hanged him?" That view was echoed in Moscow. Yuri Modin, the canny Soviet case officer, wrote: "To my mind the whole business was politically engineered. The British government had nothing to gain by prosecuting Philby. A major trial, to the inevitable accompaniment of spectacular revelation and scandal, would have shaken the British establishment to its foundations." Far from being caught out by Philby's defection, "the secret service had actively encouraged him to slip away," wrote Modin. Many in the intelligence world believed that by leaving the door open to Moscow and then walking away, Elliott had deliberately forced Philby into exile. And they may have been right.

Divining Elliott's precise motives is impossible, because for the next thirty years he carefully obscured and muddied them. To some he played the role of the sucker, describing Philby's flight as a shock and claiming that the possibility of defection had never occurred to him. But to others he gave the opposite impression: that he was entirely unsurprised by Philby's flight, because he had engineered it. In a book written years later under KGB supervision, Philby depicted his defection as the heroic checkmate move of the grand master: "I knew exactly how to handle it," he wrote. "How could they have stopped me?" The answer: very easily. Simply posting a Watcher on rue Kantari would have made it all but impossible for Philby to flee. But no such effort was made. As Modin wrote, "spiriting Philby out of Lebanon was child's play," because Elliott and MI6 had made it so easy—suspiciously easy, in Modin's mind.

There are two diametrically opposed interpretations of Philby's flight to Moscow. According to the first, Philby was the virtuoso spy and Elliott the fool; according to the second, those roles were reversed. Under the first scenario Philby made the decision, waited until British intelligence was looking the other way, and ran. The ease of his defection, he wrote, was the result of British blundering, "a mistake, simple stupidity." This version of events requires the assumption that MI6 was not merely inefficient and naive but quite astonishingly dim. A second, more plausible story goes like this: Elliott successfully extracted the confession that ensured Philby was now under MI6 control; he made it crystal clear that Philby's continued liberty was dependent on his continued cooperation; then, perhaps with the connivance of Dick White, he stepped away, spread the rumor that Lunn had gone skiing, and allowed Philby to believe the coast was clear, the road to Moscow wide open.

Among those who thought that Elliott, and not Philby, had won the last round was Kim Philby himself. He left Beirut thinking he had jumped; only later did Philby come to believe that he had been pushed.

KIM PHILBY WAS welcomed to Moscow by the KGB, given a thorough medical examination, and installed in a flat luxurious by Soviet standards. A minder was appointed to guard him. He was given a salary of about two hundred pounds a month and a promise that his children would be financially supported back in Britain. The KGB agreed to bring furniture and furnishings from Beirut, including an oak table given to him by Tommy Harris. Two of his favorite pipes were purchased on Jermyn Street and shipped to Moscow in the diplomatic bag. Guy Burgess and Donald Maclean were both living in Moscow, although they had by now fallen out, partly as a result of an incident during which a drunken Burgess had urinated in the fireplace of the Chinese embassy. The spy's circumstances had changed, but his habits not at all. In the summer of 1963 he died of liver failure, leaving Philby his four-thousand-book library. Philby did not see him before he died, though he later claimed that he had been prevented from doing so by his Russian handlers. "Burgess was a bit of an embarrassment here," he told the journalist Phillip Knightley. Philby had books, pipes, furniture, and rugs; now he wanted his wife.

In May, four months after Philby's disappearance, Eleanor Philby flew to London. The press was now rampaging all over the story of the defection of the third man and lying in wait for her. A few weeks earlier an "unmistakably Russian" man had appeared at her door and declared: "I'm from Kim. He wants you to join him. I'm here to help." She refused the offer, reported it to Elliott, and arrived in Britain in a state of utter confusion, still uncertain where her husband was and not knowing whether to believe the stories about his espionage and defection.

Nicholas Elliott sent a car to pick her up from the airport to escape the press. He found her a doctor to treat a swollen ankle and then, once she was back on her feet, took her out to lunch. When Eleanor brought up the subject of reuniting with Philby, Elliott was insistent: "Kim was an active communist agent and [she] should on no account contemplate going to Moscow." He warned her: "They probably won't let you out, if you go." Eleanor was struck once again by Elliott's "surprising tenderness" but was still reluctant to accept that Philby was a Soviet spy. Elliott offered to summon the head of MI6 himself, in order to persuade her. Dick White appeared within the hour, and Elliott installed them together in the sitting room of Wilton Street with coffee and a bottle of brandy. White was courteous, adamant, and only slightly untruthful. "We have definitely known for the last seven years that Kim has been working for the Russians without pay," he said. White had suspected Philby for far longer than that but had discovered clear-cut proof of his guilt less than a year earlier. By the end of the afternoon, Eleanor Philby was in floods of tears, woozy on sedatives and brandy, but finally convinced that her husband was indeed a spy. She had been, in her words, "the victim of a prolonged and monstrous confidence trick," yet she was still determined to join the con man in Moscow.

In September she received another letter from Kim: "All I am thinking of now is seeing you." Elliott did everything he could to dissuade her from going. One day he bought her a ticket to see Alfred Hitchcock's film *The Birds*, in which a community is attacked by avian marauders. "I don't know what he had in mind, except perhaps to demoralise me," she later wrote. This was, perhaps, Elliott's way of warning Eleanor that a life that seems calm and secure can swiftly turn to nightmare. She was unmoved and a few days later found herself in the office of the smiling Soviet consul, who told her to be ready to fly to Moscow in two days before handing over five hundred pounds in cash: "Buy yourself some very warm clothes."

When Eleanor announced she was leaving, Elliott mobilized his own wife in a last-ditch attempt to get her to see sense.

"What would *you* do if the man you loved went behind the Iron Curtain?" Eleanor asked Elizabeth as they drank tea.

The idea of Nicholas Elliott defecting to the USSR was so preposterous that Elizabeth found it hard not to laugh. But as Eleanor wrote, "she finally admitted that she would do the same thing I was planning to do."

Elliott feared that Eleanor might be trapped forever in Russia and believed that any attempt to resume her marriage to Philby was doomed. Yet he could not help admiring her bravery and the "passionate loyalty and devotion" that the betrayer could still inspire. "Although I had put the fear of God into her she was determined to return to Moscow and have it out with him. She left the next day."

Eleanor flew to Moscow on September 26, 1963, and landed at the airport disguised in a turban and dark glasses. Philby and his minder were waiting. "Eleanor, is that you?" he said.

LATE ONE NIGHT a few weeks later, Elliott heard a soft thump as a letter, delivered by hand, dropped into the letter box at 13 Wilton Street. Inside was a typewritten letter and an empty envelope addressed to Kim Philby at PO Box 509, Central Post Office, Moscow. The letter carried no postmark, date, or letterhead, but the handwriting on the envelope was unmistakable.

Dear Nick,

I wonder if this letter will surprise you. Our last transactions were so strange that I cannot help thinking that perhaps you wanted me to do a fade.

I am more than thankful for your friendly interventions at all times. I would have got in touch with you earlier, but I thought it better to let time do its work on the case.

It is invariably with pleasure that I remember our meetings and talks. They did much to help one get one's bearings in this complicated world! I deeply appreciate, now as ever, our old friendship, and I hope that rumours which have reached me about your having had some trouble on my account, are exaggerated. It would be bitter to feel that I might have been a source of trouble to you, but I am buoyed up by my confidence that you will have found a way out of any difficulties that may have beset you.

I have often thought that there are a number of questions connected with the whole story that might interest you, and it might be helpful all round if we could get together as in old times and discuss matters of mutual interest. After careful thought, I have come to the conclusion that Helsinki, which you could reach without difficulty, would be a suitable rendezvous—or perhaps Berlin?

I am enclosing an unsealed, addressed envelope. In the event of your agreeing to my proposal, would you post it, enclosing some view of Tower Bridge? On receipt of your letter, I will write again, through the same channel, and make suggestions about the admin. side of the rendezvous.

As you have probably guessed, I am sending this letter by "safe hand" to your private address for obvious reasons. You will, of course, treat this as a wholly private communication concerning only our two selves. At least, I hope you will see your way to follow my advice in this matter.

Guy's death was a bitter blow. He had been very ill for a long time, and only his ox-like constitution enabled him to live as long as he did. What a pity we shall never be able to gather à trois at Pruniers!

Let me hear from you soon.

Love to Elizabeth (to whom by the way, you had better not disclose the contents of this letter—nor to anyone else of course).

Elliott was astonished. Philby wrote as if his betrayal were no more than a hiccup in their long friendship. It was as if Vermehren, Volkov, the pixies, and the countless others betrayed to their deaths had never existed. Was he trying to lure Elliott into a trap? Or was this an attempt to persuade him to turn double agent, to change his bearings in this "complicated world"? The sending of a blank postcard of Tower Bridge would convey a message that the KGB could interpret: was this intended to show that Philby was acting without KGB approval, and therefore a hint that he was prepared to be reeled back in, to "discuss matters of mutual interest"? Elliott's initial reaction was one of outrage. "It was ridiculous to suppose that I would agree to meet him behind the backs of my boss and my wife." The old Philby charm, laced with bravado, was there in abundance, with its allusion to their valued friendship and the hope that he had not damaged his friend's career. Elliott decided that the letter must be "an incredibly clumsy piece of KGB disinformation, obviously designed to throw doubts on my loyalty." The next morning he took the letter in to MI6 headquarters and showed it to Dick White, who was equally intrigued. The strange missive prompted "many hours of discussion as to what, if anything, should be done about it." Elliott was in favor of setting up a meeting, "because first, I was certainly fitter than he was, and secondly because I could choose the rendezvous." He was overruled.

The key to Philby's intentions may lie in the first line of the letter. He wanted to know, once and for all, whether Elliott had deliberately cornered him into defecting. Trading once more on their friendship, he hoped to find out if, in the end, he had really won the battle of manipulation, whether he had outmaneuvered Elliott or the other way round.

Elliott did not give him that satisfaction, but he did send back a last, unmistakably barbed message, a blunt reference to just one "tragic episode" among so many, and just one of the many people Philby had destroyed, an epitaph for a friendship brutally betrayed: "Put some flowers for me on poor Volkov's grave."

Chapter Twenty

Three Old Spies

KIM PHILBY DID NOT LOVE MOSCOW, AND MOSCOW DID NOT LOVE him, though both tried to pretend otherwise. Philby had believed, back in 1934, that he was joining an "elite" force, but now he found he had no KGB rank and little to do. In Russian eyes he was an agent, not an officer, and one of little further use. He was welcomed, thanked, debriefed, and rewarded; but he was never quite trusted. The ease with which he had escaped from Beirut may have rekindled doubts long dormant in Moscow, the uneasy, queasy suspicion that he might yet be double-crossing the KGB. Yuri Modin found him unreadable: "He never revealed his true self. Neither the British, nor the women he lived with, nor ourselves ever managed to pierce the armor of mystery that clad him. . . . In the end I suspect that Philby made a mockery of everyone, particularly ourselves." A KGB minder accompanied him everywhere, ostensibly as protection against possible British retaliation but also as guard and jailer. He remained, in the words of one KGB officer, an "Englishman to his fingertips" and therefore innately suspect. In Britain Philby had been too British to be doubted; in Russia he was too British to be believed.

When Philby's copies of the *Times* arrived in Moscow, usually weeks after publication, he carefully ironed them and then pored over accounts of cricket matches long since over. He ate thick-cut Oxford marmalade on his toast, sipped imported English tea, and listened to the BBC World Service every evening at seven. When his children visited from the West, they brought Marmite,

Worcestershire sauce, and spices for the Indian meals he liked to cook. He wore a tweed jacket in houndstooth check and a woolen tie. He drank Johnnie Walker Red Label whiskey, often obliteratingly. He described Russia as his "homeland," insisting that he had never really "belonged" to the British ruling class and could not, therefore, have betrayed it. But more honestly, he admitted that he was "wholly and irreversibly English." At times he sounded like a retired civil servant put out to pasture (which, in a way, he was), harrumphing at the vulgarity of modern life, protesting against change. The new ways of cricket baffled and enraged him. "Aluminium bats, white balls, funny clothes . . . It is all too confusing for a gentleman of the old school like myself." In an unconscious echo of Marcus Lipton, MP, he grumbled about "the ghastly din of modern music" and "hooligans inflamed by bourgeois rock music."

Other old habits persisted. His marriage to Eleanor staggered on for a time, but it was broken inside. She found Moscow gray, cold, and lonely. One day she asked him: "What is more important in your life, me and the children, or the Communist Party?" Philby's answer was the one he always gave when asked to measure feeling against politics. "The party, of course." He demanded not only admiration for his ideological consistency, for having "stayed the course," but sympathy for what it had cost him. "If you only knew what hell it is when your political convictions clash with your personal affections," he wrote in a note to the diplomat Glen Balfour-Paul. On the few occasions he received visitors from the West, he asked hungrily after news of friends. "Friendship is the most important thing of all," he declared, as if he had not undermined every one of his own. Lorraine Copeland wrote that it was "painful to think that during the years we all loved Kim and had him constantly in our homes, he was all the while laughing at us." Philby bridled at that suggestion. "I wasn't laughing at them. I have always operated on two levels, a personal level and a political one. When the two have come into conflict I have had to put politics first. The conflict can be very painful. I don't like deceiving people, especially friends, and contrary to what others think, I feel very badly about it." But not so badly as to stop.

Philby rekindled his friendship with Donald Maclean and his wife, Melinda, and the two exiled couples were naturally thrown together. Maclean spoke fluent Russian and had been given a job analyzing British foreign policy. He often worked late. Philby and Melinda started going to the opera and then on shopping trips together. In 1964 Eleanor returned to the United States to renew her passport and see her daughter. In her absence Kim Philby and Melinda Maclean started an affair. It was a fitting liaison: Philby was secretly sleeping with the wife of an ideological comrade and cheating on his own wife, repeating once again the strange cycle of friendship and betrayal that defined his world. Eleanor returned, discovered the affair, and announced she was leaving him for good: Philby did not try to stop her. He did, however, present her with his most treasured possession, his old Westminster scarf. "It had travelled with him—from school days to exile in Moscow," wrote Elliott. This symbolic loyalty to his old school was, Elliott thought, a "supreme example of schizophrenia." At the airport a KGB officer sent Eleanor on her way with a bunch of tulips.

Like Aileen before her, Eleanor did not long survive their final breakup. She wrote a poignant, pained memoir and died three years after returning to the United States. "He betrayed many people, me included," she wrote. "Kim had the guts, or the weakness, to stand by a decision he made 30 years ago, whatever the cost to those who loved him most." Eleanor spent the remainder of her life wondering whom she had really married, and concluded: "No one can ever really know another human being."

JAMES JESUS ANGLETON's personality was transformed by the realization that he had never really known Kim Philby. His faith in his fellow men had never been strong, but he had believed in the British notion that the inner ring could always be trusted; after Philby's defection a profound and poisonous paranoia seemed to seize him. "The emotional wreckage of that close friendship made him distrust everybody and colored his life from that point on." He became convinced that a vast, overarching conspiracy must be taking place under his nose, orchestrated by Philby from Moscow. "Jim just continued to think that Philby was a key actor in the KGB grand plan," one CIA contemporary said of Angleton. "To him, Philby was never just a drunken, burned-out ex-spy. He was a leader of the orchestra." In Angleton's warped logic, if Philby had fooled him, then there must be many other KGB spies in positions of influence in the West. "Never again would he permit himself to be so badly duped. He would trust no one."

Convinced that the CIA was riddled with Soviet spies, Angleton set about rooting them out, detecting layer after layer of deception surrounding him. He suspected that a host of world leaders were all under KGB control, including British prime minister Harold Wilson, Olof Palme of Sweden, and German chancellor Willy Brandt. He drew up more than ten thousand case files on suspect individuals, antiwar protesters, and internal dissidents, often gathering information by illegal means. The damage he inflicted on the CIA reached such levels that some even accused him of being a Soviet mole himself, destroying the organization from within by creating a climate of debilitating suspicion. Uncompromising and obsessive, more than a decade after Philby's vanishing act Angleton was still ascribing every fresh sign of treachery to the man he had once idolized. "This is all Kim's work," he would mutter.

Nicholas Elliott watched and wondered as Angleton descended into his wilderness of mirrors. They remained friends from a distance, but the warmth had gone. The Philby betrayal seemed to metastasize in Angleton's mind. "He had trusted him and confided in him far beyond any routine relationship between the colleagues of two friendly countries," wrote Elliott. "The knowledge that he, Jim, the top expert in the world on Soviet espionage, had been totally deceived, had a cataclysmic effect on his personality. Jim henceforward found it difficult to trust anybody, to make two and two add up to four." Elliott believed his old friend was being devoured by distrust: "Over-suspicion can sometimes have more tragic results than over-credulity. His tragedy was that he was so often deceived by his own ingenuity, and the consequences were often disastrous."

James Angleton was forced out of the CIA in 1974, when the extent of his illegal mole hunting was revealed. He retired with his orchids, his fishing rods, and his secrets, a man of deep and enduring mystery, and a brilliant fool. In retirement he spent much of his time in the Army and Navy Club, a place strongly redolent of an old-fashioned London gentlemen's club. He continued to insist that he had suspected Kim Philby from the start; but his weeding from CIA files of every reference to his relationship with Philby was proof enough of the falsity of that claim. Philby haunted the CIA: "I don't know that the damage he did can ever be actually calculated," wrote Richard Helms, the CIA chief appointed in 1966. One CIA historian assessed the cost by means of italics: "at least 25 major, *but* major operations, were destroyed."

In 1987 Angleton attended a luncheon with former CIA officers at the Officers' Club in Fort Myer outside Washington. He was sixty-nine but looked a decade older, already suffering from lung cancer and spectrally thin. His colleagues urged him to "come clean in the Philby case." Angleton gave one of his crippled half-smiles and said: "There are some matters that I shall have to take to the grave with me, and Kim is one of them."

A week later, true to his word, he was dead.

NICHOLAS ELLIOTT'S CAREER was hobbled by his association with Philby. Some in MI6 believed he had allowed Philby to flee Beirut out of personal loyalty. Some still do. By the 1960s the Robber Barons who had come of age in the 1940s were creatures of the past. MI6 was more professional, less buccaneering, and in Elliott's view a lot less fun. Sir Stewart Menzies and Elliott remained close friends. In 1968 the former C fell off his horse while riding with the Beaufort Hunt and never recovered. Elliott was the only serving MI6 officer to attend the funeral. By now he was director of requirements at MI6, responsible for the quality and relevance of information produced by the intelligence service for other government departments. It was an important job, but bureaucratic and exactly the sort of role he had always despised. "To be in administration was, in my view, the last resort."

Elliott retired in 1968 after almost thirty years as a spy. "Rather to my surprise I did not miss the confidential knowledge which no longer filtered through my in-tray," he wrote. He joined the board of Lonrho, the international mining and media company based in Cheapside in the City of London, and led by the maverick businessman Tiny Rowland. Elliott considered Rowland "a modern Cecil Rhodes," which did not stop him from joining a boardroom coup against him. When this failed, Rowland ousted the rebels, including Elliott, whom he described as "the Harry Lime of Cheapside." Elliott was thrilled to be compared to the sinister character played by Orson Welles in Graham Greene's *The Third Man* and adopted it as his soubriquet. He joined a firm of stockbrokers but found himself "incapable of leading that kind of life without relapsing into a slough of depression and boredom" and soon gave it up to pursue a life of esoteric and eccentric interests.

Elliott bought a share in a racehorse and never missed a day of Ascot. He watched a great deal of cricket and built up a fine wine cellar. He became interested in graphology, the pseudoscientific study of handwriting, and found he had a "gift for dowsing," the ability to locate underground water, ore, and gems. He could frequently be seen marching across the English country with his divining rods and then energetically digging holes. He approached MI6 with a plan to exhume buried Nazi treasure from the grounds of a monastery in Rome. He also took up Transcendental Meditation, which he considered a spiritual "alternative to involvement in religion." Klop Ustinov turned up at Wilton Street from time to time with hot veal kidneys *à la liégeoise* in a hatbox. Elliott's daughter Claudia died tragically young but, as ever, his stiff upper lip precluded public grief. He spent much of his time in clubs, where he was admired as a raconteur of risqué anecdotes, the conversational refuge of the Englishman who does not know quite what to say or cannot say what he really knows. He was no longer in the inner ring, but he did not yet abandon the secret world.

In the early 1980s a tall, spare figure in an immaculate three-piece suit could be seen from time to time slipping without fanfare into 10 Downing Street. Nicholas Elliott had become—no one was quite sure how—an unofficial adviser on intelligence matters to Margaret Thatcher. What was discussed during these meetings has never been fully revealed, and Elliott was far too discreet to say, but his political antennae were impeccable: after the breakup of the Soviet Union, he correctly predicted the emergence of an authoritarian government in Russia, and he foresaw the growth of Islamic fundamentalism, the rise of Iranian aggression, and the growing economic and political clout of China. Thatcher undoubtedly shared his view that postimperial Britain was "showing a quite unjustified lack of self-confidence." The costume of an éminence grise fit him well.

As Elliott aged, the pain of Philby's perfidy ebbed. Unlike Angleton, he would not allow Philby's ghost to torment and destroy him. He came to see the way he had been duped not as a mark of shame but as a badge of honor. Philby had been able to manipulate Elliott's loyal constancy, his adherence to an old code of behavior, as a weapon against him, and there was no dishonor in that. Yet he never ceased to wonder how someone who had been raised and educated as he had, someone he had known "extremely well over an extended period," could have chosen such a radically different path. "I have naturally given thought to the motivations behind treachery," he wrote. In later life he found himself trying to understand "Philby the man, and make some form of analysis of the personality that evolved." Whenever he reflected on the lives Philby had wasted, his anger welled up. "Outwardly he was a kindly man. Inwardly he must have been cold, calculating and cruel—traits which he cleverly concealed from his friends and colleagues. He undoubtedly had a high opinion of himself concealed behind a veil of false modesty and thus a firm streak of egocentricity." Philby had been a two-sided man, Elliott concluded, and he had only ever seen one beguiling side, "a façade, in a schizophrenic personality with a supreme talent for deception."

Though part of Elliott detested Philby, he also mourned him. He recalled Philby's small kindnesses, the devotion he inspired in others, his enchanting mischief. He imagined him living a "sad exiled life" in Moscow, with "dreary people, a spying servant, drab clothes," and felt a twinge of something like sympathy for a man of rare talent, whose life had been "wasted in a futile cause," who had "decided to betray his friends, his family, and country for a creed that is now universally discredited." He missed the spark that had drawn him to Philby on the very first day they met in 1940. "He had charm to burn," he wrote with a reluctant wistfulness. "He is said to have it still."

Philby also found his thoughts turning to Elliott in old age and reached the firm conclusion that he had been maneuvered into fleeing Beirut: "The whole thing was staged so as to push me into escaping." Elliott had been motivated by the "desire to spare SIS another spy scandal in London" and had unloaded him on Moscow.

As the cold war raged, Philby was used as a propaganda tool by both sides. The Soviets set out to prove that he was living, in the words of one apologist, a life in Moscow of "blissful peace." In 1968, with KGB approval (and editing), he published a memoir, *My Silent War*, a blend of fact and fiction, history and disinformation, which depicted Soviet intelligence as uniformly brilliant and himself as a hero of ideological constancy. Political voices in the West insisted that the reverse was true and that Philby—drunken, depressed, and disillusioned—was getting his just deserts for a life of betrayal and adherence to a diabolical doctrine. Ronald Reagan declared: "How sleepless must be Kim Philby's nights in Moscow. . . . How profoundly he and others like him must be aware that the people they betrayed are going to be victors in the end." One former MI5 officer even claimed to know what was going through Philby's mind when he did fall asleep: "He's a totally sad man, dreaming of a cottage in Sussex with roses around the door."

The truth was somewhere in between. Philby was deeply unhappy during the early years in Moscow, a place Burgess had memorably described as "like Glasgow on a Saturday night in Victorian times." The affair with Melinda soon fizzled out; she returned to Maclean and then left the USSR for good. Philby drank heavily, often alone, and suffered from chronic insomnia. He would later admit that his life became "burdensome." At some point he tried to end it by slashing his wrists. But in 1970 his spirits began to lift when George Blake, his fellow exile, introduced him to Rufina Ivanovna, a Russian woman of Polish extraction twenty years his junior, who would become his fourth wife. The KGB sent them a tea set of English bone china as a wedding present. The lingering suspicion of the Soviet intelligence service cleared, and in 1977 Philby gave a lecture to KGB officers, in which he insisted that the secret agent should admit nothing under interrogation and on no account provide a confession. "Any confession involves giving information to the enemy. It is therefore—by definition—wrong." Some of his audience must have known that Philby had himself confessed to Nicholas Elliott back in 1963. They were much too tactful to point this out.

Philby's last years were quiet, dutiful, and domesticated. Rufina tried to wean him off the booze, with only partial success. He did odd jobs for the Soviet state, including training KGB recruits and helping to motivate the Soviet hockey team—even though, as Elliott once noted, he was addicted to cricket and "showed no interest whatsoever in any other sort of sport." He was awarded the Order of Lenin, which he compared to a knighthood, "one of the better ones." In return, he never criticized the system he had supported all his adult life, never acknowledged the true character of the organization he had served, and never uttered a word of remorse. In the officially approved Soviet style, he maintained that any errors in practical communism lay not with the ideas but with the people executing them.

Philby died in a Moscow hospital on May 11, 1988. He was given a grand funeral with a KGB honor guard, buried at Kuntsevo Cemetery outside Moscow, and lauded for his "tireless struggle in the cause of peace and a brighter future." He was commemorated with a Soviet postage stamp. In 2011 the Russian foreign intelligence service put up a plaque with two faces of Kim Philby facing one another in profile, an inadvertently apt monument to a man with two sides to his head.

Elliott hatched a plan for a different sort of memorial. He recommended to MI6 that Philby be awarded the CMG, the order of St Michael and St George, the sixth-most-prestigious award in the British honors system, awarded to men and women who render extraordinary or important nonmilitary service in a foreign country. Elliott further suggested that he write a signed obituary note to accompany the award, in which he would say only: "My lips have hitherto been sealed but I can now reveal that Philby was one of the bravest men I have ever known." The implication would be clear to Moscow: Philby had been acting for Britain all along; he was not a valiant Soviet double agent but a heroic British triple agent, and Elliott had been his spymaster. The idea that Philby had fooled the KGB would cause "a tremendous fluttering in the dovecotes of the Lubyanka," Elliott wrote, and inflict the most gratifying posthumous revenge. It would be a splendid tease at Philby's expense to which he could have no answer. Elliott's proposal was turned down. The new-style MI6 did not do jokes.

As his own end approached, Elliott reflected on a life that had been "undistinguished, albeit mildly notorious," and tremendous fun. He had known indignity, misfortune, and intimate betrayal, but his fund of natural optimism never ran out. "I feel I have been extraordinarily lucky," he wrote. "I look back on my career with some wonderment."

Elliott kept a part of Philby with him always. He treasured the old umbrella he had bought so many years ago in admiring imitation of his closest friend and his worst enemy. When Elliott died in

1994, he left behind a short memoir, mostly consisting of off-color stories, with a rueful, self-mocking title: *Never Judge a Man by His Umbrella.*

It was a joke that only two people could have fully appreciated: Nicholas Elliott and Kim Philby.

Afterword

BY *JOHN LE CARRÉ*

"God, it would be good to be a fake somebody, rather than a real nobody."

—MIKE TYSON, WORLD HEAVYWEIGHT
BOXING CHAMPION

NICHOLAS ELLIOTT OF MI6 WAS THE MOST CHARMING, WITTY, elegant, courteous, compulsively entertaining spy I ever met. In retrospect, he also remains the most enigmatic. To describe his appearance is, these days, to invite ridicule. He was a *bon viveur* of the old school. I never once saw him in anything but an immaculately cut, dark three-piece suit. He had perfect Etonian manners, and delighted in human relationships.

He was thin as a wand, and seemed always to hover slightly above the ground at a jaunty angle, a quiet smile on his face, and one elbow cocked for the martini glass or cigarette.

His waistcoats curved inwards, never outwards. He looked like a P. G. Wodehouse man-about-town, and spoke like one, with the difference that his conversation was startlingly forthright, knowledgeable, and recklessly disrespectful of authority.

During my service in MI6, Elliott and I had been on nodding terms at most. When I was first interviewed for the Service, he was on the selection board. When I became a new entrant, he was a fifth-floor grandee whose most celebrated espionage coup—the wartime recruitment of a highly placed member of the German Abwehr in Istanbul, smuggling him and his wife to Britain—was held up to trainees as the ultimate example of what a resourceful field officer could achieve.

And he remained that same glamorous, remote figure throughout my service. Flitting elegantly in and out of head office, he would deliver a lecture, attend an operational conference, down a few glasses in the grandees' bar, and be gone.

I resigned from the Service at the age of thirty-three, having made a negligible contribution. Elliott resigned at the age of fifty-three, having been central to pretty well every major operation that the Service had undertaken since the outbreak of the Second World War. Years later, I bumped into him at a party.

After a turbulent spell in the City, Elliott in the most civilised of ways seemed a bit lost. He was also deeply frustrated by our former Service's refusal to let him reveal secrets which in his opinion had long passed their keep-till date. He believed he had a right, even a duty, to speak truth to history. And perhaps that's where he thought I might come in—as some sort of go-between or cut-out, as the spies would have it, who would help him get his story into the open, where it belonged.

Above all, he wanted to talk to me about his friend, colleague, and nemesis, Kim Philby.

And so it happened, one evening in May 1986 in my house in Hampstead, twenty-three years after he had sat down with Philby in Beirut and listened to his partial confession, that Nicholas Elliott opened his heart to me in what turned out to be the first in a succession of such meetings. Or if not his heart, a version of it.

And it quickly became clear that he wanted to draw me in, to make me marvel, as he himself marvelled; to make me share his awe and frustration at the enormity of what had been done to him; and to feel, if I could, or at least imagine, the outrage and the pain that his refined breeding and good manners—let alone the restrictions of the Official Secrets Act—obliged him to conceal.

Sometimes while he talked I scribbled in a notebook, and he made no objection. Looking over my notes a quarter of a century later—twenty-eight pages from one sitting alone, handwritten on fading notepaper, a rusty staple at one corner—I am comforted that there is hardly a crossing-out.

Was I contemplating a novel built around the Philby-Elliott relationship? I can't have been. I'd already covered the ground in *Tinker Tailor Soldier Spy*. A piece of live theatre, perhaps? A two-hander, the Nick & Kim Show, spread over twenty years of mutual affection—I dare almost call it love—and devastating, relentless betrayal?

If that was what I secretly had in mind, Elliott would have none of it:

"May we not ever again think about *the play*," he wrote to me sternly in 1991. And I have tried not to ever since.

Like Philby, Elliott never spoke a word out of turn, however much he drank: except of course to Philby himself. Like Philby, he was a five-star entertainer, always a step ahead of you, bold, raunchy, and funny as hell. Yet I don't believe I ever seriously doubted that what I was hearing from Elliott was the cover story—the self-justification—of an old and outraged spy.

But where Philby's cover story was crafted to deceive his enemies, the purpose of Elliott's was to deceive himself. And as Ben Macintyre points out, over time the cover story began to appear in different and conflicting versions, of which I was treated to one.

In his monologues to me—for such they often were—he made much of his efforts, under Dick White's guidance, to winkle the "truth" out of Philby in the ten years leading up to the confrontation in Beirut: not the *whole* truth, God forbid! That would have been something that in their worst nightmares both White and Elliott had refused to contemplate.

But the limited truth, the digestible version: namely, in Elliott's jargon, that somewhere back in the war years when it was understandable, Kim had gone a bit squidgy about our gallant Russian ally and given him a bit of this and that; and if he could just get it off his chest, whatever it was he'd given them, we'd all feel a lot better, and he could get on with doing what he did best, which was beating the Russian at his own game.

Alas, Macintyre's researches prove incontrovertibly that no such cat-and-mouse game took place: rather that, as the clouds of suspicion gathered, the two friends went, not face-to-face, but shoulder to shoulder. Long drunken evenings spent together? Any number of them. Alcohol was so much a part of the culture of MI6 in those days that a non-drinker in the ranks could look like a subversive or worse.

But as to Elliott's claim that he was all the while probing for chinks in Philby's armour: well, Elliott may have believed it—and certainly he was determined that I should believe it too—because, in the world that he and Philby had inhabited together for so long, the man whose cover story is not believed is the man who is operationally dead.

"TERRIFIC CHARMER, with an impulse to shock. I knew Philby terribly well, specially the family. I really cared for them. I never knew a fellow like him for getting pissed. I'd interrogate him, he'd drink Scotch the whole time, I'd literally have to load him into a cab to send him home. Give the driver five quid to cart him upstairs. Took him to a dinner party once. Charmed everyone, then suddenly he started talking about his hostess's tits. Said she had the best breasts in the Service. Totally off-colour. I mean you don't, at a dinner party, start talking about your hostess's tits. But that's how he was. Liked to shock. I knew the father too. I had him to dinner in Beirut the night he died. Fascinating chap. Talked endlessly about his relationship with Ibn Saud. Eleanor, Philby's third wife, adored him. The old boy managed to make a pass at someone's wife, then left. A few hours later he'd died. Last words were 'God I'm bored.'"

In the absence of his wife, Elizabeth, I had already noted that Elliott consistently referred to Philby by his surname. Only in her presence did Philby become Kim.

———

"MY INTERROGATION OF Philby lasted a long time. The one in Beirut was the end of a series. We had two sources. One was a pretty good defector. The other was this mother figure. The Office shrink had told me about her. He rang me up, the shrink. He'd been treating Aileen, Philby's second wife, and he said, 'She's released me from my Hippocratic Oath. I've got to talk to you.' So I went and saw him and he told me Philby was homosexual. Never mind all his philandering, never mind that Aileen, whom I knew pretty well, said Philby liked his sex and was pretty good at it. He was homosexual, all part of a syndrome, and the psychiatrist, on no evidence he knew of, was also convinced he was bad. Working for the Russians. Or something. He couldn't be precise but he was sure of it. He advised me to look for a mother figure. Somewhere there'll be a mother figure, he said. It was this woman Solomon. [Flora Solomon, who introduced Philby to Aileen in 1939.] Jewish woman. She was working in Marks & Spencer's, a buyer or something. She was angry with Philby over the Jewish thing. Philby had been working for Colonel Teague, who was Head of Station in Jerusalem, and Teague was anti-Jewish, and she was angry. So she told us some things about him. Five [MI5] were in charge by then, and I passed it all on to Five—get the mother figure, Solomon. Wouldn't listen of course, they're too bureaucratic."

"PEOPLE WERE SO *naughty* about Philby. Sinclair and Menzies [former Chiefs of MI6]—well, they just wouldn't listen to anything against him."

"SO THIS CABLE came, saying they had the proof, and I cabled back to White saying I must go and confront him. It had been an on-going thing for so long, and I owed it to the family to get it out of him. Feel? Well, I don't think I'm an emotional sort of chap, much, but I was fond of his women and children, and I always had the feeling that Philby himself would like to get the whole thing off his chest and settle down and follow cricket, which was what he loved. He knew cricket averages backwards and forwards. He could recite cricket till the cows came home. So Dick White said okay. Go. So I flew to Beirut and I saw him and I said to him, if you're as intelligent as I think you are, and for the sake of your family, you'll come clean, because the game is up. Anyway, we could never have nailed him in court; he'd have denied it. Between you and me the deal was perfectly simple. He had to make a clean breast of it, which I thought he wanted to do anyway, which was where he fooled me, and he had to give us everything, but *everything* on damage. That was paramount. The damage limitation. After all, I mean one of the things the KGB would have been asking him was, who can we approach independently of you, who's in the Service, who might work for us? He might have suggested people. We had to know all that. Then whatever else he'd given them. We were completely firm on that."

My notes resort to straight dialogue:

Self: "So what were your sanctions if he didn't cooperate?"

Elliott: "What's that, old boy?"

"Your sanctions, Nick, what you could threaten him with in the extreme case. Could you have him sandbagged, for instance, and flown to London?"

"Nobody wanted him in London, old boy."

"Well, what about the ultimate sanction then—forgive me—could you have him killed, liquidated?"

"My dear chap. One of us."

"So what *could* you do?"

"I told him, the alternative was a *total* cut-off. There wouldn't be an embassy, a consulate, a legation, in the whole of the Middle East that would have the first bloody thing to do with him. The business community wouldn't touch him, his journalistic career would be dead in the water. He'd have been a leper. His whole life would have been over. It never even crossed my mind he'd go to Moscow. He'd done this one thing in the past, he wanted it out of the way, so he'd got to come clean. After that we'd forget it. What about his family and Eleanor?"

I mention the fate of less favoured traitors who did far less than Philby but spent years in prison for it:

"Ah well, *Vassall*—well he wasn't top league, was he?"

(John William Vassall, homosexual son of an Anglican parson and clerk to the naval attaché at the British Embassy in Moscow, was sentenced to eighteen years for spying for the KGB.)

"THAT WAS THE first session and we agreed to meet again at four o'clock and at four o'clock he turned up with a confession, sheets of it, eight or nine closely typed pages of stuff, on the damage, on everything, masses of it. Then he says, you could do me a favour actually. Eleanor knows you're in town. She doesn't know anything about me. But if you don't come round for a drink she'll smell a rat. So I say all right, for Eleanor's sake I'll come round and have a drink with you. But first of all I've got to encode this stuff and cable it to Dick White, which I did. When I got to his place for a drink, he'd passed out. Pissed. Lying on the floor. Eleanor and I had to put him to bed. She took his head, I took his feet. He never said anything when he was pissed. Never spoke a loose word in his life, far as I know. So I told her. I said to her, 'You know what this is about, don't you?' She said, 'No,' so I said, 'He's a bloody Russian spy.' He'd told me she hadn't rumbled him, and he was right. So I went home to London and left him to Peter Lunn to carry on the interrogation. Dick White had handled the case jolly well, but he hadn't said a word to the Americans. So I had to dash over to Washington and tell them. Poor old Jim Angleton. He'd made such a fuss of Philby when he was head of the Service's station in Washington, and when Angleton found out—when I told him, that is—he sort of went all the other way. I had dinner with him just a few days ago."

"MY THEORY IS, you see, that one day the KGB will publish the rest of Philby's biography. The first book sort of cut itself dead at 1947. My guess is, they've got another book in their locker. One of the things Philby *has* told them is to polish up their goons. Make 'em dress properly, smell less. Sophisticated. They're a totally different-looking crowd these days. Smart as hell, smooth, first-class chaps. Philby's work, that was, you bet your boots. No, we never thought of killing him. He fooled me, though. I thought he wanted to stay where he was."

"YOU KNOW, LOOKING back, though—don't you agree?—at all the things we got up to—all right, we had some belly-laughs—my God, we had some belly-laughs—we were terribly amateurish, in a way. I mean those lines through the Caucasus, agents going in and out, it was so *amateurish*. Well, he betrayed Volkov, of course, and they killed him. So when Philby wrote to me from Moscow and invited me to go and meet him in Berlin or Helsinki, and not tell Elizabeth or Dick White, I wrote back and told him to put some flowers on Volkov's grave for me. I thought that was rather good.

"I mean, who the *hell* did he think I was, not telling them? The first person I'd tell was Elizabeth, and *immediately* after that, I'd tell Dick White. I'd been out to dinner with Gehlen [Reinhard Gehlen, at that time director of the BND, West Germany's secret service]—did you know Gehlen?—came back late at night, and there was this plain envelope on the doormat with 'Nick' written on it. Dropped in by hand. 'If you can come, send me a postcard with Nelson's Column on it for Helsinki, Horseguards for Berlin,' some damned thing. Who the hell did he think I was? The Albanian operation? Well yes, he probably blew that too. I mean we had some fucking good assets in Russia too in the old days. Don't know what happened to them either. Then he wants to meet me because he's lonely. Well of course he's lonely. He shouldn't have gone. He fooled me. I've written about him. The Sherwood Press. The big publishers all wanted me to write about the interrogation, but I wouldn't. It's more for one's climbing friends, a memoir. You can't write about the Office. Interrogation's an art. You understand that. It went on over a long time. Where was I?"

SOMETIMES ELLIOTT DRIFTED off into reminiscences of other cases that he had been involved in. The most significant was that of Oleg Penkovsky, a GRU colonel who provided the West with vital Soviet defense secrets in the run-up to the Cuba missile crisis. Elliott was infuriated by a book concocted by the CIA as a piece of Cold War propaganda and published under the title *The Penkovsky Papers*:

"Frightful book. Made out the fellow was some kind of saint or hero. He was nothing of the sort, he'd been passed over and he was pissed off. The Americans turned him down but Shergy [Harold Shergold, controller of MI6's Soviet bloc operations] knew he was all right. Shergy had the nose. We couldn't have been less similar but we got on marvellously. *Les extrèmes se touchent.* I was in charge of Ops, Shergy was my number two. Marvellous field man, very sensitive, almost never wrong. He'd been right about Philby too, from very early. Shergold looked Penkovsky over and thought yes, so we took him on. Very brave thing, in spying, to put your faith in someone. Any fool can go back to his desk and say, 'I don't altogether trust this chap. On the one hand, on the other hand.' It takes a lot of guts to take a flyer and say, 'I believe in him.' That's what Shergy did, and we went along with him. Women. Penkovsky had these whores in Paris, we laid them on, and he complained he couldn't do anything with them: once a night and that was it. We had to send the Office doctor out to Paris to give him a shot in the bum so that he could get it up. You do get some belly-laughs, they were what one lived for sometimes. These marvellous belly-laughs. I mean, how could you crack up Penkovsky to be a hero? Mind you, betrayal takes courage. You have to hand it to Philby too. He had courage. Shergy resigned once. He was frightfully temperamental. I came in, found his resignation on my desk. 'In view of the fact that Dick White'—he put CSS of course—'has passed information to the Americans without my consent, and has therefore endangered my very sensitive source, I wish to resign as an example to other members of the Service'—something like that. White apologised and Shergy took back his resignation. I had to talk him round, though. Wasn't easy. Very temperamental chap. But a marvellous field man. And he got Penkovsky dead right. Artist."

ELLIOTT ON SIR Claude Dansey, also known as Colonel Z, deputy chief of MI6 during World War II:

"Utter shit. Stupid too. But tough and rude. Wrote these awful short minutes to people. Carried on feuds. I mean a real shit. I took over his networks when I became head of station in Bern after the war. Well, he did have these high-level business sources. *They* were good. He had a knack of getting these businessmen to do things for him. He was good at that."

On Sir George Young, vice chief to Sir Dick White during the Cold War:

"Flawed. Brilliant, coarse, always had to be out on his own. He went to Hambro's after the Service. I asked them later: How did you make out with George? Were you up or down? They said they reckoned, about even. He got them some of the Shah's money, but he made perfectly awful balls-ups that cost them about as much as he got for them."

On Professor Hugh Trevor-Roper, historian and wartime member of SIS:

"Brilliant scholar, all that, but wet and useless. Something perverse inside him. Laughed my head off when he took a dive on those Hitler diaries. The whole Service knew they were fake. But Hugh walked straight in. How *could* Hitler have written them? I wouldn't have the chap near me in the war. When I was head man in Cyprus I told my sentry at the door that if a Captain Trevor-Roper showed up, he should shove his bayonet up his arse. He showed up, the sentry told him what I'd said. Hugh was puzzled.

Belly-laughs. That's what I liked about the Service. Marvellous belly-laughs."

On providing a prostitute for a potential SIS asset from the Middle East:

"St Ermin's Hotel. She wouldn't go. Too near the House of Commons. 'My father's an MP.' She had to have fourth June off so that she could take her nephew out from Eton. 'Well, perhaps you'd rather we got someone else?' I said. Didn't hesitate. 'All I want to know is, how much?'"

On Graham Greene:

"I met him in Sierra Leone in the war. Greene was waiting for me at the harbour. 'Have you brought any French letters?' he yelled at me soon as I came within earshot. He had this fixation about eunuchs. He'd been reading the station code book and found that the Service actually had a code group for eunuch. Must have been from the days when we were running eunuchs in the harems, as agents. He was dying to make a signal with eunuch in it. Then one day he found a way. Head Office wanted him to attend a conference somewhere. Cape Town, I think. He had some operation fixed or something. Not an operation, knowing him, he never mounted one. Anyway he signalled back, 'Like the eunuch I can't come.'"

A wartime reminiscence of life in Turkey under diplomatic cover:

"Dinner at the Ambassador's. Middle of the war. Ambassadress lets out a yell because I've cut off the nose. 'Nose of what?' 'The cheese.' 'The valet *handed* me the bloody cheese,' I tell her. 'And you cut the nose off it,' she says. Hell did they get it from? Middle of the bloody war. Cheddar. And the chap who'd handed it to me was Cicero, the fellow who sold all our secrets to the Abwehr. The D-Day landing. The lot. And the Huns didn't believe him. Typical. No faith."

I am describing to Elliott how, while I was in MI5, Graham Greene's *Our Man in Havana* was published and the Service's legal advisor wanted to prosecute him under the Official Secrets Act for revealing the relationship between a head of station and his head agent.

"Yes, and he jolly nearly got done for it. Would have served him bloody right."

What for? But I didn't ask.

AND MOST MEMORABLE of all, perhaps, Elliott recalling a passage, real or imagined, from what he insisted were his early soundings of Philby concerning his Cambridge days:

" 'They seem to think you're a bit *tarnished* somehow.'

" 'By?'

" 'Oh, you know, early passions, membership—'

" 'Of?'

" 'Jolly interesting group, actually, by the sounds of it. Exactly what university is for. Lefties all getting together. The Apostles, wasn't it?' "

IN 1987, TWO years before the Berlin Wall came down, I was visiting Moscow. At a reception given by the Union of Soviet Writers, a part-time journalist with KGB connections named Genrikh Borovik invited me to his house to meet an old friend and admirer of my work. The name of the friend, when I enquired, was Kim Philby. I now have it on pretty good authority that Philby knew he was dying and was hoping I would collaborate with him on another volume of memoirs.

I refused to meet him. Elliott was pleased with me. At least I think he was. But perhaps he secretly hoped I might bring him news of his old friend.

Cornwall, England, 2014

Acknowledgments

I AM AGAIN INDEBTED TO MANY PEOPLE WHO HAVE PROVIDED guidance, encouragement, and hospitality during the writing of this book, as well as access to documents, photographs, and their own memories. I am particularly grateful to the families and descendants of people in a story that remains, for many, a painful chapter of the past. This book would have been impossible to write without the generous help of Mark and David Elliott, son and grandson of Nicholas Elliott, who have proved an endless fund of support and practical assistance. I was also privileged to meet Elizabeth Elliott, widow of Nicholas, just a few weeks before her death in 2012. The list that follows is incomplete, since many of those who were most helpful to me have understandably asked, for professional reasons, to remain anonymous: you know who you are, and how grateful I am.

I would particularly like to thank the following: Nathan Adams, Christopher Andrew, Dick Beeston, the late Rick Beeston, Paul Bellsham, Keith Blackmore, Tom Bower, Roger Boyes, Alex Brooman-White, Anthony Cavendish, Rozanne Colchester, Gordon Corera, David Cornwell, Jane Cornwell, Leo Darroch, Natasha Fairweather, Frances Gibb, Oleg Gordievsky, Peter Greenhalgh, Barbara Honigmann, William Hood, Alistair Horne, Keith Jeffery, Margy Kinmonth, Jeremy Lewis, Peter Linehan, Philip Marsden, Nick Mays, Robert McCrum, Tommy Norton, John Julius Norwich, Michael Pakenham, Roland Philipps, Harry Chapman Pincher, Gideon Rachman, Felicity Rubinstein, Jenni Russell,

John Smedley Archives, Xan Smiley, Wolfgang Suschitzky, Rupert Walters, Nigel West, and Damian Whitworth.

I am indebted to Robert Hands, Peter Martland, Richard Aldrich, and Hayden Peake for reading the manuscript and saving me from many embarrassing errors: the errors that remain are entirely my own. Once again, Jo Carlill has achieved miracles of picture research; I have enjoyed and profited greatly from working with the BBC: Janice Hadlow, Martin Davidson, Dominic Crossley-Holland, Francis Whateley, Tom McCarthy, Ben Ryder, Louis Caulfield, Adam Scourfield, Dinah Rogers, Gezz Mounter, and Jane Chan. My colleagues and friends at *The Times* (London) have provided help and advice. The generous provision of a fellow commonership by St John's College Cambridge enabled me to finish the book in the ideal scholarly surroundings.

It is a pleasure and privilege to be published by Crown: my particular thanks to Molly Stern and Kevin Doughten for their unfailing patience and efficiency. Ed Victor, as ever, has steered another huge and complicated project into port with the skill of master-mariner.

My family deserves both praise and sympathy for putting up with yet another consuming spy project without throwing me out; and to Kate, all my love.

Notes

Citations marked "KV" refer to the Security Service files, "PREM" to Prime Minister's Office files, and "FO" to Foreign Office files, all at the National Archives (TNA) at Kew, UK.

EPIGRAPHS

vii **Friends: noun, general slang:** International Spy Museum, "Language of Espionage," http://www.spymuseum.org/education-programs/spy-resources/language-of-espionage/#F.

vii **If I had to choose between:** *The Nation*, July 16, 1938.

CHAPTER ONE: APPRENTICE SPY

3 **"I am relieved":** Nicholas Elliott, *Never Judge a Man by His Umbrella* (London, 1992), p. 101.

3 **"So that was that":** Ibid.

4 **"crossed in love":** Ibid., p. 3.

4 **"the epitome of the English":** Ibid., p. 1.

4 **"effete":** Ibid., p. 88.

4 **"when dealing with foreigners":** Ibid., p. 43.

5 **"Claude was highly embarrassed":** Ibid., p. 13.

5 **"God, Disease and Below":** Ibid., p. 18.

5 **"nothing as unpleasant":** Ibid., p. 31.

5 **"sheer hell":** Ibid., p. 21.

5 **"The increased legibility":** Ibid., p. 34.

6 **"How hard should I work":** Ibid., p. 80.

6 **"He strongly advised":** Ibid.

6 **"a triumph over the examiners":** Ibid., p. 89.

7 **"languid, upper-class manner":** Peter Wright, *Spycatcher: The Candid Autobiography of a Senior Intelligence Officer* (London, 1987), p. 174.

7   "I could never be a": Elliott, *Never Judge a Man*, p. 40.

7   "obey not the order": Ibid.

7   "plug ugly": Ibid., p. 15.

7   "was no more or less": Ibid.

7   "inability to get down": Ibid., p. 91.

8   "There was no serious": Nicholas Elliott, *With My Little Eye: Observations Along the Way* (Norwich, UK, 1993), p. 16.

8   "in the diplomatic service": Elliott, *Never Judge a Man*, p. 93.

8   "opportunity to see": Ibid., p. 99.

8   "We discreetly poked": Ibid.

9   "a singularly foolhardly": Ibid.

9   "The Fuhrer is feted": Cited in James Holland, *Daily Mail*, April 18, 2009.

9   "I am tempted": Elliott, *Never Judge a Man*, p. 100.

9   "pick the bastard off": Ewan Butler, *Mason-Mac: The Life of Lieutenant-General Sir Nöel Mason-MacFarlane* (London, 1972), p. 75.

9   "strongly urged": Elliott, *Never Judge a Man*, p. 100.

9   "My mind was easily": Ibid., p. 101.

10 "just as soon as it feels": Christopher Andrew, *The Defence of the Realm: The Authorised History of MI5* (London, 2009), p. 195.

10 "the best and most ingenious": Ibid., p. 196.

11 "priceless intelligence": Ibid.

11 "I was really helping": Ibid.

11 "The English are hopeless": Ibid., p. 204.

11 "sacrificing himself": Ibid.

11 "Klop was a man": Elliott, *Never Judge a Man*, p. 149.

11 "complicated man": Ibid., p. 102.

11 "His motivation was solely": Ibid.

11 "Is Hitler going to start": Ibid.

11 "On present plans": Ibid.

11 "startling statement": Ibid.

12 "always displayed perfectly genuine": Andrew, *Defence of the Realm*, p. 246.

12 "by the autumn of 1939": Keith Jeffery, *MI6: The History of the Secret Intelligence Service 1909–1949* (London, 2010), p. 385.

12 "it could only be": Andrew, *Defence of the Realm*, p. 242.

12 "brilliant linguist": Elliott, *Never Judge a Man*, p. 103.

12 "an ostentatious ass": Ibid.

13 "overthrow the present regime": p. 382.

13 **"I have a hunch"**: Andrew, *Defence of the Realm*, p. 244.

13 **"the big man himself"**: Jeffery, *MI6*, p. 384.

13 **"No one was in sight"**: Ibid.

13 **"Our number's up"**: Sigismund Payne Best, *The Venlo Incident* (London, 1950), p. 17.

13 **"At one stroke"**: Elliott, *Never Judge a Man*, p. 103.

14 **"able to construct"**: Ibid.

14 **"intense ambition"**: Ibid.

14 **"possibility of winning"**: Ibid.

14 **"Corresponding with conceited"**: Archive Research and Document Copying, "The Venlo Incident," http://arcre.com/archive/sis/venlo.

14 **"selling everything to Moscow"**: Andrew, *Defence of the Realm*, p. 262.

15 **"as disastrous as it was"**: Elliott, *Never Judge a Man*, p. 103.

15 **"Oh what a tangled web"**: Elliott, *With My Little Eye*, p. 11.

15 **"Information has been received"**: Elliott, *Never Judge a Man*, p. 106.

15 **"It soon became apparent"**: Ibid.

15 **"We're in the final"**: Ibid., p. 109.

16 **"normality and calmness"**: Ibid.

16 **"never occurred to me"**: Ibid.

16 **"England was gripped"**: Ibid., p. 111.

16 **"give evidence of what"**: Ibid.

17 **"feeling of camaraderie"**: Ibid., p. 110.

17 **"My only moment"**: Ibid.

18 **"Basil Fisher was killed"**: Ibid., p. 111.

CHAPTER TWO: SECTION V

19 **"He was the sort of man"**: Sir Robert Mackenzie, interview with Phillip Knightley, 1967, quoted in Phillip Knightley, *The Master Spy: The Story of Kim Philby* (London, 1988), p. 119.

19 **"halting stammered witticisms"**: Graham Greene, foreword to Kim Philby, *My Silent War: The Autobiography of a Spy* (London, 1968), p. xx.

19 **"great pluck"**: E. G. de Caux to Ralph Deakin, January 14, 1938, *Times* Archives.

20 **"Many express disappointment"**: *Times* (London), November 17, 1939.

20 **"Camel-hair overcoat"**: Kim Philby, expenses claim letter, *Times* Archives.

20 **"dropped a few hints"**: Philby, *My Silent War*, p. xxviii.

20 **"A person like you"**: Knightley, *Master Spy*, p. 79.

20 **"We'll figure something":** Ibid.

21 **"war work":** Philby, *My Silent War*, p. 9.

21 **"intensely likeable":** Ibid.

21 **"I began to show off":** Ibid., p. 10.

21 **"nothing recorded against":** Ibid.

21 **"I was asked about him":** Patrick Seale and Maureen McConville, *Philby: The Long Road to Moscow* (London, 1973), p. 135.

22 **"set Europe ablaze":** Hugh Dalton, *The Fateful Years: Memoirs, 1931–1945* (London, 1957), p. 366.

22 **"I escaped to London":** Philby, *My Silent War*, p. 63.

23 **"In those days":** Nicholas Elliott, *Never Judge a Man by His Umbrella* (London, 1992), p. 111.

23 **"He had an ability":** Ibid., p. 183.

23 **"the inherent evil":** Ibid., p. 105.

23 **"very rarely discussed":** Ibid., p. 183.

23 **"the English batting":** Ibid.

23 **"Indeed," wrote Elliott:** Ibid.

23 **"pose of amiable":** Hugh R. Trevor-Roper, *The Philby Affair: Espionage, Treason, and Secret Services* (London, 1968), p. 42.

24 **"by and large pretty stupid":** Christopher Andrew, *Secret Service: The Making of the British Intelligence Community* (London, 1985), p. 249.

24 **"An exceptional person":** Ibid.

24 **"clarity of mind":** Elliott, *Never Judge a Man*, p. 183.

24 **"He was much more":** Ibid.

24 **"The old Secret Service":** Malcolm Muggeridge, *Chronicles of Wasted Time*, vol. 2 (London, 1973), p. 136.

24 **"slouching about in sweaters":** Ibid.

25 **"You'd drop in to see":** Kim Philby, interview with Phillip Knightley, 1988, cited in Knightley, *Master Spy*, p. 84.

25 **"atmosphere of *haute cuisine*":** Philby, *My Silent War*, p. 35.

25 **"out of fun rather":** Elliott, *Never Judge a Man*, p. 184.

25 **"To start with we always":** Dennis Wheatley, *The Deception Planners: My Secret War* (London, 1980), p. 30.

26 **"for an hour":** Ibid.

26 **"He was a formidable":** Elliott, *Never Judge a Man*, p. 183.

26 **"serious drinkers should never":** Ibid.

26 **"violent headache":** Ibid.

26 **"It was an organisation":** Nicholas Elliott, *With My Little Eye: Observations Along the Way* (Norwich, UK, 1993), p. 22.

26 **"They spoke the same"**: Mark Elliott, interview with the author, November 11, 2013.

27 **"negate, confuse, deceive"**: Leo D. Carl, *The International Dictionary of Intelligence* (McLean, VA, 1990), p. 83.

27 **"with a knowledge of Spain"**: Philby, *My Silent War*, p. 35.

27 **"The old boy network"**: Ibid., p. 37.

27 **"purblind, disastrous megalomaniac"**: Trevor-Roper, *Philby Affair*, p. 37.

27 **"As an intelligence officer"**: Philby, *My Silent War*, p. 46.

27 **"suspicious and bristling"**: Ibid.

28 **"personal contacts with"**: Ibid., p. 43.

28 **"He was a bit of a communist"**: Seale and McConville, *Philby*, p. 135.

28 **"active pursuit and liquidation"**: Anthony Cave Brown, *Treason in the Blood: H. St. John Philby, Kim Philby and the Spy Case of the Century* (London, 1995), p. 276.

29 **"Aileen belonged to that class"**: Flora Solomon and Barnet Litvinoff, *Baku to Baker Street: The Memoirs of Flora Solomon* (London, 1984), p. 172.

29 **"He found an avid listener"**: Ibid.

29 **"She was highly intelligent"**: Elliott, *Never Judge a Man*, p. 182.

30 **"parental pride"**: Ibid., p. 187.

30 **"long Sunday lunches"**: Greene, foreword to Philby, *My Silent War*, p. xx.

30 **"small loyalties"**: Ibid.

30 **"He had something about him"**: Seale and McConville, *Philby*, p. 133.

30 **"merry band"**: Desmond Bristow with Bill Bristow, *A Game of Moles: The Deceptions of an MI6 Officer* (London, 1993), p. 17.

30 **"a purchaser of skunk excrement"**: Ibid., p. 18.

30 **"The sense of dedication"**: Brown, *Treason in the Blood*, p. 276.

30 **"No one could have"**: Greene, foreword to Philby, *My Silent War*, p. xix.

31 **"a gentle-looking man"**: Bristow, *Game of Moles*, p. 262.

31 **"cosiness"**: Philby, *My Silent War*, p. 63.

31 **"It was not difficult"**: Ibid.

31 **"a good cricket umpire"**: Felix Cowgill, interview with Anthony Cave Brown, 1983, cited in Brown, *Treason in the Blood*, p. 275.

31 **"calculating ambition"**: Knightley, *Master Spy*, p. 119.

31 **"single-mindedness"**: Ibid.

31 **"There was something"**: Hugh Trevor-Roper, interview by Graham Turner, *Daily Telegraph*, January 28, 2003.

32 **"It was not long":** Philby, *My Silent War*, p. 53.

32 **"to good use in disrupting":** Ibid., p. 55.

32 **"mingle with the crowd":** Keith Jeffery, *MI6: The History of the Secret Intelligence Service 1909–1949* (London, 2010), p. 387.

32 **"party-goer's image":** Ibid.

33 **"This is the last time":** Charles Whiting, *Ghost Front: The Ardennes Before the Battle of the Bulge* (London, 2002), pp. 203–4.

33 **"an operational disaster":** Philby, *My Silent War*, p. 52.

33 **"virtually at will":** Ibid., p. 63.

33 **"contacts with other SIS":** Ibid.

33 **"fire-watching nights":** Greene, foreword to Philby, *My Silent War*, p. xx.

34 **"bulging briefcase and a long":** Philby, *My Silent War*, p. 63.

34 **"longhand, in neat, tiny writing":** Sir Robert Mackenzie, interview with Phillip Knightley, 1967, quoted in Knightley, *Master Spy*, p. 118.

34 **"MR NICHOLAS ELLIOTT":** Nigel West and Oleg Tsarev, *The Crown Jewels: The British Secrets at the Heart of the KGB Archives* (London, 1998), p. 311.

CHAPTER THREE: OTTO AND SONNY

35 **"Something I owe":** Rudyard Kipling, *Kim*, chapter 8.

35 **"penetration agent working":** Kim Philby, *My Silent War: The Autobiography of a Spy* (London, 1968), p. xxix.

36 **"the exquisite relish":** Anthony Cave Brown, *Treason in the Blood: H. St. John Philby, Kim Philby and the Spy Case of the Century* (London, 1995), p. 291.

36 **"My ambition is fame":** Phillip Knightley, *The Master Spy: The Story of Kim Philby* (London, 1988), p. 21.

37 **"constantly aware of his father's":** Brown, *Treason in the Blood*, p. 133.

37 **"He should always":** Ibid., p. 134.

37 **"sudden conversion":** Philby, *My Silent War*, p. xxx.

37 **"the inner fortress":** Ibid., p. xxix.

38 **"I left the university":** Ibid., p. xxxi.

38 **"I can hardly see him":** Nicholas Elliott, *Never Judge a Man by His Umbrella* (London, 1992), p. 183.

38 **"devote his life to the":** Ibid.

38 **"at a crisis point":** Knightley, *Master Spy*, p. 40.

38 **"tremendous little sexpot":** Brown, *Treason in the Blood*, p. 159.

39 **"Actually quite warm"**: Christopher Andrew, *The Defence of the Realm: The Authorised History of MI6* (London, 1994), p. 168.

39 **"Even though the basis"**: Genrikh Borovik, *The Philby Files: The Secret Life of Master Spy Kim Philby* (London, 1994) p. 22.

39 **"I do hope Kim gets a job"**: Brown, *Treason in the Blood*, p. 162.

39 **"Excess can always"**: Ibid., p. 137.

39 **"man of decisive importance"**: Andrew, *Defence of the Realm*, p. 169.

40 **"man of considerable"**: Ibid.

40 **"He was a marvellous man"**: Borovik, *Philby Files*, p. 29.

40 **"important and interesting work"**: Ibid., p. 25.

40 **"I trusted him"**: Ibid., p. 27.

40 **"prophet of the better orgasm"**: Andrew, *Defence of the Realm*, p. 170.

40 **"a poor man's sexual performance"**: Brown, *Treason in the Blood*, p. 163.

42 **"One does not look twice"**: Philby, *My Silent War*, p. xxxii.

42 **"Of all the passions"**: C. S. Lewis, "The Inner Ring" (memorial lecture at King's College, University of London, 1944), collected in C. S. Lewis, *Mere Christianity* (London, 2012).

42 **"My future looked romantic"**: Borovik, *Philby Files*, p. 28.

42 **"By background, education"**: Ibid.

42 **"The anti-fascist movement"**: Ibid.

42 **"real and palpable way"**: Ibid.

42 **"like poetry"**: Ibid., p. 33.

43 **"We have recruited the son"**: Ibid., p. 39.

43 **"What are his prospects"**: Ibid., p. 40.

43 **"the most interesting"**: Ibid., p. 52.

43 **"refers to his parents"**: Ibid., p. 147.

43 **"his marvelous education"**: Ibid., p. 31.

43 **"the remoter open spaces"**: Philby, *My Silent War*, p. xxix.

43 **"His wife was his first lover"**: Borovik, *Philby Files*, p. 148.

43 **"I sometimes felt"**: Ibid., p. 33.

43 **"I was certain that my life"**: Ibid., p. 31.

44 **"constant encouragement"**: Ibid.

44 **"Söhnchen comes from"**: Ibid., p. 43.

44 **"It's amazing that"**: Ibid., p. 55.

44 **"Once you're inside"**: Ibid., p. 56.

44 **"He has many friends"**: Ibid., p. 43.

44 **"profoundly repulsive"**: Ibid., p. 59.

44 **"in the eyes of my friends"**: Ibid.

44 **"how difficult it is to leave"**: Ibid.

45 **"It seems unlikely that"**: Ibid., pp. 52–53.

45 **"The people I could"**: Ibid., p. 46.

45 **"very serious and aloof"**: Ibid., p. 44.

45 **"Sonny has high praise"**: Ibid.

45 **"Very smart"**: Ibid., p. 44.

45 **"Do you think that"**: Ibid., p. 48.

46 **"I lost my faith"**: Elisabeth K. Poretsky, *Our Own People: A Memoir of "Ignace Reiss" and His Friends* (Oxford, UK, 1969), p. 214.

46 **"shiny grey complexion"**: Andrew, *Defence of the Realm*, p. 180.

46 **"an inspirational figure"**: Brown, *Treason in the Blood*, p. 194.

46 **"Both of them were intelligent"**: Borovik, *Philby Files*, p. 174.

46 **"handles our money"**: Ibid.

46 **"We have great difficulty"**: Ibid., p. 88.

46 **"unit strengths and locations"**: Knightley, *Master Spy*, p. 71.

47 **"a royalist of the most"**: Borovik, *Philby Files*, p. 111.

47 **"I would be lying"**: Ibid., pp. 111–12.

47 **"He works with great"**: Ibid., p. 129.

47 **"obviously been in the thick"**: Peter Wright, *Spycatcher: The Candid Autobiography of a Senior Intelligence Officer* (London, 1987), p. 260.

47 **"doing a very dangerous job"**: Ibid., p. 173.

47 **"important work for peace"**: Flora Solomon and Barnet Litvinoff, *Baku to Baker Street: The Memoirs of Flora Solomon* (London, 1984), p. 169.

47 **"he could always"**: Wright, *Spycatcher*, p. 173.

48 **"Even if he had been able"**: Borovik, *Philby Files*, p. 89.

48 **"They are very pleased"**: Ibid., p. 95.

48 **"a decent chap"**: Knightley, *Master Spy*, p. 56.

48 **"I know that as a former priest"**: Andrew, *Defence of the Realm*, p. 183.

49 **"infinite patience"**: Philby, *My Silent War*, p. xxix.

49 **"intelligent understanding"**: Ibid.

49 **"painstaking advice"**: Ibid.

49 **"marvellous men"**: Borovik, *Philby Files*, p. 29.

49 **"What's going to happen"**: Knightley, *Master Spy*, p. 71.

50 **"activity in England"**: Andrew, *Defence of the Realm*, p. 185.

50 **"I had been told in pressing"**: Philby, *My Silent War*, p. xxviii.

50 **"Where is the Café"**: Borovik, *Philby Files*, p. 143.

50 **"extraordinarily valuable"**: Ibid., p. 151.

50 **"the appropriate hands"**: Ibid.

CHAPTER FOUR: BOO, BOO, BABY, I'M A SPY

52 **"true sense of values"**: Nicholas Elliott, *Never Judge a Man by His Umbrella* (London, 1992), p. 178.

52 **"His intellectual equipment"**: Kim Philby, *My Silent War: The Autobiography of a Spy* (London, 1968), p. 109.

52 **"an utter shit"**: Cited in Anthony Read and David Fisher, *Colonel Z: The Secret Life of a Master of Spies* (London, 1985), p. 361.

53 **"Vivian was long past"**: Philby, *My Silent War*, p. 48.

53 **"He would murmur"**: Ibid., p. 69.

53 **"But behind the façade"**: Ibid.

53 **"The rewards of such unorthodoxy"**: Ibid., p. 70.

53 **"the only man in The Hotel"**: Genrikh Borovik, *The Philby Files: The Secret Life of Master Spy Kim Philby* (London, 1994), p. 205.

54 **"golden lads"**: Anthony Cave Brown, *Treason in the Blood: H. St. John Philby, Kim Philby and the Spy Case of the Century* (London, 2010), p. 470.

54 **"You know as well as I do"**: Keith Jeffery, *MI6: The History of the Secret Intelligence Service 1909–1949* (London, 2010), p. 490.

54 **"in the hurly-burly"**: Guy Liddell, *Diaries*, KV 4/466.

54 **"a pleasant personality"**: Ibid.

54 **"For every lead that produced"**: Philby, *My Silent War*, p. 48.

54 **"monstrous"**: Ibid.

54 **"a model of economy"**: Elliott, *Never Judge a Man*, p. 183.

54 **"I had the advantage"**: Ibid., p. 110.

55 **"an interesting and promising"**: Borovik, *Philby Files*, p. 167.

55 **"especially valuable"**: Philby, *My Silent War*, p. 64.

55 **"few social graces"**: Nigel West and Oleg Tsarev, *The Crown Jewels: The British Secrets at the Heart of the KGB* Archives (London, 1998), p. 312.

55 **"inclined towards inertia"**: Ibid.

55 **"weakness [for] women"**: Ibid.

55 **"the weak link"**: Ibid., p. 313.

55 **"fat briefcase"**: Philby, *My Silent War*, p. 48.

55 **"Her political views"**: Borovik, *Philby Files*, p. 208.

55 **"difficult, exhausting"**: Ibid., p. 28.

56 **"twinges of panic"**: Ibid., p. 203.

56 **"a young Englishman"**: Christopher Andrew, *The Defence of the Realm: The Authorised History of MI5* (London, 2009), p. 267.

57 **"We told him he must"**: Borovik, *Philby Files*, p. 202.

58 **"About 58, 5 feet 6 inches"**: West and Tsarev, *Crown Jewels*, p. 298.

58 **"There aren't any"**: Borovik, *Philby Files*, p. xii.

58 **"tenth on the list"**: Ibid., p. 167.

58 **"no Soviet citizens"**: Ibid., p. 210.

58 **"obvious absurdity"**: Ibid., p. 201.

59 **"highly suspicious"**: Ibid., p. 200.

59 **"dubious"**: Ibid., p. 196.

59 **"tested and retested"**: Ibid., p. 204.

59 **"upside down"**: Philby, *My Silent War*, p. 61.

59 **"to discuss the mystery"**: Ibid.

59 **"far outside the normal scope"**: Ibid.

60 **"another flood"**: Ibid.

60 **"Luck played an enormous"**: Ibid., p. 128.

60 **"cloistered"**: Ibid., p. 72.

60 **"those who sit at desks"**: Nicholas Elliott, *With My Little Eye: Observations Along the Way* (Norwich, UK, 1993), p. 15.

60 **"anxious to get away"**: Elliott, *Never Judge a Man*, p. 111.

60 **"All foreigners are bloody"**: Ibid., p. 16.

60 **"I was delighted"**: Ibid. p. 111.

61 **"who was being sent"**: Ibid., p. 112.

61 **"well-stocked bar"**: Ibid.

61 **"the tattiest army officer"**: Ibid., p. 113.

61 **"the shortage of contraceptives"**: Ibid.

61 **"managed to alleviate"**: Ibid.

61 **"roving brothel"**: Philby, *My Silent War*, p. 78.

61 **"two lonely Germans"**: Ibid.

61 **"delight"**: Elliott, *Never Judge a Man*, p. 117.

62 **"pained tolerance"**: Jeffery, *MI6*, p. 418.

62 **"great ability and energy"**: Ibid., p. 419.

62 **"one of the great espionage"**: Ibid., p. 417.

63 **"Everyone was well informed"**: Elliott, *Never Judge a Man*, p. 122.

63 **"I'm involved in a dangerous game"**: Barry Rubin, *Istanbul Intrigues* (New York, 1989), p. xvii.

64 **"not a kid glove affair"**: Jeffery, *MI6*, p. 420.

64 **"crammed from top"**: Elliott, *Never Judge a Man*, p. 120.

64 **"extremely erudite"**: Elliott, *With My Little Eye*, p.73

64 **"Its clientele"**: Elliott, *Never Judge a Man*, p. 122.

64 **"white coloured skin"**: Ibid.

65 **"a ferocious dry martini"**: Ibid., p. 123.

65 **"spoke excellent English"**: Ibid.

65 **"the capacity for friendship"**: Elliott, *With My Little Eye*, p. 15.

65 **"A large amount"**: Ibid.

65 **"One particularly remarkable man"**: Elliott, *Never Judge a Man*, p. 117.

66 **"a most unattractive"**: Ibid., p. 130.

66 **"operating a clandestine"**: Ibid.

66 **"was not altogether"**: Ibid.

66 **"more people involved"**: Elliott, *With My Little Eye*, p. 50.

66 **"All were kept under"**: Ibid., p. 51.

66 **"schoolboyish"**: Philby, *My Silent War*, p. 109.

66 **"bars, beards and blondes"**: Ibid.

67 **"the worst claret"**: Elliott, *Never Judge a Man*, p. 177.

67 **"After three of Ellie's"**: Ibid., p.123.

67 **"hoping he didn't mind"**: Ibid., p. 126.

CHAPTER FIVE: THREE YOUNG SPIES

68 **"two minutes from MI5"**: Kim Philby, *My Silent War: The Autobiography of a Spy* (London, 1968), p. 71.

68 **"the frowsty old"**: Malcolm Muggeridge, "Book Review of a Very Limited Edition," *Esquire*, May 1966, p. 84.

69 **"a notably bewildered"**: Philby, *My Silent War*, p. 74.

69 **"a bunch of amateur bums"**: Ibid., p. 75.

69 **"They lost no opportunity"**: Ibid., p. 74.

69 **"pain in the neck"**: Ibid., p. 76.

69 **"formative years"**: Tom Mangold, *Cold Warrior: James Jesus Angleton— the CIA's Master Spy Hunter* (London, 1991), p. 13.

70 **"more English than"**: Ibid., p. 12.

70 **"a mysterious person"**: Ibid., p. 13.

70 **"What a miracle"**: Michael Holzman, *James Jesus Angleton, the CIA, and the Craft of Counterintelligence* (Boston, 2008), p. 83.

70 **"arts and crafts"**: Anthony Cave Brown, *Treason in the Blood: H. St. John Philby, Kim Philby and the Spy Case of the Century* (London, 1995), p. 298.

70 **"I do remember"**: Holzman, *James Jesus Angleton*, p. 49.

70 **"earned my respect"**: Philby, *My Silent War*, pp. 150–51.

70 **"Philby may have felt"**: Holzman, *James Jesus Angleton*, p. 49.

71 **"Philby was one of Angleton's"**: Phillip Knightley, *The Master Spy: The Story of Kim Philby* (London, 1988), p. 118.

71 **"Our European friends"**: Winifred Bryher, *The Days of Mars: A Memoir, 1940–1946* (New York, 1972), pp. ix–x.

71 **"as if they contained"**: Brown, *Treason in the Blood*, p. 299.

71 **"restless appetite for organising"**: William Empson to James Angleton, February 19, 1940, quoted in Holzman, *James Jesus Angleton*, p. 22.

71 **"extremely brilliant"**: Holzman, *James Jesus Angleton*, p. 45.

71 **"Once I met Philby"**: Joseph J. Trento, *The Secret History of the CIA* (New York, 2001), p. 37.

72 **"an almost total moron"**: Nigel West and Oleg Tsarev, *The Crown Jewels: The British Secrets at the Heart of the KGB Archives* (London, 1998), p. 311.

72 **"We had achieved"**: Philby, *My Silent War*, p. 78.

72 **"in all intelligence matters"**: Ibid., p. 80.

72 **"beginning to make a career"**: Ibid., p. 79.

72 **"I regarded my SIS"**: Ibid., p. xxix.

73 **"incomprehensible"**: Christopher Andrew, *The Defence of the Realm: The Authorised History of MI5* (London, 2009), p. 272.

73 **"a straight penetration"**: Philby, *My Silent War*, p. xxix.

73 **"He is lying to us"**: Genrikh Borovik, *The Philby Files: The Secret Life of Master Spy Kim Philby* (London, 1994), p. xiv.

73 **"He was so completely"**: Yuri Modin, *My Five Cambridge Friends: Burgess, Maclean, Philby, Blunt, and Cairncross by Their KGB Controller* (New York, 1995), p. 201.

73 **"in such a manner"**: Borovik, *Philby Files*, p. 218.

74 **"single-front struggle"**: Ibid., p. xi.

74 **"modest bit towards"**: Knightley, *Master Spy*, p. 128.

75 **"Moody and nervous"**: Vermehren file, KV 2/956.

75 **"The city is riddled"**: Barry Rubin, *Istanbul Intrigues* (New York, 1989), p. 224.

75 **"specialised in making Britons"**: Ibid.

76 **"I remembered him vividly"**: Nicholas Elliott, *Never Judge a Man by His Umbrella* (London, 1992), p. 135.

76 **"small roundish man"**: Ibid.

76 **"instantly dismissed"**: Ibid.

77 **"The information obtained"**: Ibid., p. 133.

77 **"If he had not been a spy"**: Rubin, *Istanbul Intrigues,* p. 164.

77 **"penchant for involving"**: Elliott, *Never Judge a Man,* p. 120.

77 **"The names of the Azerbaijanis"**: Rubin, *Istanbul Intrigues,* p. 227.

78 **"the Arab cause depended"**: Ibid., p. 225.

78 **"Twelve-land, Twelve-land"**: Ibid., p. 201.

CHAPTER SIX: THE GERMAN DEFECTOR

79 **"unfit to represent"**: Richard Bassett, obituary of Erich Vermehren, *Independent,* May 3, 2005.

81 **"Erich Vermehren?"**: Richard Bassett, *Hitler's Spy Chief: The Wilhelm Canaris Mystery* (London, 2006), p. 280.

81 **"I had a sense"**: Ibid.

81 **"signs of instability"**: Anthony Cave Brown, *Treason in the Blood: H. St. John Philby, Kim Philby and the Spy Case of the Century* (London, 1995), p. 315.

81 **"a highly strung"**: Keith Jeffery, *MI6: The Secret History of the Secret Intelligence Service 1909–1949* (London, 2010), p. 504.

81 **"intensely anti-Nazi"**: Ibid.

81 **"fully convinced"**: Ibid.

82 **"the complete Abwehr setup"**: Ibid.

82 **"quantity of detailed information"**: Ibid.

82 **"it would not be long"**: Ibid.

83 **"a hell of a flap"**: Ibid., p. 505.

83 **"lest his disappearance"**: Barry Rubin, *Istanbul Intrigues* (New York, 1989), p. 232.

83 **"he was given breakfast"**: Ibid.

84 **"swamped by an invasion"**: Ibid.

84 **"gravely prejudiced the activities"**: Ibid., p. 229.

84 **"exceedingly tedious"**: Nicholas Elliott, *Never Judge a Man by His Umbrella* (London, 1992), p. 126.

84 **"They are so God-awful conscientious"**: Kim Philby, *My Silent War: The Autobiography of a Spy* (London, 1968), p. 42.

85 **"I don't mind telling you"**: Elliott, *Never Judge a Man,* p. 127.

85 **"obstacle race with frequent jumps"**: Ibid.

85 **"German-Turkish intelligence"**: Rubin, *Istanbul Intrigues,* p. 228.

85 **"The 24-year-old attaché"**: Associated Press, February 9, 1945.

85 **"If an enemy alien"**: Guy Liddell, *Diaries,* KV 4/466.

85 **"outstanding blow"**: Jeffery, *MI6,* p. 504.

86 **"exploded"**: Brown, *Treason in the Blood,* p. 315.

86 **"hardly surprising given":** Bassett, *Hitler's Spy Chief*, p. 282.

86 **"thrown into a state of confusion":** Jeffery, *MI6*, p. 505.

86 **"consummate skill and sympathy":** Ibid.

86 **"dine out":** David Cornwell, interview with the author, April 12, 2012.

86 **"dazzling coup":** Bassett, *Hitler's Spy Chief*, p. 279.

87 **"formidably impressed both by":** Nicholas Elliott, *With My Little Eye: Observations Along the Way* (Norwich, UK, 1993), p. 81. There is some confusion over where Elliott and Angleton first met. Elliott recalled that Angleton came to stay with him in Switzerland in 1946, but it seems more likely, according to his family and other sources, that their first encounter was in London a year earlier, during the period of the Vermehren debriefing.

87 **"Beneath the rather sinister":** Elliott, *With My Little Eye*, p. 81.

87 **"At that time, secrets":** Elliott, *Never Judge a Man*, p. 62.

87 **"Sit down, I'd like to have"** . . . **"Because the Chief told him":** Elliott, *With My Little Eye*, pp. 17–18.

88 **"For centuries the Office":** Tom Bower, *The Perfect English Spy: Sir Dick White and the Secret War, 1935–1990* (London, 1995), p. 85.

88 **"of all their contacts":** Bassett, *Hitler's Spy Chief*, p. 23.

88 **"leading Catholic activists":** Knightley, *Master Spy*, p. 110.

88 **"could have formed the backbone":** Brown, *Treason in the Blood*, p. 328.

88 **"All had been deported":** Bassett, *Hitler's Spy Chief*, p. 23.

89 **"Because Moscow had decided":** Knightley, *Master Spy*, p. 110.

89 **"drive against the Catholic Church":** KV 4/469.

89 **"I was responsible for the deaths":** Knightley, *Master Spy*, p. 128.

CHAPTER SEVEN: THE SOVIET DEFECTOR

90 **"We've been penetrated":** Tom Bower, *The Perfect English Spy: Sir Dick White and the Secret War, 1935–1990* (London, 1995), p. 66.

90 **"the next enemy":** Kim Philby, *My Silent War: The Autobiography of a Spy* (London, 1968), p. 92.

90 **"professional handling of any cases":** Nigel West and Oleg Tsarev, eds., *Triplex: Secrets from the Cambridge Five* (New Haven, CT: Yale University Press, 2009), p. 115.

91 **"provided you do not do anything":** Keith Jeffery, *MI6: The History of the Secret Intelligence Service 1909–1949* (London, 2010), p. 566.

91 **"I must do everything":** Philby, *My Silent War*, p. 94.

91 **"Cowgill must go"**: Ibid.

91 **"great warmth"**: Ibid., p. 100.

91 **"the idea was his own"**: Ibid.

92 **"At one stroke"**: Robert Cecil in Christopher Andrew and D. Dilks, eds., *The Missing Dimension: Governments and Intelligence Communities in the Twentieth Century* (London, 1984), p. 179.

92 **"The new appointment"**: Genrikh Borovik, *The Philby Files: The Secret Life of Master Spy Kim Philby* (London, 1994), p. 236.

92 **"jovial, kindly man"**: Ibid., p. 177.

92 **"a splendid professional"**: Ibid.

93 **"unburden"**: Ibid.

93 **"I must thank you"**: Ibid., p. 237.

93 **"After the gloom of London"**: Nicholas Elliott, *Never Judge a Man by His Umbrella* (London, 1992), p. 141.

94 **"not only our best source"**: Tony Paterson, "Germany Finally Honours the 'Traitor' Spy," *Independent*, September 25, 2004.

94 **"Communists and communism"**: Nicholas Elliott, *With My Little Eye: Observations Along the Way* (Norwich, UK), p. 49.

95 **"over one thousand enemy"**: Ted Morgan, *A Covert Life: Jay Lovestone: Communist, Anti-Communist, and Spymaster* (New York, 1999), p. 257.

95 **"heavily dependent on Philby"**: Anthony Cave Brown, *Treason in the Blood: H. St. John Philby, Kim Philby and the Spy Case of the Century* (London, 1995), p. 353.

95 **"enigmatic wraith"**: Michael Holzman, *James Jesus Angleton, the CIA, and the Craft of Counterintelligence* (Boston, 2008), p. 57.

95 **"haunted the streets"**: Ibid., p. 59.

95 **"You would sit on a sofa"**: David C. Martin, *Wilderness of Mirrors: Intrigue, Deception, and the Secrets That Destroyed Two of the Cold War's Most Important Agents* (Guilford, CT, 2003), p. 18.

96 **"perhaps the ablest"**: Philby, *My Silent War*, p. 105.

96 **"Was it freedom"**: Ibid., p. 108.

96 **"Not one of them"**: Ibid.

96 **"Stanley was a bit agitated"**: Borovik, *Philby Files*, p. 238.

96 **"I tried to calm him down"**: Ibid.

97 **"prank"**: Gordon Brook-Shepherd, *The Storm Birds: Soviet Post-War Defectors* (London, 1988), p. 41.

97 **"deplorably nervous state"**: Philby, *My Silent War*, p. 119.

97 **"less than rock steady"**: Ibid.

98 **"obviously been preparing"**: Ibid., p. 120.

98 **"I consider this sum"**: Jeffery, MI6, p. 525.

98 **"I know, for instance"**: Christopher Andrew, *The Defence of the Realm: The Authorised History of MI5* (London, 2009), p. 344; Peter Wright, *Spycatcher: The Candid Autobiography of a Senior Intelligence Officer* (London, 1987), p. 281.

99 **"No one's going to turn"**: Phillip Knightley, *The Master Spy: The Story of Kim Philby* (London, 1988), pp. 135–36.

99 **"copies of the material provided"**: Edward Harrison, *The Young Kim Philby: Soviet Spy and British Intelligence Officer* (Exeter, UK: 2012), p. 177.

99 **"something of the greatest importance"**: Philby, *My Silent War*, p. 121.

99 **"That evening I worked late"**: Ibid.

99 **"Don't worry, old man"**: Borovik, *Philby Files*, p. 178.

100 **"Someone fully briefed"**: Philby, *My Silent War*, p. 121.

100 **"meeting Volkov"**: Ibid., p. 120.

100 **"work the night before"**: Ibid., p. 122.

100 **"Don't you read my contract"**: Alistair Horne, *But What Do You Actually Do? A Literary Vagabondage* (London, 2011), p. 186.

101 **"with obvious relief"**: Philby, *My Silent War*, p. 122.

101 **"diplomatic couriers"**: Andrew, *Defence of the Realm*, p. 344.

101 **"this might be the last"**: Philby, *My Silent War*, p. 118.

101 **"Sorry, old man"**: Knightley, *Master Spy*, p. 138.

101 **"inexplicable delays and evasions"**: Harrison, *Young Kim Philby*, p. 178.

101 **"I thought he was just irresponsible"**: Ibid.

101 **"It wasn't Volkov"**: Philby, *My Silent War*, p. 126.

101 **"She said he was out"**: Ibid.

101 **"I asked for Volkov"**: Ibid., p. 127.

102 **"It's no bloody good"**: Ibid.

102 **"The case was dead"**: Ibid.

102 **"on stretchers and heavily sedated"**: Andrew, *Defence of the Realm*, p. 344.

102 **"brutal interrogation"**: Ibid., p. 345.

102 **"a very narrow squeak"**: Philby, *My Silent War*, p. 118.

102 **"nasty piece of work"**: Knightley, *Master Spy*, p. 138.

102 **"deserved what he got"**: Ibid.

102 **"extremely unlikely"**: Jeffery, *MI6*, p. 525.

102 **"indiscretion in the British Embassy"**: Ibid.

103 **"test the waters":** Brown, *Treason in the Blood,* p. 365.

103 **"expressed sympathy":** Holzman, *James Jesus Angleton,* p. 107.

103 **"the effect his work":** Joseph J. Trento, *The Secret History of the CIA* (New York, 2001), p. 38.

103 **"felt guilty about it":** Ibid.

103 **"He helped me to think":** Ibid.

103 **"worse for wear of the":** Brown, *Treason in the Blood,* p. 365.

103 **"warned the Center":** Andrew, *Defence of the Realm,* p. 346.

104 **"without reserve":** Ibid.

104 **"Stanley informed me":** Borovik, *Philby Files,* p. 242.

104 **"Stanley is an exceptionally valuable":** Ibid., 244.

104 **"conscientious work for over":** Ibid., 249.

105 **"I looked around":** Hugh R. Trevor-Roper, *The Philby Affair: Espionage, Treason, and Secret Services* (London, 1968), p. 42.

CHAPTER EIGHT: RISING STARS

106 **"I believed we were":** Michael Holzman, *James Jesus Angleton, the CIA, and the Craft of Counterintelligence* (Boston, 2008), p. 3.

106 **"the continuation of a civilization":** Nicholas Elliott, *With My Little Eye: Observations Along the Way* (Norwich, UK, 1993), p. 101.

106 **"I'm in it for the belly-laughs":** David Cornwell, interview with the author, April 12, 2012.

106 **"a form of defence mechanism":** Elliott, *With My Little Eye,* p. 180.

107 **"Verbal abuse is not":** Ibid., p. 61.

107 **"the British tradition":** Ibid., p. 111.

107 **"One of the joys of living":** Ibid., p. 150.

107 **"oldest and closest friends":** Ibid., p. 151.

107 **"British skiing aristocracy":** Obituary of Peter Lunn, *Daily Telegraph,* June 12, 2011.

108 **"the ideal person":** Stephen Dorril, *MI6: Fifty Years of Special Operations* (London, 2001), p. 418.

108 **"attempting to piece together":** Ibid.

108 **"superficial existence":** Ibid., p. 408.

109 **"unique opportunity":** Ibid.

109 **"blueprint for communist":** Ibid., p. 419.

109 **"lifelong communist activists":** Ibid.

109 **"not so much an ideology":** Holzman, *James Jesus Angleton,* p. 69.

109 **"like a British actor":** Tom Mangold, *Cold Warrior: James Jesus Angleton—the CIA's Master Spy Hunter* (London, 1991), p. 21.

109 **"the cadaver":** David C. Martin, *Wilderness of Mirrors: Intrigue, Deception, and the Secrets That Destroyed Two of the Cold War's Most Important Agents* (Guilford, CT, 2003).

109 **"The guy was just":** Ibid., p. 17.

110 **"Secret Documents of Vatican Diplomacy":** "Author of 'Secret Documents' Sentenced," *Catholic Herald,* July 30, 1948.

110 **"how vulnerable even":** Holzman, *James Jesus Angleton,* p. 50.

110 **"the Byzantine possibilities":** Ibid.

110 **"crawling around on his hands":** Mangold, *Cold Warrior,* p. 21.

110 **"His real love was unravelling":** Elliott, *With My Little Eye,* p. 81.

111 **"We were . . . damned good friends":** Holzman, *James Jesus Angleton,* p. 71.

111 **"Stanley reported that":** Genrikh Borovik, *The Philby Files: The Secret Life of Master Spy Kim Philby* (London, 1994), p. 241.

112 **"What a very nice chap":** Anthony Cave Brown, *Treason in the Blood: H. St. John Philby, Kim Philby and the Spy Case of the Century* (London, 1994), p. 367.

112 **"happy ending":** Flora Solomon and Barnet Litvinoff, *Baku to Baker Street: The Memoirs of Flora Solomon* (London, 1984), p. 210.

112 **"Kim, a happy and devoted father":** Ibid.

112 **"seemed to belong to the misty":** Ibid., p. 172.

112 **"Awkward of her gestures":** Ibid., p. 169.

113 **"incapable of disloyalty":** Brown, *Treason in the Blood,* p. 208.

113 **"all round experience":** Phillip Knightley, *The Master Spy: The Story of Kim Philby* (London, 1988), p. 142.

113 **"profoundly sorry":** Guy Liddell, *Diaries,* KV 4/468.

113 **"main southern base":** Kim Philby, *My Silent War: The Autobiography of a Spy* (London, 1968), p. 130.

113 **"Kim gave a large farewell party":** Liddell, *Diaries,* KV 4/468.

114 **"given permission to play":** Brown, *Treason in the Blood,* p. 382.

114 **"a white Russian":** Philby, *My Silent War,* p. 133.

114 **"a fairly free hand":** Ibid.

114 **"start weaving a spy network":** Borovik, *Philby Files,* p. 251.

115 **"energetic enthusiast":** Dorril, *MI6,* p. 210.

115 **"We knew in advance":** Ibid., p. 212.

115 **"the very mechanism through":** Holzman, *James Jesus Angleton,* p. 91.

115 **"He was totally consumed":** Mangold, *Cold Warrior,* p. 23.

116 **"We rediscovered each other":** Ibid.

116 **"I've got sitting in my jeep":** Brown, *Treason in the Blood,* p. 384.

117 **"He was both efficient and safe"**: Ibid., p. 380.

117 **"willing to back them"**: Dorril, *MI6*, p. 211.

117 **"energetic lads"**: Borovik, *Philby Files*, p. 252.

117 **"tip and run"**: Philby, *My Silent War*, p. 140.

117 **"alert and intelligent"**: Ibid., p. 143.

118 **"notably subdued"**: Ibid.

118 **"It was essential"**: Ibid.

118 **"striding through a sparse wood"**: Ibid.

118 **"The boys weren't bad"**: Borovik, *Philby Files*, p. 252.

118 **"in chains"**: Nicholas Elliott, *Never Judge a Man by His Umbrella* (London, 1992), p. 185.

119 **"dying of some mysterious ailment"**: Ibid., p. 185.

119 **"charming woman and loving wife"**: Ibid.

119 **"It was an intense affront"**: Ibid.

120 **"the marriage steadily deteriorated"**: Ibid.

120 **"It was James Jesus Angelton"**: Brown, *Treason in the Blood*, p. 386.

121 **"At one stroke"**: Philby, *My Silent War*, p. 145.

121 **"unlimited possibilities"**: Ibid.

121 **"Who am I supposed to work"**: Borovik, *Philby Files*, p. 257.

121 **"I was lunched at many"**: Philby, *My Silent War*, p. 146.

121 **"One side is open"**: Borovik, *Philby Files*, p. 261.

122 **"chain reaction that would"**: Nicholas Bethell, *The Great Betrayal: The Untold Story of Kim Philby's Biggest Coup* (London, 1978), p. 41.

122 **"formal British and American"**: Ibid., p. 57.

CHAPTER NINE: STORMY SEAS

125 **"There was no question"**: Nicholas Bethell, *The Great Betrayal: The Untold Story of Kim Philby's Biggest Coup* (London, 1978), p. 56.

125 **"all absolutely stark naked"**: David de Crespigny Smiley, interview no. 10340, Imperial War Museum, London, 1988.

127 **"We were looking only"**: Bethell, *Great Betrayal*, p. 56.

127 **"that the communists"**: Ibid., p. 83.

127 **"Brothers, you're all going"**: Ibid.

127 **"fascist terrorists"**: Ibid.

128 **"memorable send-off"**: Kim Philby, *My Silent War: The Autobiography of a Spy* (London, 1968), p. 148.

128 **"a private club afloat"**: http://cruiselinehistory.com.

128 **"disgustingly rich friend"**: Philby, *My Silent War*, p. 148.

128 **"I began to feel that"**: Ibid.

128 **"one of the few glories":** Ibid., p. 149.

129 **"admired him as a 'professional' ":** Gordon Corera, *MI6: Life and Death in the British Secret Service* (London, 2012), p. 64.

129 **"I was brought up in England":** Tom Mangold, *Cold Warrior: James Jesus Angleton—the CIA's Master Spy Hunter* (London, 1991), p. 13.

129 **"Things have gone wrong":** Bethell, *Great Betrayal*, p. 84.

130 **"Who are you?":** Ibid., p. 87.

130 **"We said we were":** Ibid., p. 141.

130 **"The sun has risen":** Ibid., p. 142.

131 **"several Albanian civilians":** Ibid., p. 110.

131 **"disappointing":** Ibid., p. 96.

131 **"judged by wartime standards":** Stephen Dorril, *MI6: Fifty Years of Special Operations* (London, 2001), p. 389.

131 **"it would be wrong to abandon":** Bethell, *Great Betrayal*, p. 97.

131 **"was the one who made":** Dorril, *MI6*, p. 385.

132 **"Philby was a great charmer":** Corera, *MI6*, p. 64.

132 **"He had charm":** James McCargar, writing as Christopher Felix, "A Second Third Man," *New York Times Book Review*, May 26, 1968.

132 **"undoubtedly devoted to his children":** Nicholas Elliott, *Never Judge a Man by His Umbrella* (London, 1992), p. 187.

132 **"by any objective standard":** Philby, *My Silent War*, p. 162.

132 **"a former FBI man":** Ibid., p. 152.

132 **"a cold, fishy eye":** Ibid., p. 180.

132 **"bumbling":** Ibid., p. 164.

132 **"puddingy":** Ibid.

132 **"He entertained a lot":** Bethell, *Great Betrayal*, p. 101.

133 **"They were long":** *The Cost of Treachery*, BBC, aired October 30, 1984.

133 **"suggestive of complicity":** McCargar as Felix, "Second Third Man."

133 **"suggest drifting out":** Phillip Knightley, *The Master Spy: The Story of Kim Philby* (London, 1988), p. 155.

133 **"Intelligence officers talk trade":** Anthony Cave Brown, *Treason in the Blood: H. St. John Philby, Kim Philby and the Spy Case of the Century* (London, 1995), p. 399.

133 **"please one party":** Philby, *My Silent War*, p. 150.

133 **"The sky was the limit":** Bruce Page, David Leitch, and Phillip Knightley, Philby: *The Spy Who Betrayed a Generation* (London, 1968), p. 211.

133 **"the driving force":** Philby, *My Silent War*, p. 150.

134 **"I got a few nibbles"**: Michael Holzman, *James Jesus Angleton, the CIA, and the Craft of Counterintelligence* (Boston, 2008), p. 132.

134 **"It was the belief"**: Ibid.

134 **"habit"**: Philby, *My Silent War*, p. 151.

134 **"He demonstrated regularly"**: Ibid.

135 **"Our close association"**: Ibid.

135 **"used to pride himself"**: Mangold, *Cold Warrior*, p. 47.

135 **"Our discussions ranged"**: Philby, *My Silent War*, p. 151.

135 **"Both CIA and SIS"**: Ibid., p. 152.

135 **"Many of Harvey's lobsters"**: Ibid.

136 **"During those long, boozy lunches"**: Mangold, *Cold Warrior*, pp. 46–47.

136 **"Everything was written up"**: Ibid., p. 44.

136 **"chaotic"**: Christopher Andrew, *The Defence of the Realm: The Authorised History of MI5* (London, 2009), p. 420.

137 **"We'll get it right next time"**: Corera, *MI6*, p. 67.

137 **"We had agents parachuting in"**: Mangold, *Cold Warrior*, p. 47.

138 **"the timing and geographical"**: Philby, *My Silent War*, p. 159.

138 **"I do not know what happened"**: Ibid.

138 **"We knew that they would"**: Bethell, *Great Betrayal*, p. 137.

138 **"The boys in London imagined"**: Ibid., p. 146.

139 **"tied to the back of a jeep"**: Ibid., p. 150.

139 **"Our famous radio game"**: Corera, *MI6*, p. 62.

139 **"It was obvious there was"**: Bethell, *Great Betrayal*, p. 104.

139 **"Our security was very"**: Corera, *MI6*, p. 63.

140 **"well and truly blown"**: Bethell, *Great Betrayal*, p. 105.

140 **"Albania would fall"**: Nicholas Bethell, "Profits and Losses of Treachery," *Independent*, September 6, 1994.

140 **"There is little question"**: Bethell, *Great Betrayal*, p. 212.

140 **"He gave us vital information"**: Yuri Modin, *My Five Cambridge Friends: Burgess, Maclean, Philby, Blunt, and Cairncross by Their KGB Controller* (New York, 1995), p. 123.

140 **"The agents we sent"**: Knightly, *Master Spy*, p. 128.

141 **"gave Philby over drinks"**: Corera, *MI6*, p. 65.

CHAPTER TEN: HOMER'S ODYSSEY

143 **"Jim and Kim were very fond"**: Tom Mangold, *Cold Warrior: James Jesus Angleton—the CIA's Master Spy Hunter* (London, 1991), p. 43.

143   **"After a year of keeping up"**: Kim Philby, *My Silent War: The Autobiography of a Spy* (London, 1968), p. 151.

143   **"If you have a lot of money"**: Genrikh Borovik, *The Philby Files: The Secret Life of Master Spy Kim Philby* (London, 1994), p. 264.

143   **"The more visitors I had"**: Philby, *My Silent War*, p. 146.

143   **"valuable agent network"**: Christopher Andrew, *The Defence of the Realm: The Authorised History of MI5* (London, 2009), p. 376.

143   **"particularly important"**: Ibid.

143   **"Philby was looking on"**: Ibid., p. 378.

144   **"genuine mental block"**: Philby, *My Silent War*, p. 167.

144   **"before the net closed in"**: Andrew, *Defence of the Realm*, p. 423.

144   **"He clearly feels"**: Guy Liddell, *Diaries*, KV 4/472.

144   **"give us more time"**: Andrew, *Defence of the Realm*, p. 379.

145   **"parental pride in being"**: Nicholas Elliott, *Never Judge a Man by His Umbrella* (London, 1992), p. 187.

145   **"I have a shock for you"**: Philby, *My Silent War*, p. 126.

145   **"for a few days"**: Anthony Cave Brown, *Treason in the Blood: H. St. John Philby, Kim Philby and the Spy Case of the Century* (London, 1995), p. 416.

145   **"I know him only too well"**: Phillip Knightley, *The Master Spy: The Story of Kim Philby* (London, 1988), p. 165.

145   **"I do not think that"**: Andrew, *Defence of the Realm*, p. 422.

145   **"was not the sort of person"**: Ibid.

146   **"eccentricities"**: Philby, *My Silent War*, p. 166.

146   **"What does he mean *worse*"**: Ibid.

146   **"Knowing the trouble"**: Elliott, *Never Judge a Man*, p. 186.

146   **"The inevitable drunken scenes"**: Ibid.

146   **"keep an eye"**: Philby, *My Silent War*, p. 166.

147   **"secure line of communication"**: Andrew, *Defence of the Realm*, p. 423.

147   **"the most outstanding historian"**: Brown, *Treason in the Blood*, p. 419.

148   **"the cheapest bourbon"**: David C. Martin, *Wilderness of Mirrors: Intrigue, Deception, and the Secrets That Destroyed Two of the Cold War's Most Important Agents* (Guilford, CT, 2003), p. 53.

148   **"a peculiar garb"**: Ibid.

148   **"for fantastic profits"**: Ibid.

148   **"a bloated alcoholic"**: Michael Holzman, *James Jesus Angleton, the CIA, and the Craft of Counterintelligence* (Boston, 2008), p. 88.

148   **"What Freudian impulse"**: Ibid., p. 121.

149   **"beastily distorted"**: Ibid.

149 **"How could you?":** Ibid.

149 **"a social disaster":** Martin, *Wilderness of Mirrors*, p. 53.

149 **"handsome":** Philby, *My Silent War*, p. 184.

149 **"Forget it":** Knightley, *Master Spy*, p. 168.

151 **"Don't you go too":** Philby, *My Silent War*, p. 171.

151 **"There's serious trouble":** Modin, *My Five Cambridge Friends*, p. 200.

151 **"Donald's now in such a state":** Andrew, *Defence of the Realm*, p. 424.

151 **"We agree to your organizing":** Modin, *My Five Cambridge Friends*, p. 201.

151 **"no predisposition to be a spy":** Ibid., p. 22.

151 **"men who are too short":** Andrew, *Defence of the Realm*, p. 335.

152 **"at Victoria, MI5's men":** Modin, *My Five Cambridge Friends*, p. 207.

152 **"Back on Monday!":** Brown, *Treason in the Blood*, p. 430.

152 **"Don't go with him":** Modin, *My Five Cambridge Friends*, p. 204.

153 **"The Centre had concluded":** Ibid.

153 **"It just happened":** Tom Bower, *The Perfect English Spy: Sir Dick White and the Secret War, 1935–1990* (London, 1995), p. 109.

153 **"I have never tasted":** Elliott, *Never Judge a Man*, p. 156.

154 **"It seems a pity":** Ibid., p. 46.

154 **"at all costs and by all means":** Press Association, news report, July 7, 1951.

154 **"6' 3", normal built":** AP/Press Association Images, "Wanted" notice, July 8, 1951, Press Association document no. PA.7587460, available at http://paimages.co.uk/preview/?urn=2.7587460.

154 **"decanter of poisoned Scotch":** Brown, *Treason in the Blood*, p. 430.

155 **"Kim," Paterson half-whispered:** Philby, *My Silent War*, p. 172.

155 **"lack of discipline":** Andrew, *Defence of the Realm*, p. 426.

155 **"crude manners":** Ibid.

156 **"a stiff drink":** Philby, *My Silent War*, p. 175.

156 **"My clear duty was":** Ibid.

157 **"There is no doubt":** Liddell, *Diaries*, KV 4/473.

157 **"There must be many people":** Philby, *My Silent War*, p. 176.

CHAPTER ELEVEN: PEACH

158 **"rapier mind":** Kim Philby, *My Silent War: The Autobiography of a Spy* (London, 1968), p. 113.

158 **"deeply subtle twists":** Ibid.

158 **"How long will you be away":** Phillip Knightley, *The Master Spy: The Story of Kim Philby* (London, 1988), p. 181.

158 **"a pleasant hour"**: Philby, *My Silent War*, p. 181.

158 **"matters of mutual concern"**: Ibid.

159 **"major sensation"**: PREM 8/1524 (no. 1792).

159 **"highly professional, perceptive and accusatory"**: Tom Mangold, *Cold Warrior: James Jesus Angleton—the CIA's Master Spy Hunter* (London, 1991), p. 44.

159 **"Philby was a Soviet spy"**: Ibid.

159 **"a retrospective exercise in spite"**: Philby, *My Silent War*, p. 185.

160 **"suffered severe concussion"**: David C. Martin, *Wilderness of Mirrors: Intrigue, Deception, and the Secrets That Destroyed Two of the Cold War's Most Important Agents* (Guilford, CT, 2003), p. 53.

160 **"conviction"**: Mangold, *Cold Warrior*, p. 45.

160 **"without reference to Philby"**: Ibid.

160 **"the bottom line was"**: Martin, *Wilderness of Mirrors*, p. 53.

160 **"he remained convinced"**: Mangold, *Cold Warrior*, p. 45.

160 **"held in high esteem"**: Ibid.

160 **"What is the rest"**: Martin, *Wilderness of Mirrors*, p. 57.

160 **"apprehensive"**: Philby, *My Silent War*, p. 182.

161 **"He did his best to put"**: Ibid.

161 **"might have views on the case"**: Guy Liddell, *Diaries*, KV 4/473.

161 **"this horrible business"**: Christopher Andrew, *The Defence of the Realm: The Authorised History of MI5* (London, 2009), p. 427.

161 **"There was no case against"**: Anthony Cave Brown, *Treason in the Blood: H. St. John Philby, Kim Philby and the Spy Case of the Century* (London, 1995), p. 438.

162 **"nondescript"**: Tom Bower, *The Perfect English Spy: Sir Dick White and the Secret War, 1935–1990* (London, 1995), p. 127.

162 **"pure trade"**: Ibid., p. 124.

162 **"establishment"**: Ibid.

162 **"very sketchy"**: Ibid.

163 **"an indiscreet, disorganised"**: Ibid., p. 125.

163 **"Kim is extremely worried"**: Liddell, *Diaries*, KV 4/473.

163 **"wholly convincing"**: Ibid.

163 **"I dined with Anthony Blunt"**: Ibid.

163 **"hard to believe"**: Ibid.

164 **"Fire Philby or we break off"**: Burton Hersh, *The Old Boys: The American Elite and The Origins of the CIA* (New York, 1992), p. 321.

164 **"severely shaken"**: PREM 8/1524 (no. 1803).

164 **"clean house regardless"**: Ibid.

164   **"In the State Department":** Ibid.

164   **"their wholehearted commitment":** Bower, *Perfect English Spy*, p. 126.

164   **"While all the points":** Liddell, *Diaries*, KV 4/473.

165   **"I'm in no particular hurry":** Bower, *Perfect English Spy*, p. 126.

165   **"subsequently converted her":** Liddell, *Diaries*, KV 4/473.

165   **"he himself had never":** Ibid.

165   **"denied emphatically":** Ibid.

165   **"nasty little question":** Philby, *My Silent War*, p. 183.

166   **"insatiable appetite for new":** Nicholas Elliott, *Never Judge a Man by His Umbrella* (London, 1992), p. 173.

167   **"guilty only of an unwise friendship":** Knightley, *Master Spy*, p. 183.

167   **"the victim of unsubstantiated":** Bower, *Perfect English Spy*, p. 127.

167   **"I'm no good to you now":** Patrick Seale and Maureen McConville, *Philby: The Long Road to Moscow* (London, 1973), p. 217.

167   **"obvious distress":** Philby, *My Silent War*, p. 184.

167   **"not possibly be a traitor":** Brown, *Treason in the Blood*, p. 439.

167   **"dedicated, loyal officer":** Chapman Pincher, *Treachery: Betrayals, Blunders and Cover-ups: Six Decades of Espionage* (London, 2012), p. 401.

167   **"great black cloud":** Philby, *My Silent War*, p. 184.

168   **"He said that he had been":** Liddell, *Diaries*, KV 4/473.

168   **"Personally I would be delighted":** Elliott, *Never Judge a Man*, p. 176.

168   **"I suppose he is not doing":** Liddell, *Diaries*, KV 4/473.

168   **"in jest":** Ibid.

168   **"it was already too late":** Ibid.

169   **"The case against Philby":** Ibid.

169   **"sticky":** Philby, *My Silent War*, p. 185.

169   **"judicial inquiry":** Andrew, *Defence of the Realm*, p. 427.

169   **"Hello Buster":** Genrikh Borovik, *The Philby Files: The Secret Life of Master Spy Kim Philby* (London, 1994), p. 297.

170   **"How would I know?":** Phillip Knightley, *The Master Spy*, p. 186.

170   **"Who was that young":** Borovik, *Philby Files*, p. 298.

170   **"How could I not help her?":** Ibid.

170   **"So far, he has admitted":** Liddell, *Diaries*, KV 4/473.

170   **"It all became a shouting match":** Bower, *Perfect English Spy*, p. 133.

171   **"The interrogation of Philby":** Liddell, *Diaries*, KV 4/473.

171   **"I find myself unable":** Andrew, *Defence of the Realm*, p. 427.

171   **"There's no hope":** Bower, *Perfect English Spy*, p. 133.

171   **"Philby's attitude throughout":** Liddell, *Diaries*, KV 4/473.

171 **"had all the cards in his hands"**: Ibid.

171 **Nicholas Elliott again referred:** Andrew, *Defence of the Realm*, p. 427.

172 **"counter-attacking"**: Liddell, *Diaries*, KV 4/473.

172 **"foremost exponent in the country"**: Andrew, *Defence of the Realm*, p. 336.

172 **"manner verging on the exquisite"**: Philby, *My Silent War*, p. 187.

172 **"two little traps"**: Ibid.

172 **"Nothing could have been more"**: Ibid.

173 **"remained open"**: Liddell, *Diaries*, KV 4/473.

173 **"hanging"**: Philby, *My Silent War*, p. 187.

173 **"I would have given"**: Ibid.

173 **"a much more favourable"**: Andrew, *Defence of the Realm*, p. 427.

173 **"unproven"**: Ibid.

173 **"Investigation will continue"**: PREM 11/4457.

173 **"We feel that the case"**: Ibid.

CHAPTER TWELVE: THE ROBBER BARONS

174 **"To whom should a wife's allegiance"**: Genrikh Borovik, *The Philby Files: The Secret Life of Master Spy Kim Philby* (London, 1994), p. 311.

174 **"suspicious"**: Guy Liddell, *Diaries*, KV 4/474.

174 **"entirely innocent"**: Ibid.

175 **"Kim's gone"**: Borovik, *Philby Files*, p. 311.

175 **"Thank God it's you at last"**: Ibid.

176 **"insane"**: Anthony Cave Brown, *Treason in the Blood: H. St. John Philby, Kim Philby and the Spy Case of the Century* (London, 1995), p. 447.

176 **"disclosed very definitely"**: Liddell, *Diaries*.

176 **"loyal ex-colleague"**: Nicholas Elliott, *Never Judge a Man by His Umbrella* (London, 1992), p. 186.

176 **"the poor man's Surrey"**: Kim Philby, *My Silent War: The Autobiography of a Spy* (London, 1968), p. xx.

176 **"Philby was under constant watch"**: Yuri Modin, *My Five Cambridge Friends: Burgess, Maclean, Philby, Blunt, and Cairncross by Their KGB Controller* (New York, 1995), p. 229.

176 **"Peach is apt to get"**: Christopher Andrew, *The Defence of the Realm: The Authorised History of MI5* (London, 2009), p. 433.

177 **"You must fight like hell"**: Tom Bower, *The Perfect English Spy: Sir Dick White and the Secret War, 1935–1990* (London, 1995), p. 292.

177 **"The whole family went through"**: Elliott, *Never Judge a Man*, p. 186.

177 **"whether he wished for"**: Liddell, *Diaries*, KV 4/474.

177 **"C seemed to have reached":** Ibid.

178 **"Philby would recover from":** Brown, *Treason in the Blood*, p. 447.

178 **"the extent to which Peach":** Andrew, *Defence of the Realm*, p. 433.

178 **"of which he was governor":** Elliott, *Never Judge a Man*, p. 187.

178 **"the intense disagreement":** Andrew, *Defence of the Realm*, p. 430.

178 **"refused to let one":** Bower, *Perfect English Spy*, p. 134.

179 **"In [Aileen's] opinion":** Andrew, *Defence of the Realm*, p. 433.

179 **"was close enough to our house":** Elliott, *Never Judge a Man*, p. 186.

180 **"in the normal way":** Liddell, *Diaries*, KV 4/474.

180 **"somewhat worried":** Ibid.

181 **"worry that Petrov had brought":** Borovik, *Philby Files*, p. 312.

181 **"had parted from his wife":** Andrew, *Defence of the Realm*, p. 430.

181 **"It will undermine Philby":** Bower, *Perfect English Spy*, p. 152.

181 **"pursuing a vendetta against Philby":** Ibid., p. 153.

181 **"desperately short of cash":** Modin, *My Five Cambridge Friends*, p. 228.

181 **"rendered us immense services":** Ibid., p. 229.

182 **"a large sum of money":** Ibid.

182 **"villainous Italian authorities":** Ibid., p. 230.

182 **"vied with one another":** Ibid., p. 231.

183 **"Excuse me":** Ibid.

183 **"Tomorrow. 8pm. Angel.":** Ibid.

183 **"a long stare":** Ibid.

183 **"Yes," he said. "Yes. Yes.":** Ibid.

183 **"I was virtually certain":** Philby, *My Silent War*, p. 190.

184 **"the dark silhouette kept pace":** Ibid., p. 232.

184 **"refreshed spirit":** Ibid., p. 190.

184 **"Petrov knew nothing":** Andrew, *Defence of the Realm*, p. 430.

184 **"I was no longer alone":** Philby, *My Silent War*, p. 190.

185 **"It is the spy who has":** George Kennedy Young, circular, 1950s, http://en.wikipedia.org/wiki/George_Kennedy_Young.

185 **"Men's minds are shaped":** Ibid.

185 **"biased":** Andrew, *Defence of the Realm*, p. 430.

185 **"victim of a miscarriage of justice":** Andrew, *Defence of the Realm*, p. 430.

186 **"The Milmo Report":** PREM 11/4457.

186 **"Produce the evidence":** Bower, *Perfect English Spy*, p. 156.

186 **"greatest defender":** Gordon Corera, *MI6: Life and Death in the British Secret Service* (London, 2012), p. 72.

186 **"We are going to have":** Bower, *Perfect English Spy*, p. 154.

187 **"I know you are the Third Man":** Andrew, *Defence of the Realm*, p. 433.

187 **"welcomed the chance":** Ibid., p. 430.

187 **"who knew him well":** Peter Wright, *Spycatcher: The Candid Autobiography of a Senior Intelligence Officer* (London, 1987), p. 44.

188 **"To call it an interrogation":** Ibid.

188 **"You may be pleased":** Borovik, *Philby Files*, p. 315.

188 **"The trail had become":** Philby, *My Silent War*, p. 192.

188 **"livid":** Bower, *Perfect English Spy*, p. 156.

188 **"belief that one of the questioners":** Andrew, *Defence of the Realm*, p. 430.

188 **"tipster":** FO 953/2165.

189 **"The house at Crowborough":** Elliott, *Never Judge a Man*, p. 186.

CHAPTER THIRTEEN: THE THIRD MAN

190 **"If pop music is going to be":** Cited in Raiford Guins and Omayra Zaragoza Cruz, *Popular Culture: A Reader* (London, 2005), p. 368.

190 **"Has the Prime Minister":** Debate in the House of Commons, October 25, 1955, published in *Hansard's Parliamentary Debates*, Commons, 6th ser., vol. 545, col. 28–29. HC Deb 25 October 1955 vol 545 cc28–9.

191 **"My name is in the newspapers":** Genrikh Borovik, *The Philby Files: The Secret Life of Master Spy Kim Philby* (London, 1994), p. 314.

191 **"might prejudice the case":** Kim Philby, *My Silent War: The Autobiography of a Spy* (London, 1968), p. 192.

191 **"We've decided that you":** Borovik, *Philby Files*, p. 314.

191 **"additional stress for Aileen":** Nicholas Elliott, *Never Judge a Man by His Umbrella* (London, 1992), p. 186.

192 **"absolutely convinced I had":** Borovik, *Philby Files*, p. 322.

192 **"leaned heavily in favour":** Phillip Knightley, *The Master Spy: The Story of Kim Philby* (London, 1988), p. 195.

192 **"Nothing would be worse":** Anthony Cave Brown, *Treason in the Blood: H. St. John Philby, Kim Philby and the Spy Case of the Century* (London, 1995), p. 454.

193 **"Mr Philby had Communist:** Harold Macmillan, debate in the House of Commons, November 7, 1956, published in *Hansard's Parliamentary Debates*, Commons, 6th ser., vol. 545, col. 1483. HC Deb 07 November 1955 vol 545 cc1483–611.

193 **"a man whose name has been smeared":** Richard Brooman-White, debate in the House of Commons, November 7, 1956, published in *Hansard's Parliamentary Debates*, Commons, 6th ser., vol. 545, col. 1483.

193 **"He [Lipton] is in favour of acting":** Ibid.

193 **"Whoever is covering up":** Frank Tomney, debate in the House of Commons, November 7, 1956, published in *Hansard's Parliamentary Debates*, Commons, 6th ser., vol. 545, col. 1483.

194 **"I will not be gagged by anybody":** Marcus Lipton, debate in the House of Commons, November 7, 1956, published in *Hansard's Parliamentary Debates*, Commons, 6th ser., vol. 545, col. 1483.

194 **"Even Mr. Philby has not":** Ibid.

194 **"Jesus Christ!":** Philby, *My Silent War*, p. 195.

194 **"Do come in":** Borovik, *Philby Files*, p. 318.

195 **"The efficiency of our security services":** The press conference can be viewed at www.youtube.com/watch?v=N2A2g-qRIaU.

196 **"I see you understand the habits":** Borovik, *Philby Files*, p. 319.

196 **"breathtaking":** Yuri Modin, *My Five Cambridge Friends: Burgess, Maclean, Philby, Blunt, and Cairncross by Their KGB Controller* (New York, 1995), p. 234.

196 **"Kim played his cards with":** Ibid.

196 **"deeply regretted":** "Colonel Lipton Withdraws," *Times* (London), November 11, 1955.

196 **"My evidence was insubstantial":** Brown, *Treason in the Blood*, pp. 457–58.

196 **"Colonel Lipton has done":** Philby, *My Silent War*, p. 197.

196 **"overjoyed":** Modin, *My Five Cambridge Friends*, p. 234.

196 **"seek his reemployment":** Tom Bower, *The Perfect English Spy: Sir Dick White and the Secret War, 1935–1990* (London, 1995), p. 158.

196 **"further service to the Soviet":** Philby, *My Silent War*, p. 198.

198 **"frogmen had popped up":** Nicholas Elliott, *With My Little Eye: Observations Along the Way* (Norwich, UK, 1993), p. 24.

198 **"a matter of high intelligence":** Ibid.

198 **"We wanted a closer look":** Ibid.

199 **"undaunted devotion to duty":** Ibid.

199 **"a most engaging man":** Ibid.

199 **"kindly bantam cock":** Rob Hoole, "The Buster Crabb Enigma," *Warship World*, January 2007.

199 **"to get m' feet wet again":** Marshall Pugh, *Commander Crabb* (London, 1956), p. 156.

199 **"supplies of whisky":** Elliott, *With My Little Eye*, p. 25.

199 **"heading for a heart attack":** Peter Wright, *Spycatcher: The Candid Autobiography of a Senior Intelligence Officer* (London, 1987), p. 74.

199   **"Crabb was still the most"**: Elliott, *With My Little Eye*, p. 25.

200   **"The dicey operations"**: Bower, *Perfect English Spy*, p. 159.

200   **"These ships are our guests"**: Chapman Pincher, *Treachery: Betrayals, Blunders and Cover-ups: Six Decades of Espionage* (London, 2012), p. 417.

200   **"We don't have a chain"**: Bower, *Perfect English Spy*, p. 160.

200   **"I am sorry, but we cannot"**: Don Hale, *The Final Dive: The Life and Death of "Buster" Crabb* (London, 2007), p. 172.

200   **"operation was mounted"**: Elliott, *With My Little Eye*, p. 24.

201   **"working holiday"**: Brown, *Treason in the Blood*, p. 460.

201   **"attached Foreign Office"**: Bower, *Perfect English Spy*, p. 160.

201   **"down to take a dekko"**: "1956: Mystery of Missing Frogman Deepens," On This Day, BBC.com, http://news.bbc.co.uk/onthisday/hi/dates/stories/may/9/newsid_4741000/4741060.stm.

202   **"an extra pound of weight"**: Elliott, *With My Little Eye*, p. 24.

202   **"A tip-off from a British"**: Gordon Corera, *MI6: Life and Death in the British Secret Service* (London, 2012), p. 78.

203   **"There will be blood"**: Wright, *Spycatcher*, p. 74.

203   **"We'll all be for"**: Ibid., p. 75.

203   **"specially employed in connection"**: Hale, *Final Dive*, p. 176.

203   **"presumed drowned"**: Ibid.

203   **"I'm afraid it rather"**: Wright, *Spycatcher*, p. 74.

203   **"missing or lost property"**: Hale, *Final Dive*, p. 172.

204   **"in trouble"**: Elliott, *With My Little Eye*, p. 24.

204   **"he hoped he was"**: Ibid.

204   **"such an unusual occurrence"**: Hale, *Final Dive*, p. 183.

204   **"regret about this incident"**: Ibid., p. 188.

204   **"completely unauthorized"**: Ibid.

204   **"paid no attention"**: Ibid., p. 183.

204   **"it can only be assumed"**: Ibid.

204   **"It would not be"**: Ibid., p. 184.

205   **"a shameful operation"**: Ibid., p. 191.

205   **"misconceived and inept operation"**: Pincher, *Treachery*, p. 421.0

205   **"Ridiculous . . . Against Orders"**: Francis Elliott, "Cold War Papers Reveal Lost Diver's Last Minutes," *Independent on Sunday*, June 11, 2006.

205   **"a typical piece of MI6"**: Wright, *Spycatcher*, p. 73.

205   **"We're still cloak and dagger"**: Bower, *Perfect English Spy*, p. 165.

205   **"one man Bay of Pigs"**: Ibid., p. 312.

205 **"A storm in a teacup":** Elliott, *With My Little Eye*, p. 25.

206 **"Crabb was both brave":** Ibid.

206 **"He almost certainly died":** Ibid.

207 **"come down to the firm":** Borovik, *Philby Files*, p. 321.

207 **"Something unpleasant again?":** Ibid.

CHAPTER FOURTEEN: OUR MAN IN BEIRUT

208 **"In those days SIS kept":** Andrew Lycett, *Ian Fleming* (London, 1996), p. 170.

208 **"Kemsley Press allowed":** Ibid., p. 169.

208 **"doing secret service stuff":** Ibid.

209 **"being re-engaged for reasons":** Patrick Seale and Maureen McConville, *Philby: The Long Road to Moscow* (London, 1973), p. 284.

209 **"The country could ill afford":** Anthony Cave Brown, *Treason in the Blood: H. St. John Philby, Kim Philby and the Spy Case of the Century* (London, 1995), p. 470.

209 **"Nick did all the negotiations":** Phillip Knightley, *The Master Spy: The Story of Kim Philby* (London, 1988), p. 199.

209 **"no appetite for reopening":** Tom Bower, *The Perfect English Spy: Sir Dick White and the Secret War, 1935–1990* (London, 1995), p. 289.

210 **"irritated that Elliott":** Ibid., p. 292.

210 **"no emotion":** Ibid.

210 **"unaware":** Ibid., p. 235.

210 **"horrified if he knew":** Ibid.

210 **"It was Nicholas Elliott":** Knightley, *Master Spy*, p. 206.

210 **"had an ersatz gaiety":** Nicholas Elliott, *Never Judge a Man by His Umbrella* (London, 1992), p. 157.

210 **"The climate of Vienna":** Ibid.

210 **"Haunted by Kim's life":** Richard Beeston, *Looking for Trouble: The Life and Times of a Foreign Correspondent* (London, 2006), p. 29.

211 **"she maintained in the hope":** Flora Solomon and Barnet Litvinoff, *Baku to Baker Street: The Memoirs of Flora Solomon* (London, 1984), p. 211.

211 **"Lebanon was the only":** Beeston, *Looking for Trouble*, p. 28.

212 **"He was quintessentially English":** Ibid., p. 29.

212 **"rangy, steady-drinking American":** Ibid.

212 **"If I should meet Kim":** Eleanor Philby, *Kim Philby: The Spy I Loved* (London, 1968), p. 28.

212 **"What touched me first":** Ibid.

213 **"Kim was a delightful companion"**: Ibid., p. 30.

213 **"My soufflés were never"**: Ibid.

213 **"sound knowledge of"**: Kim Philby, *My Silent War: The Autobiography of a Spy* (London, 1968), p. 199.

213 **"telling the British government"**: Ibid.

214 **"as conscientiously as possible"**: Ibid.

214 **"Petukhov, Soviet Trade Mission"**: Genrikh Borovik, *The Philby Files: The Secret Life of Master Spy Kim Philby* (London, 1994), p. 331.

214 **"I read your articles"**: Ibid.

214 **"total commitment"**: Kim Philby, *My Silent War*, p. xxxi.

214 **"I stayed the course"**: Ibid.

214 **"in the confident"**: Ibid., p. xxxii.

215 **"influenced and modified"**: Ibid.

215 **"a hive of activity"**: Yuri Modin, *My Five Cambridge Friends: Burgess, Maclean, Philby, Blunt, and Cairncross by Their KGB Controller* (New York, 1995), p. 234.

215 **"the intentions of the United States"**: Kim Philby, *My Silent War*, p. 199.

216 **"idleness"**: Brown, *Treason in the Blood*, p. 466.

216 **"No receipts, no money"**: Ibid.

216 **"helpful eye"**: Solomon and Litvinoff, *Baku to Baker Street*, p. 210.

216 **"poor Aileen . . ."**: Ibid., p. 211.

216 **"might have been murdered"**: Christopher Andrew, *The Defence of the Realm: The Authorised History of MI5* (London, 2009), p. 433.

216 **"considerable strength of character"**: Elliott, *Never Judge a Man*, p. 182.

216 **"a charming woman"**: Ibid., p. 185.

216 **"grave mental problem"**: Ibid.

216 **"I endeavoured to strike"**: Solomon and Litvinoff, *Baku to Baker Street*, p. 211.

217 **"I have wonderful news"**: Beeston, *Looking for Trouble*, p. 29.

217 **"wonderful escape"**: Ibid.

217 **"a wonderful American girl"**: Ibid.

217 **"stunned"**: Ibid.

217 **"Clever wonderful you fly back"**: Eleanor Philby, *Kim Philby*, p. 39.

217 **"I've come to tell you"**: Ibid.

217 **"That sounds like the best"**: *Never Judge a Man*, p. 187.

217 **"We shall take a house"**: Brown, *Treason in the Blood*, p. 482.

218 **"ringside view"**: Eleanor Philby, *Kim Philby*, p. 39.

218 **"He would sit in his terrace"**: Ibid.

218 **"leisurely daily circuit"**: Ibid., p. 52.

218 **"Kim treated the place"**: Ibid., p. 51.

218 **"to see what the other"**: Ibid.

218 **"connected with British intelligence"**: Ibid., p. 4.

218 **"He seemed to write"**: Ibid.

218 **"compelling a certain respect"**: Brown, *Treason in the Blood*, p. 491.

218 **"men whose ostensible jobs"**: Seale and McConville, *Philby*, p. 294.

219 **"The information he supplied"**: Modin, *My Five Cambridge Friends*, p. 234.

219 **"attracted much attention"**: Ibid.

219 **"There was criticism"**: Brown, *Treason in the Blood*, p. 480.

219 **"You could have read it all"**: Bower, *Perfect English Spy*, p. 292.

CHAPTER FIFTEEN: THE FOX WHO CAME TO STAY

220 **"but for his preference"**: Anthony Cave Brown, *Treason in the Blood: H. St. John Philby, Kim Philby and the Spy Case of the Century* (London, 1995), p. 470.

220 **"I have no wish to be"**: Nicholas Elliott, *Never Judge a Man by His Umbrella* (London, 1992), p. 162.

220 **"It was a most agreeable"**: Tom Bower, *The Perfect English Spy: Sir Dick White and the Secret War, 1935–1990* (London, 1995), p. 292.

220 **"excellent bouillabaisse"**: Elliott, *Never Judge a Man*, p. 167.

220 **"Fill me in, old boy"**: Eleanor Philby, *Kim Philby: The Spy I Loved* (London, 1968), p. 3.

221 **"cool, high rooms"**: Elliott, *Never Judge a Man*, p. 163.

221 **"perfect in every way"**: Ibid.

221 **"thought nostalgically of the gentle"**: Ibid.

221 **"two old friends in crown"**: Brown, *Treason in the Blood*, p. 492.

221 **"European specialist and knew"**: Philby, *Kim Philby*, p. 3.

221 **"Apart from all the political"**: Elliott, *Never Judge a Man*, p. 165.

221 **"his personal adviser"**: Patrick Seale and Maureen McConville, *Philby: The Long Road to Moscow* (London, 1973), pp. 295–96.

221 **"He was a thin, spare man"**: Ibid., p. 295.

222 **"put Kim to work"**: Ibid., p. 296.

222 **"serving two masters"**: Interview with former *Economist* correspondent.

222 **"mainly political and personality"**: Brown, *Treason in the Blood*, p. 492.

222 **"reports about political developments"**: Bower, *Perfect English Spy*, p. 292.

222 **"They used to meet"**: Philby, *Kim Philby*, p. 3.

222 **"Oh boy"**: Ibid., p. 52.

222 **"greater participation in the British"**: Seale and McConville, *Philby*, p. 298.

223 **"keep an eye on Philby"**: Bower, *Perfect English Spy*, p. 292.

223 **"Elliott's overt and innocent"**: Ibid.

223 **"seemed to relish the confidence"**: Brown, *Treason in the Blood*, p. 491.

223 **"I had begun to feel"**: Philby, *Kim Philby*, p. 3.

223 **"broker a deal with"**: Stephen Dorril, *MI6: Fifty Years of Special Operations* (London, 2001), pp. 670–71.

223 **"In all he served"**: Brown, *Treason in the Blood*, p. 480.

224 **"He was one of the few adults"**: Mark Elliott, interview with the author, October 17, 2013.

224 **"ski in the mornings"**: Elliott, *Never Judge a Man*, p. 166.

224 **"promised to look after it"**: Andrew Lycett, *Ian Fleming* (London, 1996), p. 376.

224 **"an Armenian"**: Ibid.

224 **"arranged to see a pornographic"**: Ibid.

224 **"at parties for British diplomats"**: Bower, *Perfect English Spy*, p. 292.

225 **"Out of fun rather"**: Elliott, *Never Judge a Man*, p. 184.

225 **"caused a chain reaction"**: Ibid.

225 **"It was at a cocktail party"**: Ibid.

226 **"He had no inhibitions"**: Ibid.

226 **"fierce martini"**: Ibid., p. 187.

226 **"recognized as the dominant"**: Richard Helms, *A Look Over My Shoulder: A Life in the Central Intelligence Agency* (New York, 2003), p. 275.

226 **"and used those opportunities"**: Joseph J. Trento, *The Secret History of the CIA* (New York, 2001), p. 274. No documentary record of these contacts survives, which indicates that either they did not take place or Angleton destroyed the evidence.

227 **"He travelled regularly"**: Richard Beeston, *Looking for Trouble: The Life and Times of a Foreign Correspondent* (London, 2006), p. 44.

227 **"whose brain was there"**: Brown, *Treason in the Blood*, p. 477.

227 **"all he had to do"**: Ibid., p. 478.

227 **"much too sophisticated"**: Ibid.

227 **"liked to talk to Philby"**: Genrikh Borovik, *The Philby Files: The Secret Life of Master Spy Kim Philby* (London, 1994), p. 335.

227 **"Philby was friendly"**: George Young, quoted in the *Sunday Times*, May 15, 1988.

228 **"The United States had to face"**: Miles Copeland, quoted in George Lenczowski, *American Presidents and the Middle East* (Durham, NC: Duke University Press, 1990), p. 6.

228 **"known and liked"**: Brown, *Treason in the Blood*, p. 486.

228 **"better than anyone else"**: Miles Copeland, *Without Cloak or Dagger: The Truth About the New Espionage* (New York, 1974), p. 146.

228 **"a humorous and highly intelligent"**: Nicholas Elliott, *With My Little Eye: Observations Along the Way* (Norwich, UK, 1993), p. 68.

229 **"Generous, outrageous, always fun"**: Beeston, *Looking for Trouble*, p. 106.

229 **"one of the most indiscreet"**: Elliott, *With My Little Eye*, p. 68.

229 **"I could trust him"**: Ibid.

229 **"keep an eye on Philby"**: Copeland, *Without Cloak or Dagger*, p. 212.

229 **"report signs that he might"**: Ibid., p. 146.

229 **"still practising his old tradecraft"**: Ibid., p. 212.

229 **"entertaining and colourful invention"**: Elliott, *With My Little Eye*, p. 69.

230 **"a melodious voice"**: Philby, *Kim Philby*, p. 53.

230 **"lapping up"**: Ibid., p. 5.

230 **"She was affectionate"**: Ibid.

231 **"hopelessly endearing"**: Ibid.

231 **"happiest years"**: Ibid., p. 51.

CHAPTER SIXTEEN: A MOST PROMISING OFFICER

232 **"treated with the deference"**: Eleanor Philby, *Kim Philby: The Spy I Loved* (London, 1968), p. 46.

232 **"Elizabeth and I were among"**: Nicholas Elliott, *Never Judge a Man by His Umbrella* (London, 1992), p. 188.

232 **"drew the old man out"**: Ibid.

232 **"memorable occasion"**: Ibid.

232 **"left at tea time"**: Ibid.

232 **"God, I'm bored"**: Anthony Cave Brown, *Treason in the Blood: H. St. John Philby, Kim Philby and the Spy Case of the Century* (London, 1995), p. 495.

232 **"a mixture of love and hate"**: Elliott, *Never Judge a Man*, p. 188.

233 "not completely well": Genrikh Borovik, *The Philby Files: The Secret Life of Master Spy Kim Philby* (London, 1994), p. 203.

233 "If you feel strongly enough": Elliott, *Never Judge a Man*, p. 188.

233 "thunderstruck, but by no means": Kim Philby, *My Silent War: The Autobiography of a Spy* (London, 1968), p. 132.

233 "went out of circulation": Elliott, *Never Judge a Man*, p. 188.

233 "He drank himself senseless": Eleanor Philby, *Kim Philby*, p. 47.

233 "Kim seemed overwhelmed": Richard Beeston, *Looking for Trouble: The Life and Times of a Foreign Correspondent* (London, 2006), p. 33.

234 "a most promising officer": Roger Hermiston, *The Greatest Traitor: The Secret Lives of Agent George Blake* (London, 2013), p. 221.

234 "a good-looking fellow": Brown, *Treason in the Blood*, p. 501.

234 "it was the relentless bombing": Ian Irvine, "George Blake: I Spy a British Traitor," *Independent*, October 1, 2006.

234 "I felt I was": Ibid.

234 "He doesn't belong": Tom Bower, *The Perfect English Spy: Sir Dick White and the Secret War, 1935–1990* (London, 1995), p. 261.

234 "man of no class": Hermiston, *Greatest Traitor*, p. 56.

234 "He was in love": Ibid., p. 61.

235 "90 per cent sure": Bower, *Perfect English Spy*, p. 263.

235 "to London immediately": Hermiston, *Greatest Traitor*, p. 221.

236 "whether Blake would like": Ibid.

236 "In the course of conversation": Ibid., p. 222.

236 "Moscow saw no cause": Ibid.

237 "would be more convenient": Ibid., p. 223.

237 "For a moment a shadow": Ibid.

237 "a few matters": Ibid., p. 226.

237 "I was in deep": Ibid., p. 227.

237 "It wasn't hostile": Ibid.

237 "No, nobody tortured me": Ibid., p. 229.

237 "The game was up": Ibid.

238 "the biggest hammer possible": Bower, *Perfect English Spy*, p. 268.

238 "The following name": Hermiston, *Greatest Traitor*, p. 236.

238 "It can happen to anyone": Bower, *Perfect English Spy*, p. 269.

238 "Your case is one": Hermiston, *Greatest Traitor*, p. 250.

239 "I went round": Beeston, *Looking for Trouble*, pp. 33–34.

239 "Kim would become insulting": Ibid., p. 31.

239 "not light-hearted about drink": Eleanor Philby, *Kim Philby*, p. 5.

240 "By the next day": Beeston, *Looking for Trouble*, p. 31.

240 **"I know all about"**: Patrick Seale and Maureen McConville, *Philby: The Long Road to Moscow* (London, 1973), p. 301.

240 **"You know Moyra"**: Beeston, *Looking for Trouble*, p. 32.

240 **"What would you do"**: Ibid.

240 **"something awful"**: Ibid.

240 **"What's the matter"**: Eleanor Philby, *Kim Philby*, p. 5.

241 **"Kim seemed to give"**: Ibid., p. 6.

241 **"seemed out of all proportion"**: Ibid.

241 **"shattered"**: Elliott, *Never Judge a Man*, p. 187.

241 **"Apart from when"**: Ibid.

241 **"the most valuable defector"**: Caroline Rand Herron and Michael Wright, "A KGB Defector Who May Not Be," *New York Times*, February 2, 1986.

241 **"very important spy network"**: Christopher Andrew, *The Defence of the Realm: The Authorised History of MI5* (London, 2009), p. 435.

242 **"exhibited increasing signs"**: Peter Wright, *Spycatcher: The Candid Autobiography of a Senior Intelligence Officer* (London, 1987), p. 193.

242 **"Modin had gone to Beirut"**: Ibid.

242 **"a shadow of his former"**: Yuri Modin, *My Five Cambridge Friends: Burgess, Maclean, Philby, Blunt, and Cairncross by Their KGB Controller* (New York, 1995), p. 236.

242 **"to warn Philby"**: Christopher Andrew and Vasili Mitrokhin, *The Sword and the Shield: The Mitrokhin Archive and the Secret History of the KGB* (London, 1999), p. 440.

242 **"belly laughs"**: David Cornwell, interview with the author, April 12, 2012.

243 **"Of course he's a traitor"**: Bower, *Perfect English Spy*, p. 293.

CHAPTER SEVENTEEN: I THOUGHT IT WOULD BE YOU

244 **"Russian soul, Jewish heart"**: Flora Solomon and Barnet Litvinoff, *Baku to Baker Street: The Memoirs of Flora Solomon* (London, 1984), p. 229.

244 **"To anyone with eyes"**: Ibid., p. 225.

245 **"The thought occurred to me"**: Ibid.

245 **"dangerous work in hazardous"**: *London Gazette*, April 4, 1944.

245 **"How is it the"**: Solomon and Litvinoff, *Baku to Baker Street*, p. 226.

245 **"very dangerous job for peace"**: Peter Wright, *Spycatcher*, p. 173.

245 **"intuitive feeling that Harris"**: Solomon and Litvinoff, *Baku to Baker Street*, p. 226.

246 **"the terrible way he treated":** Peter Wright, *Spycatcher: The Candid Autobiography of a Senior Intelligence Officer* (London, 1987), p. 173.

246 **"You must do something":** Solomon and Litvinoff, *Baku to Baker Street,* p. 226.

246 **"I will think about it":** Ibid.

246 **"major breakthrough":** Wright, *Spycatcher,* p. 172.

246 **"a strange, rather untrustworthy":** Ibid., p. 173.

246 **"She clearly had a grudge":** Ibid.

246 **"I will never give":** Ibid.

246 **"It will leak, I know":** Ibid.

247 **"Why didn't she tell us":** Tom Bower, *The Perfect English Spy: Sir Dick White and the Secret War, 1935–1990* (London, 1995), p. 294.

247 **"I had not volunteered":** Solomon and Litvinoff, *Baku to Baker Street,* p. 226.

247 **"how clubmanship and the old":** Ibid., p. 227.

247 **"far too wily":** Chapman Pincher, *Treachery: Betrayals, Blunders and Cover-ups: Six Decades of Espionage* (London, 2012), p. 473.

248 **"We need to discover":** Bower, *Perfect English Spy,* p. 295.

248 **"should be treated as":** Ibid.

248 **"Keep a lid on things":** Ibid., p. 294.

248 **"voluminous brief in preparation":** Wright, *Spycatcher,* p. 173.

250 **"The privately educated Englishman":** John le Carré, *The Secret Pilgrim* (London, 1990), part 2.

250 **"happily have killed him":** Mark Elliott, interview with the author, November 11, 2013.

251 **"there was more chance":** Bower, *Perfect English Spy,* p. 296.

251 **"Philby's greatest supporter":** Ibid.

251 **"a proficient, clever and determined":** Anthony Cave Brown, *Treason in the Blood: H. St. John Philby, Kim Philby and the Spy Case of the Century* (London, 1995), p. 505.

251 **"Elliott swore not to":** Andrew Boyle, *The Climate of Treason: Five Who Spied for Russia* (London, 1979), p. 436.

251 **The few of us inside MI5:** Wright, *Spycatcher,* p. 174.

252 **"We'd fully penetrated the KGB":** Bower, *Perfect English Spy,* p. 296.

252 **"vertically intoxicated":** Eleanor Philby, *Kim Philby: The Spy I Loved* (London, 1968), p. 7.

252 **"It was as if our flat":** Ibid.

252 **"He only had to smell":** Ibid.

252 **"What is the matter":** Ibid., p. 5.

252 **"very cold fish indeed":** Ibid., p. 9.

253 **"He dragged us protesting":** Ibid., p. 8.

253 **"already had a good deal":** Ibid.

253 **"He was bleeding profusely":** Ibid.

253 **"If we don't get":** Ibid.

253 **"one more ounce of alcohol":** Ibid., p. 9.

253 **"I was a bloody fool":** Ibid.

253 **"prepared himself for a battle":** Boyle, *Climate of Treason*, p. 436.

253 **"I've got an awful task":** Rozanne Colchester, interview with the author, June 11, 2013.

253 **"It was a terrible shock":** Ibid.

253 **"he always laughed about things":** Ibid.

254 **Nicholas knew he had blood:** Ibid.

254 **"in a casual voice":** Bower, *Perfect English Spy*, p. 297.

254 **"a meeting between himself":** Pincher, *Treachery*, p. 474.

255 **"The minute that call":** Philby, *Kim Philby*, p. 9.

255 **"I rather thought":** Bower, *Perfect English Spy*, p. 297.

CHAPTER EIGHTEEN: TEATIME

257 **"Perfectly tolerable"** . . . **"right up until '49":** The dialogue between Kim Philby and Nicholas Elliott is constructed from the following sources: Tom Bower, *The Perfect English Spy: Sir Dick White and the Secret War, 1935–1990* (London, 1995), pp. 297–98; Genrikh Borovik, *The Philby Files: The Secret Life of Master Spy Kim Philby* (London, 1994), pp. 3, 5, and 344; Andrew Boyle, *The Climate of Treason: Five Who Spied for Russia* (London, 1979), pp. 436–37; and interviews with individuals familiar with the transcript of that conversation.

258 **"in-house":** Peter Wright, *Spycatcher: The Candid Autobiography of a Senior Intelligence Officer* (London, 1987), p. 174.

260 **"He never once asked":** Ibid., p. 194.

260 **"Everything's OK":** Gordon Corera, *MI6: Life and Death in the British Secret Service* (London, 2012), p. 87.

261 **"The next 24 hours":** Tom Bower, *The Perfect English Spy: Sir Dick White and the Secret War, 1935–1990* (London, 1995), p. 299.

261 **"Okay, here's the scoop":** Ibid.

261 **"seen the error":** Christopher Andrew, *The Defence of the Realm: The Authorised History of MI5* (London, 2009), p. 436.

261 **"Is Nedosekin your contact":** Bower, *Perfect English Spy*, p. 299.

261 **"I've got no bloody contact":** Ibid.

261 **"very bland document"**: Anthony Cave Brown, *Treason in the Blood: H. St. John Philby, Kim Philby and the Spy Case of the Century* (London, 1995), p. 507.

261 **"limited confession"**: Andrew, *Defence of the Realm*, p. 436.

262 **"just a little stalling"**: Phillip Knightley, *The Master Spy: The Story of Kim Philby* (London, 1988), p. 217.

262 **"Our promise of immunity"**: Borovik, *Philby Files*, p. 345.

262 **"trying his manful best"**: Wright, *Spycatcher*, p. 194.

262 **"By the end"**: Ibid.

263 **"finally broken"**: Bower, *Perfect English Spy*, p. 299.

263 **"obscure hotel"**: Eleanor Philby, *Kim Philby: The Spy I Loved* (London, 1968), p. 6.

263 **"he did not want"**: Ibid.

263 **"this furtiveness was"**: Ibid.

263 **"as if nothing had intervened"**: Boyle, *Climate of Treason*, p. 438.

263 **"His greatest passion"**: Philby, *Kim Philby*, p. 6.

264 **"several names which alarmed"**: Knightley, *Master Spy*, p. 215.

264 **"Blunt was in the clear"**: Wright, *Spycatcher*, p. 194.

264 **"claimed to know nothing"**: Ibid.

264 **"the debriefing would be"**: Bower, *Perfect English Spy*, p. 299.

265 **"knew about the KGB"**: Ibid.

265 **"It became clear to me"**: Knightley, *Master Spy*, p. 215.

265 **"might stand him in"**: Ibid.

265 **"lifeline"**: Bower, *Perfect English Spy*, p. 298.

265 **"effusive in his gratitude"**: Ibid., p. 300.

265 **"He could have rejected"**: Ibid.

265 **In our judgment**: Andrew, *Defence of the Realm*, p. 436.

266 **"What makes you think"**: Chapman Pincher, *Treachery: Betrayals, Blunders and Cover-ups: Six Decades of Espionage* (London, 2012), p. 476.

266 **"He might, I suppose"**: Bower, *Perfect English Spy*, p. 300.

266 **"Nobody wanted him in London"**: David Cornwell, interview with the author, October 11, 2012.

266 **"It just didn't dawn on us"**: Bower, *Perfect English Spy*, p. 301.

267 **"unsympathetic"**: Ibid.

CHAPTER NINETEEN: THE FADE

268 **"Philby does not think"**: Tom Bower, *The Perfect English Spy: Sir Dick White and the Secret War, 1935–1990* (London, 1995), p. 301.

268 **"Your time has come"**: Genrikh Borovik, *The Philby Files: The Secret Life of Master Spy Kim Philby* (London, 1994), p. 346.

268 **"They won't leave you"**: Ibid.

268 **"had planted doubts"**: Ibid., p. 352.

268 **"Arrangements will take some time"**: Ibid., p. 347.

269 **"If you see me carrying"**: Ibid.

269 **"the question that interests"**: Ibid.

269 **"proved a helpful and friendly"**: Glencairn Balfour Paul, *Bagpipes in Babylon: A Lifetime in the Arab World and Beyond* (London, 2006), p. 187.

270 **"Daddy's going to be late"**: Eleanor Philby, *Kim Philby: The Spy I Loved* (London, 1968), p. 2.

270 **"cosy gathering"**: Ibid., p. 3.

270 **"God, what a horrible night"**: Ibid.

270 **"Don't be silly"**: Ibid.

270 **"had nothing to say"**: Clare Hollingworth, *Front Line* (London, 1990), p. 191.

270 **"Everything is fine"**: Borovik, *Philby Files*, p. 349.

271 **"a hastily summoned meeting"**: Eleanor Philby, *Kim Philby*, p. 4.

271 **"Would you like me"**: Ibid.

271 **"His advice was to do"**: Ibid.

271 **"terrible fear"**: Ibid.

272 **"last link with England"**: Yuri Modin, *My Five Cambridge Friends: Burgess, Maclean, Philby, Blunt, and Cairncross by Their KGB Controller* (New York, 1995), p. 237.

272 **"Philby had vanished"**: Nicholas Elliott, *With My Little Eye: Observations Along the Way* (Norwich, UK, 1993), p. 94.

272 **"Tell my colleagues"**: Eleanor Philby, *Kim Philby*, p. 18.

272 **"There is no question"**: Nicholas Elliott, *Never Judge a Man by His Umbrella* (London, 1992), p. 189.

272 **"in circumstances calculated"**: Ibid.

272 **"You do realise that your"**: Eleanor Philby, *Kim Philby*, p. 18.

273 **"choose a spot high up"**: Ibid., p. 19.

273 **"convinced that Kim had"**: Ibid., p. 12.

273 **"on no account to meet"**: Ibid., p. 21.

273 **"to test the system"**: Ibid.

273 **"Many people in the secret"**: Peter Wright, *Spycatcher: The Candid Autobiography of a Senior Intelligence Officer* (London, 1987), p. 174.

274 **"We should have sent"**: Ibid., p. 194.

274 **"But after lengthy interrogation"**: Ibid., p. 325.

274 **"He had been my boss"**: Desmond Bristow with Bill Bristow, *A Game of Moles: The Deceptions of an MI6 Officer* (London, 1993), p. 229.

274 **"horror"**: Ibid.

274 **"I never thought he would"**: Bower, *Perfect English Spy*, p. 304.

274 **"What a shame we reopened"**: Ibid.

274 **"disappointed"**: Ibid.

274 **"I tried to repair"**: Ibid., p. 305.

274 **"face the awful truth"**: Tom Mangold, *Cold Warrior: James Jesus Angleton—the CIA's Master Spy Hunter* (London, 1991), p. 45.

275 **"I had them burned"**: Ibid., p. 46.

275 **"He was an unforgivable traitor"**: Paul, *Bagpipes in Babylon*, p. 187.

275 **"dumbfounded"**: Anthony Cave Brown, *Treason in the Blood: H. St. John Philby, Kim Philby and the Spy Case of the Century* (London, 1995), p. 487.

275 **"unbelievable"**: Ibid., p. 488.

275 **"He was the best actor"**: Ibid.

276 **"What Philby provided"**: Michael Holzman, *James Jesus Angleton, the CIA, and the Craft of Counterintelligence* (Boston, 2008), p. 125.

276 **"Since Mr Philby resigned"**: Edward Heath (Lord Privy Seal), debate in the House of Commons, July 1, 1963, published in Hansard's Parliamentary Debates, Commons, 6th ser.

276 HELLO, MR PHILBY: Brown, *Treason in the Blood*, p. 527.

276 **"Philby was allowed to escape"**: Bristow, *Game of Moles*, p. 281.

276 **"To my mind the whole"**: Modin, *My Five Cambridge Friends*, p. 238.

277 **"the secret service had actively"**: Ibid.

277 **"I knew exactly how"**: Phillip Knightley, *The Master Spy: The Story of Kim Philby* (London, 1988), p. 217.

277 **"spiriting Philby out"**: Modin, *My Five Cambridge Friends*, p. 236.

277 **"a mistake, simple stupidity"**: Borovik, *Philby Files*, p. 323.

278 **"Burgess was a bit"**: Knightley, *Master Spy*, pp. 222–23.

278 **"unmistakably Russian"**: Eleanor Philby, *Kim Philby: The Spy I Loved*, p. 22.

278 **"I'm from Kim"**: Ibid.

279 **"Kim was an active communist"**: Ibid., p. 56.

279 **"surprising tenderness"**: Ibid.

279 **"We have definitely known"**: Ibid.

279 **"the victim of a prolonged"**: Ibid., p. xiii.

279 **"All I am thinking of now"**: Ibid., p. 59.

279   **"I don't know what":** Ibid., p. 64.

279   **"Buy yourself some very":** Ibid., p. 66.

280   **"What would *you* do":** Ibid., p. 63.

280   **"she finally admitted":** Ibid.

280   **"passionate loyalty and devotion":** Nicholas Elliott, *Never Judge a Man*, p. 182.

280   **"Although I had put":** Nicholas Elliott, *With My Little Eye*, p. 94.

280   **"Eleanor, is that you?":** Eleanor Philby, *Kim Philby*, p. 69.

280   **"Dear Nick":** Kim Philby to Nicholas Elliott, n.d., Cleveland Cram Collection, Georgetown University Library, Washington, DC.

282   **"It was ridiculous to suppose":** Elliott, *With My Little Eye*, p. 95.

282   **"an incredibly clumsy piece":** Ibid.

282   **"many hours of discussion":** Ibid.

282   **"because first":** Ibid.

282   **"tragic episode":** Ibid., p. 97.

282   **"Put some flowers for me":** Ibid., p. 98.

CHAPTER TWENTY: THREE OLD SPIES

283   **"elite":** Kim Philby, *My Silent War: The Autobiography of a Spy* (London, 1968), p. xxxii.

283   **"He never revealed":** Yuri Modin, *My Five Cambridge Friends: Burgess, Maclean, Philby, Blunt, and Cairncross by Their KGB Controller* (New York, 1995), p. 270.

283   **"Englishman to his fingertips":** Ibid.

284   **"homeland":** Genrikh Borovik, *The Philby Files: The Secret Life of Master Spy Kim Philby* (London, 1994), p. 373.

284   **"belonged":** Murray Sayle, "London-Moscow: The Spies Are Jousting," *Sunday Times* (London), January 6, 1968.

284   **"wholly and irreversibly English":** Anthony Cave Brown, *Treason in the Blood: H. St. John Philby, Kim Philby and the Spy Case of the Century* (London, 1995), p. 527.

284   **"Aluminium bats, white balls":** Phillip Knightley, *The Master Spy: The Story of Kim Philby* (London, 1988), p. 239.

284   **"the ghastly din":** Ibid., p. 253.

284   **"hooligans inflamed":** Ibid.

284   **"What is more important":** Eleanor Philby, *Kim Philby: The Spy I Loved* (London, 1968), p. 78.

284   **"The party, of course":** Ibid.

284   **"stayed the course":** Kim Philby, *My Silent War*, p. xxxi.

284 "If you only knew": Glencairn Balfour Paul, *Bagpipes in Babylon: A Lifetime in the Arab World and Beyond* (London, 2006), p. 186.

284 "Friendship is the most": Ibid.

284 "painful to think that during": Brown, *Treason in the Blood*, p. 488.

284 "I wasn't laughing at them": Knightley, *Master Spy*, p. 254.

285 "It had travelled with him": Nicholas Elliott, *Never Judge a Man by His Umbrella* (London, 1992), p. 189.

285 "supreme example of schizophrenia": Ibid.

285 "He betrayed many people": Eleanor Philby, *Kim Philby*, p. 175.

285 "No one can ever really know": Ibid., p. xiv.

286 "The emotional wreckage": Michael Holzman, *James Jesus Angleton, the CIA, and the Craft of Counterintelligence* (Boston, 2008), p. 206.

286 "Jim just continued to think": Tom Mangold, *Cold Warrior: James Jesus Angleton—the CIA's Master Spy Hunter* (London, 1991), p. 48.

286 "Never again would he permit": David C. Martin, *Wilderness of Mirrors: Intrigue, Deception, and the Secrets That Destroyed Two of the Cold War's Most Important Agents* (Guilford, CT, 2003), p. 193.

286 "This is all Kim's work": Holzman, *James Jesus Angleton*, p. 207.

286 "He had trusted him": Nicholas Elliott, *With My Little Eye: Observations Along the Way* (Norwich, UK, 1993), p. 81.

287 "I don't know that the damage": Martin, *Wilderness of Mirrors*, p. 193.

287 "come clean in the Philby case": Brown, *Treason in the Blood*, p. 565.

288 "To be in administration": Elliott, *Never Judge a Man*, p. 179.

288 "Rather to my surprise": Ibid., p. 192.

288 "a modern Cecil Rhodes": Ibid., p. 191.

288 "the Harry Lime of Cheapside": Ibid., p. 192.

288 "incapable of leading that kind": Ibid., p. 195.

288 "gift for dowsing": Ibid.

288 "alternative to involvement": Elliott, *With My Little Eye*, p. 65.

289 "showing a quite unjustified lack": Ibid., p. 109.

289 "extremely well over an": Elliott, *Never Judge a Man*, p. 182.

289 "I have naturally given thought": Ibid.

289 "Outwardly he was a kindly": Ibid., p. 183.

290 "a façade, in a schizophrenic": Ibid., p. 190.

290 "sad exiled life": Ibid., p. 189.

290 "dreary people, a spying servant": Ibid.

290 "wasted in a futile cause": Elliott, *With My Little Eye*, p. 99.

290 "decided to betray": Elliott, *Never Judge a Man*, p. 190.

290 "He had charm to burn": Ibid., p. 189.

290 **"The whole thing was staged":** Knightley, *Master Spy*, p. 215.

290 **"desire to spare SIS":** Borovik, *Philby Files*, p. 323.

290 **"blissful peace":** Ibid., p. 357.

290 **"How sleepless must be":** Ibid., p. 373.

291 **"He's a totally sad man":** Knightley, *Master Spy*, p. 5.

291 **"like Glasgow on a Saturday":** Tom Driberg, *Guy Burgess: A Portrait with Background* (London, 1956), p. 100.

291 **"burdensome":** Knightley, *Master Spy*, p. 235.

291 **"Any confession involves":** Rufina Philby with Hayden Peake and Mikhail Lyubimov, *The Private Life of Kim Philby: The Moscow Years* (London, 1999), p. 257.

291 **"showed no interest":** Elliott, *Never Judge a Man*, p. 185.

291 **"one of the better ones":** Knightley, *Master Spy*, p. 257.

292 **"tireless struggle in the cause":** Ibid., p. 260.

292 **"My lips have hitherto":** Elliott, *With My Little Eye*, p. 95.

292 **"a tremendous fluttering":** Ibid.

292 **"undistinguished, albeit mildly notorious":** Ibid., p. 10.

292 **"I feel I have been":** Ibid.

Select Bibliography

ARCHIVES

British Library Newspaper Archive, Colindale, UK

Bundesarchiv—Abteilung Militärarchiv, Freiburg, Germany

Churchill Archives Centre, Churchill College, Cambridge

IWM Archives, Imperial War Museum, London

National Archives, Kew, UK

National Archives, Washington, DC

The Times (London) Archives

PUBLISHED SOURCES

Aldrich, Richard J. *GCHQ: The Uncensored Story of Britain's Most Secret Intelligence Agency.* London, 2011.

Andrew, Christopher. *The Defence of the Realm: The Authorised History of MI5.* London, 2009.

———. *Secret Service: The Making of the British Intelligence Community.* London, 1985.

Andrew, Christopher, and David Dilks, eds. *The Missing Dimension: Governments and Intelligence Communities in the Twentieth Century.* London, 1984.

Andrew, Christopher, and Oleg Gordievsky. *KGB: The Inside Story of Its Foreign Operations from Lenin to Gorbachev.* London, 1990.

Andrew, Christopher, and Vasili Mitrokhin. *The Mitrokhin Archive II: The KGB and the World.* London, 2005.

———. *The Sword and the Shield: The Mitrokhin Archive and the Secret History of the KGB.* London, 1999.

Bassett, Richard. *Hitler's Spy Chief: The Wilhelm Canaris Mystery.* London, 2006.

Beeston, Richard. *Looking for Trouble: The Life and Times of a Foreign Correspondent.* London, 2006.

Bennett, Gill. *Churchill's Man of Mystery: Desmond Morton and the World of Intelligence.* London, 2007.

Bennett, Ralph. *Behind the Battle: Intelligence in the War with Germany 1939–45.* London, 1999.

Best, Sigismund Payne. *The Venlo Incident.* London, 1950.

Bethell, Nicholas. *The Great Betrayal: The Untold Story of Kim Philby's Greatest Coup.* London, 1978.

Borovik, Genrikh. *The Philby Files: The Secret Life of Master Spy Kim Philby.* Edited by Phillip Knightley. London, 1994.

Bower, Tom. *The Perfect English Spy: Sir Dick White and the Secret War, 1935–1990.* London, 1995.

Boyle, Andrew. *The Climate of Treason: Five Who Spied for Russia.* London, 1979.

Bristow, Desmond, with Bill Bristow. *A Game of Moles: The Deceptions of an MI6 Officer.* London, 1993.

Brook-Shepherd, Gordon. *The Storm Birds: Soviet Post-War Defectors.* London, 1988.

Brown, Anthony Cave. *Bodyguard of Lies.* Vol. 1. London, 1975.

———. *Treason in the Blood: H. St. John Philby, Kim Philby and the Spy Case of the Century.* London, 1995.

Bryher, Winifred. *The Days of Mars: A Memoir, 1940–1946.* New York, 1972.

Butler, Ewan. *Mason-Mac: The Life of Lieutenant-General Sir Nöel Mason-MacFarlane.* London, 1972.

Carl, Leo D. *The International Dictionary of Intelligence.* McLean, VA, 1990.

Carter, Miranda. *Anthony Blunt: His Lives.* London, 2001.

Cavendish, Anthony. *Inside Intelligence.* London, 1990.

Copeland, Miles. *The Game of Nations: The Amorality of Power Politics.* New York, 1970.

———. *The Game Player: Confessions of the CIA's Original Political Operative.* London, 1989.

———. *Without Cloak or Dagger: The Truth About the New Espionage.* New York, 1974.

Corera, Gordon. *MI6: Life and Death in the British Secret Service.* London, 2012.

Crowdy, Terry. *Deceiving Hitler: Double Cross and Deception in World War II.* London, 2008.

Curry, J. *The Security Service 1908–1945: The Official History.* London, 1999.

Dalton, Hugh. *The Fateful Years: Memoirs, 1931–1945*. London, 1957.

Doerries, Reinhard R. *Hitler's Intelligence Chief: Walter Schellenberg*. New York, 2009.

Dorril, Stephen. *MI6: Fifty Years of Special Operations*. London, 2001.

Driberg, Tom. *Guy Burgess: A Portrait with Background*. London, 1956.

Elliott, Nicholas. *Never Judge a Man by His Umbrella*. London, 1992.

———. *With My Little Eye: Observations Along the Way*. Norwich, UK, 1993.

Foote, Alexander. *Handbook for Spies*. London, 1949.

Gilbert, Martin. *Winston S. Churchill*. Vol. 6, *Finest Hour, 1939–1941*. London, 1983.

Hale, Don. *The Final Dive: The Life and Death of "Buster" Crabb*. London, 2007.

Hamrick, S. J. *Deceiving the Deceivers: Kim Philby, Donald Maclean, and Guy Burgess*. New Haven, CT, 2004.

Harris, Tomás. *Garbo: The Spy Who Saved D-Day*. Introduction by Mark Seaman. London, 2004.

Harrison, Edward. *The Young Kim Philby: Soviet Spy and British Intelligence Officer*. Exeter, UK, 2012.

Hastings, Max. *Finest Years: Churchill as Warlord 1940–45*. London, 2009.

———. *Overlord: D-Day and the Battle for Normandy 1944*. London, 1984.

Helms, Richard. *A Look Over My Shoulder: A Life in the Central Intelligence Agency*. New York, 2003.

Hermiston, Roger. *The Greatest Traitor: The Secret Lives of Agent George Blake*. London 2013.

Hersh, Burton. *The Old Boys: The American Elite and the Origins of the CIA*. New York, 1992.

Hollingworth, Clare. *Front Line*. London, 1990.

Holt, Thaddeus. *The Deceivers: Allied Military Deception in the Second World War*. London, 2004.

Holzman, Michael. *James Jesus Angleton, the CIA, and the Craft of Counterintelligence*. Boston, 2008.

Horne, Alistair. *But What Do You Actually Do? A Literary Vagabondage*. London, 2011.

Jeffery, Keith. *MI6: The History of the Secret Intelligence Service 1909–1949*. London, 2010.

Kahn, David. *Hitler's Spies: German Military Intelligence in World War II*. New York, 2000.

Knightley, Phillip. *The Master Spy: The Story of Kim Philby*. London, 1988.

———. *The Second Oldest Profession*. London, 1986.

Lenczowski, George. *American Presidents and the Middle East*. Durham, NC: Duke University Press, 1990.

Liddell, Guy. *The Guy Liddell Diaries, 1939–1945*. Vols. 1 and 2. Edited by Nigel West. London, 2005.

Lycett, Andrew. *Ian Fleming*. London, 1996.

Mangold, Tom. *Cold Warrior: James Jesus Angleton—the CIA's Master Spy Hunter*. London, 1991.

Martin, David C. *Wilderness of Mirrors: Intrigue, Deception, and the Secrets that Destroyed Two of the Cold War's Most Important Agents*. Guilford, CT, 2003.

Modin, Yuri. *My Five Cambridge Friends: Burgess, Maclean, Philby, Blunt, and Cairncross by Their KGB Controller*. New York, 1995.

Morgan, Ted. *A Covert Life: Jay Lovestone: Communist, Anti-Communist, and Spymaster*. New York, 1999.

Muggeridge, Malcolm. *Chronicles of Wasted Time*. Vols 1 and 2. London, 1973.

Page, Bruce, David Leitch, and Phillip Knightley. *Philby: The Spy Who Betrayed a Generation*. London, 1968.

Paine, Lauran. *The Abwehr: German Military Intelligence in World War II*. London, 1984.

Paul, Glencairn Balfour. *Bagpipes in Babylon: A Lifetime in the Arab World and Beyond*. London, 2006.

Philby, Eleanor. *Kim Philby: The Spy I Loved*. London, 1968.

Philby, Kim. *My Silent War: The Autobiography of a Spy*. London, 1968.

Philby, Rufina, Mikhail Lyubimov, and Hayden Peake. *The Private Life of Kim Philby: The Moscow Years*. London 1999.

Pincher, Chapman. *Treachery: Betrayals, Blunders and Cover-Ups: Six Decades of Espionage*. London, 2012.

Poretsky, Elisabeth K. *Our Own People: A Memoir of "Ignace Reiss" and His Friends*. Oxford, UK,, 1969.

Pugh, Marshall. *Commander Crabb*. London, 1956.

Read, Anthony, and David Fisher. *Colonel Z: The Secret Life of a Master of Spies*. London, 1985.

———. *Operation Lucy: Most Secret Spy Ring of the Second World War*. London, 1981.

Rose, Kenneth. *Elusive Rothschild: The Life of Victor, Third Baron*. London, 2003.

Rubin, Barry. *Istanbul Intrigues*. New York, 1989.

Seale, Patrick, and Maureen McConville. *Philby: The Long Road to Moscow*. London, 1973.

Sisman, Adam. *Hugh Trevor-Roper: The Biography.* London 2011.

Solomon, Flora, and Barnet Litvinoff. *Baku to Baker Street: The Memoirs of Flora Solomon.* London, 1984.

Trento, Joseph J. *The Secret History of the CIA.* New York, 2001.

Trevor-Roper, Hugh. *The Philby Affair: Espionage, Treason, and Secret Services.* London, 1968.

Weiner, Tim. *Legacy of Ashes: The History of the CIA.* London, 2007.

West, Nigel. *At Her Majesty's Secret Service: The Chiefs of Britain's Intelligence Agency, MI6.* London, 2006.

———. *Mask: MI5's Penetration of the Communist Party of Great Britain.* London, 2005.

———. *MI5: British Security Service Operations 1909–45.* London, 1981.

———. *Venona: The Greatest Secret of the Cold War.* London, 1999.

West, Nigel, and Oleg Tsarev, eds., *The Crown Jewels: The British Secrets at the Heart of the KGB Archives.* London, 1998.

———. *Triplex: Secrets from the Cambridge Five.* New Haven, CT: Yale University Press, 2009.

Wheatley, Dennis. *The Deception Planners: My Secret War.* London, 1980.

Whiting, Charles. *Ghost Front: The Ardennes Before the Battle of the Bulge.* London, 2002.

Wright, Peter. *Spycatcher: The Candid Autobiography of a Senior Intelligence Officer.* London, 1987.

Index

About the Author

BEN MACINTYRE is a writer-at-large for *The Times* of London and the bestselling author of *Double Cross, Operation Mincemeat, Agent Zigzag, The Napoleon of Crime,* and *Forgotten Fatherland,* among other books.